SECOND EDITION

Human Sexuality

Contemporary Perspectives

Edited by
Eleanor S. Morrison
and
Vera Borosage

Michigan State University

with the assistance of
Judith Arrigo O'Donnell

 MAYFIELD PUBLISHING COMPANY

Library of Congress Catalog Card Number: 76-56509
International Standard Book Number: 0-87484-381-2

Manufactured in the United States of America
Mayfield Publishing Company
285 Hamilton Avenue, Palo Alto, California 94301

This book was set in Palatino by Lehmann Graphics and was printed
and bound by the George Banta Company. Sponsoring editor was
Alden C. Paine, Carole Norton supervised editing, and Alice Rosen-
dall was manuscript editor. Michelle Hogan supervised production,
the book was designed by Nancy Sears, and the cover and part title
page artwork is by Ireta Cooper.

CONTENTS

iii

CONTENTS

271 *Part 4* SOME PUBLIC ISSUES

377 *Part 5* TOWARD A NEW SEXUALITY

PREFACE

One student generation of four years separates this new edition from the first one. In that short time, emphases in the field of human sexuality have shifted and concerns have changed. Therefore, although this textbook continues to embody an interdisciplinary collection broad in scope but focused on the sociocultural aspects of human sexuality, most of the readings it contains are new. They were chosen in response to recommendations made in a survey of professors who teach courses in human sexuality, and because they address questions students everywhere raise in the classroom. We are especially grateful to our students, who continually provide us with their perspectives, criticisms, and enthusiasms.

In the university courses, community workshops, and professional in-service training events taught by the editors of this book, teaching and learning occur primarily in small peer groups of men and women, with a trained group facilitator. Selections from this book and others are read prior to each group session and serve as a prompting script for interaction among the group members. Group sessions include a variety of learning activities such as role playing, reacting to film clips, and exchanging childhood memories. These activities stimulate personal interaction, listening, and self-disclosure, and at the same time provide an all-too-rare chance for direct, serious *talk* about sexual concerns.

Our continuing goal is to stimulate reaction, thought, and discussion, and to encourage each student to make a reflective, personal assessment of the meaning, style, and direction of his or her unique sexuality.

INTRODUCTION

The only thing my mother ever told me about was my period. No mention of the male sex organs or intercourse was ever made. When I came to college, the shock of the let's-jump-in-the-sack men really floored me. I had been brought up that my body was nothing to be ashamed of, but it wasn't to be flaunted either.

I was one evening pulled aside by my father and told how living matter reproduces itself. Out of this explanation, I gained a rather sound understanding of cellular divisions, embryology, and fertilizations. Yet there was no mention of human sexuality and its relationship with love, lust, gratification, or fulfillment.

I'm the kind of girl who doesn't have to take any money to the bar because someone is always buying me drinks. I'm a manipulator, and, of course, it's fake. I want to be genuine, but when you are part of a contrived and often phoney social situation, whether it's a bar, a t.g.,[1] or whatever . . . .

Maybe it's because I'm a man and gay—but I am very afraid of losing my youth to the merry-go-round. Each wrinkle that appears on my face will represent an irreversible defeat. I can think of nothing more pitiable than two aged faggots clinging to each other because no one else will have them.

These excerpts from anonymous student papers illustrate how little we understand and how much we need to learn, not only about human sexuality as a whole but about our own sexual selves. The editors of this textbook hope that the readings it contains and the various perspectives these readings present will clarify misconceptions, encourage dialogue, and help each student reader to define an individual, personal, and unique sexuality.

In recent years, the findings of researchers such as Masters and Johnson have illuminated the physiology of human sexual response and uncovered a wealth of information about the dynamics of sexual interactions. Our base of factual knowledge is expanding, but the field of human sexuality is still replete with tenaciously believed fallacies and myths, many of which are perpetrated by reputable practitioners in medicine and education. Although an understanding of the physiology of sex is important to a mature sexuality, this textbook is concerned less with clinical research data than with the psychological, social, and cultural aspects of human sexuality.

By making explicit a diversity of current assumptions about the psycho-socio-cultural dimensions of human sexuality, the readings in this volume will help students to compare and contrast—and thus to define—their own presently held assumptions. Among the viewpoints represented here, the reader will find these assumptions:

1 Sexuality is far more encompassing than genital or reproductive activity. "Sexuality is everything that has to do with your being a man or a woman. . . . [E]ducation for sexuality is every experience you have had up to your particular stage of development as a male or as a female."[2]
2 All of us are sexual beings from birth to death—through infancy, childhood, puberty, young adulthood, the middle years, and old age.
3 Sexuality has many styles and forms: marital and nonmarital, celibate and participative, active and inactive, homosexual and heterosexual, solitary and interactive, committed and casual—and what is appropriate for a given person depends on the interaction of personal choice and cultural setting.
4 Sexuality has a tremendous power in our lives that is sometimes inordinate in relation to the rest of our experience. Because it is associated at the core of personality with such qualities as self-esteem and identity, sexuality is sometimes seen as *the* key to personal worth and viability.
5 Contrary to popular mythology, sexual behavior is neither instinctual nor intuitive but is a subtly learned, complex process that is defined largely by one's culture. Sexuality is not an immutable, rigid, predetermined entity that proceeds uncontrollably along some predestined course, but is a malleable set of behaviors, fantasies, beliefs, and attitudes that can be changed and shaped by learning, choice, and action. All human beings, whether men or women, are very similar in

their biological sexual response, and the specific ways in which we make that response—with whom, when, where, how many, how long, using what orifices and what body positions—are learned and relearned.

6 Sexuality is defined primarily by the interaction of our biological gender with the interpretations and meanings we give it and the messages we receive about it from our family, peers, and culture. These meanings and interpretations are amenable to relearning.[3]

7 Sexuality is paradoxical in its completeness-in-itself and completeness-in-sharing-with-another aspects. Some feminists insist that a women's sexuality (and by implication, a man's) exists in and of itself irrespective of whether she ever interacts with a man. The classical *yin–yang* imagery portrays sexuality as incomplete without the complementarity of male and female in union. There is truth in both viewpoints.

8 Sexuality is fraught with worry, isolation, loneliness, and fear for many otherwise sophisticated and knowledgeable persons— especially those who have no opportunity to talk seriously about sexuality with respected peers. Many persons enter adulthood with a burden of guilt, fear, and anxiety about sexuality that results from childhood impressions, misinformation, and the all-too-frequent silence and avoidance patterns of their parents. Fears of having a perverted or abnormal sexuality plague persons who are unaware of the universality of sexual curiosity, exploration, and experimentation that is associated with childhood and youth between persons of the same and of opposite genders.

In addition to the personal aspects, there are many public issues concerning human sexuality—for example, abortion, pornography, rape, marriage and divorce laws, homosexuality, rights to privacy and to sexual information, contraceptives, and equality between the sexes in employment, promotion, and pay. These issues affect the quality of family and community life, and the economy. They require disciplined study, sophisticated judgment, and citizen decision and action in the elective, legislative, and judicial arenas. How much power and jurisdiction should the state have in defining guidelines? Are sexual behaviors "private matters between consenting adults" with which the state should not interfere?

Whether in the public or private scene, however, every student approaches the study of human sexuality with personal opinions about all kinds of matters from the proper time to teach children about sex to the acceptability of oral-genital sex. In our view, learning about human sexuality must take account of these opinions and provide the opportunity for students to engage in serious and sustained interchange of ideas. That interaction must be based on accurate information as well as on careful reflection about personal convictions, prejudices, beliefs, and values. The readings in this volume were selected to trigger such reaction and interaction. If some of them appear too polemical, too "radical," too "traditional," too "feminist," or too "subjective," our catalytic purpose will have been achieved.

NOTES

1 A "thank-God-it's-Friday" party.

2 Harold Lief, "An Interview with Mary Calderone, M.D.," *Medical Aspects of Human Sexuality*, August 1968, pp. 42, 46.

3 For two fascinating explorations of this thesis, see John Money and Anke Ehrhardt, *Man and Woman, Boy and Girl* (Baltimore: Johns Hopkins University Press, 1972); and John Gagnon and William Simon, *Sexual Conduct* (Chicago: Aldine Publishing Co., 1973).

Development

and sexuality

PART 1 / DEVELOPMENT AND SEXUALITY

The development of human sexuality is a controversial subject even today. Freudian theory still pervades contemporary thought, despite the scientific approach of sex researchers in this century. Freud believed that human sexual behavior is the necessary physical expression of a basic drive or instinct that must be controlled by society. He saw the child as a biological organism whose instinctual urges needed taming by the family, the first socializing agents.[1] Alfred Kinsey, whose monumental work was published in 1948 and 1953, also believed in a physiologically based sexual drive, but concentrated his research on yielding quantitative data on sexual behaviors such as the frequency of orgasm, premarital and extramarital sex, and homosexual experiences. His books exposed the true sexual behavior of a large sample of the American population and removed the veil from our apparently conventional sexuality.[2] Later, research by Masters and Johnson provided surprising facts about the sexuality of women, especially regarding their capacity for multiple orgasms.[3]

The readings in this part do not attempt to explain the biological bases of human sexuality, but are concerned instead with its psychological, cultural, and social dimensions. Simon and Gagnon disavow Freudian theory and believe human sexuality to be learned behavior dominated by sociocultural influences and based on the "social script" internalized

3

during an individual's development. Some interesting and controversial issues are raised by this reading: (1) During courtship and dating, men and women train each other to be sexual in new ways; the man trains the woman to be genitally sexual, and the woman trains the man to be emotionally and relationally sexual. How will women's increasing assertiveness affect this phase of sexual development? (2) Both male and female adolescents are physically equipped to experience sexual pleasure. Why, then, in view of the consciousness-raising effects of the feminist movement, do females still have to be taught to be sexual? Will male and female sexuality have to be redefined?

Can you identify and respond to other controversies associated with Simon and Gagnon's reading?

In the excerpt from their extensively researched book, *The Psychology of Sex Differences*, Maccoby and Jacklin attempt to identify and elucidate the persistent beliefs about boy–girl differences that pervade song and story—and even academic literature. The behavior of some children and adolescents contradicts many of the authors' conclusions because behavioral characteristics of the sexes overlap, and Maccoby and Jacklin are dealing with statistical averages. Furthermore, the gender-role aspects of sexual behavior are becoming increasingly complex. Do you think that the "sexual revolution" will eliminate sex-role stereotypes?

The women's liberation movement and the gradual removal of social, economic, and legal constraints against women in our society are bound to affect not only male–female relationships but how we socialize our children. Mothers of young boys still say, "Big boys don't cry," no matter how much the son may hurt. What other subtle stereotypic socialization practices can you describe? Will the push for equality between the sexes foster unisex socialization practices in rearing boys and girls? Would such child rearing affect the diversity of family life styles that now exist in this country?

Calderone's reading focuses on eroticism, which comprises feelings, thoughts, and fantasies associated with body pleasure and love of self and others. Because attitudes toward sex are instilled early in a child's life, Calderone believes that parents should be aware of any negative feelings they may have toward normally occurring erotic behavior and must become comfortable with their own sexuality before they can help their children internalize positive attitudes about sexual identity. Both parents and teachers should keep up with changing social attitudes toward sexual behaviors that were until recently not discussed openly—for example, masturbation, homosexual behavior, and nonmarital coitus.

Children acquire gender identity primarily through learning in the context of surrounding social influences. *Gender identity* and *masculinity* or *femininity* describe psychological aspects of sexuality but are distinctly separate terms. A child who says, "I'm a boy," is expressing his gender identity, which is a social identity that will not change even if he acquires "feminine" interests such as cooking or dancing. *Masculinity* and *femininity* are behavioral terms that refer to the sex-role characteristics a particular culture assigns as appropriate to each sex. If an aberration occurs in sex hormone distribution, the affected infant may look like a female even if it is a genetic male. Such a child can be reared and socialized to be a *psychosocial* female and acquire a *girl* gender identity, but will lack ovaries and a vagina. (The latter, however, can be provided by plastic surgery.) This anomaly occurs rarely, but it illustrates the complexity of the processes that develop and pattern human sexuality.

Katchadourian and Lunde point out that masturbation is part of normal human sexual development and a universal experience. In some societies, sexual stimulation of infants is acceptable as a pacifier, and children are encouraged to masturbate and play at having intercourse.[4] In our society, we no longer think that masturbation is wrong, or that it causes insanity, impotence, or falling hair; but we are slow to accept opinions of religious and medical leaders that masturbation can be beneficial in releasing sexual tensions, even when a sex partner is available.

The facts presented in this reading are based largely on Kinsey's research and on a later study by *Playboy* magazine. The data show a high incidence of masturbation across social classes and support the theory that masturbation promotes learning about human sexuality. Of special interest is the information about the incidence of masturbation among females. Will society now remove the remaining taboos against masturbation, especially for girls, and let them explore their bodies without guilt?

Hettlinger addresses college students, many of whom are caught in the dilemma between the "new morality" of sexual permissiveness and the more traditional restraints they may have internalized while growing up. He points out the importance of cultural learning to the development of human sexuality and describes Kohlberg's model of how moral reasoning develops from childhood to adulthood. This developmental process of achieving ethical maturity makes it possible for us to make enlightened decisions about our personal sexual behavior.

Changing attitudes toward sexual experience sometimes create a peer pressure that makes it almost as reprehensible to be a virgin today as it once was to be sexually experienced before marriage. As a result, students may enter an intimate sexual relationship expecting a high quality of sexual and emotional intimacy, only to feel a general cynicism, disillusionment, and bitterness rarely experienced by students twenty years ago.[5] Such a circumstance can be especially traumatic for the woman student who is committed to the idea of marriage and having a family. And what about students who are not part of the subculture of permissive sex—students who are "unattractive," career-oriented, inhibited by religious or family values, or simply too shy for intimate relationships? Some of these students express feelings of inadequacy, of not belonging, and of hopelessness for the future. Why should talk of others' sexual exploits make them feel this way? What sexual pressures have you experienced, or exerted? Did the way you felt as a result make you change your behavior—and if so, why?

A solution to these problems may be found in Hettlinger's proposal that each student be allowed to make free choices based on individual values and rational thinking independent of pressures imposed by others. This is a reasonable and desirable guideline, but will our society allow individuals to arbitrate their own sexual behavior, discard the norm, and "march to the tune of a different drummer"?

Sex researchers have neglected the years of life from 40 to 60 until the past decade, when they began to examine middle age for the causes of old-age problems such as health and decreasing capacities for sex, work, and intimate relationships. Generalizing about middle-aged people is difficult because of the wide range of life styles surfacing in today's world: some couples are at the peak of their earning capacity and, freed from child-rearing responsibilities, are "having a ball"; others add to the climbing divorce rate by seeking new alliances or freedom from the bonds of marriage; still others are burdened with the high cost of educating their college-age children, the products of the "baby boom" of the fifties. In any case, the role that sex plays in the lives of the aging may diminish, sometimes because the menopause-related problems of both women and men are repressed. Although psychological attitudes such as boredom with sameness and fear of impotence can play havoc with sexual performance, there is no apparent physiological reason why frequent and satisfying sex should not continue throughout middle and old age.

In her reading, de Beauvoir convicts Western society for its treatment of aging citizens. Unwilling to acknowledge the existence of sex among the aged, we either idealize the serenity we imagine they have achieved in their freedom from carnal desire, or we denigrate old-age sexuality in expressions such as "dirty old man." We seem to think there is something indecent about old people enjoying sexual intercourse or other acts of intimacy. Old age can be a time of "zest for life" despite the vicissitudes of coming to terms with diminishing sexual powers and the decreasing availability of sex partners, as shown by de Beauvoir's accounts of several literary and political figures who maintained their youthful libido into very old age. To the author, "sexuality, vitality, and activity are indissolubly linked" and together keep human beings involved in life instead of on the shelf. This reading gives young people a glimpse into their futures with its delightful and discerning anecdotes about sexuality in the aged, still a rare subject in professional literature and the media. A positive value of sex in a young person's total personality may well augur sexual satisfaction and zest in the later years, and youth's relaxed and permissive attitudes now surrounding people entering old age may enable the aging to opt for increased sexual activity and diversity in sexual alliances. Will the progress of sexual development end on an upbeat?

NOTES

1 Sigmund Freud, "Three Essays on Sexuality," *Complete Psychological Work* (London: Hogarth, 1953) v. 7: 135–245.

2 Alfred C. Kinsey, W. B. Pomeroy and C. E. Martin, *Sexual Behavior in the Human Male* (Philadelphia: W. B. Saunders Co., 1948); Alfred C. Kinsey, W. B. Pomeroy, C. E. Martin, and P. H. Gebhard, *Sexual Behavior in the Human Female* (Philadelphia: W. B. Saunders Co., 1953).

3 W. H. Masters and V. E. Johnson, *Human Sexual Response* (Boston: Little, Brown and Co., 1966).

4 W. N. Stephens, *The Family in Cross-Cultural Perspective* (New York: Holt, 1963).

5 Herbert Hendin, "The Revolt Against Love," *Harper's*, August 1975, p. 20.

Psychosexual Development

William Simon and John Gagnon

Erik Erickson has observed that, prior to Sigmund Freud, "sexologists" tended to believe that sexual capacities appeared suddenly with the onset of adolescence. Sexuality followed those external evidences of physiological change that occurred concurrent with or just after puberty. Psychoanalysis changed all that. In Freud's view, libido—the generation of psychosexual energies—should be viewed as a fundamental element of human experience at least beginning with birth, and possibly before that. Libido, therefore, is essential, a biological constant to be coped with at all levels of individual, social, and cultural development. The truth of this received wisdom, that is, that sexual development is a continuous contest between biological drive and cultural restraint, should be seriously questioned. Obviously sexuality has roots in biological processes, but so do many other capacities, including many that involve physical and mental competence and vigor. There is, however, abundant evidence that the final states which these capacities attain escape the rigid impress of biology. This independence of biological constraint is rarely claimed for the area of sexuality, but we would like to argue that the sexual is precisely that realm where the sociocultural forms most completely dominate biological influences.

It is difficult to get data that might shed much light on the earliest aspects of these questions: Adults are hardly equipped with total recall and the preverbal or primitively verbal child does not have ability to report accurately on his own internal state. But it seems obvious—and it is a basic assumption of this paper—that with the beginnings of adolescence many new factors come into play, and to emphasize a straight-line developmental continuity with infant and childhood experiences may be seriously misleading. In particular, it is dangerous to assume that because some childhood behavior appears sexual to adults, it must be sexual. An infant or a child engaged in genital play (even if orgasm is observed) can in no sense be seen as experiencing the complex set of feelings that accompanies adult or even adolescent masturbation.

A part of the legacy of Freud is that we have all become remarkably adept at discovering "sexual" elements in nonsexual behavior and symbolism.

Therefore, the authors reject the unproven assumption that "powerful" psychosexual drives are fixed biological attributes. More importantly, we reject the even more dubious assumption that sexual capacities or experiences tend to translate immediately into a kind of universal "knowing" or innate wisdom—that sexuality has a magical ability, possessed by no other capacity, that allows biological drives to be expressed directly in psychosocial and social behaviors.

The prevailing image of sexuality—particularly that of the Freudian tradition—is that of an intense, high-pressure drive that forces a person to seek physical sexual gratification, a drive that expresses itself indirectly if it cannot be expressed directly. The available data suggest to us a different picture—one that shows either lower levels of intensity, or, at least, greater variability. We find that there are many social situations or life-roles in which reduced sex activity or even deliberate celibacy is undertaken with little evidence that the libido has shifted in compensation to some other sphere.

A part of the legacy of Freud is that we have all become remarkably adept at discovering "sexual" elements in nonsexual behavior and symbolism. What we suggest instead (following Kenneth Burke's three-decade-old insight) is the reverse—that sexual behavior can often express and serve nonsexual motives.

NO PLAY WITHOUT A SCRIPT

We see sexual behavior therefore as *scripted* behavior, not the masked expression of a primordial drive. The individual can learn sexual behavior as he or she learns other behavior—through scripts that in this case give the self, other persons, and situations erotic abilities or content. Desire, privacy, opportunity, and propinquity with an attractive member of the opposite sex are not, in themselves, enough; in ordinary circumstances, nothing sexual will occur unless one or both actors organize these elements into an appropriate script. The very concern with foreplay in sex suggests this. From one point of view, foreplay may be defined as merely progressive physical excitement generated by touching naturally erogenous zones. The authors have referred to this conception elsewhere as the "rubbing of two sticks together to make a fire" model. It would seem to be more valuable to see this activity as symbolically invested behavior through which the body is eroticized and through which mute, inarticulate motions and gestures are translated into a sociosexual drama.

A belief in the sociocultural dominance of sexual behavior finds support in cross-cultural research as well as in data restricted to the United States. Psychosexual development is universal—but it takes many forms and tempos. People in different cultures construct their scripts differently; and in our own society, different segments of the population act out different psychosexual dramas—something much less likely to occur if they were all reacting more or less blindly to the same superordinate urge. The most marked differences occur, of course, between male and female patterns of sexual behavior. Obviously, some of this is due to biological differences, including differences in hormonal functions at different ages. But the significance of social scripts predominate; the recent work of Masters and Johnson, for example, clearly points to far greater orgasmic capacities on the part of females than our culture would lead us to suspect. And within each sex—especially among men—different social and economic groups have different patterns.

Let us examine some of these variations, and see if we can decipher the scripts.

CHILDHOOD

Whether one agrees with Freud or not, it is obvious that we do not become sexual all at once. There is continuity with the past. Even infant experiences can strongly influence later sexual development.

But continuity is not causality. Childhood experiences (even those that appear sexual) will in all likelihood be influential not because they are intrinsically sexual, but because they can affect a number of developmental trends, including the sexual. What situations in infancy—or even early childhood—can be called psychosexual in any sense other than that of creating potentials?

The key term, therefore, must remain potentiation. In infancy, we can locate some of the experiences (or sensations) that will bring about a sense of the body and its capacities for pleasure and discomfort and those that will influence the child's ability to relate to others. It is possible, of course, that through these primitive experiences, ranges are being established—but they are very broad and overlapping. Moreover, if these are profound experiences to the child—and they may well be that—they are not expressions of biological necessity, but of the earliest forms of social learning.

In childhood, after infancy there is what appears to be some real sex play. About half of all adults report that they did engage in some form of sex play as children and the total who actually did may be half again as many. But, however the adult interprets it later, what did it mean to the child at the time? One suspects that, as in much of childhood role-playing, their sense of the adult meanings attributed to the behavior is fragmentary and ill formed. Many of the adults recall that, at the time, they were concerned with being found out. But here, too, were they concerned because of the real content of sex play, or because of the mystery and the lure of the forbidden that so often enchant the child? The child may be assimilating outside information about sex for which, at the time, he has no real internal correlate or understanding.

A small number of persons do have sociosexual activity during preadolescence—most of it initiated by adults. But for the majority of these, little apparently follows from it. Without appropriate sexual scripts, the experience remains unassimilated—at least in adult terms. For some, it is clear, a severe reaction may follow from falling "victim" to the sexuality of an adult—but, again, does this reaction come from the sexual act itself or from the social response, the strong reactions of others? (There is some evidence that early sexual activity of this sort is associated with deviant adjustments in later life. But this, too, may not be the result of sexual experiences in themselves so much as the consequence of having fallen out of the social main stream and, therefore, of running greater risks of isolation and alienation.)

In short, relatively few become truly active sexually before adolescence. And when they do (for girls more often than boys), it is seldom immediately related to sexual feelings or gratifications but is a use of sex for nonsexual goals and purposes. The "seductive" Lolita is rare but she is significant: she illustrates a more general pattern of psychosexual development—a commitment to the social relationships linked to sex before one can really grasp the social meaning of the physical relationships.

Of great importance are the values (or feelings, or images) that children pick up as being related to sex. Although we talk a lot about sexuality, as though trying to exorcise the demon of shame, learning about sex in our society is in large part learning about guilt; and learning how to manage sexuality commonly involves learning how to manage guilt. An important source of guilt in children comes from the imputation to them by adults of sexual appetites or abilities that they may not have but that they learn, however imperfectly, to pretend they have. The gestural concomitants of sexual modesty are learned early. For instance, when do girls learn to sit or pick up objects with their knees together? When do they learn that the bust must be covered? However, since this behavior is learned unlinked to later adult sexual performances, what children must make of all this is very mysterious.

The learning of sex roles, or sex identities, involves many things that are remote from actual sexual experience, or that become involved with sexuality only after puberty. Masculinity or femininity, their meaning and postures, are rehearsed before adolescence in many nonsexual ways.

A number of scholars have pointed, for instance, to the importance of aggressive, deference, dependency, and dominance behavior in childhood. Jerome Kagan and Howard Moss have found that aggressive behavior in males and dependency in females are relatively stable aspects of development. But what is social role, and what is biology? They found that when aggressive behavior occurred among girls, it tended to appear most often among those from well-educated families that were more tolerant of deviation. Curiously, they also reported that "it was impossible to predict the character of adult sexuality in women from their preadolescent and early adolescent behavior," and that "erotic activity is more anxiety-arousing for females than for males" because "the traditional ego ideal for women dictates inhibition of sexual impulses."

The belief in the importance of early sex-role learning for boys can be viewed in two ways. First, it may directly indicate an early sexual capacity in male children. Or, second, early masculine identification may merely be an appropriate framework within which the sexual impulse (salient with puberty) and the socially available sexual scripts (or accepted patterns of sexual behavior) can most conveniently find expression. Our bias, of course, is toward the second.

But, as Kagan and Moss also noted, the sex role learned by the child does not reliably predict how he will act sexually as an adult. This finding also can be interpreted in the same two alternative ways. Where sexuality is viewed as a biological constant which struggles to express itself, the female sex-role learning can be interpreted as the successful repression of sexual impulses. The other interpretation suggests that the difference lies not in learning how to handle a preexistent sexuality but in learning how to *be* sexual. Differences between men and women, therefore, will have consequences both for *what* is done sexually, as well as *when*.

Once again, we prefer the latter interpretation, and some recent work that we have done with lesbians supports it. We observed that many of the major elements of their sex lives—the start of actual genital sexual behavior, the onset and frequency of masturbation, the time of entry in sociosexual patterns, the number of partners, and the reports of feelings of sexual deprivation—were for these homosexual women almost identical with those of ordinary women. Since sexuality would seem to be more important for lesbians— after all, they sacrifice much in order to follow their own sexual pathways—this is surprising. We concluded that the primary factor was something both categories of women share—the sex-role learning that occurs before sexuality itself becomes significant.

Social class also appears significant, more for boys than girls. Sex-role learning may vary by class; lower-class boys are supposed to be more aggressive and put much greater emphasis on early heterosexuality. The middle and upper classes tend to tolerate more deviance from traditional attitudes regarding appropriate male sex-role performances.

Given all these circumstances, it seems rather naive to think of sexuality as a constant pressure, with a peculiar necessity all its own. For us, the crucial period of childhood has significance not because of sexual occurrences but because of nonsexual developments that will provide the names and judgments for later encounters with sexuality.

ADOLESCENCE

The actual beginnings and endings of adolescence are vague. Generally, the beginning marks the first time society, as such, acknowledges that the individual has sexual capacity. Training in the postures and rhetoric of the sexual experience is now accelerated. Most important, the adolescent begins to regard those about him (particularly his peers, but also adults) as sexual actors and finds confirmation from others for this view.

For some, as noted, adolescent sexual experience begins before they are considered adolescents. Kinsey reports that a tenth of his female sample and a fifth of his male sample had experienced orgasm through masturbation by age 12. But still, for the vast majority, despite some casual play and exploration that post-Freudians might view as masked sexuality, sexual experience begins with adolescence. Even those who have had prior experience find that it acquires new meanings with adolescence. They now relate such meanings to both larger spheres of social life and greater senses of self. For example, it is not uncommon during the transition between childhood and adolescence for boys and, more rarely, girls to report arousal and orgasm while doing things not manifestly sexual—climbing trees, sliding down bannisters, or other activities that involve genital contact—without defining them as sexual. Often they do not even take it seriously enough to try to explore or repeat what was, in all likelihood, a pleasurable experience.

> **Within two years of puberty all but a relatively few boys have had the experience of orgasm, almost universally brought about by masturbation.**

Adolescent sexual development, therefore, really represents the beginning of adult sexuality. It marks a definite break with what went on before. Not only will future experiences occur in new and more complex contexts, but they will be conceived of as explicitly sexual and thereby begin to complicate social relationships. The need to manage sexuality will rise not only from physical needs and desires but also from the new implications of personal relationships. Playing, or associating, with members of the opposite sex now acquires different meanings.

At adolescence, changes in the developments of boys and girls diverge and must be considered separately. The one thing both share at this point is a reinforcement of their new status by a dramatic biological event—for girls, menstruation, and for the boys, the discovery of the ability to ejaculate. But here they part. For boys, the beginning of a commitment to sexuality is primarily genital; within two years of puberty all but a relatively few have had the experience of orgasm, almost universally brought about by masturbation. The corresponding organizing event for girls is not genitally sexual but social: they have arrived at an age where they will learn role performances linked with proximity to marriage. In contrast to boys, only two-thirds of girls will report ever having masturbated (and, characteristically, the frequency is much less). For women, it is not until the late twenties that the incidence of orgasm from any source reaches that of boys at age 16. In fact, significantly, about half of the females who masturbate do so only after having experienced orgasm in some situation involving others. This contrast points to a basic distinction between the developmental processes for males and females: males move from privatized personal sexuality to sociosexuality; females do the reverse and at a later stage in the life cycle.

THE TURNED-ON BOYS

We have worked hard to demonstrate the dominance of social, psychological, and cultural influences over the biological: now, dealing with adolescent boys, we must briefly reverse course. There is much evidence that the early male sexual impulses—again, initially through masturbation—are linked to physiological changes, to high hormonal inputs during puberty. This produces an organism that, to put it simply, is more easily turned on. Male adolescents report frequent erections, often without apparent stimulation of any kind. Even so, though there is greater biological sensitization and hence masturbation is more likely, the meaning, organization, and continuance of this activity still tends to be subordinate to social and psychological factors.

Masturbation provokes guilt and anxiety among most adolescent boys. This is not likely to change in spite of more "enlightened" rhetoric and discourse on the subject (generally, we have shifted from stark warnings of mental, moral, and physical damage to vague counsels against nonsocial or "inappropriate" behavior). However, it may be that this very guilt and anxiety gives the sexual experience an intensity of feeling that is often attributed to sex itself.

Such guilt and anxiety do not follow simply from social disapproval. Rather, they seem to come from several sources, including the difficulty the boy has in presenting himself as a sexual being to his immediate family, particularly his parents. Another source is the fantasies or plans associated with masturbation—fantasies about doing sexual "things" to others or having others do sexual "things" to oneself; or having to learn and rehearse available but proscribed sexual scripts or patterns of behavior. And, of course, some guilt and anxiety center around the general disapproval of masturbation. After the early period of adolescence, in fact, most youths will not admit to their peers that they did or do it.

Nevertheless, masturbation is for most adolescent boys the major sexual activity, and they engage in it fairly frequently. It is an extremely positive and gratifying experience to them. Such an introduction to sexuality can lead to a capacity for detached sex activity—activity whose only sustaining motive is sexual. This may be the hallmark of male sexuality in our society.

Of the three sources of guilt and anxiety mentioned, the first—how to manage both sexuality and an attachment to family members—probably cuts across class lines. But the others should show remarkable class differences. The second one, how to manage a fairly elaborate and exotic fantasy life during masturbation, should be confined most typically to the higher classes, who are more experienced and adept at dealing with symbols. (It is possible, in fact, that this behavior, which girls rarely engage in, plays a role in the processes by which middle-class boys catch up with girls in measures of achievement and creativity and, by the end of adolescence, move out in front. However, this is only a hypothesis.)

The ability to fantasize during masturbation implies certain broad consequences. One is a tendency to see large parts of the environment in an erotic light, as well as the ability to respond, sexually and perhaps poetically, to many visual and auditory stimuli. We might also expect both a capacity and need for fairly elaborate forms of sexual activity. Further, since masturbatory fantasies generally deal with relationships and acts leading to coitus, they should also reinforce a developing capacity for heterosociality.

The third source of guilt and anxiety—the alleged "unmanliness" of masturbation—should more directly concern the lower-class male adolescent. ("Manliness" has always been an important value for lower-class males.) In these groups, social life is more often segregated by sex, and there are, generally, fewer rewarding social experiences from other sources. The adolescent therefore moves into heterosexual—if not heterosocial—relationships sooner than his middle-class counterparts. Sexual segregation makes it easier for him than for the middle-class boy to learn that he does not have to love everything he desires and therefore to come more naturally to casual, if not exploitative relationships. The second condition—fewer social rewards that his fellows would respect—should lead to an exaggerated concern for proving masculinity by direct displays of physical prowess, aggression, and visible sexual success. And these three, of course, may be mutually reinforcing.

In a sense, the lower-class male is the first to reach "sexual maturity" as defined by the Freudians. That is, he is generally the first to become aggressively heterosexual and exclusively genital. This characteristic, in fact, is a distinguishing difference between lower-class males and those above them socially.

But one consequence is that although their sex lives are almost exclusively heterosexual, they remain homosocial. They have intercourse with females, but the standards and the audience they refer to are those of their male fellows. Middle-class boys shift predominantly to coitus at a significantly later time. They, too, need and tend to have homosocial elements in their sexual lives. But their fantasies, their ability to symbolize, and their social training in a world in which distinctions between masculinity and femininity are less sharply drawn, allow them to withdraw more easily from an all-male world. The difference between social classes obviously has important consequences for stable adult relationships.

One thing common in male experience during adolescence is that while it provides much opportunity for sexual commitment in one form or another, there is little training in how to handle emotional relations with girls. The imagery and rhetoric of romantic love is all around us; we are immersed in it. But whereas much is undoubtedly absorbed by the adolescent, he is not likely to tie it closely to his sexuality. In fact, such a connection might be inhibiting, as indicated by the survival of the "bad-girl-who-does" and "good-girl-who-doesn't" distinction. This is important to keep in mind as we turn to the female side of the story.

WITH THE GIRLS

In contrast to males, female sexual development during adolescence is so similar in all classes that it is easy to suspect that it is solely determined by biology. But, while girls do not have the same level of hormonal sensitization to sexuality at puberty as adolescent boys, there is little evidence of a biological or social inhibitor either. The "equipment" for sexual pleasure is clearly present by puberty but tends not to be used by many females of any class. Masturbation rates are fairly low, and among those who do masturbate, fairly infrequent. Arousal from "sexual" materials or situations happens seldom, and exceedingly few girls report feeling sexually deprived during adolescence.

Basically, girls in our society are not encouraged to be sexual—and may be strongly discouraged from being so. Most of us accept the fact that while "bad boy" can mean many things, "bad girl" almost exclusively implies sexual delinquency. It is both difficult and dangerous for an adolescent girl to become too active sexually. As Joseph Rheingold puts it, where men need only fear sexual failure, women must fear both success and failure.

Does this long period of relative sexual inactivity among girls come from repression of an elemental drive or merely from a failure to learn how to be sexual? The answers have important implications for their later sexual development. If it is repression, the path to a fuller sexuality must pass through processes of loss of inhibitions, during which the girl unlearns, in varying degrees, attitudes and values that block the expression of natural internal feelings. It also implies that the quest for ways to express directly sexual behavior and feelings that had been expressed nonsexually is secondary and of considerably less significance.

On the other hand, the "learning" answer suggests that women create or invent a capacity for sexual behavior, learning how and when to be aroused and how and when to respond. This approach implies greater flexibility: unlike the repression view, it makes sexuality both more and less than a basic force that may break loose at any time in strange or costly ways. The learning approach also lessens the power of sexuality altogether; all at once, particular kinds of sex activities need no longer be defined as either "healthy" or "sick." Lastly, subjectively, this approach appeals to the authors because it describes female sexuality in terms that seem less like a mere projection of male sexuality.

If sexual activity by adolescent girls assumes less specific forms than with boys, that does not mean that sexual learning and training do not occur. Curiously, though girls are, as a group, far less active sexually than boys, they receive far more training in self-consciously viewing themselves—and in viewing boys—as desirable mates. This is particularly true in recent years. Females begin early in adolescence to define attractiveness, at least partially, in sexual terms. We suspect that the use of sexual attractiveness for nonsexual purposes that marked our preadolescent "seductress" now begins to characterize many girls. Talcott Parsons' description of how the wife "uses" sex to bind the husband to the family, although harsh, may be quite accurate. More generally, in keeping with the childbearing and child-raising function of women, the development of a sexual role seems to involve a need to include in that role more than pleasure.

To round out the picture of the difference between the sexes, girls appear to be well-trained precisely in that area in which boys are poorly trained—that is, a belief in and a capacity for intense, emotionally-charged relationships and the language of romantic love. When girls during this period describe having been aroused sexually, they more often report it as a response to romantic, rather than erotic, words and actions.

In later adolescence, as dates, parties, and other sociosexual activities increase, boys—committed to sexuality and relatively untrained in the language and actions of romantic love—interact with girls committed to romantic love and relatively untrained in sexuality. Dating and courtship may well be considered processes in which each sex trains the other in what each wants and expects. What data are available suggest that this exchange system does not always work very smoothly. Thus, ironically, it is not uncommon to find that the boy becomes emotionally involved with his partner and therefore lets up on trying to seduce her, at the same time that the girl comes to feel that the boy's affection is genuine and therefore that sexual intimacy is more permissible.

In our recent study of college students, we found that boys typically had intercourse with their first coital partners one to three times, while with girls it was ten or more. Clearly, for the majority of females first intercourse becomes possible only in stable relationships or in those with strong bonds.

"WOMAN, WHAT DOES SHE WANT?"

The male experience does conform to the general Freudian expectation that there is a developmental movement from a predominantly genital sexual commitment to a loving relationship with another person. But this movement is, in effect, reversed for females, with love or affection often a necessary precondition for intercourse. No wonder, therefore, that Freud had great difficulty understanding female sexuality—recall the concluding line in his great essay on women: "Woman, what does she want?" This "error"—the assumption that female sexuality is similar to or a mirror image of that of the male—may come from the fact that so many of those who constructed the theory were men. With Freud, in addition, we must remember the very concept of sexuality essential to most of nineteenth century Europe—it was an elemental beast that had to be curbed.

It has been noted that there are very few class differences in sexuality among females, far fewer than among males. One difference, however, is very relevant to this discussion—the age of first intercourse. This varies inversely with social class—that is, the higher the class, the later the age of first intercourse—a relationship that is also true of first marriage. The correlation between these two ages suggests the necessary social and emotional linkage between courtship and the entrance into sexual activity on the part of women. A second difference, perhaps only indirectly related to social class, has to do with educational achievement: here, a sharp border line seems to separate from all other women those who have or have had graduate or professional work. If sexual success may be measured by the percentage of sex acts that culminate in orgasm, graduate and professional women are the most sexually successful women in the nation.

Why? One possible interpretation derives from the work of Abraham Maslow: Women who get so far in higher education are more likely to be more aggressive, perhaps to have strong needs to dominate; both these characteristics are associated with heightened sexuality. Another, more general interpretation would be that in a society in which girls are expected primarily to become wives and mothers, going on to graduate school represents a kind of deviancy—a failure of, or alienation from, normal female social adjustment. In effect, then, it would be this flawed socialization—not biology—that produced both commitment toward advanced training and toward heightened sexuality.

For both males and females, increasingly greater involvement in the social aspects of sexuality—"socializing" with the opposite sex— may be one factor that marks the end of adolescence. We know little about this transition, especially among noncollege boys and girls; but our present feeling is that sexuality plays an important role in it. First, sociosexuality is important in family formation and also in learning the roles and obligations involved in being an adult. Second, and more fundamental, late adolescence is when a youth is seeking, and experimenting toward finding, his identity—who and what he is and will be; and sociosexual activity is the one aspect of this exploration that we associate particularly with late adolescence.

Young people are particularly vulnerable at this time. This may be partly due to the fact that society has difficulty protecting the adolescent from the consequences of sexual behavior that it pretends he is not engaged in. But, more importantly, it may be because, at all ages, we all have great problems in discussing our sexual feelings and experiences in personal terms. These, in turn, make it extremely difficult to get support from others for an adolescent's experiments toward trying to invent his sexual self. We suspect that success or failure in the discovery or management of sexual identity may have consequences in personal development far beyond merely the sexual sphere—perhaps in confidence and feelings of self-worth, belonging, competence, guilt, force of personality, and so on.

ADULTHOOD

In our society, all but a few ultimately marry. Handling sexual commitments inside marriage makes up the larger part of adult experience. Again, we have too little data for firm findings. The data we do have come largely from studies of broken and troubled marriages, and we do not know to what extent sexual problems in such marriages exceed those of intact marriages. It is possible that, because we have assumed that sex is important in most people's lives, we have exaggerated its importance in holding marriages together. Also, it is

> **About half of all married men and a quarter of all married women will have intercourse outside of marriage at one time or another.**

possible that, once people are married, sexuality declines relatively, becoming less important than other gratifications (such as domesticity or parenthood); or it may be that these other gratifications can minimize the effect of sexual dissatisfaction. Further, it may be possible that individuals learn to get sexual gratification, or an equivalent, from activities that are nonsexual or only partially sexual.

The sexual desires and commitments of males are the main determinants of the rate of sexual activity in our society. Men are most interested in intercourse in the early years of marriage—woman's interest peaks much later; nonetheless, coital rates decline steadily throughout marriage. This decline derives from many things, only one of which is decline in biological capacity. With many men, it is more difficult to relate sexually to a wife who is pregnant or a mother. Lower-class adult men receive less support and plaudits from their male friends for married sexual performance than they did as single adolescents; and we might also add the lower-class disadvantage of less training in the use of auxiliary or symbolic sexually-stimulating materials. For middle-class men, the decline is not as steep, owing perhaps to their greater ability to find stimulation from auxiliary sources such as literature, movies, music, and romantic or erotic conversation. It should be further noted that for about 30 percent of college-educated men, masturbation continues regularly during marriage, even when the wife is available. An additional (if unknown) proportion do not physically masturbate but derive additional excitement from the fantasies that accompany intercourse.

But even middle-class sexual activity declines more rapidly than bodily changes can account for. Perhaps the ways males learn to be sexual in our society make it very difficult to keep it up at a high level with the same woman for a long time. However, this may not be vital in maintaining the family, or even in the man's personal sense of well-being, because, as previously suggested, sexual dissatisfaction may become less important as other satisfactions increase. Therefore, it need seldom result in crisis.

About half of all married men and a quarter of all married women will have intercourse outside of marriage at one time or another. For women, infidelity seems to have been on the increase since the turn of the century—at the same time that their rates of orgasm have been increasing. It is possible that the very nature of female sexuality is changing. Work being done now may give us new light on this. For men, there are strong social-class differences—the lower class accounts for most extramarital activity, especially during the early years of marriage. We have observed that it is difficult for a lower-class man to acquire the appreciation of his fellows for married intercourse; extramarital sex, of course, is another matter.

In general, we feel that far from sexual needs affecting other adult concerns, the reverse may be true: adult sexual activity may become that aspect of a person's life most often used to act out other needs. There are some data that suggest this. Men who have trouble handling authority relationships at work more often have dreams about homosexuality; some others, under heavy stress on the job, have been shown to have more frequent episodic homosexual experiences. Such phenomena as the rise of sadomasochistic practices and experiments in group sex may also be tied to nonsexual tensions, the use of sex for nonsexual purposes.

It is only fairly recently in the history of man that he has been able to begin to understand that his own time and place do not embody some eternal principle or necessity but are only dots on a continuum. It is difficult for many to believe that man can change, and is changing, in important ways. This conservative view is evident even in contemporary behavioral science; and a conception of man as having relatively constant sexual needs has become part of it. In an ever-changing world, it is perhaps comforting to think that man's sexuality does not change very much and therefore is relatively easily explained. We cannot accept this. Instead, we have attempted to offer a description of sexual development as a variable social invention—an invention that in itself explains little and requires much continuing explanation.

What We Know and Don't Know About Sex Differences

Eleanor Emmons Maccoby and Carol Nagy Jacklin

The physical differences between men and women are obvious and universal. The psychological differences are not. Yet people hold strong beliefs about sex differences, even when those beliefs fail to find any scientific support.

Some popular views of sex differences are captured in a scene from the Rodgers and Hammerstein musical *Carousel*. A young man discovers he is to be a father. He rhapsodizes about the kind of son he expects to have. The boy will be tall and tough as a tree, and no one will dare to boss him around. It will be all right for his mother to teach him manners, but she mustn't make a sissy out of him. The boy will be good at wrestling, and able to herd cattle, run a riverboat, drive spikes.

Then the prospective father realizes, with a start, that the child may be a girl. The music moves to a gentle theme. She will have ribbons in her hair. She will be sweet and petite, just like her mother, and suitors will flock around her. There's a slightly discordant note, introduced for comic relief from sentimentality, when the expectant father brags that she'll be half again as bright as girls are meant to be. But then he returns to the main theme: his daughter will need to be protected.

The lyrics in this scene reflect some common cultural stereotypes in the social science literature on sex differences. We believe there is a great deal of myth in both the popular and scientific views about male–female differences. There is also some substance.

In order to find out which generalizations are justified and which are not, we spent three years compiling, reviewing, and interpreting a very large body of research—over 2,000 books and articles— on the sex differences in motivation, social behavior, and intellectual ability. We examined negative as well as positive evidence. At the end of our exhaustive and exhausting search, we were able to determine which beliefs about sex differences are supported by evidence, which beliefs have no support, and which are still inadequately tested.

First, the myths:

MYTH ONE: GIRLS ARE MORE "SOCIAL" THAN BOYS

There is no evidence that girls are more likely than boys to be concerned with people, as opposed to impersonal objects or abstract ideas. The two sexes are equally interested in social stimuli (e.g., human faces and voices), and are equally proficient at learning by imitating models. They are equally responsive to social rewards, such as praise from others, and neither sex consistently learns better for this form of reward than for other forms.

In childhood, girls are no more dependent than boys on their caretakers, and boys are no more willing than girls to remain alone. Girls do not spend more time with playmates; the opposite is true, at least at certain ages. The two sexes appear to be equally adept at understanding the emotional reactions and needs of others, although measures of this ability have been narrow.

Any differences that do exist in the sociability of the two sexes are more of kind than of degree. Boys are highly oriented toward a peer group and congregate in larger groups; girls associate in pairs or small groups of children their own age, and may be somewhat more oriented toward adults, although the evidence on this is weak.

MYTH TWO: GIRLS ARE MORE SUGGESTIBLE THAN BOYS

Boys are as likely as girls to imitate other people spontaneously. The two sexes are equally susceptible to persuasive communications, and in face-to-face situations where there is social pressure to conform to a group judgment about an ambiguous situation, there are usually no sex differences in susceptibility. When there are, girls are somewhat more likely to adapt their own judgments to those of the group, although some studies find the reverse. Boys, on the other hand, appear to be more likely to accept peer group values when these conflict with their own.

MYTH THREE: GIRLS HAVE LOWER SELF-ESTEEM THAN BOYS

Boys and girls are very similar in overall self-satisfaction and self-confidence throughout childhood and adolescence. (The information on childhood is meager, but what there is indicates no sex difference.) The sexes do differ in the areas in which they report greatest self-confidence. Girls rate themselves higher in the area of social competence, while boys more often see themselves as strong, powerful, dominant, potent.

Through most of the school years, boys and girls are equally likely to believe they can influence their own fate, as opposed to falling victim to chance. During the college years (not earlier or later), men have a greater sense of control over their destiny, and are more optimistic in predicting their own performance on a variety of school-related tasks. However, this does not imply a generally lower level of self-esteem among women of this age.

MYTH FOUR: GIRLS LACK MOTIVATION TO ACHIEVE

In the pioneering studies of achievement motivation, girls were more likely to report imagery about achievement when asked to make up stories to describe ambiguous pictures, as long as the instructions did not stress either competition or social comparison. Boys need to be challenged by appeals to their ego or competitive feelings, for their achievement imagery to reach the level of girls'. Although boys' achievement motivation does appear to be more responsive to competitive arousal, that does not imply that they have a higher level of achievement motivation in general. In fact, when researchers observe behavior that denotes a motive to achieve, they find no sex differences or find girls to be superior.

MYTH FIVE: GIRLS ARE BETTER AT ROTE LEARNING AND SIMPLE REPETITIVE TASKS. BOYS ARE BETTER AT HIGH-LEVEL TASKS THAT REQUIRE THEM TO INHIBIT PREVIOUSLY LEARNED RESPONSES

Neither sex is more susceptible to simple conditioning, in which stimuli become connected with responses in what is assumed to be a rather automatic process. Neither sex excels in rote-learning tasks, such as learning to associate one word with another. Boys and girls are equally proficient at tasks that call on them to inhibit various responses, e.g., discrimination of certain items from others, a task requiring the subject to avoid attending or responding to irrelevant cues.

Boys are somewhat more impulsive during the preschool years, but after that the sexes do not differ in ability to wait for a delayed reward or inhibit early, incorrect responses, or on other measures of impulsivity.

MYTH SIX: BOYS ARE MORE "ANALYTIC" THAN GIRLS

The sexes do not differ on tests of cognitive style that measure one's ability to analyze, i.e., the ability to respond to a particular aspect of a situation without being influenced by the context, or restructure the elements of a problem in order to achieve a solution. Boys and girls are equally likely to respond to contextual aspects of a situation that are irrelevant to the task at hand. Boys are superior only on problems that require visual discrimination or manipulation of objects set in a larger context; this superiority seems to be accounted for by spatial ability, which we discuss below, and does not imply a general analytic superiority.

MYTH SEVEN: GIRLS ARE MORE AFFECTED BY HEREDITY, BOYS BY ENVIRONMENT

Male identical twins are intellectually more alike than female identical twins, but the two sexes resemble their parents to the same degree.

> **In all cultures in which aggressive behavior has been observed, boys are more aggressive physically and verbally.**

Boys are more vulnerable to damage by a variety of harmful agents in the environment both before and after birth, but this does not mean that they are more affected by environmental influences in general.

The two sexes learn with equal facility in a wide variety of situations. If learning is the primary means by which the environment affects us, then the two sexes are equivalent in this regard.

MYTH EIGHT: GIRLS ARE "AUDITORY," BOYS "VISUAL"

Male and female infants do not seem to respond differently to sounds. At most ages, boys and girls are equally adept at discriminating speech sounds. There is no sex difference in memory for sounds previously heard.

No study shows a sex difference among newborns in time spent looking at visual stimuli. During the first year of life, neither sex emerges clearly as more responsive to what they see. From infancy to adulthood, the sexes exhibit a similar degree of interest in visual stimuli. They also seem to be alike in ability to discriminate among objects, identify shapes, estimate distances, and perform on a variety of other tests of visual perception.

Our examination of the social science literature also revealed some sex differences that are fairly well-established:

DIFFERENCE ONE: MALES ARE MORE AGGRESSIVE THAN FEMALES

A sex difference in aggression has been observed in all cultures in which aggressive behavior has been observed. Boys are more aggressive physically and verbally. They engage in mock-fighting and aggressive fantasies as well as direct forms of aggression more frequently than girls. The sex difference manifests itself as soon as social play begins, at age two or two and a half. From an early age, the primary victims of male aggression are other males, not females.

Although both sexes become less aggressive with age, boys and men remain more aggressive through the college years. Little information is available for older adults.

DIFFERENCE TWO: GIRLS HAVE GREATER VERBAL ABILITY THAN BOYS

Girls' verbal abilities probably mature somewhat more rapidly in early life, although a number of recent studies find no sex differences. During the period from preschool to early adolescence, the sexes are very similar in their verbal abilities. But at about age 11, they begin to diverge; female superiority increases through high school, and possibly beyond. Girls score higher on tasks that involve understanding and producing language, and on "high-level" verbal tasks (analogies, comprehension of difficult written material, creative writing) as well as "lower-level" measures (such as fluency and spelling).

DIFFERENCE THREE: BOYS EXCEL IN VISUAL-SPATIAL ABILITY

Visual-spatial ability involves the visual perception of figures or objects in space and how they are related to each other. One visual-spatial test has the subject inspect a three-dimensional pile of blocks, and estimate the number of surfaces visible from a perspective different than his own. Another has him look at a figure, then select one from a set of four that matches the original if rotated in a plane. Male superiority on visual-spatial tasks is not found in childhood, but appears fairly consistently in adolescence and adulthood, and increases through the high-school years. The sex differences are approximately equal on analytic tasks (those that require separation of an element from its background) and nonanalytic ones.

DIFFERENCE FOUR: BOYS EXCEL IN MATHEMATICAL ABILITY

The two sexes are similar in their early acquisition of quantitative concepts and their mastery of arithmetic in grade school. Beginning at about age 12 or 13, however, boys' mathematical skills increase faster than girls'. The greater rate of improvement does not seem to be entirely due to the fact that boys take more math courses, although the question has not been extensively studied.

The magnitude of the sex difference varies depending on the study, and is probably not as great as the difference in spatial ability. Both visual-spatial and verbal processes are sometimes involved in solving math problems; some problems can be solved in either way, while others cannot, a fact that may help to explain why the size of the sex difference varies from one study to another.

On some questions, we found ambiguous findings or too little evidence on which to base conclusions. These questions are still open to further research.

QUESTION ONE: ARE THERE DIFFERENCES IN TACTILE SENSITIVITY?

Most studies of tactile sensitivity in infancy or ability to perceive by touch at later ages do not show sex differences. When differences are found, girls are more sensitive, but since this finding is rare, we cannot be confident that it is meaningful. Most studies in which the results are analyzed by sex deal with newborns; more work is needed with other ages.

QUESTION TWO: ARE THERE DIFFERENCES IN FEAR, TIMIDITY, AND ANXIETY?

Studies that involve direct observation of fearful behavior usually do not find sex differences. But teacher ratings and self-reports usually reveal girls as more timid or more anxious. The problem with self-reports is that we do not know whether the results reflect real differences, or only differences in people's willingness to report anxiety.

Since the very willingness to assert that one is afraid may lead to fearful behavior, the problem may turn out to be unimportant. But it would be desirable to have measures other than self-reports, which now contribute most of the data from early school age on.

QUESTION THREE: IS ONE SEX MORE ACTIVE THAN THE OTHER?

Sex differences in activity level do not appear in infancy. They begin to show up when children reach the age of social play. Some studies find that during the preschool years, boys tend to be more active, but many studies do not find a sex difference. This discrepancy may be partially traceable to the kind of situation in which measurements are made. Boys appear to be especially stimulated to bursts of high activity when other boys are present. But the exact way in which the situation controls activity level remains to be established.

Activity level is also affected by motivational states—fear, anger, curiosity—and therefore is of limited usefulness in identifying stable individual or group differences. We need more detailed observations of the vigor and quality of children's play.

QUESTION FOUR: IS ONE SEX MORE COMPETITIVE THAN THE OTHER?

Some studies find boys to be more competitive than girls, but many find the sexes to be similar in this regard. Almost all the research on competition has involved situations in which competition is maladaptive. For example, two people might be asked to play the prisoner's dilemma game, in which they have to choose between competitive strategies that are attractive to the individual in the short run, and cooperative strategies that maximize both players' gains in the long run. In such situations, the sexes are equally cooperative.

In settings where competitiveness produces greater individual rewards, males might be more competitive than females, but this is a

> **The two sexes are highly alike in their willingness to explore a novel environment.**

guess based on common-sense considerations, such as the male interest in competitive sports, and not on research in controlled settings. The age of the subject and the identity of the opponent no doubt make a difference too; there is evidence that young women hesitate to compete against their boyfriends.

QUESTION FIVE: IS ONE SEX MORE DOMINANT THAN THE OTHER?

Dominance appears to be more of an issue in boys' groups than in girls' groups. Boys make more attempts to dominate each other than do girls. They also more often attempt to dominate adults.

But the dominance relations between the sexes are complex. In childhood, the segregation of play groups by sex means that neither sex frequently tries to dominate the other; there is little opportunity. When experimental situations bring the two sexes together, it is not clear whether one sex is more successful in influencing the behavior of the other. In mixed adult groups or pairs, formal leadership tends to go to the males in the early stages of an interaction, but the longer the relationship lasts, the more equal influence becomes.

QUESTION SIX: IS ONE SEX MORE COMPLIANT THAN THE OTHER?

During childhood, girls tend to be more obedient to the commands and directions of adults. But this compliance does not carry over into relationships with peers. Boys are especially concerned with maintaining their status in their peer group, and therefore are probably more vulnerable than girls to pressures and challenges from that group, although this has not been well-established. It is not clear that in adult interactions, one sex is consistently more willing to comply with the wishes of the other.

QUESTION SEVEN: ARE NURTURANCE AND "MATERNAL" BEHAVIOR MORE TYPICAL OF ONE SEX?

There is very little information about the tendencies of boys and girls to be nurturant or helpful toward younger children or animals. Cross-cultural work does indicate that girls between six and 10 are more often seen behaving nurturantly. In our own society, the rare studies that report nurturant behavior involve observation of free play among nursery-school children. These studies do not find sex differences, but the setting usually does not include children who are much younger than the subjects being observed. It may be that the presence of younger children would elicit sex differences in nurturant behavior.

Very little information exists on how adult men respond to infants and children, so we can't say whether adult females are more disposed to behave maternally than adult males are to behave paternally. But if there is a sex difference, it does not generalize to a greater female tendency to behave altruistically. Studies of people's willingness to help others in distress have sometimes found men to be more helpful, sometimes women, depending on the identity of the person needing help and the kind of help that is required. Overall, the sexes seem similar in degree of altruism.

QUESTION EIGHT: ARE FEMALES MORE PASSIVE THAN MALES?

The answer is complex, but for the most part negative. The two sexes are highly alike in their willingness to explore a novel environment, when they both have freedom to do so. Both sexes are highly responsive to social situations of all kinds, and although some individuals tend to withdraw from social interaction and simply watch from the sidelines, they are as likely to be male as female.

We said earlier that girls are more likely to comply with adult demands, but compliance can take an active form; running errands and performing services for others are active process. Young boys seem more prone than girls to put out energy in bursts of strenuous physical activity, but the girls are not sitting idly by while the boys act; they are simply playing more quietly. Their play is fully as organized and planned, possibly more so. When girls play, they actively impose their own design upon their surroundings as much as boys do.

It is true that boys and men are more aggressive, but this does not mean that females are the passive victims of aggression—they do not yield or withdraw in the face of aggression any more frequently than males do, at least during the phases of childhood that have been observed. We have already noted the curious fact that while males are more dominant, females are not especially submissive, at least not to boys and girls their own age. In sum, the term "passive" does not accurately describe the most common female personality attributes.

We must conclude from our survey of all the data that many popular beliefs about the psychological characteristics of the two sexes have little or no basis in fact. Yet people continue to believe, for example, that girls are more "social" than boys, or are more suggestible than boys, ignoring the fact that careful observation and measurement show no sex differences.

The explanation may be that people's attention is selective. It is well documented that whenever a member of a group behaves the way an observer expects him to, the observer notes the fact, and his prior belief is confirmed and strengthened. But when a member of the group behaves in a way that is not consistent with the observer's expectations, the behavior is likely to go unnoticed, so the observer's prior belief remains intact.

This probably happens continually when those with entrenched ideas about sex differences observe male and female behavior. As a result, myths live on that would otherwise rightfully die out under the impact of negative evidence.

Eroticism as a Norm

Mary S. Calderone

The nature of this presentation is that of speculative and philosophical comments.

As in other fields, the rate at which knowledge about human sexuality is increasing has been markedly accelerated in the past ten years, i.e., the time intervals between such landmarks as Freud, Kinsey, and the two books of Masters and Johnson have been decreasing in length. What is new one year tends toward obsolescence the next. At the same time, from the point of view of the ordinary person, information about sex is more and more available—incorrect or distorted or sound—but at least available. In the past decade this has been largely due to the awareness of professionals of its importance, with its consequent integration into the bodies of knowledge assumed to be basic to the practice of their disciplines.

Like a picture puzzle, the outlines of human sexuality as it exists are beginning to emerge, with little bits and pieces of information being added here and there from the research and findings of many indi-

Revised version of a paper presented at the Annual Meeting of the National Council on Family Relations, Toronto, Ontario, Canada, October 18, 1973. Reprinted from *The Family Coordinator,* October 1974, pp. 337–342. Copyright (1974) by The National Council on Family Relations. Reprinted by permission.

viduals. What we see is far from being what we have imagined or postulated human sexuality was or ought to be.

THE PICTURE IN THE PAST

I should like here to remind you of the picture that we had of human sexuality even ten or fifteen years ago, a picture that now, as a society, we are still in the process of giving up.

The Child

The child used to be considered totally nonsexual, "innocent" (i.e., ignorant), "pure in mind" (i.e., no sexual thoughts, questions, fantasies) and in body (no erotic feelings or actions). When any of these occurred there were classical ways of dealing with them:

> "You're too young to ask about such things."
> "When you grow up you'll know."
> "Don't ever mention that word to me again."
> "Don't let me catch you doing that again."

The Adolescent

Adolescents, full of burgeoning sexual feelings, were expected to receive gratefully such information as was doled out by their parents, usually at a one time, rather ceremonious occasion called "having a little talk." They were not supposed to be sexual or to have sexual feelings, and the general attitude of the society was reflected in the shallow way in which parents usually dealt with what, to each adolescent, was a most profound, unique, and sometimes shaking self-experience of sex.

> "Now you are a little woman."
> "Now you are a man."
> "Playing with yourself is self-abuse."
> "Don't let a boy near you."
> "Don't get a girl into trouble."

"Nice girls aren't supposed to feel that way."
"Boys will be boys."
"When you get married you'll understand."
"Marriage is the beginning of true bliss."

The Adult

To be an adult was considered equivalent to being married, for it was inconceivable that anyone should not wish to be married and therefore the single state simply had to be involuntary. The aphorisms here were usually of the following order:

"If your wife 'comes' right from the beginning it shows she's experienced."
"If your wife doesn't come it shows she's frigid."
"You won't know true ecstasy until you both come at the same time every time."
"The woman's role is to satisfy the man."
"The man has a right to have his wife whenever he wants."

Over 50

To be over 50 was old, to be over 65 was aged. In either case, sex was not considered to exist.

"After the change women lose their interest in sex."
"Men go downhill after 50."
"It's disgusting and perverted for old men and women over 60 to be still interested in sex."
"I tell my husband I'm 60 and through with all that foolishness."

With our increased knowledge about and understanding of what it really means to be human and sexual, too many of us still hold on to such beliefs.

In the midst of repudiating these palpably false beliefs, however, the difficulty is to arrive at a societal consensus of what constitutes acceptable replacements. I should like to consider the most difficult area of all, the replacement of the "purity" concept—purity of mind meaning no sexual thoughts or fantasies, purity of body meaning no erotic feelings or actions, particularly in relation to the child and adolescent. How realistically is this concept of "purity" applicable?

GENDER IDENTITY AND PSYCHOSEXUAL DEVELOPMENT

Masters and other obstetricians and gynecologists have attested to the signs of functioning of the sexual system long before reproductive maturation. One of the earliest things a boy baby does after the first cry is to have an erection; the girl baby's vagina lubricates within 24 hours of birth. However, research and clinical experience

> **The work of the sex chromosomes is limited to determining whether or not the individual will be a genetic male or a genetic female.**

(Money and Ehrhardt, 1973) have shown that a great deal occurs before the moment of birth that will have a direct bearing not only on eventual capacity to respond erotically, but also on gender of the individual eventually chosen to respond to and with, and specifically on gender identity and role.

The genetic sex of the child is determined from the moment of conception. Genetically the child can be XX (female), XY (male), or other variations. At the moment of conception, either configuration XX or XY determines, in early embryonic life, whether the still-to-be-developed gonadal tissue will become testes or ovaries. It is difficult for most parents and even professionals to realize that thereafter, "the sex chromosomes will have no known direct influence on subsequent sexual and psychosexual differentiation" (Money and Ehrhardt, 1973). The work of the sex chromosomes is limited to determining whether or not the individual will be a genetic male or a genetic female, but it remains for the gonadal tissue, differentiating as a result of the influence of the chromosomes, to elaborate the hormonal secretions that will determine whether or not the anatomical sex of the baby will match the genetic sex so that the gender of the child can be correctly assigned at birth.

In the absence of the effects of testicular or male sex secretions, the embryo whether genetically XX (female) or XY (male) will always be female. Even if there were no ovarian or testicular hormones (a rare condition) the anatomy would still differentiate as female. "Testicular hormones are imperative for the continuing differentiation of the reproductive structures of a male" (Money and Ehrhardt, 1973). There are interesting clinical conditions that verify these findings: for instance, a hereditary trait in certain families may be passed on by the mother to some of her male children. This is androgen insensitivity—regardless of how much androgen the testicles produce before or after birth, or how much androgen is artificially given after birth, the cells of that particular individual are forever totally unresponsive to it. Therefore the XY or male individual (probably identified as a female at birth because the testicles are usually located in the abdomen) will arrive at puberty with a fully formed female personality, and will develop breasts because of estrogen produced by the adrenals, but cannot menstruate as there are no ovaries or uterus. Chromosomal studies will then reveal that she is a genetic male, but because her identity and behavior have been psychosocially fixed as female and in almost all aspects she is clearly female except that she cannot bear children, no effort should be made to change her sex of assignment and rearing. The testicles are removed, not because they can exert any hormonal influence but because they may possibly undergo later malignant degeneration, a functioning vagina can be surgically constructed, and she can marry and continue life as the female that she is, perhaps never having been made aware that she in fact was a genetic male.

Ultimately it is clear that the truly controlling factor in the development of gender identity and role is the psychosexual differentiation brought about by the parents and other adults in their treatment—

that is, the programming in the post natal 36 months—of the child. A striking example cited by Money was the identical twin boys whose circumcision shortly after birth resulted in a tragic accident causing total loss of the penis of one child. Under the advice of the Johns Hopkins Gender Identity Clinic, the parents, with full understanding of all the later implications of not providing definitive treatment, brought the sixteen month old infant to the hospital as a male, and took her away as a female following appropriate surgery. As the child approached puberty she would be given additional female sex hormones which she would have to receive for the rest of her life. The interesting factor here is that the mother kept a full diary and reported how early in the lives of the otherwise identical twins, even before the second birthday, the little girl began her psychosexual differentiation as a female.

All parents should be helped to understand that nothing assures that a genetic male or genetic female will grow up to acquire gender identity/role behavior congruent with the genetic gender, and that their own role is paramount in the achievement of correct gender identity. This is acquired and fixed by the time the child is eighteen months or two years old at the latest, and is thereafter probably not subject to change without severe psychosexual trauma.

The parents are also the unconscious primary programmers of the gender role behavior that their particular culture considers appropriate for a male or a female. Thus by the age of five, one should recognize that a child comes to school with the primary part of his or her sex education completed and fixed. The secondary part consists of imparting appropriate and useful information, and the development of positive attitudes about one's sex identity and role.

Closely integrated with these in that first five year period are the attitudes children will develop regarding the erotic drive that makes itself manifest, regardless of gender identity, very early in life. As boy or girl baby moves through the first year of life and begins to explore the body, the genitals are found to be pleasurable to touch and to fondle. Masturbation and almost unmistakable signs of orgasm have been identified by observers for boy and girl babies under one year (Kinsey, 1948 and 1953). Many men and some women testify that their first remembered masturbation to orgasm was at four or five years of age, others in preadolescence, still others at puberty. Yet by the age of eighteen, Kinsey found that, although practically 100 percent of males had experienced orgasm, only 40 percent of females, regardless of coital experience or gender of partner, had done so. The percentage for females rose steadily through their 20's and 30's, a few not experiencing first orgasm until their 40's. (Is this difference due to the attitudes of parents who punish their girl babies for signs of erotic interest more than they do boys?) However, in old age the situation is often reversed, with women retaining capacity for orgasm later than males. Masters and Johnson (1970) and other researchers have found that the primary requisite for continuing an already well established sexual life is an interested and interesting partner. Newman and Nichols (1960) found that a primary criterion was the social—that is, legal—acceptability of the partner. Among married couples over 60 in their sample, 54 percent continued to experience orgasm, among unmarried people only seven percent.

WHICH EXPRESSIONS ARE NORMS?

If erotic expressions can be accepted as norms throughout life, and I think such acceptance should now be recognized as inevitable, the primary question then becomes which erotic expressions, and under what conditions, especially in childhood? The American Law Institute, in the development of its Model Penal Code, used as a criterion for acceptability whether "social harm" resulted from a given act, meaning that it should not harm the individual, another individual involved in the act, or society as a whole. This is a useful criterion with which to examine various forms of erotic behaviors. Without awareness of this criterion, the United States society has been carrying out just such an examination, with gradual change of attitudes as a result. Considering three forms of erotic behavior on a three point scale UPD (unthinkable, permissible, desirable), masturbation, homosexual behavior, and nonmarital coitus can be plotted for changing acceptability in the general society for four age groups over the past six decades. (See Table.)

Author's estimation of changes in broad societal attitudes regarding three forms of sexual behavior, at four life stages, by 20 year periods. 1910–1970+.

Non-marital intercourse

	1910–30	1930–50	1950–70	1970+
Aging	U	U	(P)	D?
Adult	(P)	(P)	(P)	D
Adolescent	U	U	(P)	P?
Child	U	U	U	U

Masturbation

	1910–30	1930–50	1950–70	1970+
Aging	U	U	(P)	D
Adult	U	U	P	D
Adolescent	U	(P)	P	D
Child	U	(P)	P	D

Homosexual or bisexual behavior

	1910–30	1930–50	1950–70	1970+
Aging	U	U	U	P?
Adult	U	U	(P)	P
Adolescent	U	U	U	P?
Child	U	U	(P)	P?

Code: U = unthinkable
P = permissible
D = desirable
( ) = probably equivocal

The point to be made here is not only the change in societal attitudes about eroticism from negative towards positive, but the acceleration of this change in the past decade. Will this acceleration continue into the next two decades as sex for pleasure as distinct from sex for reproduction is accepted? It probably will, as people discover that even unfriendly sexual experiences need not be the disastrous, shattering, forever maiming agents that they were once thought to be. Rather, the possible negative effects of such experiences are being recognized as more likely to arise out of the very fear of and reaction against sex that are expressed, especially by parents, at the time of the event. The price paid by individuals, both as children and as adults, for the ignorance and fear inflicted upon them by the society because of their normally occurring erotic behavior is very high, whether in terms of eventual sexual inadequacy in marriage, or of compulsive behavior such as promiscuousness (heterosexual or homosexual), sadomasochism, fetishism, voyeurism, exhibitionism, or repetitious recourse to hard core pornography for the only sexual reactions many sexually crippled individuals are able to achieve.

CONCLUSION

In a society replete with human beings increasingly alienated, depressed, and lonely, the sexual malconditioning of many adults is double punishment, by the crimes of ignorance and silence that were actually committed against them in their own childhood or youth, and because the resulting compulsive sexual behavior of such individuals may render them vulnerable to punishment by the law.

Once professionals get past the barrier of accepting the eroticism of children and youth as legitimate, it should become far easier for them to devise ways to help parents understand their roles—first in accepting and then in helping their children in the responsible socialization of these erotic drives from infancy onward, so as to facilitate rather than minimize ultimate erotic responsiveness in adult life.

REFERENCES

American Law Institute Model Penal Code, Philadelphia, Pennsylvania, Tentative Draft No. 4, 1955.

Kinsey, Alfred C., Wardell B. Pomeroy, Clyde E. Martin, and Paul H. Gebhard. *Sexual Behavior in the Human Female.* Philadelphia: W. B. Saunders Company, 1953.

Kinsey, Alfred C., Wardell B. Pomeroy, and Clyde E. Martin, *Sexual Behavior in the Human Male.* Philadelphia: W. B. Saunders Company, 1948.

Masters, William H. and Virginia E. Johnson. *Human Sexual Inadequacy.* Boston: Little Brown and Company, 1970.

Money, John and Anne A. Ehrhardt. *Man & Woman, Boy & Girl.* Baltimore: The Johns Hopkins University Press, 1972.

Newman, G. and C. R. Nichols. Sexual Activities and Attitudes in Older Persons. *Journal of the American Medical Association,* 1960, 173, 33–35.

Masturbation

Herant A. Katchadourian and Donald T. Lunde

As infants explore their bodies, sooner or later they discover the pleasurable potential of their genitals. Some infants and preadolescent children do masturbate, in effect, but deliberate masturbation usually does not become common until the early teens. Most boys, for instance, are 10 to 12 years old when they begin; at age 13, when most girls have experienced menarche, only about 15 percent have masturbated. These percentages reported by Kinsey have undergone considerable changes as referred to further on.

Most boys seem to learn to masturbate from one another. In the Kinsey sample nearly all males reported having heard about the practice before trying it themselves, and quite a few had watched companions doing it. (Three out of four boys were led to masturbating by hearing or reading about it. About 40 percent mentioned observing others as their primary inspiration.) Pubescent boys thus appear to be much more communicative about their sexual activities than are

From *Fundamentals of Human Sexuality*, Second Edition, by Herant A. Katchadourian and Donald T. Lunde. Copyright © 1975 by Holt, Rinehart and Winston. Reprinted by permission of Holt, Rinehart and Winston.

girls, and are also bolder in seeking information. Fewer than one in three boys reported discovering this outlet by himself, and fewer than one in ten was led to it through homosexual contact.

Females learn to masturbate primarily through accidental discovery of the possibility (two out of three in the Kinsey sample), and they may begin as late as their thirties. Apparently females do not discuss their own sexual behavior as openly as males do; some women who know of male masturbation are startled to discover that the practice also occurs among females. Occasionally a woman may masturbate for years before she realizes the nature of her act, though such innocence was perhaps more common in the past.[1]

Verbal and printed sources, though less important than for males, continue to provide important leads for females (43 percent), and so does observation (11 percent). Furthermore, slightly more than 10 percent of girls are initiated into masturbation through petting, which is true for very few males. After a girl experiences orgasm through petting (usually as a result of manipulation by the male) she may then use the same methods autoerotically. Occasionally foreplay leading to coitus fulfills the same function. Homosexual contacts account for very few initiations into masturbation for females.

PREVALENCE AND FREQUENCY

Even those who decry the practice concede that masturbation is very prevalent among males and much more common among females than is widely recognized. Prevalence figures from various studies differ somewhat, but all have been high.

In the Kinsey sample, 92 percent of males and 58 percent of females were found to have masturbated to orgasm at some time in their lives. An additional 4 percent of women had masturbated without reaching orgasm. If we try also to include those who have the experience while oblivious of its "true nature," about two of three women may be supposed to have masturbated. Males rarely masturbate without ejaculating, and when they ejaculate there is no mistake about it. The male percentages do not therefore really change much when those with experiences stopping short of orgasm are also included. . . .

What was the weekly frequency of masturbation among men? As we noted in connection with total outlet, age, and marital status made a great deal of difference. In boys from puberty to 15 years old, among whom this practice reached a peak, the mean frequency of masturbation was twice a week. If we consider the "active population" only—that is, only those who actually had masturbated sometime or other—then the weekly mean was 2.4 times. These figures decreased steadily with age: In the total unmarried population, the 46–50-year-old group averaged fewer than one orgasm every two weeks; in the active population the mean was 1.2. Frequencies for married men were very small. There was no mean higher than once every two or three weeks.

How often did the average male masturbate? In the active unmarried population frequencies ranged from almost twice a week (in the post pubertal group up to 15 years) to about once every two weeks (in the 46–50-year-old group). In "active" married groups the rates were much lower. In no age group did an average married male masturbate more than once a month. Medians were consistently lower than were means, and both averages declined with age.

These frequencies must be understood within the context of the wide range of variation. There were men (apparently healthy) who never masturbated or did so only once or twice in their lives. Others may have averaged twenty or more such orgasms a week over many years.

The average (mean and median) frequencies for the active female sample were quite uniform at various age levels (up to the mid-50) and did not show the steady decline with age that was characteristic of males. The average unmarried woman, if she masturbated at all, did so about once every two or three weeks; the median for her married counterpart was about once a month.

The range of variation in frequency of female masturbation was very wide. In addition to many who never masturbated, some masturbated yearly, monthly, weekly, or daily; and some occasionally reached staggering numbers of orgasms in a single hour. These few individuals inflated the female means to two or three times the corresponding medians.

In the *Playboy* married sample, every other male and one out of three females reported having masturbated during the preceding year. For both sexes there was a distinct and similar correlation between age and prevalence of the practice. The highest rates were in the 25–34-year group (about 70 percent for males, 45 percent for females). The prevalence among 18–24-year-olds was almost as high (about 65 and 35 percent respectively), but the rates for both sexes steadily declined among older persons. By age 55 and over, only about 20 percent of males and 10 percent of females were engaging in the practice.

The prevalence rates for singles were higher than for marrieds for both sexes. The overall rate for single males was almost 85 percent. The rate for 18–24-year-olds was slightly lower, that for 25–34-year-olds somewhat hgher. The overall female rate was about 45 percent; that for 18–24-year-olds a bit lower, but the rate for the 25–34-year group was almost 70 percent. . . . The cumulative totals otherwise come very close to the Kinsey percentages and show that 94 percent of modern males and 63 percent of females have masturbated at some time in their lives.

Additional changes in masturbatory behavior since the time of Kinsey are moderately impressive. Attitudes have become more liberalized, but remain ambivalent. There is a distinct change in that boys and girls appear to start masturbating earlier. In the Kinsey sample the incidence of masturbation among boys of 13 years of age was about 45 percent. In the *Playboy* survey sample the corresponding percentage figure had increased to 65 percent. The rates for girls were lower than those for boys in both the Kinsey and *Playboy* studies. But the same pattern described for boys was also present among girls. Thus, while in the Kinsey sample the incidence of masturbation by age 13 was about 15 percent, in the *Playboy* sample the corresponding percentage had increased to close to 40 percent.

This increase in prevalence rates in masturbation since the Kinsey survey was not restricted to adolescents. Prevalence rates for single young males have gone up moderately, and for single females more markedly. Currently, 60 percent of women between the ages of 18–24 report some masturbatory experience as opposed to a quarter of single girls in their upper teens and a third in their early 20's among the

Kinsey females. There is also an increase in the frequency rates: Kinsey males between 16–25 averaged 49 times a year against 52 times among modern 18–24-year-olds. The corresponding rise for females is from 21–37 times a year.[2]

Additional current information has been reported from the Sorensen survey pertaining to masturbation.[3] In this sample 58 percent of boys and 39 percent of girls between 13 and 19 years of age reported having masturbated one or more times in their lives. Girls generally had had their first experience a year or so earlier than boys, and for most girls this occurred before they were 13.

While quite prevalent masturbation was not very frequent. Only 28 percent reported having masturbated during the preceding month. Of

> **Of all the alternatives to marital coitus (other than abstinence and nocturnal orgasm) masturbation is the least threatening to the marital relationship.**

these, 30 percent had done so only once or twice, 18 percent at least eleven times, and 7 percent twenty or more times during the past month. Boys were generally more active in this regard than girls.

Masturbation and Social Class

The better-educated person in the Kinsey sample (especially if female) was more likely to masturbate. Only 89 percent of males with only grade-school educations masturbated sometime in their lives. In the group with no education beyond high school 95 percent masturbated; for those with college educations the figure was 96 percent. The corresponding figures for females were 34, 59, and 60 percent.

The frequency of masturbation showed definite correlation with education among males and was highest among college-educated groups. Females did not show this correlation. Although a woman's social background (as measured by education) may have influenced her decision whether or not to masturbate, it did not affect the frequency.

Masturbation was clearly a very important outlet for the better educated. It was used by almost all college-educated males and nearly two-thirds of the females. It constituted not only the chief source (60 percent) of male orgasms before marriage but also almost 10 percent of orgasms following marriage. More than two-thirds of college-educated men masturbated at least some time after marriage.

These differences in fequency of masturbation can be explained by several factors. First, better-educated people are less fearful of masturbation as a health hazard. In their social circles masturbation may be openly condoned or at least not seriously condemned. At less-educated levels there are strong taboos against masturbation and for that matter against all sexual practices other than coitus. To many in this group masturbation seems not only unhealthy but also unnatural and unseemly. They find it difficult to understand, for instance, why a married man with ready access to a woman would ever want to masturbate.

An additional factor is the difference in class attitudes toward premarital coitus. Although better-educated people have gradually relaxed restrictions against premarital relations, they are probably still less permissive than are their counterparts in the lower classes. The greater reliance on masturbation may then arise partly from aversion to its alternatives rather than from direct preference for it.

Currently, these class-related differences (as measured by occupational and educational status) appear less significant, although they still persist even among the younger generation.

Adult masturbation is sometimes viewed as a product of "hypocritical" attitudes and sexual inhibitions characteristic of Western (particularly Anglo–Saxon) societies. The less educated among these groups are assumed to be less handicapped by such cultural distortions and closer to living under more "primitive" and therefore more "natural" conditions. The data from other cultures (and from behavioral studies of animals) do not substantiate these allegations.

Masturbation and Marriage

. . . masturbation accounted for far greater shares of total outlet for single people than for those who were married—as would be expected. In fact, we may ask why married people masturbate at all.

Current data indicate that there is an apparent increase in the prevalence of masturbation among young married men and women compared to the Kinsey sample: Whereas about 40 percent of husbands in their late twenties and early thirties masturbated in the past (median rate 6 times a year), now about 70 percent do so (median rate 24 times a year). For wives of corresponding ages the percentages have gone up from 30 percent to 70 percent, but the median rate has not changed (10 times a year). These data when viewed in the larger context of the study do not suggest that increased masturbation is in compensation for frustrations in marital coitus. . . . this is far from the case. Rather, modern married persons, especially those who are younger, appear relatively freer to rely on masturbation as an auxiliary outlet for sexual and related needs.[4]

The predominant reason for both sexes is the temporary unavailability of the spouse—through absence, illness, pregnancy, disinclination, and so on. Of all the alternatives to marital coitus (other than abstinence and nocturnal orgasm) masturbation is the least threatening to the marital relationship.

There are other instances in which masturbation may actually be preferable to coitus. A man may then be able to give freer reign to his fantasies, whereby, if he is simply after sexual release, he may circumvent lengthy and tedious courting of a demanding and exacting wife. If he has potency problems it saves him repeated humiliation. A woman, on the other hand, may find coitus unsatisfying and may attend to her own sexual needs through self-stimulation. As an autoerotic activity masturbation provides a person with full and complete control without the obligations and restraints necessary in dealing with another person.

Masturbation and Religion

As most interpreters of Jewish and Christian moral codes have condemned masturbation, let us see what effect this condemnation has had on actual behavior. Interestingly, men and women seem to have been influenced differently. The very high prevalence of masturbation among males indicates that religious belief has not had a significant effect. A man may feel less or more guilty about masturbating, but sooner or later more than nine out of ten men indulge in the practice. There is a difference, however, in how often they do so. The more religious men (particularly Orthodox Jews and practicing Roman Catholics) in the Kinsey sample did masturbate somewhat less often. The highest frequencies were among religiously inactive Protestants.

Among women, masturbation was definitely less widespread among the more devout (41 percent) than among the nondevout (67 percent). The degree of devotion seemed more important than the particular denomination. In contrast to men, once a woman had engaged in this practice she did not seem influenced by her religious beliefs in how often she used it.

Even though the devout females was less likely to masturbate, this practice accounted for a higher proportion of her total sexual outlet than it did for her nondevout counterpart. Masturbation still apparently provided a "lesser evil" in comparison with alternatives like premarital coitus.

Hunt reports that religious devoutness continues to have a significant influence on the practice of masturbation today: The nonreligious are more likely to masturbate, start doing so at a younger age, and are more likely to continue it into adult life and also into marriage.[5] But these differences between the devout and the nondevout are operating less effectively among the young. The effect of religion is generally much more marked among women than men.

Miscellaneous Factors

Boys who reached puberty at a younger age were more likely to masturbate and to do so more frequently than were boys who reached puberty later. The same did not apply to girls.

Women born after 1920 were more likely (by about 10 percent) to masturbate than those born before 1900. Among males there was a slight increase in the lower-educational groups in these two age categories. Otherwise, no substantial changes seem to have occurred in the masturbatory activities of successive generations.

Differences in background seemed to make some difference for women, but not for men: Urban women were more likely to masturbate, but there were no differences in how often they did so. The practice also accounted for a smaller percentage of the total outlet of urban women. . . .

MASTURBATION AND HEALTH

"There is really no end to the list of real or supposed symptoms and results of masturbation," according to Havelock Ellis, who was himself ambivalent about the practice.[6] Insanity; epilepsy; various forms of headaches (in addition to "strange sensations at the top of the head"); numerous eye diseases (including dilated pupils, dark rings around the eyes, "eyes directed upward and sideways"); intermittent deafness; redness of nose and nosebleeds; hallucinations of smell and hearing; "morbid changes in the nose"; hypertrophy and tenderness of the breasts; afflictions of the ovaries, uterus, and vagina (including painful menstruation and "acidity of the vagina"); pains of various kinds, specifically "tenderness of the skin in the lower dorsal region"; asthma; heart murmurs ("masturbator's heart"); and skin ailments ranging from acne to wounds, pale and discolored skin, and "an undesirable odor of the skin in women" are all supposed consequences of masturbation.

There is no evidence to support any of these or any other claims of physical harm resulting from masturbation. Yet for more than 200 years (from the dawn of the Age of Enlightenment) and until recently these dire effects have held an unshakable place in the beliefs of the medical elite in the Western world. The historical emergence of these notions is worth reviewing.

From the time of Hippocrates physicians have voiced their concern that overindulgence in sex is detrimental to health . . . . Only in the last 250 years, however, has masturbation been singled out as a particularly harmful activity. Before the eighteenth century we can find only occasional references to masturbation in medical texts. Early in the eighteenth century a book entitled *Onania, or the Heinous Sin of Self-Pollution* appeared in Europe. The author was probably a clergyman turned quack who peddled a remedy along with the book. Although the work became very popular throughout Europe (and is referred to in Voltaire's *Dictionnaire Philosophique*), it appears to have had no immediate impact upon medical opinion.

Then in 1758 *Onania, or a Treatise upon the Disorders Produced by Masturbation* by the distinguished Swiss physician Tissot appeared. It reiterated and amplified the claims of the former work. Tissot's views, coming from an unimpeachable authority, seem to have found ready acceptance. Despite rebuttals and accusations that he was exploiting his medical reputation to further his private moral points of view, the book became a standard reference. By the end of the eighteenth century the "masturbatory hypothesis" of mental disease and assorted ills was well entrenched. The further progress and eventual discrediting of these notions have been described by Hare.[7]

What about the psychological aspects of masturbation? As current views have been strongly influenced by psychoanalytic concepts, it may be best to examine first the reasoning behind some answers to questions about what masturbation means and what its consequences are.

Masturbation has received a great deal of attention in psychoanalytic theory. There are references to it in almost every one of the twenty-three volumes of Freud's collected works. The same is true of the writings of other analysts, and W. Stekel has devoted an entire volume to this topic.[8]

Freud believed that autoeroticism involves much more than Ellis envisaged when he proposed the term. Freud included, for instance, activities like thumb-sucking. As for masturbation, he divided it into several phases . . .: first, the self-stimulation of early infancy, which lasts only a short while; then further such activity before the age of 4; next suppression until the onset of puberty and the beginnings of adult sexuality; and finally, either continuation into adulthood or replacement by heterosexual coitus.

Freud found childhood masturbation (the second phase) of critical importance as a potential cause of neurosis. He believed that its effects "leave behind the deepest (unconscious) impressions in the subject's memory, determine the development of his character, if he is to remain healthy, and the symptomatology of his neurosis, if he is to fall ill after puberty."[9]

His reasoning is that early infantile masturbation is no more than innocent self-exploration, that the infant obtains pleasure from it but is too young to be blamed or even to comprehend blame, and that masturbation is therefore conflict-free. During the next phase the child (at about 3 years old) is going through the critical oedipal stage; he is now capable of fantasies, and when he resumes masturbation incestuous wishes become linked to it so that he feels guilty and fears punishment.

In addition to these inner changes, the environment also now treats him differently: A child of 4 is expected to behave properly, and masturbation is considered improper. He is told to stop, threatened, perhaps ultimately punished. Parents may actually imply that harm will come to his genitals if he persists. The child is bewildered. Are the threats directed at the act or at the fantasies (of which most parents are quite oblivious)? What will happen to him? What should he do? From this welter of unconscious conflicts under a façade of childhood innocence his psychological future takes shape.

At puberty, infantile conflicts reemerge and must be resettled, this time for adaptation to the world of adults. Masturbation now becomes a testing ground for adult sexual behavior, a way of becoming acquainted with one's equipment, of rehearsing future sexual behavior, and of releasing sexual tensions. In time, there is a gradual switch from the autoerotic to the sociosexual sphere: Masturbation is abandoned for the more mature and fulfilling outlet of coitus, but is resumed when coitus is unavailable.

Masturbation, viewed within the framework of psychoanalytic theory, is thus a universal normal activity of childhood and adolescence and a legitimate adult outlet when coitus is not possible. It is considered harmful, however, when it engenders guilt and anxiety—and symptomatic of sexual immaturity when it is preferred to heterosexual intercourse.

It is possible to argue that, on the basis of the phylogenetic and crosscultural record, masturbation is a biologically and psychologically legitimate sexual outlet. Population researchers may point out that by condemning adult masturbation psychoanalysts impute at least some degree of emotional disturbance to a vast segment of the population with no other independent evaluation of their behavior and feelings.

Currently no informed person has any real concern about the

deleterious effects of masturbation in a physical sense. Whatever concerns exist pertain to psychological and moral issues. Psychological judgments in this regard are based on the motivations behind the practice, the degree of dependency on this outlet, and the extent to which the practice excludes sociosexual relationships.

The relief of sexual tension is the most frequently verbalized motivation for masturbation (claimed by four out of five men and two out of three women in the *Playboy* survey sample). The need for such release is often to compensate for the lack of a sexual partner or temporary unavailability of one because of illness, absence, or some other reason. But masturbation is also relied on as an auxiliary source of gratification, even by the apparently happily married. The fantasy gratification functions of masturbation were discussed earlier. Other motivations behind the practice are nonsexual. In the *Playboy* sample over a quarter of males and a third of females reported that they masturbated to combat feelings of loneliness. Not frequently,

> **People generally seem to feel ashamed and secretive about the practice and ". . . almost no adults, not even the very liberated can bring themselves to tell friends, lovers, or mates that they still occasionally masturbate."**

people also resort to the practice to release tensions caused by occupational or personal problems or to simply relax in order to go to sleep.

A listing of motives such as these does not in itself provide an adequate basis for making judgments. A proper evaluation of masturbatory behavior, as with any other type of behavior, eventually has to be made in the context of the individual's overall life. In this regard it is clear that masturbation can become a liability if it is compulsively relied on at the expense of ultimately more rewarding interpersonal encounters. It is a convenient shortcut that carries the potential of shortchanging oneself. The problem in these cases is not primarily the result of masturbation but rather other, more fundamental psychological conflicts. In these cases masturbation becomes one more facet of the general picture of maladaptation. It must be recognized, however, that even in these pathological conditions it may provide one of the few readily available forms of sexual release and psychological comfort to the disturbed individual.

Despite the general condoning of the practice (at least for adolescents) by the medical profession, doctors often conclude that one should not carry the practice "to excess." Excess is not defined, and what the harm will be is not specified. This vagueness reflects the discredited but not discarded notions of former times.[10]

Masturbation is still not quite "respectable." Ambivalence in this regard appears to characterize even modern youths who have been generally spared the horror stories of former times. Sorensen reports that of all the sexual practices queried, masturbation elicited the most reticence and defensiveness.[11]

The problem was partly one of guilt. Among the adolescents currently masturbating, only 19 percent claimed never to have felt guilty (32 percent did so rarely, 32 percent sometimes, and 17 percent often). There was also an element of shame, since masturbation implied that one is not mature enough, attractive enough, or sophisticated enough to have a sexual partner. Yet, paradoxically, masturbation was found to be more common among those also engaging in coitus, than in those who were not.

Similar attitudes have been reported from the Playboy Foundation survey. People generally seem to feel ashamed and secretive about the practice and ". . . almost no adults, not even the very liberated can bring themselves to tell friends, lovers, or mates that they still occasionally masturbate."[12]

Though a remarkable percentage of people still feel that masturbation is wrong, there is a clear association between the prevalence of such attitudes and age. In the 55 and older age group, 29 percent of males and 36 percent of females agree that "masturbation is wrong." These percentages steadily decrease so that in the 18–24-year-old bracket only 15 percent of males and 14 percent of females still agree with this statement. These figures indicate not only a relative change in attitude but the disappearance of sex discrepancy in such attitudes.[13]

The general social acceptability of the practice is also clearly on the rise, as can be judged by the explicit discussions of masturbation in popular and literary works (notably *Portnoy's Complaint*).[14] The polite tolerance of earlier marriage manuals toward the practice has also given way to unabashed endorsement by writers of some of the currently popular sex manuals.[15]

NOTES

1 "A married lady who is a leader in social-purity movements and an enthusiast for sexual chastity, discovered, through reading some pamphlet against solitary vice, that she had herself been practicing masturbation for years without knowing it. The profound anguish and hopeless despair of this woman in face of what she believed to be the moral ruin of her whole life cannot well be described." (Ellis, H. [1942], Vol. I, Part One, p. 164.)
    One of our own students reported that she only realized that she masturbated after attending the course in human sexuality in college.

2 Hunt (February 1974), pp. 54–55.

3 Sorenson, R. C. (1973), pp. 129–145.

4 Hunt (February 1974), pp. 176–177.

5 For denominational differences in this regard *see* Hunt (1974), pp. 87–88.

6 Ellis, H. (1942), Vol. I, Part One, p. 249.

7 Hare (1962). *See also* Comfort (1967) and Schwartz (1973).

8 Stekel (1950).

9 Freud, *Three Essays on the Theory of Sexuality* (1905), in Freud (1957-1964), Vol. VII, p. 189.

10 For a range of medical opinions *see* Medical Aspects of Human Sexuality (April 1973), pp. 12–24.

11 Sorenson (1973), p. 143.

12 Hunt (February 1974), p. 54.

13 Hunt (February 1974), p. 55.

14 Roth (1967).

15 "*J*" (1969), pp. 38–52; "*M*" (1971), pp. 60–68.

REFERENCES

Comfort, A. *The Anxiety Makers*. New York: Delta Publishing Co., 1967.

Ellis, H. *Studies in the Psychology of Sex*. 2 vols. New York: Random House, 1942. (Originally published in 7 volumes, 1896-1928.)

Freud, S. *The Standard Edition of the Complete Psychological Works of Sigmund Freud* (1957-1964), ed. James Strachey. London: Hogarth Press and Institute of Psychoanalysis.

Hare, E. H. "Masturbatory Insanity: The History of an Idea," *Journal of Mental Science*, 452 (1962): 2–25.

Hunt, M. *Sexual Behavior in the 1970's*. Chicago: Playboy Press, 1974.

"J." *The Sensuous Woman*. New York: Lyle Stuart, 1969.

Kinsey, A. C., Pomeroy, W. B., Martin, C. E., and Gebhard, P. H. *Sexual Behavior in the Human Female*. Philadelphia: W. B. Saunders Co., 1953.

"M." *The Sensuous Man*. New York: Lyle Stuart, 1971.

Roth, P. *Portnoy's Complaint*. New York: Random House, 1967.

Schwarz, G. S. "Devices to Prevent Masturbation," *Medical Aspects of Human Sexuality*, 7, no. 5 (May 1973).

Sorenson, R. C. *Adolescent Sexuality in Contemporary America* (The Sorenson Report). New York: World Publishing, 1973.

Stekel, W. *Auto-eroticism*. New York: Liveright Publishing Corp., 1950.

Values on Campus

Richard Hettlinger

"I think that sex is just one of the greatest pleasures of life, and that your body is ready for it and needs it at the age of puberty, be it ten or thirteen or fifteen, and that when the body needs it you should accommodate the body's needs and your own desires." Underlying this statement, made to me by a student in a recording for a filmstrip (Hettlinger, 1969), is the widespread view that sex is a simple physical need that ought to be satisfied without concern over questions of ethics or social convention. A common analogy is drawn between sex and eating: both are responses to instinctual needs, and it is as absurd (and dangerous) to deny ourselves sex as it is to deny ourselves food. A failure to satisfy the sexual urge, it is frequently supposed, will lead to emotional damage and to sexual inadequacy in adulthood. Ellis (1963) has said dogmatically that "when a young man does, for any considerable period of time, remain even moderately (not to mention completely) abstinent, there is every reason to believe that he may do himself considerable harm and that he is practically never likely to do himself any good" (p. 14).

If this is the case a discussion of values is irrelevant in a book on sex: for values imply some criteria by which to determine when and how sexuality should be expressed. If sex is a physical need to which one should respond immediately the only "value" to be considered is that of satisfying the demands of the body.

If we look more closely at the analogy, however, it turns out to be far from conclusive. While one cannot live without eating anything, one can live very well without eating *some* things: indeed abstention from certain foods is essential to the life of many people, and the human system adapts without any ill effects to dietary restrictions or other situations when particular foods are unavailable. We do not think the immediate satisfaction of physical hunger a good thing in all circumstances. An alcoholic or a member of a group with limited supplies who fails to control an intense desire for drink or food is not applauded. Equally, even if it is true (and the fact has not been demonstrated) that abstinence from *all* forms of sexual release is necessarily harmful, it does not follow that abstinence from *some* forms of sexual release is harmful. A conscious choice, based on reasonable principles, to abstain from intercourse and to be satisfied temporarily with petting or masturbation may be entirely healthy.

Masters (1968) has pointed out that "there must be countless lifetime celibates who have not become neurotic." *The Playboy Advisor*, in reply to a query from two anxious readers, put it this way:

> Abstinence, as such, is neither good nor bad for the health. What does affect the individual's well-being are the circumstances of, and the motivations for, his abstention. Kinsey points out that men who are physically incapacitated, natively low in sex drive, sexually unawakened in their early years or separated from their usual sources of sexual stimulation can abstain indefinitely without appreciable harm. Even when these conditions do not prevail, if the motivation for abstention is conscious and rational, no harm will be done (*Playboy*, November 1967).

The studies of Ardrey (1966), Lorenz (1967) and Morris (1967) have been interpreted by many as giving support to the view that instincts must inevitably exert a decisive power in human relationships. Beneath the surface gloss, according to Morris, the naked ape is "still very much a primate" subject to the irresistible urges of raw animal need. Ardrey takes it as axiomatic that human beings are largely controlled by animal instinct and bound to be aggressive. These reminders of the fragility of human societies and the danger that the quality of our relationships may be debased by less than human behavior are timely. But they should not be taken to mean that sexual values are unimportant, or that we can remain human beings and abandon ourselves unthinkingly to the satisfaction of our physical needs. A movie called *The Fear* was promoted by an ad showing a man apparently raping a woman, with the caption: "There are hungers no man can deny." But few of us think for a moment that the analogy holds in this case. It must be remembered that the very concept of

> **Sex is deeply associated with cultural expectations since, except for masturbation, it always involves another person.**

"instinct" (at least in man) as an inherent disposition or impulse which determines behavior and is beyond conscious control is repudiated by many responsible scientists (Ashley Montagu, 1968).

Lorenz, while stressing the value of aggression or initiative in man, has complained of the misinterpretation that attributes to him the view that man is controlled by instinct: "I tried to show the existence of internal forces that man must know in order to master. I said that reason could conquer aggression." And in a specific reference to the sexual implications of his theories Lorenz warned that taking "the theoreticians of complete sexual promiscuity" at their word would involve enormous damage to human culture (*The New York Times Magazine*, July 5, 1970). For Lorenz the absolutely new and critical factor in the human situation is the appearance of language, the possibility of a cumulative tradition or culture, and "the greatest gift of all, rational responsible morality," which gives man the power to control his animal inheritance (1967, p. 232).

Man is indeed an animal, and the ethologists are right to remind us that a recognition of that fact is vital if human existence is to be preserved. But man is an animal whose physical needs have been given more than purely physical significance. Sex in particular has come to have emotional and social associations that are absent from other activities, such as eating.[1] Even eating is surrounded by many social customs which, in normal civilized circumstances, involve considerable restraints on the immediate satisfaction of hunger. But sex is even more deeply associated with cultural expectations since, except for masturbation, it always involves another person. In a unique sense this particular physical urge has been transformed in the course of human history.

The role played in human sexuality by cultural development makes it impossible to hide behind any simple identification of sex and hunger, and makes responsible decisions about values unavoidable. "Because all complex human behavior is heavily dependent upon cortical processes it is automatically open to modification through the influences of previous experience. This explains why, in human beings more than in any other species, sexuality is structured and patterned by learning" (Ford and Beach, 1951, p. 259). As Arieti (1972) points out, "When an animal reacts to hunger, thirst, sexual desire, it does not choose; it responds. It has no alternative; it has to follow the urge. Although these animal functions are motivated, they are not willed and do not imply conscious selection. Can a man revert to the stage of simple appetite? Only in extreme rare cases, the existence of which are doubted: the cases of so-called irresistible impulses. These cases occur only in conditions of severe pathology, mental illness, or early infancy" (pp. 36–37).

Studies of the development of moral reasoning (Piaget, 1932; Kohlberg, 1964; Maddock, 1972; O'Connor and Wrightsman, 1972) suggest that people pass through several stages in the process of achieving mature, integrated ethical standards. At first a child accepts the distinction between right and wrong simply in terms of the physical consequences associated with the words. That is good which results in pleasurable experience; that is bad which is associated with pain, punishment or parental disapproval. Authority figures are obeyed and their edicts followed without any awareness of principles or any sense of a general moral order. Purely pragmatic and hedonistic interests are at work.

At a second level the expectations and approval of the group (initially the family) become significant factors, sometimes outweighing the values of personal pleasure. Thus immediate private advantage may be subordinated to the sense of loyalty to others and to the satisfaction of approval by society. Rules are obeyed for their own sake in the interests of the common good. Only at a third level of maturity, at what Kohlberg calls the "postconventional" stage, is the ideal of personal value embraced and the possibility affirmed of challenging social definitions of right and wrong in the name of one's own understanding of good and evil. While this is theoretically the foundation of our society it is by no means embraced by all. The opposition to the Vietnam war represented a significant assertion of postconventional moral judgment by many; but a large proportion of the population still give loyalty to "my country—right or wrong." In sexual matters the great majority of adults still feel it important to uphold the traditional ideal of premarital chastity even though many of them did not practice it themselves.[2]

The transition from conventional moral reasoning to postconventional independence takes place during adolescence and may often only be fully achieved during the years at college. But it does not represent the full development of the human capacity for ethical maturity. This comes only when a person is able to define the right in terms of self-chosen moral principles based on universal applicability and logical consistency. This involves more than the acceptance of a set of laws or rules of even the most demanding kind (such as the Ten Commandments). It is a decision of conscience to live, as far as possible, by an ideal such as that of Kant (always treat another person as an end, not only as a means: act on that maxim which you would will to become a universal law) or of the Sermon on the Mount (love your neighbor as yourself: always treat others as you would like them to treat you).

The achievement of postconventional morality should surely be the concern of any mature person, and most students *claim* to have achieved independence from the purely traditional standards of society. But I suspect that sexual behavior on campus is more often less free of convention than it appears. Rather than being based on independent values it frequently seems to be motivated by a continuing need to reject traditional mores. It continues to be an extension of the necessary adolescent celebration of escape from the confines of establishment anti-sexualism, rather than a mature and considered pattern based on reflection and critical judgment.

Not infrequently, submission to the authority of parents or church is replaced by tutelage to a new, dogmatic ideal of sexual expertise. For the dedicated pursuit of "organ grinding" can be as destructive of personal freedom and of human relationships as the most rigid Victorianism. One experienced psychiatrist has stated: "Some of the people whom I knew who had great, vivid, violent orgastic potency could not fit into any psychiatric description of an emotionally mature person in relationship with other people" (Granatir, 1968). Masters (1968) has warned that "the greatest mistake a male can make is to feel that because he has a certain amount of technical competence, he is an effective sexual entity." Schaefer (1973) makes it clear that the same is true for a female: "The ability to experience orgasm through heterosexual sex does not necessarily ensure an ability to achieve warm and satisfying heterosexual relationships and vice versa" (p. 17).

Conflict between adolescents and their parents very frequently focuses on the question of sexual behavior because the necessary task of asserting one's own individuality against the family requires that one's freedom as a sexual person be affirmed. According to Storr (1968) self-esteem is *chiefly* rooted in sexuality:

> A confident belief in one's own masculinity or femininity is a fundamental part of human identity. . . . The normal person, if such exists, constantly renews a sense of value through loving and being loved; and the object of physical passion is thus not only a means whereby the drive of sexuality can be expressed and assuaged, but also a vital source of self-esteem. We cannot escape our physical natures; and a proper pride in oneself as a human being is rooted in the body through which love is given and taken (pp. 68–69).

Interference by parents in the freedom to engage in sexual activity can easily appear to be an infringement on the right to independence. But at a deeper level adolescence means the re-ordering of the infantile sexual relationship to one's parents. It has been said that you can only fall in love with a girl (or boy) when you fall out of love with your mother (or father). And unconsciously the repudiation of parental sexual standards involves a rift between the generations that it is almost impossible to handle on a rational level. It is therefore inevitable that rebellion against adult ideals of chastity can take on something of the quality of a crusade, and independence and freedom seem to be synonymous with unrestrained sexuality. But this is surely a fallacy. Rebellion for its own sake can be a conformity as rigid as unques-

> During the past decade there has been a marked increase in the percentage of women engaging in intercourse at college, but there is little evidence of a similar modification of parental attitudes towards the sexual freedom of their daughters.

tioning obedience to authority. To sleep around just because the adult world says it is forbidden is no more a truly mature thing to do than it is to preserve your virginity just because your mother told you to. True freedom is the capacity to develop one's own individual values as a sexual being, questioning what is erroneous in the standards of the past, but embracing whatever wisdom the experience of others conveys.[3]

Most people have in the past eventually worked out a reasonable accommodation between their parents' values and their own life styles. Reiss (1967) found that two out of three college students saw their sexual *standards* as similar to those of their parents—though a large proportion felt guilt about their sexual *behavior*. He also found that as people came to assume the responsibilities of marriage and family their standards became more conservative: the degree of permissiveness was markedly lower among married than among unmarried adults, and lower yet among parents with teenaged children. But Reiss's study was conducted ten years ago, and two developments in the past decade make it less likely that today's students will eventually adopt their parents' standards.

First, those who (understandably) dismiss the moral authority of a society that bombed Hanoi and Cambodia, failed to distinguish between the seriousness of marijuana and heroin and produced the Watergate scandals are more likely to reject the sexual mores of their parents. "Once you have taken drugs and broken that rule, it's easier to break all the others," commented one college senior.

Second, there has been a significant new development separating the generations since about 1965. Up to that time the number of male students engaging in intercourse (while, as we shall see, not as high as is popularly assumed) was much greater than the number of women students doing so. But parental standards, while technically uniform, were often perceived as permitting much more liberty for men to experiment. The possibility of an accommodation between the two was therefore open. During the past decade there has been a marked increase in the percentage of women engaging in intercourse at college (Davis, 1971), but there is little evidence of a similar modification of parental attitudes towards the sexual freedom of their daughters. Not only do parents not communicate any expectation that their female children will engage in intercourse; they frequently refuse to face or discuss the fact that they have done so when it is obviously the case.

One recent study of the attitudes of unmarried upperclass women at the University of Oregon and of their mothers found them so far apart on the specific issue of premarital intercourse that the author argued that attempts at communication on the subject would exacerbate rather than alleviate generational conflict (LoPiccolo, 1973). Many women tell me that their fathers find it impossible to imagine their involvement in any sexual experience, and one student who was planning to live with her male friend while they attended graduate school at the same institution found that her parents simply failed to acknowledge the situation, despite her broad hints. In such circumstances the possibility remains that sex on campus may be an expression of revolt rather than based on consistent principle.

If freedom from, rather than reaction to, parental or other traditional authorities is difficult to achieve, submission to new but equally binding external standards is difficult to avoid. The peer group plays a valuable role in providing support for the individual in the necessary adolescent process of establishing personal independence. But it can, in its turn, be a threat to the development of mature standards. There is a persuasive pressure towards uniformity and against individual judgment on every campus. Loss of virginity is represented as the norm and the (considerable) minority who prefer to delay the experience of intercourse are often made to feel inadequate. One female student confided to a counselor that her virginity was such a burden to her that: "On a trip to Greece, I found any old Greek and did it so it wouldn't be an issue any more." Another woman reported, "It isn't the boys who pressure you into bed, but it's the other girls. Not that they say anything, but just by being around them I feel like some kind of nut" (Steinem, 1972).

The authority of campus experts has been given new status and apparently objective support in recent years. A group of sexual prophets, as unqualified in their dogmatism as the religious teachers of the past, now assure the doubtful that sexual restraints are demonstrably ridiculous and orgasmic pleasure the universal test of maturity. Thus Ellis (1969) states: "Among enlightened and educated young people today, I would call the preservation of virginity before marriage an overt display of arrant masochism." A widely read sex guide contains the assertion that "if marriage is not possible (for any number of reasons), then sex without marriage is the only alternative. (*No sex is so stupid it is not even worth considering as a possibility.*)" (Reuben, 1969, pp. 107–8).[4]

The result is a reversed sexual anxiety, a guilt about feeling guilty, a new dogmatism to which many subscribe because of external pressure. There is a new puritanism of the sexually emancipated which can just as easily discourage honest and independent thinking. "Sin," writes Rollo May (1969), "used to mean giving in to one's sexual desires; it now means not having full sexual expression. Our contemporary puritan holds that it is immoral *not* to express your libido. . . . A woman used to be guilty if she went to bed with a man, now she feels vaguely guilty if after a certain number of dates she still refrains" (pp. 45–46).

The results can be tragic for those whose preference or persuasion or physical qualities exclude them from the experiences that the more vocal libertarians take for granted. A graduate student in a letter to *Sexual Behavior* (March, 1972) complained that magazines like *Playboy* are "more frustrating than helpful because they give the impression that everybody but me has a good, active sexual life" and declared that his constant obsession with the problem of his own virginity had contributed to a difficult time in college. "What has the so-called sexual revolution meant for those too homely, too disagreeable, too sheltered, or too inhibited to participate in the sexual economy?" asked Christopher Jencks (1964). "My guess is that they are the real losers as campus mores change. For every suicide brought on by sexual intercourse, there are probably a dozen precipitated by lack of dates; for every psychiatric patient burdened with an unwanted marriage or an unforgotten abortion, there are probably two suffering from the absence of invitations to such disasters."

While figures for intercourse on campus are notoriously hard to estimate because of great variations between different institutions depending on their location and cultural background, they are lower than many students assume. At a large midwestern state university the actual percentage of campus virgins was underestimated by 78 percent of the women interviewed (Jackson and Potkay, 1973). A reasonable estimate, based on recent studies,[5] is that on a national average about 65 percent of today's male college students engage in coitus and about 50 percent of today's college women. All in all the picture is *not* one in which students universally regard the question of virginity as closed. Whether an individual's decision is to engage in intercourse or not should be based on responsible consideration of the issues involved and the values he or she wants to preserve, *not* on a sense of inevitability artificially produced by misinformation about statistics, or on the loudly touted myth of the disappearing virgin. One out of every three men and one out of every two women on campus today will probably fall in that category at graduation.

Virginity or non-virginity, however, is not the only issue of importance. What is more significant is the quality of sexual intimacy; and here again the student, particularly the freshman, is likely to be influenced by the popular impression that on campus "anything goes." Unfortunately this assumption vitiates several widely read studies of student sexual activity. By failing to distinguish between intercourse in a purely casual situation and its occurrence as an expression of affection and commitment, they succeed in giving an unbalanced picture of the moral climate on campuses. A survey carried out by Daniel Yankelovich Inc. (1972) concluded that in recent years there had been a major change in sexual morality because "casual premarital sexual relations" had increased. A book by the sociologist Vance Packard had the significant title *The Sexual Wilderness* (1968); but, while it contained some valuable material, it too gave a false impression of moral irresponsibility by treating all acts of intercourse outside of marriage as equally promiscuous. Packard exclaimed in dismay at the discovery that 58 percent of American college males and 43 percent of American college women admitted to coital experience. But a careful reading of his figures shows that only 30 percent of the males and only 7 percent of the females had ever engaged in a "one night affair involving coitus," and he admitted that the figure for promiscuity among college women was "practically insignificant" since most of the 7 percent came from one university in New York City.

It is difficult to know what to make of those who thus exaggerate the degree of irresponsible sex on campus. One Catholic college chaplain suggested that "the image of large numbers of college students 'sleeping around,' indiscriminately indulging in sex for kicks and pleasure without any concern for consequences or permanence, appears to reflect more the frustrated yearnings of writers and readers than it does actual campus life" (Walsh, 1967). A British writer has put it more bluntly. The older generation, he suggests, have "an almost obscene obsession with the sexuality of the young . . . prompted by envious rancour and a bullying intention to interfere" (MacInnes, 1963).

But whatever the reason, reports on student sexual behavior that suggest a morass of indulgence can obviously have the effect of pressuring some people into casual sex they do not really want because they perceive it to be expected of them at college. That it is a false, or at least an oversimplified, impression is clear. Kinsey (1948) found, for example, that a much smaller percentage of students ever visited a prostitute than was the case among the less educated groups, and students almost always find the experience degrading. The Katz study (1968) concluded that "sexual intimacy seems to take place in the context of a relationship that is serious rather than casual" (p. 56). The number of male and female students having their first coital experience in a non-committed relationship or having coitus with more than one person *declined* significantly in the midwestern United States between 1958 and 1968 (Christensen and Gregg, 1970).

Vreeland (1972), who studied the dating patterns of Harvard men, comparing their interests in 1960 and 1970, found that while the desire for sexual intimacy remained constant, and the likelihood that it would include intercourse increased, companionship was more highly rated than sexual conquest. "Our evidence does not suggest the sexual revolution that has been publicized," she writes. "The Har-

> **One barrier to the establishment of mature values is overconcern with measurable sexual behavior.**

vard men of the '70s are much more interested in the *companion* pattern of dating, characterized by an intense emotional relationship with a woman that, although containing a sexual component, is similar to a same-sex peer relationship. Girls are sought as friends in their own right rather than partners for recreation or status achievements. . . . Students today date more frequently and become more committed to one woman than did their counterparts of the 1960s . . . we found less evidence of unbridled promiscuity than a relaxation of restrictions on sexual intercourse for couples involved in a more or less stable relationship." Arafat and Yorburg (1973a), who questioned several hundred female students using drugs in 1970–71, reported that "the modal sexual pattern even among heavy drug users is that of fidelity to a single partner at any time . . . the promiscuity pattern is a minority pattern among drug users in our study."

The point of all this is not to argue for the adoption of a less permissive set of values because most students are less casual in their sexual behavior than their image suggests. To do that would be to attempt to impose another statistical tyranny. Nor am I denying that there is a good deal of impersonal and exploitative sex on campus. The aggressive obsession with sexual conquest represented by Jonathan and Sandy in the movie *Carnal Knowledge* was a caricature—but a caricature of an attitude one frequently encounters among students. What I am urging is the importance of each individual's establishing his or her own personal, coherent, rational basis for sexual behavior without being pressured by a need to comply with any dogmatic authority, old or new, or with any supposed uniform values characteristic of the student community.

Another barrier to the establishment of mature values is overconcern with measurable sexual behavior. Figures and percentages can undoubtedly contribute enormously to freedom from false fears and unnecessary guilt. To know that 95 percent of all males masturbate, or that the great majority of women are capable of enjoying orgasm, or that 5 percent of the population is homosexual, can be truly liberating. I do not want in any way to question the value of such studies as those of Kinsey and of Masters and Johnson. Accurate factual information about sexual practices of various people, and about the physiology of sexual response, is essential. Unfortunately some treatments of the ethical and personal aspects of the subject have been guilty of gross neglect of the scientific findings. But the simple fact that coitus and orgasm are relatively clear identifiable experiences makes these the natural criteria for statistical measurement, and as a result these particular elements of human sexuality tend to be isolated from the whole gamut of personal relationships. Kinsey, for example, in listing the number of sexual "outlets" (a peculiarly masculine phrase) experienced by different people drew no statistical distinction between an orgasm resulting from intercourse with a farm animal or one enjoyed in the context of a deeply human love-relationship. The result is a distorted focusing of attention on sex as a target-oriented activity. The ease with which we identify "sex" and coitus in ordinary speech illustrates the trend. We can say, quite absurdly, of a couple who are in love and enjoying every form of intimacy short of intercourse that they are *not* "having sex together."

The authors of the major research works were themselves quite aware of the limitations of their treatment of sexuality. Kinsey (1948) repeatedly pointed out that he had not identified *the* American sexual pattern and after a full statement of the arguments pro and con premarital intercourse concluded with this warning: "The resolution of these conflicting claims can come only through some recognition that certain of these problems lie in areas which belong to the biologic, psychologic, and social sciences, while others are moral problems which the student of moral philosophies most solve" (1953, p. 309).

Masters and Johnson (1968) have freely acknowledged that their work was intentionally restricted to the physical aspects of sexuality and that the *why* of sexual response is far more important than the *what*. In an article, "A Defense of Love and Morality" (*McCalls*, November 1966), they stressed that sex as a physical phenomenon is only a small part of sexuality. But popular interpretation has all too often assumed that factual research has settled, or made irrelevant, questions of personal judgment: and as a result instead of students working out their own standards with honesty and consistency they can easily fall into an uncritical and oversimplified search for the perfect orgasm, ignoring the psychological, social and ethical issues that are inseparable from *human* sexuality.

A particular problem arises for many women as a by-product of the new understanding of female sexuality. The search for what has been called "the liberated orgasm" (Seaman, 1972) can turn out to be yet another compulsive obsession. The impression that all women who fail to enjoy multiple orgasms are sexually inadequate can be as serious a barrier to the development of independent values as the older assumption that all women who enjoyed sex were "nymphomaniacs."[6] "The sexual revolution—liberated orgastic women, groupies, communal lovemaking, homosexuality—has made us feel that we must be able to have sex with impunity, without anxiety, under any conditions and with anyone, or we're uptight freaks. These alienating, inhuman expectations are no less destructive or degrading than the Victorian puritanism we all so proudly rejected" (*Our Bodies, Our Selves*, 1973, p. 23).

Two women participants in a discussion expressed their anxieties thus:

Sara: I will tell you something that I feel is unacceptable. Right now there is a lot of pressure on women to function well sexually. People feel it is unacceptable for a woman not to be able to have an orgasm because of all the literature and all the studies that are going on. That makes me nervous. That bothers me because it is in such contradiction to the way I was raised. It is like telling a girl to switch all of a sudden. After not being allowed to, you are *supposed* to perform, and not just perform but to enjoy yourself. That is very hard for me. I am having some problems in that area, so all the talk about women having many orgasms at once just adds to it for me.

Sally: Right. If you experience orgasms with one person, and you don't experience them with another one, the pressure is on you to try to figure out why. It is sort of like trying to figure out what you are doing every moment. You can make the appropriate sounds at the appropriate times, but in fact you know you are acting. Then you begin to wonder, first of all, why you are acting. Secondly, you are wondering why you are not experiencing all these ecstatic feelings you had experienced before.

It is like anything else—you are supposed to measure up to the normal. What is normal for me is not normal for you. Why I am not normal like the rest of the people who are in the studies I don't know (Gadpaille, 1972).

One source of this concern is the assumption that the male pattern of orgasm should be the norm for women. Because we now know that the female is capable of orgasmic experience as intense as that of the male (Masters and Johnson, 1966), it is taken for granted that women should and can enjoy orgasm as readily and in the same circumstances as men. Because the biological identity of male and female orgasm has been established there is now an expectation that the woman will normally experience a dramatic, vigorous climax similar to the man's. Her failure to do so may be taken as a lack of sexual responsiveness or as a slight on her partner's masculinity. Some women feel it necessary to fake orgasm to impress the man.

Some men will blame a woman for being "frigid"[7] if she fails to perform as he expects and according to his standards of sexual pleasure. Indeed there is a reason to believe that it is the male's anxiety about his own sexual capacity that leads him to demand *his* kind of sexual response from his partner (Schaefer, 1973). "If the male is secure with his own feelings about himself as a man, he need not feel threatened nor feel inadequate if his partner does not achieve orgasm. An important side effect of the female's lack of orgasm may be the development of secondary impotence or premature ejaculation on the part of the male. This may come about from the anxiety generated by his 'need to perform,' his fear of failure to bring his partner to orgasm, and by the memory of previous unsuccessful achievements" (Adelson et al., 1973).

Marcus (1966) argues that women have too easily allowed themselves to be persuaded to identify their sexual capacities with those of men, thus failing to achieve the real liberation they seek. He points out that in the nineteenth century women as well as men were convinced that there was a female ejaculation parallel to that during male orgasm. This shows us, he suggests, that women's idea of their own sexuality is "historically a response to what men want and demand that sexuality to be, and that in general women are content to accept whatever model of their own sexuality men offer to and demand of them. *Mutatis mutandis,* a little reflection will yield the insight that the same thing is happening today" (p. 113).

Another source of confusion about the "norm" of female sexual response arises from popular misreading of the Masters and Johnson studies. To take the results of their study of *Human Sexual Response* (1966) and use them as a standard by which to judge the experiences of college women is to submit to another statistical tyranny. It must be remembered that all but two of their sample were over twenty-one, *all were required as a condition of participation to have experienced orgasm during intercourse* and 357 out of the 382 female subjects were or had been married.[8] Furthermore, it is not sufficiently noted that while Masters and Johnson identified only one sexual response pattern for men, they diagrammed three cycles for their female research population and described even this as an oversimplification of the "infinite variety" of female orgasmic experience.

Rather than expecting orgasmic satisfaction similar to that of the male, women should realize that "orgasm can be a very mild experience, almost as mild as a peaceful sigh, or it can be an extreme state of ecstasy with much thrashing about and momentary loss of awareness. It can last a few seconds or half a minute or longer. There is, in brief, no right or wrong way to have one" (*Our Bodies, Our Selves*, 1973, p. 33).

Reuben (1969) has taken it upon himself to tell women what they want sexually, even when women deny that orgasm is all that important to them. "Some women tell it that way," he admits, "but 'enjoying' sex without orgasm is about as satisfying as 'enjoying' a nice dinner without being able to swallow it" (p. 124). I do not question at all the importance of the recognition of female orgasmic capacity: virtually every woman, given the right conditions, can enjoy orgasm. An increasingly large number of women will do so in the future, and they will do so at an earlier age than their older sisters did. Failure to reach orgasm, once a certain level of arousal has been passed, is as frustrating and even physically painful for a woman as for a man. But most women take much longer than men to reach that level (Gebhard, 1966). Most women are more dependent than men on the emotional and personal circumstances for erotic arousal. And many women, despite Reuben's *obiter dictum*, report that they are sometimes sexually satisfied by hugging, petting or intercourse without orgasm (Bardwick, 1971; Sherfey, 1972; Stanley et al., 1973; Bell and Bell, 1972; Fisher, 1973).

Schaefer (1973) came to the conclusion that "the experience of orgasm, in and of itself, is *not* always an integral part of sexual contentment" (p. 18), and quotes this example among several: "I'm pleased and feel good whether I have an orgasm or not. It's all extremes. If I feel that he has tried to communicate with me and give something to me emotionally, that he's enjoying me and I'm enjoying him, then I don't care whether I have a climax or not. It's not that important. Of course, I wouldn't like to go every night without one. Then I would feel very frustrated and want something more" (p. 147).

No woman, then, need feel that she has to comply with some model of sexual behavior imposed by others. She is free to be a sexual person in accordance with whatever values and ideals she chooses to adopt. She can act in whatever way expresses her own inner convictions, without any obligation to perform or respond in a manner

> **Healthy sexuality depends on** *both* **sexes freeing themselves from a goal-oriented concern with achieving orgasm, and on enjoying different experiences of sexual intimacy for their own worth rather than as mere "foreplay" to coitus.**

dictated by men or by other women. Schaefer (1973) sums up the situation thus: "The more thoughtful woman will realize that she must become her own authority in matters regarding her sexual conduct. She is obliged to create reasonable rules for herself. She must weigh every edict, liberal or conservative, and discard those that do not make sense for her life. The only alternative is to succumb mindlessly to the latest fashions in sexuality—which may be as repressive as earlier, orthodox styles of sexual abstinence, and may introduce anxieties considerably more difficult to dismiss" (p. 129).

Healthy sexuality depends on *both* sexes freeing themselves from a goal-oriented concern with achieving orgasm, and on enjoying different experiences of sexual intimacy for their own worth rather than as mere "foreplay" to coitus. Mature sexual values can only be established by the man or woman who is free of a sense of obligation to conform to some predetermined pattern of behavior. We have examined some of the forces that tend to inhibit that freedom by imposing new sexual uniformities. The idea that animal instincts are our masters, and that sexuality is determined by the genitals fails to do justice to the distinctness of man. We must be concerned with what Maslow has called "the farther reaches of human nature" rather than with the minimal satisfaction of physical needs. We must seek a postconventional morality which is neither the passive acceptance of nor the arbitrary rejection of what society has to teach us. There is no true freedom in conforming to peer group expectations or to the popular misrepresentation of the campus as a perpetual orgy. Statistical studies provide us with the raw material for responsible decision making, not with conclusions.

NOTES

1 This is the point that Theodor Reik (1957) ignored in his rigid distinction between sex and love. He was obviously right in questioning a simplistic identification of the two terms. We do have sexual experiences with people we do not love, and we all love people with whom we have no (genital) sexual relationship. But in human culture sex does have emotional and volitional associations that are absent from other physical activities. Despite Reik's prophecy it is unlikely that in the near future we shall think of libido "in chemical terms only."

2 Kinsey (1953) found that the major change in sexual behavior (as distinct from sexual ideals) came with the generation which went to college immediately after the *first* World War.

3 Personally I believe that the perpetuation of rules governing private sexual behavior on campus tends to encourage immaturity. Many sexual adventures are motivated by a need to assert self-identity against the authority figures of college administrators *in loco parentis*. If this motive were defused and personal sexual freedom recognized, I think more students would be ready to learn from the experience and ideas of faculty members and administrators (Hettlinger, 1972).

4 The emphasis is mine. By "sex" Reuben specifically means intercourse.

5 Lucky and Nass, 1969; Bell and Chaskes, 1970; Christensen and Gregg, 1970; Kaats and Davis, 1970; Davis, 1971; Robinson et al., 1972; Freedman and Lozoff, 1972; Jackson and Potkay, 1973; Arafat and Yorburg, 1973a.

6 The word is best avoided. It does have a proper technical application to a condition which is symptomatic of mental disorder. But in popular use it is simply a pejorative term by which men (and women) label any woman who exhibits more sexual interest than they possess themselves. Most authorities now agree that many women who have in the past been classified as nymphomaniacs were just highly sexed and in no way emotionally disturbed (Levitt, 1973).

7 Another word best avoided. There is a very uncommon technical condition of frigidity due to physical or psychological causes and requiring therapy (McCary,

1973), but the layman wrongly uses the term indiscriminately to put down any woman who fails to respond sexually as he desires.

8 A similar misunderstanding may arise from reading *The Sensuous Woman* by "J" (1969). Despite its sexist orientation the book contains a lot of useful information. But what many readers fail to note is that the women cited as successful exponents of the art of the sensuous were mostly married (more than once) and in the late twenties or thirties—and some of their partners were in the forties or fifties!

REFERENCES

Adelson, Edward R. et al., "How do you advise the Man who is Overly Concerned about
1973   Female Orgasm?" *Medical Aspects of Human Sexuality*, March.

Arafat, Ibtihaj and Yorburg, Betty, "Drug Use and the Sexual Behavior of College
1973   Women," *Journal of Sex Research*, February.

Ardrey, Robert, *The Territorial Imperative*, Delta (1968).
1966

Arieti, Silvano, *The Will to Be Human*, Quadrangle.
1972

Bardwick, Judith, *Psychology of Women: A Study of Bio-Cultural Conflicts*, Harper & Row.
1971

Bell, Robert R. and Bell, Phyllis, "Sexual Satisfaction among Married Women," *Medical
1972   Aspects of Human Sexuality*, December.

Bell, Robert R. and Chaskes, Jay, "Premarital Sexual Experience among Coeds, 1958 and
1970   1968," *Journal of Marriage and the Family*, February.

Boston Women's Health Book Collective, *Our Bodies, Our Selves*, Simon & Schuster.
1973

Christensen, Harold T. and Gregg, Christina, "Changing Sex Norms in America and
1970   Scandinavia," *Journal of Marriage and the Family*, November.

Davis, Keith E., "Sex on Campus: Is there a revolution?" *Medical Aspects of Human
1971   Sexuality*, January.

Ellis, Albert,
1963   *Sex and the Single Man*, Lyle Stuart.
1969   "The Use of Sex in Human Life," a dialogue between Albert Ellis and
        David Mace, *Journal of Sex Research*, February.

Fisher, Seymour, "Female Orgasm," Medical Aspects of Human Sexuality, April.
1973

Ford, Clellan S. and Beach, Frank, *Patterns of Sexual Behavior*, Harper (1970).
1951

Freedman, Mervin B. and Lozoff, Marjorie, ". . . Some statistical background," *Sexual
1972   Behavior*, November.

Gadpaille, Warren J., "What Is Acceptable Sexual Behavior?" *Sexual Behavior*, July.
1972

Gebhard, Paul H., "Factors in Marital Orgasm," *The Social Dimensions of Human Sexuality*
1966   (eds. Bell, Robert R. and Gordon, Michael), Little, Brown (1972).

Granatir, William, "Female Orgasm," *Medical Aspects of Human Sexuality*, April.
1968

Hettlinger, Richard F.
1969   *"Everything But . . . ,"* Guidance Associates.
1972   "Sex and the College Student," *Sexual Behavior*, November.

"J", *The Sensuous Woman*, Dell.
1971

Jackson, Erwin D. and Potkay, Charles A., "Precollege Influences on Sexual Experiences
1973   of Coeds," *Journal of Sex Research*, May.

Jencks, Christopher, "Sex and the College Girl," *The New Republic*, April 4.
1964

Kaats, Gilbert R. and Davis, Keith, "The Dynamics of Sexual Behavior of College
1970   Students," *Journal of Marriage and the Family*, August.
1972   "The Social Psychology of Sexual Behavior," *Social Psychology in the Seventies*
        (ed. Wrightsman, Lawrence S.), Brooks/Cole.

Kinsey, A. C., Pomeroy, W. B. and Martin, C. E., *Sexual Behavior in the Human Male*,
1948   Saunders.

Kinsey, A. C., Pomeroy, W. B., Martin, C. E. and Gebhard, P. H., *Sexual Behavior in the*
1953   *Human Female*, Saunders.

Kohlberg, Lawrence, "Development of Moral Character and Moral Ideology," *Review of*
1964   *Child Development Research*, vol. I (eds. Hoffman, Martin and Hoffman,
        Lois Wladis), Russell Sage Foundation.

Levitt, Eugene E., "Nymphomania," *Sexual Behavior*, March.
1973

LoPiccolo, Joseph, "Mothers and Daughters: Perceived and Real Difference in Sexual
197   Values," *Journal of Sex Research*, May.

Lorenz, Konrad, *On Aggression*, Bantam.
1967

Luckey, Eleanore B. and Nass, Gilbert D., "A Comparison of Sexual Attitudes and
1969   Behavior in an International Sample," *Journal of Marriage and the Family*, May.

MacInnes, Colin, "Coming of Age in Great Britain," *The Spectator* (London), May 3.
1963

Maddock, James, "Morality and Individual Development: A Basis for Value Education,"
1972   *The Family Coordinator*, July.

Marcus, Steven, *The Other Victorians*, Basic.
1966

Maslow, Abraham, *Toward a Psychology of Being*, Van Nostrand.
1962

Masters, William H. and Johnson, Virginia E.,
1966   *Human Sexual Response*, Little, Brown.
1968   "Playboy Interview: Masters and Johnson," *Masters and Johnson Explained*
        (Lehrman, N.), Playboy Press (1970).

May, Rollo, *Love and Will,* Norton.
1969

McCary, James Leslie, *Human Sexuality* (second edition), Van Nostrand Reinhold.
1973

Montagu, M. F. Ashley, ed., *Man and Aggression,* Oxford.
1968

Morris, Desmond, *The Naked Ape,* McGraw-Hill.
1967

O'Connor, John and Wrightsman, Lawrence S., "Moral Development and the Devel-
1972   opment of Motives," *Social Psychology in the Seventies* (ed. Wrighsman,
Lawrence S.), Brooks/Cole.

Packard, Vance, *The Sexual Wilderness,* McKay.
1968

Piaget, Jean, *The Moral Judgment of the Child,* Free Press (1965).
1932

Reik, Theodor, *Of Love and Lust,* Bantam (1967).
1957

Reiss, Ira L., *The Social Context of Premarital Sexual Permissiveness,* Holt, Rindhart and
1967   Winston.

Reuben, David, *Everything you always wanted to know about sex,* McKay.
1969

Robinson, Ira E., King, Karl and Balswick, Jack O., "The Premarital Sexual Revolution
1972   Among College Females," *The Family Coordinator,* April.

Schaefer, Leah Cahan, *Women and Sex,* Pantheon.
1973

Seaman, Barbara, *Free and Female,* Coward, McCann and Geoghegan.
1972

Sherfey, Mary Jane, *The Nature and Evolution of Female Sexuality,* Random House.
1972

Stanley, Elizabeth et al., "Can Women Enjoy Sex without Orgasm?" *Medical Aspects of*
1973   *Human Sexuality,* January.

Steinem, Gloria, "The Moral Disarmament of Betty Coed," *Esquire,* September.
1972

Storr, Anthony, *Human Aggression,* Atheneum.
1968

Suggs, Robert C., "Sex and Personality in the Marquesas," *Human Sexual Behavior*
1971   (eds. Marshall, Donald S. and Suggs, Robert C.), Basic.

Vreeland, Rebecca S., "Sex at Harvard," *Sexual Behavior,* February.
1972

Walsh, Joseph L., "Sex on Campus," *Commonweal,* February 24.
1967

Yankelovitch Inc., Daniel, *The Changing Values on Campus,* Washington Square.
1972

Joie de Vivre

Simone de Beauvoir

ON SEXUALITY AND OLD AGE

Those moralists who vindicate old age claim that it sets the individual free from his body. The purification of which the moralists speak
consists for them essentially in the extinction of sexual desires: they are
happy to think that the elderly man escapes from his slavery and
thereby achieves serenity. In his well-known poem, "John Ander-
son My Jo," Robert Burns described the ideal old couple in whom carnal passion has died quite away. The pair has climbed the hill of
life side by side; once they tasted blissful hours; now with trembling
steps but still hand in hand they must go together along the road that
leads to the end of the journey. This stereotype is deeply imprinted
upon the hearts of young and middle-aged people because they met
it countless times in the books of their childhood and because their respect for their grandparents persuades them of its truth. The idea
of sexual relations or violent scenes between elderly people is deeply
shocking.

Yet there also exists an entirely different tradition. The expres-

Reprinted from the January, 1972 issue of *Harper's Magazine* by permission of the author.

sion, "dirty old man," is a commonplace of popular speech. Through literature and even more through painting, the story of Susanna and the Elders has taken on the value of a myth. The comic theater has endlessly repeated the theme of the ancient lover. As we shall see, this satirical tradition is closer to the truth than the edifying speeches of idealists who are concerned with showing old age as it ought to be.

In childhood, sexuality is polymorphous: it is not centered upon the genital organs. "Only at the end of a complex and hazardous evolution does the sexual drive assume a preeminently genital aspect; at this point it takes on the apparent fixity and finality of an instinct."[1] From this we may at once draw the conclusion that a person whose genital functions have diminished or become nonexistent is not

> **An inquiry into the sexuality of the aged amounts to asking what happens to a man's relationship with himself, with others, and with the outside world when the preeminence of the genital aspect of the sexual pattern has vanished.**

therefore sexless: he is a sexed being—even eunuchs and impotent men remain sexed—and one who must work out his sexuality in spite of a given mutilation.

An inquiry into the sexuality of the aged amounts to asking what happens to a man's relationship with himself, with others, and with the outside world when the preeminence of the genital aspect of the sexual pattern has vanished. Obviously it would be absurd to imagine that there is a simple return to infantile sexuality. Never, on any plane, does the aged person lapse into "a second childhood," since childhood is by definition a forward, upward movement. And then again, infantile sexuality is in search of itself, whereas the aged man retains the memory of what it was in his maturity. Lastly, there is a radical difference between the social factors affecting the two ages.

The enjoyment the individual derives from his sexual activities is rich and manifold to a very high degree. It is understandable that a man or woman should be bitterly unwilling to give it up, whether the chief aim is pleasure, or the transfiguration of the world by desire, or the realization of a certain image of oneself, or all this at the same time. Those moralists who condemn old age to chastity say that one cannot long for pleasures one no longer desires. This is a very short-sighted view of the matter. It is true that normally desire does not arise as desire in itself: it is desire for a particular pleasure or a particular body. But when it no longer rises spontaneously, reflection may very well regret its disappearance. The old person retains his longing for experiences that can never be replaced and is still attached to the erotic world he built up in his youth or maturity. Desire will enable him to renew its fading colors. And again it is by means of desire that he will have an awareness of his own integrity. We wish for eternal youth, and this youth implies the survival of the libido.

Its presence is found only among those who have looked upon their sexuality as something of positive value. Those who, because of complexes rooted in their childhood, took part in sexual activities only with aversion eagerly seize upon the excuse of age to withdraw. I knew an old woman who got her doctor to supply her with certificates so that she could avoid her disagreeable "conjugal duties": as she grew older, the number of her years provided her with a more convenient alibi. A man, if he is half impotent, or indifferent, or if the sexual act worries him badly, will be relieved when age allows refuge in a continence that will seem normal for that time onward.

People who have had a happy sexual life may have reasons for not wishing to prolong it. One of these is their narcissistic relationship with themselves. Disgust at one's own body takes various forms among men and women; but in either, age may provoke it, and if this happens they will refuse to make their body exist for another. Yet there exists a reciprocal influence between the image of oneself and one's sexual activity: the beloved individual feels that he is worthy of love and gives himself to it unreservedly; but very often he is loved only if he makes a conscious effort to be attractive, and an unfavorable image of himself stands in the way of his doing this. In this event a vicious circle is created, preventing sexual relations.

Another obstacle is the pressure of public opinion. The elderly person usually conforms to the conventional ideal. He is afraid of scandal or quite simply of ridicule, and inwardly accepts the watchwords of propriety and continence imposed by the community. He is ashamed of his own desires, and he denies having them; he refuses to be a lecherous old man in his own eyes, or a shameless old woman. He fights against his sexual drives to the point of thrusting them back into his unconscious mind.

As we might on the face of it suppose, seeing that there is so great a difference between them in their biological destiny and their social status, the case of men is quite unlike that of women. Biologically men are at the greater disadvantage; socially, it is the women who are worse off, because of their condition as erotic objects. In neither case is their behavior thoroughly understood. A certain number of inquiries into it have been carried out, and these have provided the basis for something in the way of statistics. The replies obtained are always of dubious value, and in this field the notion of an average has little meaning.

THE FEAR OF RIDICULE

As far as men are concerned, the statistics, as it so often happens, merely confirm what everybody knows—sexual intercourse diminishes in frequency with age. This fact is connected with the degeneration of the sexual organs, a degeneration that brings about a weakening of the libido. But the physiological is not the only factor that comes into play. There are considerable differences between the behavior patterns of individuals, some being impotent at sixty and others very sexually active at over eighty. We must try to see how these differences are to be explained.

The first factor, and one of perfectly obvious importance, is the subjects' marital status. Sexual intercourse is much more frequent among married men than among bachelors or widowers. Married life encourages erotic stimulus; habit and "togetherness" favor its appeasement. The "psychological barriers" are far easier to overcome. The wall of private life protects the elderly husband from public opinion, which in any case looks more favorably upon legitimate love than upon unlawful connections. He feels that his image is less endangered. The word image in this context must be thoroughly understood. Whereas the woman object identifies herself with the total image of her body from childhood on, the little boy sees his penis as an alter ego; it is in his penis that his whole life as a man finds its image, and it is here that he feels himself in peril. The narcissistic trauma that he dreads is the failure of his sexual organ—the impossibility of reaching an erection, or maintaining it, and of satisfying his partner. This fear is less haunting in married life. The subject is more or less free to choose the moment for making love. A failure is easily passed over in silence. His familiarity with his partner makes him dread her opinion less. Since he is less anxious, the married man is less inhibited than another. That is why many aged couples continue sexual activities.

The loss of his wife will often cause a trauma that shuts a man off from all sexual activities, either for a long or short period or forever. Widowers and elderly bachelors obviously have much more difficulty in finding an outlet for their libido than married men. Most have lost their charm; if they try to have an affair, their attempts come to nothing. All that remains is venal love; many men have shrunk from it all their lives, and it would seem to them a kind of giving-in, an acquiescence in the decline of age. Yet some do turn to it: they either go with prostitutes or they have a liaison with a woman they help financially. Their choice, continence or activity, depends on the balance between the urgency of their drive and the strength of their resistance.

Many find an answer in masturbation. A quarter of the subjects questioned by *Sexology* magazine said they had indulged in it either for many years or since the age of sixty: the latter were therefore brought back to it by aging. Statistical cross-checks show that even among married men, many turn to this practice. No doubt many elderly men prefer their fantasies to their wife's age-worn body. Or it may happen that either because deep-rooted complexes or awareness of age turn her against physical love, the companion refuses. Masturbation is then the most convenient outlet.

The subject's sexual activities are also influenced by his social condition. They go on far longer among manual workers, among men with a low standard of living than among those who are well to do. Workers and peasants have more straightforward desires, less dominated by erotic myths, than the middle classes; their wives' bodies wear out early, but they do not stop making love to them. When a working man's wife is old, she seems to him less spoiled than would be the case with a richer husband. Then again he has less idea of himself than the white-collar worker. And he does not take so much notice of public opinion, which has less and less force as one goes down the social scale. Old men and women who live almost entirely outside convention—tramps of both sexes, and inmates of institutions—lie together without any shame, even in front of others.

Finally, the happier and richer sexual life has been, the longer it goes on. If the subject has valued it because of the narcissistic satisfaction it gives him, he will break it off as soon as he can no longer see a flattering reflection of himself in his partner's eyes. If he has intended to assert his virility, his skill, or the power of his charm, or if he has meant to triumph over rivals, then he may sometimes be glad of the excuse of age to relax. But if his sexual activities have been spontaneous and happy, he will be strongly inclined to carry them on as long as his strength lasts.

Yet the elderly man does not take so vehement a pleasure in intercourse as a youth does, and this is because the two stages of ejaculation are reduced to one; he no longer has that piercing sensation of imminence which marks the passage from the first to the second, nor yet the triumphant feeling of a jet, an explosion—this is one of the myths that gives the male sexual act its value. Even when the aged man is still capable of normal sexual activity, he often seeks indirect forms of satisfaction; even more so if he is impotent. He takes pleasure in erotic literature, licentious works of art, dirty stories, the company of young women, and furtive contacts; he indulges in fetishism, sadomasochism, various forms of perversion, and, particularly after the age of eighty, in voyeurism. These deviations are readily comprehensible. The fact is, Freud has established that there is no such thing as a "normal" sexuality: it is always "perverted' insofar as it does not break away from its origins, which required it to look for satisfaction not in any specific activity but in the "increase of pleasure" attached to functions dependent upon other drives. Infantile sexuality is polymorphically perverse. The sexual act is considered "normal" when the partial activities are merely preparatory to the genital act. But the subject has only to attach too much importance to these preliminary pleasures to slip into perversion. Normally, seeing and caressing one's partner plays an important part in sexual intercourse. It is accompanied by fantasy; sadomasochistic elements appear; and often fetishism, clothes, and ornaments evoking the presence of the body. When genital pleasure is weak or nonexistent, all these elements rise to the first place. And frequently the elderly man prizes them very highly because they are manifestations of that erotic world that is still of the greatest value to him. He continues to live in a certain climate, his body still existing in a world filled with other bodies. Here again it is often timidity, shame, or difficulties from the outside that prevent him from indulging in what are called his vices.

We have a fair amount of evidence about elderly men's sexual life. It depends on their past and also upon their attitude toward their old age as a whole and toward their image in particular. Chateaubriand so loathed his aged face that he refused to sit for his portrait. In the first part of *Amour et vieillesse—chants de tristesse*, which he wrote when he was sixty-one, he rejects the amorous advances of a young woman: "If you tell me you love me as a father, you will fill me with horror; if you claim to love me as a lover, I shall not believe you. I shall see a happy rival in every young man. Your deference will make me feel my age, your caresses will give me over to the most furious jealousy . . . . Old age makes a man as ugly as can be wished. If he is unhappy, it is even worse . . ." He was cruelly sensitive to the "insult of the years" and his refusal was dictated by a kind of inverted narcissism.

Old men's loves are not always doomed to failure: far from it. Many of them have a sexual life that goes on very late. The Duc de Bouillon was sixty-six when his son Turenne was born. The famous Duc de Richelieu's father married for the third time in 1702, at the age of seventy. When his son was sixty-two and governor of Guienne, he led a life of debauchery. In his old age he seduced a great many young women. At seventy-eight, bewigged, made-up, and very thin, he was said to look like a tortoise thrusting its head out of its shell; this did not prevent him from having affairs with the actresses of the *Comédie française*. He had an acknowledged mistress, and he spent his evenings with whores; sometimes he used to bring them home—he liked listening to their confidences. He married when he was eighty-four and had recourse to aphrodisiacs: he made his wife pregnant. Furthermore, he deceived her too. He continued his sexual activities right up until his death, at the age of ninety-two.

Tolstoy is a well-known example of sexual vitality. Toward the end of his life he preached total continence both for men and for women. Nevertheless, when he was sixty-nine or seventy he would come back from a very long ride and make love to his wife. All the next day he would walk about the house looking pleased with himself.

> **It may happen that a man who has been indifferent to women for most of his life discovers the delights of sex in his later years.**

Sexuality was of great importance in Victor Hugo's youth and during his middle years. The image of old age that he had always set up for himself allowed him to accept his sexual desires until he was very old: no doubt he thought of Boaz when a young woman offered herself to him. In his view, age was by no means a blemish, but rather an honor; it brought one nearer to God and it was in harmony with everything that is sublime, with beauty and innocence. The aged Hugo certainly suffered from no feeling of inferiority whatsoever. In his opinion he was answerable to no one but himself: at no time in his life did he ever yield to public opinion—if he had desires, he satisfied them.

There are many other examples to show that an elderly man may be importuned by the most urgent sexual desires. H.G. Wells was sxity when he fell in love with Dolores after they had corresponded; he fell passionately in love and found himself possessed of unsuspected sexual powers. "For the first time in my life it was revealed to me that I was an astonishing fellow, an extraordinary chap, an outstanding virtuoso. Casanova certainly could never have held a candle to me," he wrote with a smile. The affair turned sour; there were ugly scenes; in the end he could no longer bear Dolores and when he was sixty-six he broke with her. Having done so he met the girl he called Brylhil; this was the most violent passion of his life, a mutual passion that lasted many years.

Among our contemporaries there are a very great many examples of elderly men married or attached to young women: Charlie Chaplin, Picasso, Casals, Henry Miller. These examples confirm the notion that if it has been rich, sexual life goes on for a long time. But it may also happen that a man who has been indifferent to women for most of his life discovers the delights of sex in his later years. Trotsky had looked upon himself as old since the age of fifty-five, but at fifty-eight he had an odd outburst of eroticism. Bernard Berenson, who died at ninety-four, wrote, "I only really became aware of sex and of women's physical, animal life at the period that might be called my old age."

Many elderly men look for younger partners. Those subjects for whom sex continues to play an important part gifted with excellent health and lead an active life. Impotence does not exclude desire; desire is most often satisfied through deviations in which the fantasies of middle age are accentuated.

L'APRÈS-MIDI D'UN FAUNE

We have one most remarkable piece of evidence concerning an old man's relationship with his body, his image, and his sex: this is Paul Léautaud's *Journal*. [2] He provides us with a living synthesis of the various points of view we have considered in this study.

Léautaud always looked at himself with a certain approval. It was from the outside that he learned he was aging, and it made him very angry. In 1923, when he was fifty-three, a railway official referred to him as "a little old gentleman." Furious, Léautaud wrote in his *Journal*, "Little old man! Old gentleman? What the devil—am I as blind as all that? I cannot see that I am either a little or an old gentleman. I see myself as a fifty-year-old, certainly, but an exceedingly well preserved fifty-year-old. I am slim and I move easily. Just let them show me an *old gentleman* in such good shape!" At fifty-nine he looked at himself with a critical eye: "Mentally and physically I am a man of forty. What a pity my face does not match! Above all my lack of teeth! I really am remarkable for my age: slim, supple, quick, active. It is my lack of teeth that spoils everything; I shall never dare to make love to a woman again."

In him we see with remarkable clarity how impossible it is for an old man to realize his age. On his birthday he wrote: "Today I begin my sixty-fourth year. In no way do I feel an old man." The old man is Another, and this Other belongs to a certain category that is objectively defined; in his inner experience Léautaud found no such person. There were moments, however, when his age weighed upon him. On April 12, 1936, he wrote, "I do not feel happy about my health nor about my state of mind; and then there is the sorrow of aging, too. Aging above all!" But at sixty-nine he wrote, "During my seventieth year I am still as lively, active, nimble and alert as a man can be."

Léautaud had every reason to be pleased with himself: he looked after his house and cared for his animals; he did all the shopping on foot, carrying heavy baskets of provisions; wrote his *Journal*; and he did not know what it was to be tired. "It is only my sight that is failing. I am exactly as I was at twenty. My memory is as good as ever and my mind as quick and sharp."

This made him all the more irritable when other people's reactions brought the truth home to him. He was seventy when a young woman lost her balance as an underground train started off with a jerk; she cried out, "I'm so sorry, Grandpa, I nearly fell on you." He wrote angrily, "Damn it all! My age must show clearly in my face. How impossible it is to see oneself as one really is!"

The paradox lies in the fact that he did not really dislike being old. He was one of those exceptional cases I have mentioned, where old age coincides with childhood fantasy: he had always been interested in old people. On March 7, 1942, when he was seventy-two, he wrote, "A kind of vanity comes over you when you reach old age—you take a pride in remaining healthy, slim, supple and alert, with an unaltered complexion, your joints in good order, no illness and no diminution in your physical and mental powers."

But his vanity demanded that his age be invisible to others: he liked to imagine that he had stayed young in spite of the burden of his years.

He only gave way to discouragement at the very end of his life, when his health failed. On February 25, 1945, he wrote, "I am very low indeed. My eyesight. The horrible marks of age I see on my face. My *Journal* behindhand. The mediocrity of my life, I have lost my energy and all my illusions. Pleasure, even five minutes of pleasure, is over for me." He was then seventy-five, and his sexual life had come to an end. But except in his very last years one of the reasons for his pride was that he still felt desire and was still capable of satisfying it. We can follow his sexual evolution in his *Journal*.

Léautaud only became fully aware of women when he was approaching his fiftieth year. At thirty-five he wrote, "I am beginning to regret that my temperament allows me to enjoy women so little." He lacked the "sacred fire." "I always think too much of other things—of myself, for example." He was afraid of impotence if his lovemaking was over very quickly: "I give women no pleasure since I have finished in five minutes and can never start again. . . . Shamelessness is all I really like in love. . . . There are some things not every woman can be asked to do." He had a lasting affair with a woman called Bl——. He says he loved her very much, but he also says that living with her was hell. When he was about forty, although he was still rather indifferent, since he could give his partner no pleasure, he delighted in looking at pictures of naked women. Yet a few years later he speaks sadly of the "rare love-scenes in my life which I really enjoyed." He reproaches himself for being "timid, awkward, brusque, oversensitive, always hesitant, never able to take advantage of even the best opportunities" with women. All this changed when at fifty he met "a really passionate woman, wonderfully equipped for pleasure and exactly to my taste in these matters," and he showed himself to be "almost brilliant," although up until then he had thought that he was not very good—as he had only known women who did not suit him. From this time on, sex became an obsession to him: on December 1, 1923, he wrote, "Perhaps Madame [one of the names he gave to his mistress] is right: my perpetual desire to make love may be somewhat pathological. . . . I put it down to a lifetime's moderation—it lasted until I was over forty—and also to my intense feeling for her, which makes me want to make love to her when I see so much as a square inch of her body. . . . I think it is also because I have been deprived of so many things, such as that female nakedness for which I have acquired such a liking. I am quite amazed when I think of what has happened to me in all this. . . . Never have I caressed any other woman as I caress Madame." In the summer they parted, and abstinence lay heavy upon him: he masturbated, thinking of her. "Of course I am delighted to be such an ardent lover at my age, but God knows it can be troublesome."

Madame was a little older than he: all his life he had loved only mature women. A twenty-three-year-old virgin threw herself at his head, and he agreed to have an affair with her; but it did not give him the least pleasure and he broke immediately. Except for this one fling he was faithful to Madame for years. He liked watching himself and her in a mirror during their lovemaking. From 1927—age fifty-seven—on, he was forced to take care not to make love too often; he found consolation in bawdy talk with the Panther (another name he gave to his mistress). He did not get on well with her; "we are attached to each other only by our senses—by vice—and what remains is so utterly tenuous!" But in 1938 he did recall with great satisfaction the "seventeen years of pleasure between two creatures the one as passionate and daring as the other in amorous words and deeds." When he was fifty-nine his affair with the Scourge, as he now called her, was still going on, though she was already sixty-four. He was shocked by couples where the woman was much younger than the man. "I myself at fifty-nine would never dare to make any sort of advance to a woman of thirty."

He was still very much attracted to the Scourge, and he took great pleasure in his "sessions" with her. Yet he did complain, "What a feeble ejaculation when I make love: little better than water!" Later he wrote "I am certainly better when I do not make love at all. Not that it comes hard—far from it—but it is always a great effort, and I do not get over it as quickly as I did a few years ago. . . . What I miss most is female nakedness, licentious attitudes, and playing amorous games."

"Until I was sixty-six or sixty-seven I could make love two or three times a week." Now he complained that his brain was tired for three or four days after making love, but he still went on, and he corresponded with three of his former mistresses.

When he was seventy Léautaud wrote, "I miss women and love terribly." He remembered how he used to make passionate love to the Scourge from the age of forty-seven to sixty-three, and then for two years with CN₁ (another mistress).

"It was only three years ago that I noticed I was slowing down. I can still make love, and indeed I quite often feel sad at being deprived of it; though at the same time I tell myself that it is certainly much better for me to abstain."

At seventy-two he was still planning idylls that never came to anything, and he had erotic dreams that gave him an erection. "At night I still feel ready for anything." But that same year he observed that his sexual powers were declining. "It is no use giving yourself over to lovemaking when the physical side is dead or nearly so. Even the pleasure of seeing and fondling is soon over, and there is not the least eagerness to begin again. For a real appreciation of all these things, there must be the heat of physical passion." It is clear that Léautaud's greatest pleasure was visual. He retained it longer than any other form of sensual enjoyment, and after the age of forty he prized it very highly indeed. When he lost it he considered that his sexual life was over. It is also clear how a man's image of himself is bound up with sexual activity. He was "in the depths of sorrow" when he could no longer experience these pleasures. Still, his narcissism did survive his sexual decline at least for some time.

THE FEMININE DISADVANTAGE

Biologically women's sexuality is less affected by age than men's. Brantôme bears this out in the chapter of his *Vies des dames galantes* that he dedicates to "certain old ladies who take as much pleasure in love as the young ones." Whereas a man of a certain age is no longer capable of erection, a woman "at no matter what age is endowed with as it were a furnace. . . all fire and fuel within." Popular tradition bears witness to this contrast. In one of the songs in the Merry Muses of Caledonia[3] an old woman laments her elderly husband's impotence. She longs for "the wild embraces of their younger days" that are now no more than a ghostly memory, since he no longer thinks of doing anything in bed except sleeping, while she is eaten up with desire. Today scientific research confirms the validity of this evidence. According to Kinsey, throughout their lives women are sexually more stable than men; when they are sixty their potential for pleasure and desire is the same as it was at thirty. According to Masters and Johnson, the strength of the sexual reaction diminishes with age; yet a woman can still reach orgasm, above all if she is regularly and properly stimulated. Those who do not often have physical relations sometimes find coition painful, either during the act or after, and sometimes suffer from dyspareunia or dysuria; it is not known whether these troubles are physical or psychological in origin. I may add that a woman can take great pleasure in making love even though she may not reach orgasm. The "preliminary pleasures" count even more perhaps for her than they do for a man. She is usually less sensitive to the appearance of her partner and therefore less worried by his growing old. Even though her part in lovemaking is not as passive as people sometimes make out, she has no fear of a particular failure. There is nothing to prevent her from going on with her sexual activities until the end of her life.

Still, all research shows that women have a less active sexual life than men. Kinsey says that at fifty, 97 per cent of men are still sexually active compared with 93 per cent of women. At sixty it is 94 per cent of men and only 80 per cent of women. This comes from the fact that socially men, whatever their age, are subjects, and women are objects, relative beings. When she marries, a woman's future is determined by her husband's; he is usually about four years older than she, and his desire progressively lessens. Or if it does continue to exist, he takes to younger women. An old woman, on the other hand, finds it extremely difficult to have extramarital relations. She is even less attractive to men than old men are to women. And in her case gerontophilia does not exist. A young man may desire a woman old enough to be his mother but not his grandmother. A woman of seventy is no longer regarded by anyone as an erotic object. Venal love is very difficult for her to find. It would be most exceptional for an old woman to have both the means and the opportunity of getting herself a partner; and then again shame and fear of what people might say would generally prevent her from doing so. This frustration is painful to many old women, for they are still tormented by desire. They usually find their relief in masturbation; a gynecologist told me of the case of one woman of seventy who begged him to cure her of this practice—she was indulging in it night and day.

When Andrée Martinerie was conducting an inquiry for *Elle* magazine (March 1969) she gathered some interesting confidences from elderly women. Madame F., a rich middle-class sixty-eight-year-old, a militant Catholic, mother of five and grandmother of ten, told her, "I was already sixty-four. . . . Now just listen: four months after my husband's death I went down into the street just like someone who is going to commit suicide. I had made up my mind to give myself to the very first man who would have me. Nobody wanted me. So I went home again." When she was asked whether she had thought of remarrying, she answered, "That is all I ever do think of. If I dared I would put an advertisement in *Le Chasseur fran-çais*. . . . I would rather have a decrepit invalid of a man than no man at all!" Talking of desire, Madame R., sixty years old and living with her sick husband, said, "It is quite true that you don't get over it." She sometimes felt like beating her head against the wall. A woman reader of this inquiry wrote to the magazine, "I must tell you that a woman remains a woman for a very long time in spite of growing older. I know what I am talking about, because I am seventy-one. I was a widow at sixty; my husband died suddenly and it took me at least two years to realize fully what had happened. Then I started to answer advertisements in the matrimonial column. I admit that I did miss having a man—or rather I should say I do miss it: this aimless existence is terrifying, without affection or any outlet for one's own feelings. I even began wondering whether I was quite normal. Your inquiry was a great relief. . . ." This correspondent speaks modestly of "affection," an "outlet for one's own feelings." But the context shows that her frustration had a sexual dimension. The reaction of a young woman who wrote to *Elle* is typical: "In our group of young people we laughed heartily about the passionate widow (the member of the Action Catholique) who cannot 'get over it.' I wish you would now hold an inquiry on love as it appears to the fourth age of women, in other words those between eighty and a hundred and twenty." Young people are very shocked if the old, especially old women, are still sexually active.

A woman, then, continues in her state as erotic object right up to the end. Chastity is not imposed upon her by a physiological destiny but by her position as a relative being. Nevertheless it may happen that women condemn themselves to chastity because of the "psychological barriers" that I have mentioned, which are even more inhibiting for them than for men. A woman is usually more narcissistic in love than a man; her narcissism is directed at her body as a whole. She has a delightful awareness of her body as something desirable, and this awareness comes to her through her partner's caresses and his gaze. If he goes on desiring her she easily puts up with her body's aging. But at the first sign of coldness she feels her ugliness in all its horror; she is disgusted with her image and cannot bear to expose her poor person to others. This lack of assurance strengthens her fear of other people's opinions: she knows how censorious they are toward old women who do not play their proper role of serene and passion-free grandmothers.

Even if her husband wants to make love with her again later, a deeply rooted feeling of shame may make her refuse him. Women make less use of diversion than men. Those who enjoyed a very active and uninhibited sexual life before do sometimes compensate for their enforced abstinence by extreme freedom in conversation and the use of obscene words. They become something very like bawds, or at least they spy upon the sexual life of their young women friends with a most unhealthy curiosity, and do all they can to make them confide their secrets. But generally speaking their language is as repressed as their lovemaking. Elderly women like to appear as restrained in their conversation as they are in their way of life. Their sexualiy now shows only in their dress, their jewelry and ornaments, and in the pleasure they take in male society. They like to flirt discreetly with men younger than themselves and they are touched by attentions that show they are still women in men's eyes.

However, it is clear from pathology that in women, too, the sexual drive is repressed but not extinguished. Psychiatrists have observed that in asylums female patients' eroticism often increases with age. Senile dementia brings with it a state of erotic delirium arising from lack of cerebral control. Repressions are also discarded in some other forms of psychosis. Dr. Georges Mahé recorded twenty cases of extreme eroticism out of 110 sixty-year-old female patients in an institution; the symptoms included public masturbation, make-believe coition, obscene talk, and exhibitionism. Unfortunately he gives no idea of the meaning of these displays: he puts them

> **Neither history nor literature has left us any worthwhile evidence on the sexuality of old women. It is an even more strictly forbidden subject than the sexuality of old men.**

into no context and we do not know *who* the patients were who indulged in these practices. Many of the inmates suffer from genital hallucinations such as rape and physical contact. Women of over seventy-one are convinced that they are pregnant. Madame C., seventy and a grandmother, sings barrack-room songs and walks about the hospital half-naked, looking for a man. Eroticism is the most important factor in many delirious states; it also triggers off some cases of melancholia. E. Gehu speaks of an eighty-three-year-old grandmother who was looked after in a convent. She was an exhibitionist, showing both homosexual and heterosexual tendencies. She fell upon the younger nuns who brought her meals; during these crises she was perfectly lucid. Later she became mentally confused. She ended up by regaining her mental health and behaving normally once more. Here again, we should like a more exact, detailed account of her case. All the observations that I have just quoted are most inadequate; but at least they do show that old women are no more "purified of their bodies" than old men.

Neither history nor literature has left us any worthwhile evidence on the sexuality of old women. It is an even more strictly forbidden subject than the sexuality of old men.

There are many cases of the libido disappearing entirely in old people. Ought they to rejoice in it, as the moralists say? Nothing is less certain. It is a mutilation that brings other mutilations with it: sexuality, vitality, and activity are indissolubly linked. When desire is completely dead, emotional response itself may grow loose at its edge. At sixty-three Rétif de La Bretonne wrote, "My heart died at the same time as my senses, and if sometimes a tender impulse stirs me, it is as erroneous as that of a savage or a eunuch: it leaves me with a profound feeling of sorrow." It seemed to Bernard Shaw that when he lost interest in women he lost interest in living. "I am aging very quickly. I have lost all interest in women, and the interest they have in me is greater than ever and it bores me. The time has probably come for me to die."

Even Schopenhauer admitted, "It could be said that once the sexual urge is over life's true centre is burnt out, leaving a mere shell." Or again, "life is like a play acted at first by live actors and then finished by automata wearing the same costumes." Yet at the same time he says that the sexual instinct produces a "benign dementia." The only choice left to men is that between madness and sclerosis. In fact what he calls "dementia" is the spring of life itself. When it is broken or destroyed a man is no longer truly alive.

The link that exists between sexuality and creativity is striking: it is obvious in Hugo and Picasso and in many others. In order to create there must be some degree of aggression—"a certain readiness," says Flaubert—and this aggressivity has its biological source in the libido. It is also necessary to feel united with the world by an emotional warmth; this disappears at the same time as carnal desire, as Gide understood very clearly when on April 10, 1942, he wrote, "There was a time when I was cruelly tormented, indeed obsessed by desire, and I prayed, 'Oh let the moment come when my subjugated flesh will allow me to give myself entirely to . . .' But to what? To art? To pure thought? To God? How ignorant I was! How mad! It was the same as believing that the flame would burn brighter in a lamp with no oil left. If it were abstract, my thought would go out; even today it is my carnal self that feeds the flame, and now I pray that I may retain carnal desire until I die."

It would not be truthful to state that sexual indifference necessarily brings inertia and impotence. There are many examples to prove the contrary. Let us merely say there is one dimension of life that disappears when there is no more carnal relationship with the world; those who keep this treasure to an advanced age are privileged indeed.

NOTES

1 J. Laplanche and J. B. Pontalis, *Vocabulaire de la psycho-analyse.*
2 Léautaud was a critic and an editor of *Mercure de France,* a literary journal.
3 Popular Scottish songs collected in the 18th century.

Part 2

Male/female roles
in transition

PART 2 / MALE/FEMALE ROLES IN TRANSITION

Today male and female roles in American society and in the family itself are in a state of transition. The Women's Liberation Movement has reached women (and some men) in all social classes, making them conscious of the economic, legal, educational, political, and interpersonal inequities between the sexes. As women struggle to free themselves from overt and covert discrimination, male–female role stereotypes are being questioned, and definitions of male and female sexuality are being reexamined. Both women and men are struggling to define individual, humane, and personally chosen sex roles, although not everyone is dissatisfied with the traditional ones. This part therefore presents divergent positions and considers both the widespread determination of many women (and men) to eliminate sexism in our society, and the equally strong determination of some women (and men) to continue the status quo.

The Roszaks present a tongue-in-cheek, biting parallelism of the masculinity/femininity game men and women play. This reading is depressing, deadly in its accuracy, and disconcerting because probably neither "he" nor "she" realizes what is happening, so internalized and subconscious are many of their feelings and actions. Do you play the game? How can you call it off?

Gilder is a strong spokesman for continuing traditional sex roles, especially in the family: men in the dominant role of husband, father, and breadwinner; women subordinate as wives, mothers, and homemakers. His reading will raise hackles among femininists, as he blames the Women's Liberation Movement for the "sexual suicide" he identifies in contemporary American society. Gilder apparently sees no particular necessity for women to be treated along with men as human beings. He does, however, make a case for the biological inferiority, subordination, and even irrelevancy of a man to a woman, who "conceives, bears, and suckles the child." Perhaps Gilder is unaware of the emphasis of research in the last decade on the importance of the father in child rearing.[1]

Gilder claims that the "natural" superiority of the male must be upheld in society's marketplace so that men can enter the marriage market and express their masculinity through procreative sexuality and parental roles. What Gilder neglects to mention is that the increasing divorce rate results in many one-parent families, often headed by women left to shift for themselves. Where is "the committed socialized male" in these cases?

Will Gilder's version of procreative sexuality and role separation promote happier married life? Do men have to "validate their masculinity" by becoming fathers in this overpopulated world? Does masculinity require that men be forever tied to the work ethic? Are women's liberation, marital openness, and sexual equity the denials of male and female sexuality Gilder claims them to be?

Masters and Johnson's belief that women will ultimately join men as full partners presents a vivid contrast to Gilder's philosophy. These noted sex researchers assure men that they have much to gain from liberal options granted to women, who will be freer and more comfortable in expressing delight in sex as well as in sharing companionship. This belief echoes a statement made by Florence Woolston, a journalist, in 1923: "Ultimately the woman movement should result in the emancipation of men."[2] More recently, the well-known feminist Gloria Steinem wrote that liberating women from age-old second-class roles need not threaten men, for they too will feel the release of liberation: no more living up to the *machismo* concept of an aggressive, powerful male who bears all the "strain of power and responsibility."[3]

Masters and Johnson focus their discussion on the private, intimate bond—a relationship that most women and men plan and hope for in the context of marriage, home, and family. Their sober reflections on sexuality contrast with the extreme positions sometimes voiced by militant feminists and offer positive encouragement to young people today. Can you mediate the Gilder and Masters-Johnson messages?

LeFevre traces the problems women encounter during their most productive years when they try to juggle a career, marriage, and children. She identifies two problems that still resist solution: (1) the burden of the double work load, and (2) the feelings of guilt a mother has on leaving her children to go to work. Although research has found that the greatest satisfactions apparently come to women who work throughout adulthood and that both daughters and sons of working mothers tend to gain in independence, achievement, and competence, it is still apparently difficult for mothers not to feel guilty about leaving their children. Other difficulties result from male control of work-role assignments in America, from limited societal arrangements to make it easier for women to work outside the home, and from the discontinuities women suffer throughout their life cycles as compared to the temporal stability of the male role.

This reading raises several questions:

1 LeFevre is obviously biased in favor of women being educated to work outside the home. Isn't there the danger of a reverse pressure for women to fit a working-wife-and-mother role stereotype? What benefits, if any, would there be to a society that disapproves of women who choose personal fulfillment as full-time homemakers?

2 A man usually gives up some privileges when his wife works. What stresses might this entail for the individuals involved?

3 What individual and societal changes would be necessary to make it possible for men to choose being househusbands while their wives work? Is this life style feasible?

4 A more recent aspect of the career–marriage syndrome is the dual-career marriage. What if both partners cannot find suitable positions in the same town? What if

the wife gets the better position, or if one partner is offered a promotion involving a transfer? What does this life style bode for the future?

Bem asserts that men and women need the freedom to express both the nurturant, reflective qualities traditionally ascribed to women and the aggressive, assertive qualities usually ascribed to men. Bem feels that the resulting *androgyny* (from *andro*, "male," and *gyne*, "female") would promote greater psychological health in individuals because their actions would not then be limited by traditional sex-role stereotypes.

The Bem Sex Role Inventory of college students has consistently indicated that rigid sex-role patterns restrict behavior, often to the detriment of personality. Students tied to rigidly prescribed sex roles were found to be more uncomfortable, more nervous, and less flexible than less role-stereotyped students. Bem believes that being androgynous therefore enables individuals to expand behavior options and cope more comfortably with our complex society. Do you think this is a valid premise? If children no longer have clear-cut and unambiguous male and female role models, will they be confused about their own identity? What impact would androgynous socialization have on marriage and the family?

In his reading, Davids makes some controversial predictions about the directions present trends indicate for marriage in North America. He goes beyond equality between husband and wife, liberalization of abortion and contraception laws and practices, lower birth rates, and the trial marriages without children originally suggested by Margaret Mead,[4] to an extrapolation for the future suggestive of Orwellian *1984*[5] concepts of regulated marriage, licensing for parenthood, screening out those "unfit" for parenthood—all to be done by "society." Is such regulation by fiat consistent with the democratic principles undergirding individual rights in our society? Is licensing people for certain roles appropriate to any but a totalitarian society?

Although Davids is concerned about how the criteria for the changes he envisions will be determined, he is hopeful that young people will become aware of the awesome responsibility of parenthood, that equalization between the sexes will become a reality in every facet of life, and that individuals will be free to choose the style of life most attractive and suitable to them

NOTES

1 David B. Lynn, *The Father: His Role in Child Development* (Belmont, CA: Wadsworth Publishing Co., 1974).

2 Florence Guy Woolston, "The Sheltered Sex," *New Republic,* 4 April 1923, pp. 161–163.

3 Gloria Steinem, "What It Would Be Like If Women Win," *Time,* 31 August 1970.

4 Margaret Mead, "Marriage in Two Steps," *Redbook,* July 1966, pp. 48ff.

5 George Orwell, *1984* (New York: Harcourt Brace, 1949).

Masculine/Feminine:
A Look at Sexuality

Betty Roszak and Theodore Roszak

He is playing masculine. She is playing feminine.

He is playing masculine *because* she is playing feminine. She is playing feminine *because* he is playing masculine.

He is playing the kind of man that she thinks the kind of woman she is playing ought to admire. She is playing the kind of woman that he thinks the kind of man he is playing ought to desire.

If he were not playing masculine, he might well be more feminine that she is—except when she is playing very feminine. If she were not playing feminine, she might well be more masculine than he is—except when he is playing very masculine.

So he plays harder. And she plays . . . softer.

He wants to make sure that she could never be more masculine than he. She wants to make sure that he could never be more feminine than she. He therefore seeks to destroy the femininity in himself. She therefore seeks to destroy the masculinity in herself.

Reprinted from *Masculine/Feminine: Readings in Sexual Mythology & the Liberation of Women*, edited by Betty Roszak and Theodore Roszak, 1969. Reprinted by permission of the publisher, Harper Colophon Books, and the authors.

She is supposed to admire him for the masculinity in him that she fears in herself. He is supposed to desire her for the femininity in her that he despises in himself.

He desires her for her femininity which is *his* femininity, but which he can never lay claim to. She admires him for his masculinity which is *her* masculinity, but which she can never lay claim to. Since he may only love his own femininity in her, he envies her her femininity. Since she may only love her own masculinity in him, she envies him his masculinity.

The envy poisons their love.

He, coveting her unattainable femininity, decides to punish her. She, coveting his unattainable masculinity, decides to punish him. He denigrates her femininity—which he is supposed to desire and which he really envies—and becomes more aggressively masculine. She feigns disgust at his masculinity—which she is supposed to admire and which she really envies—and becomes more fastidiously feminine. He is becoming less and less what he wants to be. She is becoming less and less what she wants to be. But now he is more manly than ever, and she is more womanly than ever.

Her femininity, growing more dependently supine, becomes contemptible. His masculinity, growing more oppressively domineering, becomes intolerable. At last she loathes what she has helped his masculinity to become. At last he loathes what he has helped her femininity to become.

So far, it has all been very symmetrical. But we have left one thing out.

The world belongs to what his masculinity has become.

The reward for what his masculinity has become is power. The reward for what her femininity has become is only the security which his power can bestow upon her. If he were to yield to what her femininity has become, he would be yielding to contemptible incompetence. If she were to acquire what his masculinity has become, she would participate in intolerable coerciveness.

She is stifling under the triviality of her femininity. The world is groaning beneath the terrors of his masculinity.

He is playing masculine. She is playing feminine.

How do we call off the game?

The Suicide of the Sexes

George Gilder

There's an extraordinary chorus in the land these days—all bouncing between water beds and typewriters and talk shows—making sexual liberation ring on the cash registers of revolution. They haven't much in common—these happy hookers, Dr. Feelgoods, answer men, evangelical lesbians, sensuous psychiatrists, pornographers, dolphins, swinging priests, polymorphous perverts, and playboy philosophers—but they are all at one in proclaiming the advent of a new age of freedom between the sexes.

Nothing is free, however, least of all sex, which is bound to our deepest sources of energy, identity, and emotion. Sex can be cheapened, of course, but then it becomes extremely costly to the society as a whole. For sex is the life force and cohesive impulse of a people, and their very character will be deeply affected by how sexuality is sublimated and expressed, denied or attained. When sex is devalued and deformed, as at present, the quality of our lives declines and the social fabric unravels.

Even our attitude toward the concepts "sex" and "sexuality" illustrates the problem. The words no longer evoke a broad pageant of relations and differences between men and women, embracing every aspect of their lives. Instead, "sex" and "sexuality" are assumed to refer chiefly to copulation, as if our sexual lives were restricted to the male limits, as if the experiences of motherhood were not paramount sexual events. In fact, sexual energy animates most of our activities and connects every individual to a family and a community, and through these to a past and future. Sexuality is best examined not as sexology, physiology, or psychology, but as a study encompassing all the deepest purposes of a society.

> **Without long-term commitments to and from women—without the institution of marriage—men are exiles from the procreative chain of nature.**

The differences between the sexes are perhaps the most important condition of our lives. With the people we know best, in the moments most crucial in our lives together, sexual differences become all-absorbing. Intercourse, marriage, conception of a child, childbearing, breast-feeding are all events when our emotions are most intense, our lives most thoroughly changed, and society perpetuated in our own image. And they are all transactions of sexual differences reaching in symbol or consequence into the future.

These differences are embodied in a number of roles. The central ones are mother-father, husband-wife. They form neat and apparently balanced pairs. But in the most elemental sexual terms, there is little balance at all. In most of the key sexual events of our lives, the male role is trivial, easily dispensable. Although the man is needed in intercourse, artificial insemination can make his participation rudimentary indeed. Otherwise the man is completely unnecessary. It is the woman who conceives, bears, and suckles the child. Males are the sexual outsiders and inferiors. A far smaller portion of their bodies is directly erogenous. A far smaller portion of their lives is devoted to specifically sexual activity. Their own distinctively sexual experience is limited to erection and ejaculation; their primary sexual drive leads only toward copulation. Beside the socially indispensable and psychologically crucial experiences of motherhood, men are irredeemably subordinate.

The nominally equivalent role of father is in fact a product of marriage and other cultural contrivances. There is no biological need for the father to be around when the baby is born and nurtured, and in many societies the father has no special responsibility to support the children he sires; in some, paternity isn't even acknowledged. Without long-term commitments to and from women—without the institution of marriage—men are exiles from the procreative chain of nature.

One of the best ways to enrage a young feminist today is to accuse her of having a maternal instinct. In a claim contrary to the evidence of all human history and anthropology—and to an increasing body of hormonal research[1]—most of these women assert that females have no more innate disposition to nurture children than do men. The usual refrain is, "I know lots of men with far more interest in babies than I have." But whether instinctual or not, the maternal role originates in the fact that only the woman is necessarily present at birth and has an easily identifiable connection to the child—a tie on which society can depend. This maternal feeling is the root of human sexuality. If it is not deeply cultivated among the women, it does not emerge among the men. The idea that the father is inherently equal to the mother within the family, or that he will necessarily be inclined to remain with it, is nonsense. The man must be made equal by the culture; he must be given a way to make himself equal.

A man's predicament begins in his earliest years. A male child is born, grows, and finds his being in relation to his own body and to the bodies of his parents, chiefly his mother. In trusting her he learns to trust himself, and trusting himself he learns to bear the slow dissolution of the primary tie. He moves away into a new world, into a sometimes frightening psychic space between his parents; and he must then attach his evolving identity to a man, his father. From almost the start, the boy's sexual identity is dependent on acts of exploration and initiative. Before he can return to a woman, he must assert his manhood in action. The Zulu warrior had to kill a man, the Irish peasant had to build a house, the American man must find a job. This is the classic myth and the mundane reality of masculinity, the low comedy and high tragedy of mankind.

Female histories are different. A girl's sexuality normally unfolds in an unbroken line, from a stage of utter dependency and identification with her mother through stages of gradual autonomy. Always, however, the focus of female identification is clear and stable. In a woman, moreover, sexual expression is not limited to a series of brief performances: her gender is affirmed and demonstrated monthly in menstruation, her breasts and womb further represent an extended sexual role. Even if a woman does not in fact bear a child, she is continually reminded that she can, that she is capable of performing the crucial act in the perpetuation of her family and the species. She alone can give sex an unquestionable meaning, an incarnate result.[2]

Regardless, then, of any other anxieties she may have in relation to her sexual role and how to perform it, she at least knows that she has a role. Her knowledge, indeed, is ontological: it is stamped in her very being—with the result that women rarely appreciate the significance of the absence of an extended sexual identity in men. Women take their sexuality for granted, when they are aware of it at all, and assume that were it not for some cultural peculiarity, some unfortunate wrinkle in the social fabric, men too might enjoy such deep-seated sexual authenticity.

Throughout the literature of feminism, in fact, there runs a puzzled complaint, "Why can't men *be* men, and just relax?" The reason is that, unlike femininity, relaxed masculinity is at bottom empty, a limp nullity. While the female body is full of internal potentiality, the male is internally barren (from the Old French *bar*, meaning man). Manhood at the most basic level can be validated and expressed only in action. For a man's body is full only of undefined energies. And all these energies need the guidance of culture. He is therefore deeply dependent on the structure of the society to define his role in it.

Of all society's institutions that work this civilizing effect, marriage is perhaps the most important. All the companionship, love, and inspiration that have come to be associated with marriage are secondary to its crucial social role. Marriage attaches men to families, the source of continuity, individuality, and order. As we should have long ago discovered from the frequent ineffectiveness of schools, prisons, mental hospitals, and psychiatric offices, the family is the only agency that can be depended upon to induce enduring changes in its members' character and commitment. It is, most importantly, the only uncoercive way to transform individuals, loose in social time and space, into voluntary participants in the social order.

Of course, families can exist without marriage. Almost always, they consist of women and children. The problem is this leaves the men awash in what one set of marriage counselors approvingly terms the "nowness of self." And the problem with *that* is the willingness with which men grasp their "nowness." Throughout history, societies have recognized the great price to be paid in securing family commitments from men. The alternative male pattern of brief sexual exploits and predatory economics accords very nicely indeed with the many millions of years of male evolution as a hunter. Women have had to use all their ingenuity, all their powers of sexual attraction and discrimination to induce men to create and support families. And the culture has had to invest marriage with all the ceremonial sanctity of religion and law. This did not happen as a way to promote intimacy and companionship. It evolved and survived in the course of sustaining civilized societies, where love, intimacy, and companionship might flourish.

MEN AND WORK

Every society has a sexual constitution that undergirds its economy, politics, and culture. Although its central concerns are marriages and families, nearly every contact among human beings contains a sexual charge. How all these charges are organized—the nature of the sexual constitution—will deeply influence the productivity and order of the community. It will determine whether social energies are short-circuited and dissipated, or whether they are accumulated and applied to useful pursuits. It will determine whether the society is a fabric of fully integrated citizens or whether it is an atomized flux, with disconnected individuals pursuing sex and sustenance on the most limited and anti-social scale.

At every job site, in every classroom, in every store, office, and factory, this system comes into play. To anyone else, a man at work is performing an economic task, subject to legal and political regulation. But to the man himself, this formal role probably seems incidental. To him the job is chiefly important because of the connections it affords with his co-workers and with the existing or prospective women and children in his life.

A job is thus a central part of the sexual constitution. It can affirm the masculine identity of its holder, it can make it possible for him to court women in a spirit of commitment; it can make it possible for him to be married and thereby integrated into a continuing community.

Crucial to the sexual constitution of employment is that, in one way or another, it assures that over the whole society, class by class, most men will make more money than most women. Above an absolute minimum that varies from country to country, pay and poverty are relative. And for most men, most importantly, that means relative to women. A man who does not make as much money as the significant women in his life—his girlfriend, wife, and closest co-workers—will often abandon his job and will pursue women in the plundering masculine spirit that the women's movement so woefully condemns.

The feminist contention that women do not generally receive equal pay for equal work, correct in statistical terms, may reflect a preference for male need and aggressiveness over female credentials. In any case, this tendency should be considered in light of the greater cost to the society of male unemployment. The unemployed male can contribute little to the society and will often disrupt it, while the unemployed woman may perform valuable work in creating and maintaining families. In effect, the system of discrimination, which the movement is perfectly right in finding nearly ubiquitous, tells women that if they enter the marketplace they will probably receive less pay than men, not because they could do the job less well but because they have an alternative role of incomparable value to the society

119

as a whole. The man, on the other hand, is paid more, not because of his special virtue, but because of the key importance of taming his naturally disruptive energies. The male job advantage, therefore, is based on the real costs of female careerism to raising children and socializing men. The society will have to pay these costs one way or another.

It is vital here to understand the sexual role of money. Particularly in relatively poor communities, a woman with more money than the men around her tends to demoralize them. Undermining their usefulness as providers, she weakens their connections with the community and promotes a reliance upon other, anti-social ways of confirming their masculinity: the priapic modes of hunting and fighting. A society of relatively wealthy and independent women will be a society of sexually and economically predatory males, or a society of narcotized drones who have abandoned sexuality entirely.

A male's money, on the other hand, is socially affirmative. If the man is unmarried, a much higher proportion of his money than a woman's will be spent on the opposite sex. His money gives him the wherewithal to undertake long-term sexual initiatives. It gives him an incentive to submit to female sexual patterns, for he knows he will retain the important role of provider. His sexual impulses can assume a civilizing, not a subversive, form.

The women's movement argues that most women work because they *need* the money. That is precisely the point, and these women must be permitted to earn it. (They will not be helped, incidentally, by the competition of increasing numbers of non-poor women for jobs.) Those who support children should receive child allowances. But men also need the money—and need an increment above the woman's pay—for unfortunately nonrational uses: for the "luxury" spending on women that is necessary if men are to establish and support families. The more men who are induced to serve as providers, the fewer women who will be left to support children alone.

Nothing is so important to the sexual constitution as the creation and maintenance of families. And since the role of the male as principal provider is a crucial prop for the family, the society must support it one way or the other. Today, however, the burdens of childbearing no longer prevent women from performing the provider role; and if day care becomes widely available, it will be possible for a matriarchal social pattern to emerge. Under such conditions, however, the men will inevitably bolt. And this development, an entirely feasible one, would probably require the simultaneous emergence of a police state to supervise the undisciplined men and a child care state to manage the children. Thus will the costs of sexual job equality be passed on to the public in vastly increased taxes. The present sexual constitution is cheaper.

Of course, the male responsibility can be enforced in many other ways, coercively or through religious and social pressures. It is perfectly possible to maintain male providers without taking social

> **The society no longer recognizes, let alone communicates forcefully, the extraordinary social costs incurred when women neglect their role in male socialization.**

costs into account in determining wages and salaries. In modern American society, however, the "social pressures" on women for marriage and family are giving way to pressures for career advancement, while the social pressures on men are thrusting them toward sexual hedonism. The society no longer recognizes, let alone communicates forcefully, the extraordinary social costs incurred when women neglect their role in male socialization. In fact, it has begun to actively promote the delights of easy sex, while indulging a pervasive cynicism toward married love.

At this point, therefore, any serious governmental campaign for equal pay for equal work would be destructive. It would endorse the false feminist assumption that a greatly expanded female commitment to careers would be economical—using "human resources" that are now "wasted." The fact is that the triumph of a careerist ideology among American women would impose ultimate costs to the society far greater than the net contribution of the additional women in the work force. Already, save for the exceptional minority, female careerism is imposing heavy psychological penalties on women themselves, since most of them will not be able to fulfill themselves in careers. The feminists would establish an ideal chiefly practicable for themselves. The rest of womankind would be told, preposterously, that they are inferior to men unless they make comparable salaries.

Perhaps the most quixotic of all feminist demands is that men at work treat women first as "human beings." Male psychology is in large part a reaction formation, shaped in relation to women. As women further invade realms conventionally regarded as masculine—and as masculine technology further transforms other male roles—men will increasingly define themselves as *not*-women, and their responses will be increasingly sexual. If all the usual job stresses are intensified by sexual competition, the men will retaliate through bureaucratic sabotage or overt viciousness on the job, or they will desperately try to escape—either to the street or to higher levels of the bureaucracy. Already subject to severe sexual strains from women, men will not easily endure professional ones.

In all these economic questions the feminists are right in virtually every superficial way. Men *do* get paid more than women; women *are* persistently discouraged from competing with men; the minority of women who are sufficiently motivated *can* perform almost every important job in society as well as men; job assignments by sex *are* arbitrary and illogical; most women *do* work because they have to; the lack of public child care facilities *does* prevent women from achieving real financial equality or opportunity.

But at a deeper level feminist women are terribly wrong. For they fail to understand their own sexual power; and they fail to perceive the sexual constitution of our society, or if they see it, they underestimate its importance to civilization and to their own interests. In general, the whole range of the society, marriage, and careers—and thus social order—will be best served if most men have a position of economic superiority over the relevant women in the community, and if in most jobs the sexes tend to be segregated by either level or function.

These practices are seen as oppressive by some; but they make possible a society in which women can love and respect men and sustain durable families. They make possible a society in which men can love and respect women and treat them humanely.

What is happening in the United States today is a steady undermining of the key conditions of male socialization. From the hospital, where the baby is abruptly taken from its mother; to early childhood, when he may be consigned to public care; to the home, where the father is frequently absent or ineffectual; to the school, where the boy is managed by female teachers and is often excelled by girls; possibly to a college, where once again his training is scarcely differentiated by sex; to a job, which, particularly at vital entry levels, is often sexually indistinct and which may not even be better paid than comparable female employment—through all these stages of development the boy's innately amorphous and insecure sexuality may be further subverted and confused.

In the end his opportunity to qualify for a family—to validate in society his love and sex through becoming a husband and provider—may be jeopardized. The man discovers that manhood affords few wholly distinctive roles except in the military, which is less inviting than ever. The society prohibits, constricts, or feminizes his purely male activities. Most jobs reward obedience, regularity, and carefulness more than physical strength; and the amount of individual initiative and assertiveness that can be accommodated by the average enterprise is very small indeed. Thus the man will find few compensatory affirmations of masculinity to sexual and social rhythms; and without a confident manhood he feels a compulsive need to prove it sexually, which he will do in ways that feminists, like the respectable women they are, fear and despise.

The American woman, meanwhile, becomes increasingly self-sufficient. While men are almost completely dependent upon women for a civilized role in the society and for biological and sexual meaning, women are capable of living decent—though often discontented—lives without men. The culture no longer much disapproves of unmarried mothers. The state affords them welfare and, increasingly, day care and maternity leave. In any case, birth control and legalized abortion give women complete control of procreation; and sexual liberation—not to mention masturbation and lesbianism—opens sexual enjoyment to them with only the most tenuous commitment to males. In fact, women are more than ever willing to adopt as their own an impulsive male sexuality, and although men may consequently find sexual partners more readily than before the meaning of their sexuality is diminished and they can derive less assurance from it. How could it be otherwise when more and more men and women now confront each other, *Joy of Sex* manuals in hand, joined in a grim competition of orgasmic performance. The barely discriminate ruttings of the liberated woman find a nice complement in the stud vanity of the swinging male.

The stud, like his chief activity, is without significance except in dramatizing the largely spurious glamour of primitive masculinity: the love-'em-and-leave-'em style of most of our male heroes in novels and films. But the ordinary man may also come to feel his sexual role devalued in a context of overt sexual liberation. And he too will turn away from the family. He watches televised football and other sports for hours on end and argues about them incessantly. He becomes easy prey to jingoism and the crudest appeals for law and order. And he is obsessed with women. He tries as much as possible to reduce them to their sexual parts, and to reduce their sexuality to his own limited terms: to meaningless but insistent copulation. Exiled from the world of women, he tries to destroy consciousness of its superiority by reducing it to his own level. He insists—against all his unconscious and ulterior knowledge—that women are as sexually contemptible as his society tells him he is.

He turns to pornography, with fantasies of sex and violence. His magazines—*Male* and *Crime* and *Saga* and *True Detective*, even respectably prurient publications like *Playboy* and its refined imitators—are preoccupied with barren copulation, or with war, perversion, and crime. He is an exile, an outlaw under the sexual constitution. Often he becomes a literal outlaw as well.

What he is *not* is a powerful oppressor, with hypertrophied masculinity. Such men lead impotent lives, and, as Rollo May asserts, violence is the product of impotence grown unbearable. Their problem is a society inadequately affirmative of masculinity: a society seduced by an obsessive rationalism and functionalism—a cult of efficiency, and a fetish of statistical equality—to eliminate many of the male affirmations which all human societies have created throughout history to compensate for male sexual insecurity and female sexual superiority. The women's movement seems determined to create more and more such exiled "chauvinist" males, all the while citing their pathetic offenses as a rationale for feminism.

Thus the society both provides for its own disruption and leaches itself of positive male energies. Engels said that marriage is the handmaiden of capitalism; one could say, however, that it is the handmaiden of any productive society. For male insecurity is also the "divine unease" that in socialized males, strong enough to submit to women, produces the driving force behind a society's achievements in industry, art, and science. It is wrong to suggest that either women's liberation or male irresponsibility is chiefly to blame for our current predicament. Both phenomena are reflections of larger trends in the society hostile to enduring love.[2]

LOVE VS. SEX

The "Love that dare not speak its name" used to be homosexual. Today, it's the love between men and women, especially husbands and wives. Feminists are not alone in their embarrassed confusion over this subject, but as usual they are a highly visible symptom of the general condition. They often avoid the problem by deferring a definition to some post-revolutionary stage—to be achieved after the withering away of masculinity—when people will at last recognize each other as "human beings."

Until then they offer an alternative, appealing to many people who are both disillusioned with their adolescent images of love and excited by a sense of new possibilities of sexual freedom and variety. For while love, in the form of euphoric monogamy, seems increasingly elusive, sex as a way of communicating warmth and exchanging pleasures seems increasingly available. It even appears that sex is best when it is spontaneous: exempt from the psychological complications of a deep love.

The movement women, with the strong support of the counselors of sex technique, go on to argue that sexual relations will be most gratifying if the conventional roles of the two sexes are not closely observed. They advise that the old "missionary position" be frequently abandoned (a male chauvinist relic, say the pamphleteers of *Out From Under*). And they give the impression that ineffable pinnacles of pleasure can be reached if couples are just willing, with the advice of the new sex manuals, to overcome inhibitions and role-stereotypes—leaving no erogenous zone unexplored, or orifice unfathomed. The "tyranny of genital sex" is to be exuberantly overthrown, and oral and anal access affirmed.

Pleasures, of course, can be given and received by a variety of people, and since variety is refreshing there is seen to be little physical or psychological reason for restricting sex to a single partner. And since sexual orgasm, the supreme pleasure, is in fact considered crucial to mental health, there seems little moral sanction either for depriving those who have failed to find a long-term lover.

These attitudes are also convenient for homosexuals, who have long since abandoned sexually determined roles and escaped from the genital tyranny of the missionary position. The view that sex is best when the partners perform in psychologically similar, if versatile, ways, in fact leaves little grounds at all for objecting to inversion. It comes as no surprise then that the proponents of gay liberation, as well as some literary avatars of that movement such as Gore Vidal and Kate Millett, should seem to be moving beyond a claim on our tolerance and compassion to an advocacy of the wonderful benefits of a homosexual style of life.

It would be a great mistake, however, to identify this fashionable concept of sex chiefly with feminism and gay liberation. For, ironically enough, it is also the essential ideology of male chauvinism: the playboy philosophy. Although the chauvinists may secretly nurse visions of male dominance, they are delighted with the prospect of female liberation. Like that *Cosmopolitan* girl and the "human beings" of *Ms.*, the playboy philosophers want to "finally and unanswerably break the connection between sexual intercourse and reproduction." Like the feminist writers, the male chauvinists fantasize polymorphously aggressive women, free of inhibitions and fixations. And also like the feminists, the male chauvinists do not like to envisage their women dependent or—God forbid—pregnant.

In practice, this popular image of spontaneous and carefree "love between mature and equal human beings" is often workable. Mutual needs are fulfilled lovingly, as long as is mutually desired, and the couple parts amicably. Each partner is defined as autonomous: neither, in theory, can be deeply hurt by the departure of the other. In a mature relationship no one is believed to suffer the mawkish toils of dependency. The two partners are free. They are liberated at once *from* expectations of lifelong enchantment, rarely fulfilled, and *for* deep physical gratifications more easily attained. Thus, according to the theory, they will be happier and less vulnerable, dealing not with fantasies but with possibilities in the real world.

With respect to marriage, the feminists offer a similar blueprint. A recent best-selling book, *Open Marriage*, by two anthropologists, George and Nena O'Neill, is a representative vision. Much of the prospectus is remarkably silly. The O'Neills invite us to transcend "mere togetherness" and reach "the ultimate in cooperation. . . that creates, through expanding feedback and growth, a *synergic couple*" (their italics). If some of us are not yet ready for the "opening expanding energy system" of the "now" marriage, if "high points" and "peak experiences" and "super moments" inspire only vertigo, the authors will understand. They concede that there may be those who might prefer to "ignore the peaks [and] huddle in the narrow valleys" of "conditional and static trust, unequal status, limited love, and a closed, self-limiting energy system." But, if one really wants to have a fulfilling union, they are firm in declaring that only an "open marriage" will do.

Oddly, however, the terms of the O'Neill marriage contract turn out to be extremely strict. As in the image of sexual relations between "human beings," so the open marriage envisages two partners with completely flexible and reversible roles. The O'Neills categorically dismiss the notion of sex-assigned functions and responsibilities, for unless the woman earns money (preferably as much as the hus-

127

band) and the man keeps house (also on equal terms) the O'Neills fear the the couple will have too little in common to "grow together." When one actually scrutinizes their notion, equality turns out to mean sameness. The man earns money; so must the woman. The man philanders; so must his wife. The man initiates sex; so must she. The woman decorates the house, cooks a meal, or makes a bed; the man must eventually reciprocate.

Children, of course, are rather awkward in this scheme and the O'Neills would have as little to do with them as possible. They positively celebrate the childless marriage and declare that "the importance of motherhood has been inflated out of all proportion." "Motherhood," they argue, "must be disentangled from the wife's role." It should be "optional" in an overpopulated world, rather than "glorified."

Actually, the danger of overpopulation has little to do with the O'Neills' advocacy of the optional status of children. What they really fear is the snare of domesticity. The home, they assert, "may have its pleasures, but none of them makes sufficient demands to bring about real growth." Domestic life programs the woman for "mediocrity and dulls her brain." Far better to get out into the world of business and the professions with all their "inspiring challenges" and "broadening vistas."

This view of the way to find both good sex and reasonably enduring love seems plausible to most sophisticated Americans. The feminists are not more daringly rebellious in their usual sexual imagery than is Hugh Hefner in his mock-heroic battle against the dread forces of American puritanism. Nonetheless, the feminists—as well as the playboy philosophers, the *Joy of Sex* technicians, and the gay liberationists—are grotesquely wrong about both love and sex.

These groups have at least this in common: an eagerness to divorce sex from procreation. This desire is hardly extraordinary. It is resisted only by the Catholic and Baptist churches and Norman Mailer, among major American institutions; and in the general alarm about overpopulation, it has gained the moral momentum of a crusade and the financial support of the major foundations. To a considerable extent, this effort is reasonable enough.

The members of the new sex coalition, however, go well beyond the search for a better contraceptive. They also want to eliminate the psychological and symbolic connections between intercourse and childbirth. They may reluctantly acknowledge that in a sense procreation is the most important current role of intercourse—and certainly the key role in the history of mankind. They may even recognize that during the millions of years when the species evolved and our sexuality was formed, fertility determined survival. Nevertheless, they look forward to a time, not too far distant, when artificial means may be employed for human reproduction.

This ideology of non-procreative sex is not a trivial matter. We all know that in the age of contraception all sexual activity does not have to be intentionally procreative, if indeed it ever did. But it hardly follows that sexual pleasure is totally unrelated to the complex of drives and desires that converge to reproduce the species in a loving and secure environment. Nor does it follow that a complete break between procreative and erotic instincts will not ultimately undermine

> **The beginning of a man's love in a civilized society lies in his desire, whether conscious or not, to have and keep his progeny.**

all forms of sexual pleasure. To state the question directly: does sex that is wholly detached from a procreative mode—that violates its genital focus and sense of futurity—does this kind of sex ultimately reduce sexual energy and undermine love? Does the separatist ideal of polymorphous pleasures so fail to correspond to the inner syntax of sexuality that it strains the bonds of human personality, becoming disintegrative, not integrative, of body and mind and spirit? To answer these questions, one must explore the ties between sexual pleasure, procreation, and love.

The beginning of a man's love in a civilized society lies in his desire, whether conscious or not, to have and keep his progeny. For this he must choose a particular woman. His love defines his choice. His need to choose evokes his love. His sexual drive lends energy to his love, and his love gives shape, meaning, and continuity to his sexuality. When he selects a specific woman, he in essence defines himself both to himself and to society. Afterwards, every sex act celebrates that definition and social engagement.

The sex act then becomes a human affirmation, involving a man's entire personality and committing it, either in fact or in symbol, to a long-term engagement in a meaningful future. In fact, one can say that the conscious or unconscious desire to have children with a specific partner is a workable definition of sexual love. It is not, in bold specific terms, the only definition. But across the range of sexual experience in a civilized society, this motive seems to run strongest in the phenomenon of love.

This concept of sexual love, originating in the desire for children and symbolized in genital intercourse, again emphasizes the differences between the sexes. A man's love is focused on the symbols and associations of a woman's procreative powers—embodied in her womb and her breasts and elaborated in her nurturant sentiments, her tenderness, and her sense of futurity. The woman loves the man for his strength and protectiveness, for temperamental qualities that provide an ability to support and protect her while she bears their children—or while she surrenders to orgasm. She loves him for his ability to control her in sexual intercourse and for his submission to the extended demands of her sexuality.

Beyond these primal attractions, of course, both the man and woman will seek a companionable and compatible partner. Both, that is, will seek someone whom they can imagine enjoying over time and who respects the values they want to transmit to their children. Such a relationship, it should go without saying, will accommodate a wide range of sexual activity, from deliberate attempts to conceive children to casual sex play.

SENSUOUS MASSAGE

There is a mode of sex, however, that is not affirmative, that tends to tear apart the armature of sexuality and identity. That sort of sex oc-

curs when the sex act does not express love, is not associated even unconsciously or symbolically with the aspiration to conceive children, and does not subordinate male instant gratification to female
futurity. Then the sex act becomes a transient pleasure, an ephemeral
kick, which, if pursued, leads to emotional fragmentation rather
than to a sense of continuity with nature and society. If this kind of sex
prevails, the male circuit of impulsive and predatory sexuality can become the dominant rhythm in the culture.

The women's movement, the male chauvinists, the gay
liberationists, the sexologists, and the pornographers all tend to indulge and promote such a disintegration. All present alternatives
to loving sexuality. The man and woman who are attempting to fulfill
their sexual natures in an affirmative way are bombarded with contrary
ideologies. The pornographer pervasively advertises the potential
joys of promiscuity, of unknown but shapely bodies—continuously
stimulates primal male impulses and subverts the effort to maintain
monogamous ties. The sex manuals present utopian images of the
bliss that comes with an abandonment of "inhibitions" and
"stereotypes" that may be important to affirmative sexuality. The
women's movement offers visions of a spurious sexual equality, in
which women are to be considered as erotically impulsive as men,
or more so. The gay liberationists romanticize a pattern in which ultimate sexual fulfillment is impossible and in which temporary
gratification is paramount.

The danger in the sexual separatist program is that unsocialized
men will become culturally dominant, while the civilized will have
to resist the pressures of the society at large. A civilization dependent on families, on long-term commitments, will be confronted by a
powerful mass culture propagating a sexuality of immediate
gratifications. A society profoundly reliant on monogamy will face a culture advertising promiscuity. We find ourselves close to that situation
today.

The effect on men is most immediate and far-reaching because
their identities and secondary sexual behavior are more dependent on
culture and therefore more vulnerable to shifts in social pressures.
But ultimately the impact on women is just as tragic. Women face a cruel
dilemma, exemplified in part by the current women's movement.

Some have responded to the increasing abdication of men from civilized social and sexual patterns by trying to play both key roles, sustaining long-term commitments as well as familial responsibilities. The most talented and stable will succeed, thus perpetuating civilized behavior in the face of a hostile culture. Other women have chosen careers alone, while either forgoing sex or halfheartedly adopting the male pattern. Still others have enthusiastically embraced an essentially male chauvinist ethic of promiscuous "openness," narrowing their expectations of men and of the potentialities of their own bodies.

In the end, the sexuality of both men and women and the spirit of the community are reduced to the limited, barren, compulsive circuitry of uncivilized males. Confined in a shallow present, with little hope for the future or interest in the past, neither sex works or loves devotedly. While sex is given a steadily larger role, it loses contact with its procreative sources and becomes increasingly promiscuous and undifferentiated, homosexual and pornographic. It becomes what in fact our current liberationists—male and female—already imagine it to be, essentially a form of sensuous massage—a shapeless, dissolute, and destructive pursuit of ever more elusive pleasures by ever more drastic techniques. In the quest for a better orgasm or more intense titillation, a frustrated population goes on ever wilder goose chases in "little-known erogenous zones"—on ever more futile scavenger hunts for sexual erotica, picking up a whip here, an orgy there, but always returning to the sterile and shapeless lump of their own sexuality. Such are the aporias of carnal knowledge—the dead ends of "spontaneity."

Our sexual potentialities are to a great extent fixed. But what we do with them is determined by culture, which is shaped by us. The first and most important step in restoring a sense of order and purpose and community is to reestablish the social pressures and cultural biases in favor of durable monogamous love and marriage—the long-term feminine sexual patterns—that the women's movement and the playboy philosophers find so "oppressive." It is women who will most benefit in the beginning, for their discomfort in the toils of male sexuality is already inducing a revulsion toward sex altogether. But ultimately the whole society gains. For as we cultivate more profound patterns of love and sexuality, we will create a deeper sense of community, a more optimistic embrace of the future, and a more productive society.

The differences between the sexes are the single most important fact of human society. The drive to deny them—in the name of women's liberation, marital openness, sexual equality, erotic consumption, homosexual romanticism—must be one of the most quixotic crusades in the history of the species. Yet in a way it is typical of crusades. For it is a crusade against a particular incarnate humanity—men and women and children—on behalf of a metaphysical "humanism." It seems unlikely, however, that the particular men and women one meets in the real world will ever voluntarily settle for long in an open house of barren abstractions.

NOTES

1 The increasingly conclusive evidence that the two sex roles originate in pro found biological differences is summarized and appraised in a brilliant new scholarly study by Steven Goldberg, *The Inevitability of Patriarchy* (Morrow).

2 Doris Lessing, a writer frequently praised and published in *Ms.*, states the case with her usual vehemence. Speaking of feminist characters in her own work, she said in a recent interview, "We're very biological animals. We always tend to think that if one is in a violent state of emotional need, it is our unique emotional need or state, when in matter of fact it's probably just the emotions of a young woman whose body is demanding that she have children. . . . Anna and Molly [in *The Golden Notebook*] are women who are conditioned to be one way and are trying to be another. I know a lot of girls who don't want to get married or have children. And very vocal they are about it. Well, they're trying to cheat on their biology. . . . It will be interesting to see how they're thinking at thirty."

What Men Stand to Gain from Women's Liberation

William H. Masters and Virginia E. Johnson

Diane Dollinger: As a girl I never felt it would become me to be physically aggressive toward a guy. If he wanted me, that was fine; and if he wanted me at the same time I wanted him, I would have to hope he could get the right cues from me. . . .

Virginia Johnson: . . .Here is another double-standard residual—a reflection of the traditional view of the woman's role, with the culture assigning her the responsibility of meeting the man's needs. . . . Today we are in transition, and we'll assume that a young couple don't want to live in accord with that traditional standard. But can they make progress toward sexual equality without undermining the sexual relationship itself?

The increasing acceptance of American women as independent persons is an irreversible process. And the final outcome seems clear: women will join men as full partners.

This prospect evokes uneasiness and even anxiety in many people, women as well as men. Change is never more unsettling than when it raises questions about fundamental matters that have always been taken for granted. And few matters seem less open to question than the nature of sexual identity and the importance of differences between the sexes. Both women and men are thus understandably disturbed to find themselves confronted with the possibility that much of what they believe about the female sex may be inaccurate or untrue. The new outlook introduces a disconcerting and troubling element into their world.

Such alarm is groundless, based for the most part on confusion and misconceptions that need clarification. Not all aspects of the problem can be dealt with in this limited space, but several important considerations can be raised as a contribution to the dialogue now going on between women and men all over the world.

A primary and rather obvious distinction must first be made. The common basis on which men and women cooperate in society at large is not the same as the unique basis on which a specific couple coexist in private. The two worlds are separate realms of experience with radically different requirements for success—performance at work, fulfillment at home—and they involve different risks and rewards. For any woman determined to develop her independence beyond traditional lines, there is no possibility of weighing the consequences without taking into account whether the steps she takes will influence the life she leads in public or in private. The Liberation Movement possesses a different significance in each of these worlds. To overlook this distinction is to blur the meaning of the movement and to transform any discussion of the matter into a futile debate.

Both worlds, of course, do interact. A self-assured woman who works on a basis of equality with male colleagues, for example, is likely to find it easier to establish a personal relationship with a man based on mutual needs than if she were in the usual subordinate position at work, dominated by males. This highly complex crossover effect—from public to private life—deserves further careful study. All that can be noted now is that public attitudes influence private relationships.

Our intention here is to focus on the private relationship in an effort to trace some of the ways in which the equal rights movement may affect the intimate man–woman bond. For this, after all, is the crux of the matter. While feminism today is moving forward with all the fervor of a fad, for how long will women continue to pursue the principle of sex equality if it does not lead to emotional fulfillment in their private worlds? And fulfillment for the overwhelming majority of women requires an enduring relationship with a man.

Militant Women's Liberation advocates may deplore that fact, but a fact it remains. Marriage is now more popular than at any time in the nation's history. Two out of three Americans of marriageable age are married; more marriages were performed in 1970 than in any year since the 1946 postwar boom; and the number of marriages continued to rise during the first nine months of 1971, the last period to be studied. These statistics alone refute those social observers who,

> **If some of the leaders of the women's movement make the strategic mistake of attacking marriage as part of a male plot to keep women under control, they will almost surely find themselves out of touch with most other women.**

with no sociological evidence to offer, have been prophesying the decline of marriage.

Furthermore the statistics do not reflect the full extent to which men and women choose to be united as couples, since living together without being legally wed seems an accelerating trend. All things considered, we have ample persuasive proof that the man–woman bond still plays a crucial role in the lives of individuals of both sexes—and appears likely to continue in importance in the future.

If some of the leaders of the women's movement make the strategic mistake of attacking marriage as part of a male plot to keep women under control, they will almost surely find themselves out of touch with most other women. Any attempt to persuade the average woman that she too has an important stake in the outcome of the present campaign to extend women's rights will fall on deaf ears if that campaign projects the concept that equality and independence are assets only for the unmarried and the childless.

Such a misconception is regrettable. The emancipation movement has much to contribute to society as a whole, but it cannot succeed without widespread support from the general public, men as well as women. Before the feminists can hope to win over any substantial number of the opposite sex, however, they must first find ways to convince most members of their own. The nonconformist minority must be joined by the traditionalist majority.

But what have Liberation spokeswomen to say to a woman who dreams of having a husband, a home and a family? This woman wants to know what part, if any, sexual equality can play in helping her to find happiness in the world she shares with friends and family.

Her questions are simple, personal and practical. If she is single and acts with more self-reliance and initiative than most men are accustomed to, and she wants to be accepted as a person first and a female second, she may wonder whether her attractiveness will be diminished. If she selects a job not usually performed by a female, makes friends with men as naturally as with women, and accepts premarital sex as a healthy consequence of emotional commitment, will she jeopardize the future she desires?

Or if she is married and has as much to say as her husband in making decisions that concern them both, if she chooses to work or be of service in the community even though this takes her out of the house during the day, and if she makes it clear that she enjoys being an active partner in marital sex, she may worry about undermining her marriage.

There are good reasons to believe that such fears are groundless. By disregarding outdated social stereotypes and searching instead to discover what she can do and wants to do, a woman improves her chances of becoming a happier and more fulfilled person—and this improves her chances of achieving and maintaining a rewarding marriage.

This is a general principle, of course, and what happens in any given case can never be predicted. A woman can always make an unfortunate choice of partner, for example—although such an error of judgment is less likely if she respects herself as an individual in her own right. Secure in her identity as a female, she won't feel compelled to marry to prove that she is a woman; confident of her worth as a person, she won't be vulnerable to the man who needs to dominate a woman to prove his masculinity.

In seeking a partner to marry or to live with, she will be looking for her male counterpart: a man who rejects the sex stereotypes that prevail in society, who will accept her as his equal and will prize her individuality. With such a man she can avoid the trap in which so many wives are caught, where roles are assigned on the basis of sex alone, where both man and woman act on cue in standardized ways according to a script written centuries ago, no matter how awkward or compromised they may feel, and where, barred from the kind of sharing relationship that would extend their sense of themselves as individuals, they live out their lives locked side by side in separate cells labeled His and Hers.

Any woman who has the will and the courage to break out of the cell that historically has been considered appropriate for females, a cell comfortably padded with privileges, has something of tremendous value to offer a man—the key to his own prison door. For wherever equality of the sexes exists, and especially in the intimate world of marriage, liberation of the female liberates the male.

This can be seen with striking clarity in the sexual relationship. Traditionally sex has been something a man does to a woman. During a considerable period in history this arrangement served its purpose. It offered the man release from physical tension whenever he needed it so that he could concentrate on earning a living for himself and his family. And it resulted in pregnancy and children for the woman, which represented justification of her existence. Under these circumstances most husbands could perform adequately because nothing was required beyond a brief coupling. They themselves were led to expect little pleasure from marital sex; and their wives, none at all.

Attitudes began changing in this century in response to complex social and cultural influences. Men—and, to a lesser degree, women—began hoping to achieve sexual gratification in the marriage bed. Since they still adhered to the old active-male/passive-female philosophy, however, a woman could not cooperate sexually without compromising her standing as a respectable woman, in her husband's eyes as well as her own. And because she could not contribute her own sexual feelings, success depended entirely upon the man.

Over the years, pressures on him increased. At first he was expected only to be gentle and considerate; then, to make his wife feel loved and desired; next, to assure her of an orgasm, possibly simultaneous with his own; and finally, to trigger a whole series of orgasms. It is only fair to point out that these were not female ultimatums. Most of them, in fact, were articulated by male writers—novelists, psychotherapists, sexologists and the like—whose recommendations often depended more on imagination than on research and were influenced more by prevailing cultural beliefs than by secure, scientific knowledge. They envisioned the sexual function less as an authentic expression of a total relationship than as a personal achievement test with specific performance goals.

Their unrealistic sex-performance standards, which filtered into the expectations of many men and women confused by shifting ethical and moral codes, were still based on the insidious notion that sex is the mark of the man. This lopsided approach to the sexual relationship persisted through the 1940s, fifties and even the sixties, despite the fact that more and more young women were rejecting the double standard, accepting—and even initiating—premarital sex.

Sex with affection was their byword, and they saw it as part of an exchange. If they could learn to be more open, more flexible and more encouraging, they would then be rewarded with male performances guaranteed to deliver ecstasy. They did not realize that this attitude was simply a new variation on the old theme of active-male/passive-female; they didn't understand what it meant to be a full and equal partner.

In that sense they are no more liberated than their mothers, and today's young men are under greater pressure than ever before. In the past, men at least had escape hatches. Inexperienced females had a limited ability to respond, were further inhibited by fear of pregnancy and settled, not ungratefully, for warmth and tenderness in place of passion. But once morality and birth-control methods evolve to a point where the woman feels free to grant herself permission to enjoy sexual relations, she turns to a particular man to make good on the promise made in his name by the male sex in general—to deliver pleasure on demand. What acceptable excuse can he offer if he cannot produce the promised delight? Whom can he blame but himself?

Thus sex often looms like Mount Everest before many a man—he is expected to reach the peak, pulling his partner up with him, and, if he is married, to do so with regularity. If intercourse does not proceed according to plan most of the time—if it does not reach the five-minute mark, for example, or does not include the programmed orgasm—a man may come to believe that he is sexually incompetent. No wonder some husbands, unwilling to make the effort or to risk being considered sexually inadequate or perhaps impotent, retreat behind the defense of indifference.

What a great many men and women must learn is that they cannot achieve the pleasure they both want until they realize that the most effective sex is not something a man does to or for a woman but something a man and woman do together *as equals*.

This deceptively simple truth points to one of the most valuable contributions a woman can make to a man's ability to function effectively, from which she, of course, benefits. The sexually liberated woman learns, among other things, the importance of being free, as men have always been free, to express openly the full range of her sexual excitement and involvement—the delight of wanting and being wanted, touching and being touched, seeing and being seen, hearing words and uttering them, of fragrances and textures, silences and sounds. Her spontaneous feelings, spontaneously communicated, stimulate her partner and heighten his tensions, impelling him to act on his own impulses. Whatever she gives him returns to her and whatever he gives her comes back to him.

More than half the pleasure of the sexual experience depends on a partner's response. If there is virtually no reaction at all, or at best passive acceptance, the emotional current steadily weakens and eventually flickers and goes dead. In too many marriages the wife may never say no but never really says yes—and then is puzzled later in life that when she goes to bed, her husband stays up to watch television.

But even saying yes—and meaning it—is not the answer. Active participation does not consist of merely initiating matters which the man is then expected to complete. The woman who wholeheartedly commits herself as an equal in the sexual union is involved in continuous response to her husband's changing needs and desires, as he is involved in hers. Like him, she values freshness and variety and from time to time willingly experiments with the many modes of arousal as an expression of her personality and mood of the moment, not as an artificial contrivance to resuscitate flagging desire.

The responsiveness of both partners is based on their mutual acceptance as vulnerable human beings with unique needs, expectations and capabilities. The wife does not assume that her husband wants what all men are supposed to want. Sensitive to what he says or reveals without words, she responds to his actual feelings at a specific moment—and she counts on him to do the same for her. Emotional needs, which vary with the mood, time and place, are not

> **A woman cannot be sexually eman- cipated without first becoming per- sonally emancipated.**

labeled "masculine" and "feminine." If he enjoys it when she manifests a strong sexual urge, that is fine; and if—as inevitably happens at times—their needs are not complementary, they will gently make their way to the best solution they can negotiate, not as representatives of two different sexes but as two separate partners united by a mutual concern.

Together they succeed or together they fail in the sexual encounter, sharing the responsibility for failure, whether it is reflected in his performance or hers. While conclusive proof is still lacking, there are firm grounds for believing that the female who esteems herself as something more than a collector's item, who has a positive appreciation of her biological nature and enters into sex as a free and equal partner—and who is as responsive to her partner's needs as she wants him to be to hers—will do more to eliminate male fears of functional failure than all the therapy in the world.

But a woman cannot be sexually emancipated without first becoming personally emancipated. If she is nothing to herself, she has nothing to give to anyone. For such a woman, to give herself to a man is to give him nothing, and so she expects nothing in return. Sexually she receives him and perhaps considers herself useful, as an object is useful.

The more she sees in herself and values herself as a person, however, the more able she is to establish an equitable relationship with a man. Thus before any woman can play a constructive role in a man's life as an equal, before she can join him as a partner, contribute to his sexual pleasure and, by sharing it, relieve him of some of the performance pressures placed on him by society, she must have a strong sense of who she is and what she can do and of her worth as a human being. She must have pride in herself as an individual who happens to be, and is happy to be, a woman.

She cannot achieve this goal by wishful thinking or her own solitary efforts; she does not exist in a cultural vacuum. In her earliest years her personal integrity is best served if it is safeguarded by those closest to her—parents, relatives, teachers, friends—and if somewhere, somehow, the outside world permits her to glimpse examples of what she can become, if she chooses to make the effort. The very society that currently tries to bribe her with special privileges to accept subordinate status also offers her a chance, no matter how small, to struggle toward independence and equality.

This is no less true outside the realm of sex. An interesting example of how husbands who accept their wives as equals gain from being united in a mutual effort can be found, surprisingly enough, in the trucking industry. On long-distance hauls, where drivers must operate in pairs so that one can spell the other at the steering wheel, a small but growing number of husbands and wives have been teaming up. Less than ten years ago the idea would have been inconceivable. For it to be happening today in an industry generally regarded as a stronghold of male chauvinism is striking evidence that the principle of equality of the sexes is spreading more rapidly than is generally realized.

The advantages of such a joint venture—to the couple as a pair, to the husband as a man and the wife as a woman—seem transparently clear. By sharing the driving they reject the old, stereotyped division of labor into "a man's job" and "woman's work." Since both receive salaries, they reject the traditional view that only the man should be the provider. The husband, secure as a male, accepts his wife's cooperation in carrying a burden that, as life-insurance statistics make shockingly plain, literally has cost other men their lives. Thus not only can a couple like this enjoy being together—they also can enjoy being together longer.

The wife, no less female for driving a truck, gains the security of a closer relationship with her husband, strengthened by sharing responsibilities and sharing experiences. Knowing that she is respected for what she can do, valued for what she contributes, and appreciated for the woman she is, her sense of her self cannot help flourishing.

She may never have heard of the Women's Liberation Movement, but she exemplifies it. And if an image is needed to characterize the relationship between husband and wife today, perhaps it can be found here: codrivers of a vehicle taking both to the same destination, each trusting the other to help steer in the direction they want to go, traveling together because they do not want to be apart.

This is the significance of the Liberation Movement today. For in the past it was only the most exceptional women in the most exceptional of circumstances who could transcend the rigid limitations placed on their sex. Today, and certainly tomorrow, that opportunity must be available to women with less privileged backgrounds—and this can happen only if the social structure itself is changed so that discrimination is not enforced by law and only if public opinion and private attitudes can be changed so that discrimination is not perpetuated by a "gentleman's agreement." These are the obstacles which women in the vanguard of the struggle for equality must concentrate on eliminating.

This struggle, which is echoed in discussions and arguments in homes all over the country, is too often conceived in terms of a misleading image: two on a seesaw. Power is the pivot, and if one sex goes up, the other must come down. What women gain, men lose.

But the sexual relationship itself shows the analogy to be false. What a man and a woman achieve together benefits both—the very quality of life, *as it is individually experienced*, can be immeasurably augmented by a fully shared partnership.

On Being Female in America

Carol LeFevre

In the last decade, our attitudes toward traditional expressions of male–female sexuality have been in a remarkable ferment. The young women of the 1950s who committed themselves wholeheartedly to staying home and raising large families are now middle-aged matrons seeking alternatives to the empty nest. Their young-adult daughters are questioning the primacy of a woman's commitment to home and family, and many are seeking careers outside the home. In a 1973 poll of New Jersey college women, for example, 2 out of 3 did not think that being a wife and mother is the most important role for a woman, 4 out of 5 felt that a wife's career is as important as her husband's, and 3 out of 4 expected their husbands to share the housework.[1] Some women are choosing not to have children, and current research suggests that children strain, rather than cement, a marriage.[2]

POLARIZED STEREOTYPES

In the traditional American view of male and female sexuality, men

---

Published by permission of the author.

are the active, aggressive providers for and protectors of their families. Women are the weaker, passive, nurturant sex—biologically designed, if not divinely ordained, to care for men and children. As providers, men can work at any of a variety of tasks. Women, however, have one proper vocation: that of homemaker. For men, vocation and parenthood are separate; for women, the two roles are fused in image and in practice. Man's work and woman's place are biologically determined and socially necessary for the maintenance of the family and of society.

The radical feminists who have emerged during the last decade argue that marriage and children trap women into economic, social, and emotional dependence on, and consequent submission to, men. They see little evidence other than childbearing ability to support the traditional contention that innate differences exist between the sexes. They believe that abilities and personality traits considered typical of men and women in our society result not from biology but from

> **Women in our culture are taught that their main goal in life and the proof of their femininity lie in attracting and securing a man.**

socialization, which prepares men to dominate and women to submit to and serve men and children. Furthermore, men's superior economic and political power results from an unjust discrimination against women solely on the basis of sex.

Although proponents of each view agree that serious strains on men and women exist in modern society, the traditionalists fear that the liberation of women will destroy the already fragile bonds between the sexes, lead to the neglect of children, and complete the disintegration of the family. Conversely, the feminists argue for speedy reforms; they point out the greater incidence among women of mental illness and poverty, and the earlier deaths of men attributed to their lifelong responsibility for the support of women and children.

While traditional patterns provide satisfying lives for some people in our society, they fail to meet crucial needs of others. Threatened by the demands of the women's movement, a militant group of housewives defends the indispensability and privilege of their at-home status and attacks the most visible harbinger of change, the Equal Rights Amendment, while 1 out of every 2 women votes with her feet by going out to work every day.

TO BE A WOMAN, GET A MAN

Women in our culture are taught that their main goal in life and the proof of their femininity lie in attracting and securing a man. Conventional wisdom, repeated in innumerable cartoons and jokes, urges women to catch men, and men to beware of being caught. Is marriage the solution to all of life's problems for women, and is it the liability for men that we have been led to expect?

When a man and woman marry, the continuity of the husband's life is nearly always maintained, while the wife usually subordinates her own life, needs, and preferences to his.[3] His vocation is undisturbed and even abetted by marriage, while hers typically becomes secondary or is exchanged for homemaking. They live where his work takes them, and she adjusts her life to his hours and job demands, to his car and clothing needs, and often to his preference in friends, food, sex, and leisure activities. The higher her social class, the more the wife becomes involved in her husband's business and social world, and the more her identity becomes tied to his.[4] His work supports the family, and she becomes acutely aware of her financial dependence on him. In one survey, 84 percent of the urban housewives and 91 percent of the suburban housewives questioned listed the role of breadwinner among the most important roles of the man of the family, and two-thirds put that role in first place.[5]

In spite of the adjustments they must make, most women fare quite well when they are first married, and both husband and wife are likely to report a high level of marital satisfaction. If they had jobs when they were married, most middle-class wives continue to work until the event they anticipate with romantic pleasure—the

147

birth of their first child. Surely now they will be completely fulfilled as women. They have been told since childhood that this is their crowning glory in life. Or is it?

MOTHERHOOD: FULFILLMENT OR TRAP?

Lopata's extensive study of 571 housewives of all social levels concludes:

> The event causing the greatest discontinuity of personality in American middle-class women is the birth of the first child, particularly if it is not immediately followed by a return to full-time involvement outside of the home. It is not just a "crisis" which is resolved by a return to previous roles and relations, but an event marking a complete change in life approach. All other changes, except widowhood, are more gradual.[6]

Clearly the impact of the first child is far greater on the wife than on the husband. Although he loses his place as the center of his wife's attention in the family, his major role outside the home continues unchanged. For her, however, motherhood is a whole new way of life and a long-term commitment. If marriage does not live up to her expectations, there is a way out; but children cannot be divorced or returned.

Middle-class mothers   For some young women, motherhood is the happy, fulfilling experience they have been taught to expect. In a survey by Rossi, the most home-oriented of a nationwide sample of young married women three years out of college reported great happiness and a transforming sense of fulfillment from their home and early motherhood role.[7] Not a few young women are glad to escape routine or unsatisfying jobs, enjoy managing their own time, and find home and children meaningful and rewarding. Nearly all women form a strong attachment to their children and are deeply concerned for their healthy, wholesome development.

Some women, however, find motherhood traumatic. If they have had satisfying careers, the shift to full-time child care and housewifery may require a sharp adjustment, especially for professional women.[8] Usually they have had little education for motherhood and may be overwhelmed to find themselves suddenly responsible for the around-the-clock care of a tiny, totally dependent baby whose demands are immediate and urgent. Furthermore, these women often have strong convictions about the importance of a mother's loving care; they hold high standards for themselves and are fearful of the damaging psychological consequences of every mistake. Although they may quickly develop a new maturity and selflessness, their anxiety level is likely to be high.

Many women see themselves as changing with the birth of their children from initiating persons actively controlling their own lives ("I could come and go as I pleased") to reacting persons adjusting to and "tied down" by the demands of children and a heavy workload, with limited adult contacts and little intellectual stimulation.[9] These feelings are expressed by Mike McGrady, who reversed roles with his wife for a year:

> At the heart of my difficulty was this simple fact: for the past two decades I had been paid for my work. I had come to feel my time was valuable. Suddenly my sole payment was a weekly allowance given to me with considerable fanfare by my breadwinning wife. I began to see that as a trap, a many-strings-attached offering that barely survived a single session in the supermarket. . . . The pay was bad and the hours were long but what bothered me most was my own ineptitude, my inability to apply myself to the business of managing a home. . . . I never quite mastered that most basic task, the cleaning of the house. Any job that requires six hours to do and can be undone in six minutes by one small child carrying a plate of crackers and a Monopoly set . . . . No longer do I feel guilty about my failure as a homemaker. I would no more applaud the marvelously efficient and content housewife than I would applaud the marvelously efficient and content elevator operator. . . . it is always someone else who goes up, someone else who gets off.[10]

While the wife is home alone adjusting to her new role, her young husband is away many hours each week working hard to get ahead in his career; he has little time or energy to understand his wife's problems. And the wife, having relinquished her own career aspirations, is often busily pushing him up the corporate ladder and urging a move to the suburbs "because it would be better for the children." "The suburbs," Lopata says, "have become symbolically connected with the American dream of upward mobility and 'the good life' in the eyes of many people. 'Better for the children' may mean that suburbs offer a chance for such mobility, for starting life on a higher rung than the parent."[11]

Once ensconced in her dream home, the young wife finds herself in a "bedroom community" of women and children—separated from the resources, conveniences, and problems of city life, and further separated from her husband. The responsibilities for running the household, raising the family, and creating ties to the community are virtually hers alone. In such a situation, developing the skills for her role as housewife/mother/estate manager and finding and using the resources the family and their property need require considerable initiative. The dependent, passive woman may have a difficult time at this stage in her life, and she sometimes ends up overwhelmed and depressed in a psychiatric ward. However, the very complexity of her role and her relatively high level of education may lead to the development of "a new type of housewife: one who works competently and creatively in the role and who opens the home to societal participation."[12] Although confinement with small children may be difficult even for the mature, competent, independent woman, her role during the children's school years may lead her to develop organizational, administrative, and social skills that not only enrich her family and the community, but will help her to find alternative roles to fill her life as her children grow older.

Working-class mothers   The working-class wife, being oriented toward the traditional male–female roles, moves more naturally than the middle-class wife into an early enclosed "woman's world" during the period of early motherhood. There, she is more likely to have her mother and other female relatives nearby, providing advice and support. Because she and her husband tend to be strongly oriented toward kin and toward friends of the same sex, their relationship with each other is different from that of the middle-class companionate marriage.[13] While middle-class women often feel that children interfere with marital closeness, working-class wives say that children provide a bond to hold husbands in the relationship.[14]

Because her life is more narrowly circumscribed by home, family, and relatives, and her intellectual abilities less developed by education, the working-class wife tends to be more deeply involved with her children, seeking her satisfaction in life through them, yet fearful of her ability to understand and control either them or the outside world. Her anxious devotion puts a premium on conservative moral codes, and is threatened by new ideas and changing social roles.[15] She too is home alone with her children most of the day—subject to the same stresses of confinement and children's demands as her more affluent sisters. However, her husband is less likely to provide relief or help when he is home because children are definitely her business.

The High Cost of Staying Home

Despite the fact that a mother who stays at home to care for her children performs a valuable and difficult job and makes an important economic

> **Working women have generally better mental health than housewives.**

contribution to the family and to society, she receives no pay, gets no disability or retirement benefits, can build up no personal savings, and receives Social Security only through her husband—if she is not divorced before her twentieth wedding anniversary. Too few women realize that they are only one man away from welfare.

In addition to the economic costs of staying home, the psychological costs are, for many women, excessive—greater than for the man or woman who works. Married women are more likely than either married men or single women to have a nervous breakdown or to feel that one is impending, and to experience nervousness, inertia, insomnia, fainting, and heart palpitations.[16]

The results of the isolation our culture imposes on mothers with small children, where fathers are absent most of the week and no other adults are in the household, are not always benign. Anthropological studies tell us that mothers who raise children under such conditions show less affection and more physical aggression toward their offspring.[17] The suburban tract house or the urban duplex can become a pressure cooker from which fretful children and harried mothers have no relief. One-fourth of the working-class mothers interviewed by Komarovsky expressed considerable anxiety about their irritability and "hollering" at the children. One mother said, "I know they've got to be spanked sometimes but I spank them when I get mad. I shake and beat them and then I feel lousy."[18]

Every year in this country, a million cases of child neglect and abuse occur at all socioeconomic levels.[19] Clearly something is wrong. Neither husbands away at work nor child care experts telling women to be consistent and loving toward their children have any real idea of the pressures many young mothers experience at this stage of their lives.

THE WORKING WOMAN

In 1940, 1 of every 4 American women worked outside the home. By 1970, 1 of every 2 women was employed, including 6 million mothers with children under the age of 6, and 11 million with children between the ages of 6 and 11.[20] How do women fare when they work outside the home?

Working women have generally better mental health than housewives. Professional women especially find their work satisfying. Employed mothers report good relationships with their children more often than unemployed mothers, and have a stronger decision-making position in the marriage.[21] But there are stresses.

In the early 1960s, many career-oriented women a few years out of college were beset with problems; one-third reported discrimination on account of sex.[22] There is ample documentation of the frustration of ambitious young women because of overt and covert discrimination, and low-paying, dead-end jobs. Of all working women, only 15 percent hold professional and technical jobs, and most of these are in the relatively low-paid professions of teaching or nursing.

Even in "non-female" professions, women tend to remain at lower levels than men and to receive lower pay. Young people, however, appear ready for change. A 1975 survey of entering freshmen college women showed that 16.9 percent planned to become business executives, doctors, lawyers, or engineers—occupations planned by only 5.9 percent of women students 10 years ago[23]—and admission of women to graduate schools in these fields has risen proportionately. Ninety-two percent of all college freshmen in another 1975 survey believed women should have job equality[24]—but the battle to achieve it has only begun.

The so-called "women's occupations" (clerical, sales, office work, and so forth) have always been less well paid than men's, and the differential has been increasing. Whereas women earned 63 cents for every dollar men earned in 1958, they now earn 57 cents. Despite these inequities, many women report considerable satisfaction with their clerical jobs and are glad for the paychecks and the peer companionship. But paychecks that provide ample spending money for the "girl" waiting to marry are meager indeed for the woman supporting a family.

In the past women who did not marry in their twenties might turn to serious career preparation in their thirties. But in the 1970s, as careers for women have become a more accepted way of life, many young women plan from college or earlier to combine a career and marriage. How do women who make this choice fare?

Carrying a Double Load

The stress element most commonly found among employed married women, especially if they have children, is work overload. This is much the greatest for the mother without a husband, and is abetted by the psychological and financial strains of carrying the total responsibility alone. But the married woman, too, usually continues to carry all or virtually all of the responsibility for household and children in addition to her outside job. Even when she can afford to hire services, she remains responsible for seeing that the work is done. A study of professional-psychologist couples found that the men with professional wives took no more responsibility at home than husbands in a control group of male psychologists whose wives were homemakers,[25] and only 3 of 35 husbands of women graduate students with families shared responsibility for household tasks, although several others gave some help.[26] However, in an English study of 5 couples who considered each other's careers of equal importance, 3 shared the domestic responsibilities equally.[27]

While allocating the housework is a major struggle for some "liberated" wives who try to get their men to help with dishwashing, cooking, and cleaning, the trend toward equal sharing is growing among young couples. If the wife continues working, these early patterns may become a firmly established part of the marriage. If she drops out of the labor market to care for children, however, the pattern may quickly change. Returning to work later, she may face a considerable struggle to get husband and children to share the household responsibilities, as many housewives returning to school or work have found.[28] As McGrady pointed out, "Even the most loving family hates to lose that trusted servant, that faithful family retainer, that little old homemaker, you. No one enjoys it when the most marvelous appliance of them all breaks down."[29]

Carrying a Double Load Alone

One of every 6 mothers—whether married, widowed, separated, divorced, or single—is the sole source of her family's economic support.[30] She usually has full responsibility for her children's care, education, and housing, for housekeeping, budgeting, maintaining a car (if she can afford one), and for the family's social life and relationship with the community—often in addition to her full-time employment. Yet she earns little more than half the salary her husband commands, and if she is divorced her husband is likely to default on child-support payments within two years.

Children of Working Mothers

Half the mothers with school-age children, and 3 of 10 with pre-school-age children, are employed. Do these children suffer when mother is away for part of the day? Surprisingly, the first carefully controlled research in this area, begun by Nye and Hoffman in the late 1950s, showed that the harmful effects seem to be related to whether or not mother likes her work. If the mother in their research study was unhappy in her job (usually a lower-class mother working out of necessity rather than choice in a low-level job), she was likely to be more demanding and neglectful of her children than her unemployed peers. If the mother was highly satisfied in her work (usually a middle-class mother who worked by choice in a higher-level position), she sometimes compensated for her feelings of guilt by overindulging her children and by asking them for less help than did nonworking mothers. The children of dissatisfied working mothers were more likely to be hostile and aggressive, while children of satisfied working mothers had somewhat less mature social behavior and lower academic performance than children of homemakers.[31] However, another researcher found that mothers who wanted to work but conscientiously forced themselves to stay at home with their children were often the most dissatisfied of all;[32] these children may pay a considerable price for their mothers' sacrifices.

A number of positive effects of mothers' employment have been found. Hoffman reports that working mothers worried about whether they were spending enough time with their children, but they reported better relationships with them than did housewives who felt less sympathetic and more hostile toward their offspring. Adolescent daughters of working mothers, particularly in the middle class or above, were more active and autonomous, more often identified with and admired their mothers, and had a more egalitarian and varied view of women's roles and abilities. Sons as well as daughters of mothers who were professionally employed tended to be high achievers themselves, suggesting that such mothers serve as role models.[33]

Fathers in egalitarian families with working mothers are more involved in raising the children, often having a good relationship with their daughters and encouraging their independence and achievement while accepting them as females.[34] Fathers in traditional patriarchal families, in contrast, are likely to encourage and enjoy cute, flirtatious, cuddly behavior and a feminine appearance in their daughters, placing more emphasis on the girl's ability to please than to do.[35] Tyler found that these strongly feminine-oriented girls were more "ladylike," better behaved, and better liked in grade school, but that in high school the girls who had been more active, talkative, and spent more time reading became more confident and better adjusted, and held career expectations in addition to their typical "feminine" interests. Similarly, boys who strongly adopted "masculine" values closed their range of interests early.[36]

Studies of college-age women confirm these findings. Rossi found a lack of intellectual development among strongly home- and person-oriented, "feminine" college graduates,[37] and Murphy and Raushenbush found that Sarah Lawrence women from traditional families were less confident, less self-determining, and more subject to family pressures than other students. They had no career motivation, profited less from college, and were less clear about their own roles as women. Although they planned early marriage and a homemaking role, the choice resulted less from a distinctly feminine orientation than from a desire to escape from or comply with family

> Despite the popular image of middle-aged women sadly pining away in the empty nest, most women welcome the freedom from family responsibilities as children leave home.

pressures. Their lack of autonomy and lower sense of competence made them unable to direct their own lives.[38]

The results of these studies appear to be related to the different child-rearing values expressed by career mothers and housewives. The former stress and take pride in developing their children's independence and competence, whereas the latter tend to emphasize the importance of mothers sacrificing their own wishes for their children and to be overconcerned about their childrens' health and safety.[39] Other studies have found that the woman who was a high achiever in college but stays home with her children often seeks vicarious satisfaction by pressuring her children toward achievement. As the children get older, the mother's need for achievement rises but her self-esteem is low. She has feelings of self-sacrifice and depression, is particularly anxious about her competence in general and about her children, is guilty about occasional losses of self-control, and yet is ambivalent about her children's growing independence.[40] Obviously the whole family would be better off if she got out of the house and achieved for herself.

Not all of the findings of our present research on working women, especially on professional women, may apply to the present generation of young people and their children. Most of these studies were done on women who entered motherhood at the height of the "feminine mystique," were taught to feel guilty if they worked by choice, and consequently tried especially hard to be good mothers. As cultural attitudes shift and the number of young women with working mothers grows, both the guilt feelings and the extra maternal effort may disappear. Furthermore, younger couples are sharing the major household and family responsibilities, a development that should reduce the stress on mother and bring father closer to the children. There is some evidence that young fathers are becoming less success oriented, are seeking a better balance of work and family, and tend to encourage rather than to frustrate their wives' careers. However, it remains to be seen whether these changing attitudes will lead to better, more relaxed parenting or only to greater careless-ness in arranging adequate child care and in meeting children's needs.

DOES LIFE BEGIN AT FORTY?

Whether or not mother works, children grow up and leave home. And whether or not a woman marries, middle age will arrive in due time. How do women with different orientations—"feminine" family-oriented, family-plus-work-oriented, or career-oriented— fare when they reach this stage of life?

Despite the popular image of middle-aged women sadly pining away in the empty nest, most women welcome the freedom from family responsibilities as children leave home, and enjoy more time for their own interests and for companionship with their husbands.[41] Marital satisfaction is often higher among couples at this stage of family life than during the child-rearing years—perhaps partly because the most unhappy couples are likely to be divorced by this time.[42] First admissions to mental hospitals, which rise through early family life and peak among the 25- to 34-year-old age group, drop gradually throughout middle age.[43] And the much-touted "crisis" of menopause is easily managed by most women.[44] For many middle-aged women, self-concepts rise as interests, talents, and capabilities laid aside during the years of heavy responsibility reemerge and are put to use in new directions.[45]

More than half the women at this stage of life now use their experience and talents in the labor market, while others return to school to update or develop their credentials and competence. These women gain a new usefulness and status in society and in their own families, as the value of their work is recognized by a paycheck. Their worth is no longer based primarily on female biological functions and physical attributes that diminish with age, but on a new identity earned through productive, paid work.

Some middle-aged women, however, are clearly more satisfied than others; the differences seem to be directly related to the choice they made earlier in life. Mulvey found that middle-aged women of the traditional feminine orientation tended to center their lives on marriage and to be "unproductive"; they felt frustrated, defeated, and constricted by life, and followed others' expectations regardless of personal desires. Women who combined traditional feminine interests with a professional orientation tended to be "productive"—career directed or active in volunteer activities; they were well-adjusted, felt satisfied with their lives, reported a sense of fulfillment, and saw their lives as expanding. The small number of least-feminine, strongly career-oriented women were highly adjusted and "productive."

It is apparent from the high school records of the women in Mulvey's study that the main factor distinguishing "productive" from "unproductive" middle-age was not youthful scholastic achievement or personality ratings, but educational preparation. Many of the dissatisfied women had once dreamed of a nursing or science career but had not obtained the necessary education. At middle age, they were either at home or working in low-level jobs.[46]

Other studies confirm that women who devote themselves to home and family and engage in no activities outside the home are more likely to become dissatisfied and depressed when the children are grown.[47, 48] A fifty-year follow-up of 430 gifted women originally studied by Terman as schoolgirls in the 1920s found that working women without children reported the greatest life satisfaction— especially those who pursued professional careers. Although the women who devoted themselves to homemaking were less satisfied with their lives, they greatly valued their children—so much so, that most would have liked more children than they had.[49]

Work seems to be a central value that most women feel makes for a fuller, happier life. When more than 400 well-placed wives were questioned, four-fifths of the wives of scientists and engineers, two-thirds of the university faculty wives, more than one-half of the wives of middle-level business managers, and even one-fourth of the older senior management wives (median income $59,000) said they would work if they could relive their lives; virtually all of those who had been employed agreed that they would make the same choice again. Women in every group, employed or not, expressed a strong desire for more education, better career preparation, and a worth-while career.[50]

As women age, the life style they have built up through the years determines the possibilities open to them. The personalities developed through the choices and experiences of a lifetime become even more central to their behavior patterns and satisfaction level.[51] The dismal picture of lonely, failing, institutionalized old age applies to only a small fraction of the aging population. The current generation of elderly still includes a large number of poor, uneducated persons in poor health, but with every passing year more of the 65-and-over population are well educated, healthy, relatively well off, and politically active. Neugarten predicts that this growing group of "young–old" will develop a wide range of patterns in work, education, leisure, and housing.[52]

It has been suggested that women may be better able than men to cope with aging, retirement, and widowhood because the repeated discontinuities in their lives make them more flexible and adaptable. Certainly the woman who has kept herself alive and developing is better able to enrich her own and her husband's retirement, to make a life for herself if necessary, to relate to her children and grandchildren, and to live in a continuously changing world.

SUGAR AND SPICE ARE NOT ENOUGH

The implications of all these findings for girls and women are quite clear. The girl who is brought up by a dominant father and a submissive housewife–mother to fit the "sugar and spice and everything nice" image of femininity is likely to be stunted in her development. She tends to be less autonomous, less competent, and more dependent than her less traditional sisters. She is more likely to marry young but is less ready to assume the mature responsibility for household, children, and community that life demands of the contemporary woman. Her socialization fits her very well for Life With Father—but father is seldom present during the week and mother had better be capable of handling things herself. She is apt to put aside her own interests to focus on her children and to make a poor adjustment when the children leave home.

The woman who works throughout adulthood, whether married or single, with or without children, reports higher life satisfaction and better adjustment than women following more traditional patterns. A close second is the woman who stays home during at least some of the child-rearing years, gradually enlarging her interests and activities, often returning to work somewhere along the way. She develops a wide variety of social skills and competencies and is capable of creating a satisfying life for herself and others whether she pursues her own creative interests, engages in community work or politics, or enters paid employment. The wisdom of her choice lies in its satisfaction and meaningfulness to her and to those around her, not in whether or not she is paid. Nonetheless, few women are so secure that they will never need to earn a salary, and it is prudent to be prepared.

WHERE DO WE GO FROM HERE?

If the strains and constraints that modern society imposes on both women and men are to be removed and the pain they cause alleviated, individuals not only must seek alternatives in their own lives, but must demand corrective social and political action. There is much to be done:

1 We need to examine the way in which we socialize the sexes from early childhood and our expectations concerning appropriate adult sex-role behavior—and then change the attitudes and practices that no longer fit our world.

2 The media, educational materials, and so forth should be stopped from portraying men as typically strong, intelligent, insensitive, and often violent knowers and doers, and women as typically stupid, silly, subordinate, and domestic sex objects.

3 Women need to be taught from childhood to articulate their needs, to develop their interests and abilities, to create satisfying environments for themselves, and to take full advantage of their emerging opportunities and freedoms.

4 Girls and women need better guidance to help them recognize the importance of serious vocational preparation, whether or not they plan to spend some years at home with children.

5 Long-term social and political pressure is needed to achieve true equality of educational and economic opportunities for women—an accomplishment that would alleviate the serious economic deprivation of many women, especially older women and mothers of single-parent families.

6 The remaining legal inequities that affect women's employment and penalize the housewife must be removed.

7 Every woman should take a long view of her life, preparing for both predictable and extraordinary changes in her role over her life span.

8 Women need to plan for their own financial security in widowhood, divorce, or old age. Too often they are unaware of inheritance laws, hold no funds or property in their own names, or make disadvantageous divorce settlements.

9 Couples should reconsider whether their particular marital roles are the best for them, or whether responsibilities might be more equitably and satisfyingly allocated. (Perhaps both husband and wife are overworked, and a simpler lifestyle or living closer to employment would relieve some of the burden.)

10 Parents, especially young mothers and single parents, need

more help with the responsiblity for children. Solutions to this problem can be both public and private, including education for parenthood, baby-sitting exchange, public day care, and cooperative living arrangements (especially helpful for single-parent families).

11 Women who have internalized traditional sex-role expectations should be helped to realize that it is not particularly virtuous to be "content" with inequitable situations, and encouraged to recognize and exercise their options.

Women as well as men are individuals—unique members of the vast and varied human species. In a society that is as complex and filled with possibilities for diverse expressions of sexuality as ours, no one needs to conform to a single stereotype. Work needs doing and children need nurturing. Both men and women need caring human relationships, a sense of usefulness and worth, and possibilities for renewal and growth. The opportunities and challenges that are becoming available to women in this century are unprecedented in human history. As more women develop their full, mature, human, and sexual potential, as men release themselves from the traditional "male" stereotype, and as both men and women are able to express their individuality more freely, life in our society should become happier, more productive, and more fulfilling for everyone.

NOTES

1   Ann P. Parelius, "Emerging Sex-role Attitudes, Expectations, and Strains Among College Women," *Journal of Marriage and the Family* 37 (1975): 146–153.

2   Jessie Bernard, *The Future of Marriage* (New York: World Publishing, 1972), ch. 4.

3   Ibid., ch. 3.

4   Helena Z. Lopata, *Widowhood in an American City* (Cambridge, Mass.: Schenkman, 1973), pp. 42–43.

5   Lopata, *Occupation: Housewife* (New York: Oxford University Press, 1971), p. 92.

6   Ibid., pp. 200–201.

7   Alice Rossi, "The Roots of Ambivalence in American Women" (Paper delivered to the Continuing Education for Women Section of the Adult Education Association of the U.S.A., Chicago, November 15, 1966), pp. 18–19.

8   E. E. LeMasters, "Parenthood as Crisis," in *Sourcebook in Marriage and the Family*, 2nd ed., ed. M. S. Sussman (Boston: Houghton Mifflin, 1963), pp. 194–198.

9 Lopata, *Occupation: Housewife*, ch. 4.

10 Mike McGrady, "Let 'em Eat Leftovers," *Newsweek*, 2 February 1976, p. 13.

11 Lopata, *Occupation: Housewife*, p. 202.

12 Ibid., p. 152.

13 Mirra Komarovsky, *Blue-collar Marriage* (New York: Random House, 1962), ch. 2.

14 Lopata, *Occupation: Housewife*, ch. 4.

15 Lee Rainwater, Richard P. Coleman, and Gerald Handel, *Workingman's Wife* (New York: Oceania, 1959), ch. 5.

16 Bernard, *The Future of Marriage*, ch. 3.

17 Bernard, *The Future of Motherhood* (New York: Dial Press, 1974), pp. 37, 89.

18 Komarovsky, *Blue-collar Marriage*, p. 80.

19 Georgie Anne Geyer, "U. S. Child Care Still in Make-believe World," *Chicago Daily News*, 14 January 1976, p. 18.

20 "Women Who Work Outside the Home," *Women's Lobby Quarterly*, October 1975, p. 2.

21 Robert O. Blood and Donald M. Wolfe, *Husbands and Wives* (New York: Free Press, 1960), ch. 2.

22 Rossi, "Roots of Ambivalence," pp. 18–19.

23 "Documenting the Expanding Roles for Women," *New York Times*, 25 January 1976, IV, 8:2.

24 Attitudes of First-time Students," *Chronicle of Higher Education*, 12 January 1976, p. 3.

25 Rebecca B. Bryson, Jeff B. Bryson, Mark H. Licht, and Barbara G. Licht, "The Professional Pair: Husband and Wife Psychologists," *American Psychologist* 31 (1976): 10–16.

26 Carol LeFevre, "The Mature Woman as Graduate Student: A Study of Changing Self-conceptions" (doctoral diss., University of Chicago, 1971), ch. 7.

27 Rhona Rapoport and Robert N. Rapoport, *Dual-Career Families* (England: Penguin, 1971), pp. 280–281.

28 LeFevre, "The Mature Woman," ch. 7; Blood, "The Husband–Wife Relationship," in *The Employed Mother in America*, eds. F. Ivan Nye and Lois W. Hoffman (Chicago: Rand McNally, 1963), pp. 285–290.

29 McGrady, "Let 'em Eat Leftovers," p. 13.

30 "Women Who Work," p. 2.

31 Lois Wladis Hoffman, "Mother's Enjoyment of Work and Effects on the Child," in *Employed Mother*, pp. 95–105.

32 Catherine Arnott, "Exchange Theory and the Role Choice of Married Women" (master's thesis, University of Southern California, 1969), pp. 59–60.

33 Hoffman, "The Professional Woman as Mother," in *Women and Success: The Anatomy of Achievement*, ed. Ruth B. Kundsin (New York: William Morrow, 1974), pp. 222–228.

34 *Ibid.*

35 Eleanor Emmons Maccoby and Carol Nagy Jacklin, *The Psychology of Sex Differences* (Stanford, CA: Stanford University Press, 1974), ch. 9.

36 Leona E. Tyler, "The Antecedents of Two Varieties of Vocational Interests," *Genetic Psychology Monographs* 70 (1964): 177–227.

37 Rossi, "Roots of Ambivalence," pp. 13–15.

38 Lois B. Murphy and Esther Raushenbush, *Achievement in the College Years* (New York: Harper, 1960).

39 Hoffman, "Professional Woman," p. 225.

40 *Ibid.*

41 Irwin Deutscher, "The Quality of Postparental Life," in *Middle Age,* pp. 263–268.

42 Boyd C. Rollins and Kenneth L. Cannon, "Marital Satisfaction Over the Family Life Cycle: A Reevaluation," *Journal of Marriage and the Family* 36 (1974): 271–282.

43 Neugarten and Nancy Datan, "The Middle Years," in *American Handbook of Psychiatry* (Vol. I, 2nd ed.), ed. Silvano Arieti (New York: Basic Books, 1974), p. 604.

44 Neugarten, Vivian Wood, Ruth J. Kraines, and Barbara Loomis, "Women's Attitudes Toward the Menopause," in *Middle Age,* pp. 195–200.

45 Neugarten, "The Awareness of Middle Age," in *Middle Age,* pp. 93–98.

46 Mary C. Mulvey, "Psychological and Sociological Factors in Prediction of Career Pattérns of Women," *Genetic Psychology Monographs* 68 (1963): 309–386.

47 Arnott, "Exchange Theory," pp. 57, 61–63.

48 Pauline Bart, "Depression in Middle-aged Women," in *Women in Sexist Society,* eds. Vivian Gornick and Barbara K. Moran (New York: Basic Books, 1971), pp. 163–186.

49 "Score One for Careers Over Homemaking," *Sun–Times,* 9 November 1975, p. 45.

50 Miriam K. Ringo, "The Well-placed Wife: What She Thinks; What She Wants" mimeographed (Chicago: John Paisios & Associates, Center for Urban Affairs, Northwestern University, May 1970), pp. 1–35.

51 Neugarten, Robert J. Havighurst, and Sheldon S. Tobin, "Personality and Patterns of Aging," in *Middle Age,* pp. 173–177.

52 Neugarten, "The Future and the Young–Old," Gerontologist 15 supplement (1975): 4–9.

Androgyny vs. the Tight Little Lives of Fluffy Women and Chesty Men

Sandra Lipsitz Bem

In American society, men are supposed to be masculine, women are supposed to be feminine, and neither sex is supposed to much like the other. If men are independent, tough and assertive, women should be dependent, sweet and retiring. A womanly woman may be tender and nurturant, but no manly man may be so.

For years we have taken these polar opposites as evidence of psychological health. Even our psychological tests of masculinity and femininity reflect this bias: a person scores as *either* masculine *or* feminine, but the tests do not allow a person to say that he or she is both.

I have come to believe that we need a new standard of psychological health for the sexes, one that removes the burden of stereotype and allows people to feel free to express the best traits of men and women. As many feminists have argued, freeing people from rigid sex roles and allowing them to be *androgynous* (from "andro," male, and "gyne," female), should make them more flexible in meeting new situations, and less restricted in what they can do and how they can express themselves.

In fact, there is already considerable evidence that traditional sex typing is unhealthy. For example, high femininity in females consistently correlates with high anxiety, low self-esteem, and low self-acceptance. And although high masculinity in males has been related to better psychological adjustment during adolescence, it is often accompanied during adulthood by high anxiety, high neuroticism, and low self-acceptance. Further, greater intellectual development has quite consistently correlated with cross-sex typing (masculinity in girls, femininity in boys). Boys who are strongly masculine and girls who are strongly feminine tend to have lower overall intelligence, lower spatial ability, and show lower creativity.

In addition, it seems to me that traditional sex typing necessarily restricts behavior. Because people learn, during their formative years, to suppress any behavior that might be considered undesirable or

> **Only 33 percent of the feminine women were very independent, compared to 70 percent of the masculine and androgynous students.**

inappropriate for their sex, men are afraid to do "women's work," and women are afraid to enter "man's world." Men are reluctant to be gentle, and women to be assertive. In contrast, androgynous people are not limited by labels. They are able to do whatever they want, both in their behavior and their feelings.

A MEASURE OF ANDROGYNY

I decided to study this question, to see whether sex-typed people really were more restricted and androgynous people more adaptable. Because I needed a way to measure how masculine, feminine, or androgynous a person was, I developed the Bem Sex Role Inventory (BSRI), which consists of a list of 60 personality characteristics: 20 traditionally masculine (ambitious, self-reliant, independent, assertive), 20 traditionally feminine (affectionate, gentle, understanding, sensitive to the needs of others); and 20 neutral (truthful, friendly, likable). I gave a list of 400 such traits to a group of undergraduates, who rated the desirability of each characteristic either "for a man" or "for a woman." I drew the final list for the BSRI from those characteristics that both males and females rated as being significantly more desirable for one sex than for the other.

The masculine, feminine and neutral characteristics appear in random order on the test, and a person indicates on a scale of one ("never or almost never true") to seven ("always or almost always true") how accurate each word is as a self-description. The difference between the total points assigned to masculine and feminine adjectives indicates the degree of a person's sex typing. If masculinity and femininity scores are approximately equal, the individual has an androgynous sex role.

My colleagues and I have given the BSRI to more than 1,500 undergraduates at Stanford University. Semester after Semester, we find that about 50 percent of the students adhere to "appropriate" sex roles, about 15 percent are cross-sex typed, and about 35 percent are androgynous.

With the BSRI in hand, we were in a position to find out whether sex-typed people really were restricted and androgynous people really more adaptable. Our strategy was to measure a number of behaviors that were stereotypically either masculine or feminine. We selected these particular actions to represent the very best of what masculinity and femininity have come to stand for, and we felt that any healthy adult should be capable of them. We predicted that sex-typed people would do well only when the behavior was traditionally considered appropriate for his or her sex, whereas those who were androgynous would do well regardless of the sex-role stereotype attached to the particular action.

The masculine behaviors that we selected were independence and assertiveness. The study of independence brought students to the lab for what they thought was an experiment on humor. In fact,

167

they were there to test conformity versus independence of judgment. Karen Rook and Robyn Stickney placed each person in a booth equipped with microphones and earphones, and showed him or her a series of cartoons that had been rated earlier for humorous quality. As a new cartoon appeared on the screen, the students heard the experimenter call on each person in turn for his or her rating. Although they believed that they were hearing each other's voices, they were in fact listening to a preprogrammed tape. To provoke the students into conformity, the tape included 36 trials during which the taped voices answered the experimenter falsely, agreeing that a particular cartoon was funny when it wasn't, or vice versa.

THE LIMITATIONS OF FEMININITY

We predicted that feminine women would be less independent than anyone else, and we were right. They were far more likely to conform to the incorrect taped judgments than masculine men or androgynous students of either sex. Only 33 percent of the feminine women were very independent (more independent than the average of all students), compared to 70 percent of the masculine and androgynous students.

Jeffrey Wildfogel carried out a similar study to measure assertiveness. He called students on the telephone with an unreasonable request: when would they be willing to spend over two hours, without pay, to fill out a questionnaire about their reactions to various insurance policies for students? At no time did he actually ask *whether* the people he called would be willing to participate. He simply assumed that they would, and asked them to indicate when they would be available.

In this situation, agreeing would cost a person time, effort and inconvenience, but refusing required the student to assert his or her preferences over those of the caller. The preliminary results confirmed our expectation that feminine women would find it harder to be assertive than anyone else. When Wildfogel asked the students later how difficult it was to turn the caller down, 67 percent of the feminine women said that they found it very difficult, compared to only 28 percent of the masculine men and androgynous students.

The feminine behaviors that we selected all measured the extent to which a person was willing to be responsible for or helpful toward another living creature. We expected that this time the masculine men would be at a disadvantage.

In the first study, Jenny Jacobs measured how responsive people were toward a six-week-old kitten. When students came to the lab, Jacobs explained that she wanted to see how different activities would affect their moods. Actually, we wanted only to determine their reaction to the kitten. For one of the activities, therefore, we put a kitten into the room and asked the student to respond to it in any way he or she wished. We simply recorded how often the student touched or petted the kitten. Later on in the experiment, we gave each person the opportunity to do anything in the lab room that he or she wanted: play with the kitten, read magazines, work puzzles, play with a three-dimensional tilting maze, or whatever. This time we measured how much the students played with the kitten when they didn't have to.

As expected, the masculine men were less playful than anyone else. Only nine percent of them showed a high level of playfulness with the kitten, compared to 52 percent of all the other students. But there was an unexpected result: the androgynous women played with the kitten more often than feminine women, who are presumably so fond of small, cuddly things, 64 percent to 36 percent.

MACHO MALES AND CUDDLY BABIES

We conducted two further tests—this time with human beings instead of kittens. Carol Watson and Bart Astor measured how responsive people would be toward a six-month-old baby. The student thought the study was about babies' reactions to strangers, but actually we observed the students' reactions to the baby. We left each person alone with the infant for 10 minutes while the experimenter and one of the baby's parents watched from a one-way mirror. We recorded what each person did, such as how often he or she talked to the baby, smiled at it, or picked it up. Once again, the masculine men were the least likely to play much with the baby. Only 21 percent of them were highly responsive, compared to half of all the other students. And this time the feminine women did respond warmly, but no more than the androgynous women.

The last experiment, conducted by Wendy Martyna and Dorothy Ginsberg, explored people's reactions to a person with emotional problems. The students came to the lab in pairs for what they thought was a study of acquaintance, and they drew lots so that one would be a "talker" and the other a "listener." In fact, the talker was our confederate who delivered a memorized script of personal problems. The listener was allowed to ask questions or to make comments, but never to shift the focus of the conversation away from the talker. We recorded the listener's reactions, such as how often he or she nodded and made sympathetic comments, and later we asked each listener how concerned he or she felt about the talker's problems.

Again, the masculine men were the least responsive; only 14 percent of them were above average in reacting sympathetically or in showing concern, compared to 60 percent of the other students. And the feminine women reacted most strongly to the talker, showing more concern than even the androgynous women.

The pattern of results for these five experiments suggests that rigid sex roles can seriously restrict behavior. This is especially the case for men. The masculine men did masculine things very well, but they did not do feminine things. They were independent and assertive when they needed to be, but they weren't responsive to the kitten, or the baby, or to a person in need. In other words, they lacked the ability to express warmth, playfulness, and concern, important human—if traditionally feminine—traits.

Similarly, the feminine women were restricted in their ability to express masculine characteristics. They did feminine things—played with the baby, responded with concern and support for the troubled talker—but they weren't independent in judgment or assertive of their own preferences. And for some reason, they didn't respond to the kitten; perhaps feminine women also are afraid of animals.

In contrast, the androgynous men and women did just about everything. They could be independent and assertive when they needed to be, and warm and responsive in appropriate situations. It didn't matter, in other words, whether a behavior was stereotypically masculine or feminine; they did equally well on both.

THE RIGID BARS OF SEX ROLES

In order to find out whether sex-typed people actually avoid opposite-sex behavior, Ellen Lenney and I designed a study in which people could choose an action to perform for pay. We said that we were going to photograph them for a later study, and that we didn't care at all how well they did each activity. In fact, we gave them only one minute for each performance, long enough for a convincing photo, but not long enough for them to complete the task.

Then we gave the students 30 pairs of activities, and asked them to select one from each pair to act out for pay. Some of these pairs pitted masculine activities against feminine ones (oiling a hinge versus preparing a baby bottle); some pitted feminine against neutral (winding yarn into a ball versus sorting newspapers by geographical area); and some pitted masculine against neutral (nailing boards together versus peeling an orange).

We predicted that masculine men and feminine women would consistently avoid the activity that was inappropriate for their sex, *even though it always paid more.* We were right. Such individuals were actually ready to lose money to avoid acting in trivial ways that are characteristic of the opposite sex. That was particularly true when the person running the experiment was a member of the opposite sex. In that case, fully 71 percent of the sex-typed students chose highly stereotyped activities compared to only 42 percent of the androgynous students.

We went one step further, because we wondered how sex-typed people would feel about themselves if they *had* to carry out an opposite-sex activity. We asked all the students to perform three masculine, three feminine, and three neutral activities while we photographed them, and then they indicated on a series of scales how each activity made them feel about themselves. Masculine men and feminine women felt much worse than androgynous people about doing a cross-sex task. Traditional men felt less masculine if they had to, say, prepare a baby bottle, and traditional women felt less feminine if they had to nail boards together. When the experimenter was a member of the opposite sex, sex-typed students were especially upset about acting out of role. They felt less attractive and likeable, more nervous and peculiar, less masculine or feminine, and didn't particularly enjoy the experience.

ANDROGYNY IS DESTINY

This research persuades me that traditional concepts of masculinity and femininity do restrict a person's behavior in important ways. In a modern complex society like ours, an adult has to be assertive, independent and self-reliant, but traditional femininity makes many women unable to behave in these ways. On the other hand, an adult must also be able to relate to other people, to be sensitive to their needs and concerned about their welfare, as well as to be able to depend on them for emotional support. But traditional masculinity keeps men from responding in such supposedly feminine ways.

Androgyny, in contrast, allows an individual to be both independent and tender, assertive and yielding, masculine and feminine. Thus androgyny greatly expands the range of behavior open to everyone, permitting people to cope more effectively with diverse situations. As such, I hope that androgyny will some day come to define a new and more human standards of psychological health.

North American Marriage: 1990

Leo Davids

As a preamble for this attempt to predict the options and regulations defining marriage and family life in North America a generation from
now, let us consider some of the powerful long-term trends in this area
which can be discerned either at work already, or coming very soon.
These provide the casual principles that will be extrapolated here
to provide a scientific indication of what the mating and parenthood
situation is going to look like in another two decades. The remainder of
the paper is essentially a working-out of this prediction exercise so
that an account of the new situation is built up, which is the best way we
have to predict the nature of marriage in 1990.

"PARENTHOOD IS FUN" MYTH WILL DIE

1   The foundation of almost everything else that is occurring in the
sphere of marriage and family life today is a process which will go right

Reprinted from *The Futurist: A Journal of Forecasts, Trends and Ideas About the Future,* October
1971. Published by World Future Society, An Association for the Study of Alternative Futures, 4916 St.
Elmo Avenue, Washington, D.C. 20014, 301-656-8274.

ahead in the next decade or two, and will continue to have a vast effect on people's thinking and their behavior. This process is what Max Weber called the *entzäuberung*, the "demystification" or "disenchantment" of human life, which is a hallmark of the modern orientation. Young people, especially, are continually becoming more sophisticated—due to television, modern education, peergroup frankness about all spheres of life, etc.—and they are no longer accepting the myths, the conventional folklore, upon which ordinary social in-

> Young people are gradually rejecting the myth of "parenthood is fun," realizing that parenthood is a very serious business and one which ought to be undertaken only when people are ready to plunge in and do a good job.

interaction has been based during the past few decades. Thus, for instance, young people are gradually rejecting the myth of "parenthood is fun," realizing that parenthood is a very serious business and one which ought to be undertaken only when people are ready to plunge in and do a good job.

Another grand complex of myths that is gradually being rejected is that of romantic love, under which it is perfectly acceptable to meet a person, form a sudden emotional attachment to that person without any logic or contemplation, and to marry that person on no other basis than the existence of this cathexis. Similarly, the whole institution of "shot-gun weddings," in which an unwanted, unintended pregnancy (usually occurring with a lower class girl) leads to what is called "necessary" marriage, is going to become a quaint piece of history which will be considered with the same glee that modern readers feel when they read about "bundling" in Colonial America. With young men and women who are all fully-informed about reproduction and what can be done to prevent it, such things will occur very rarely; romantic mate-selection, likewise, is going to continue only among the impoverished and marginally-educated segment of society.

Insofar as family life remains almost the only area of modern behavior that has not yet become rational and calculated but is approached with unexamined, time-honored myths, we can expect that this area is "ripe" for fundamental change. When serious, critical examination of all this really gets moving, very great changes will come about in quite a short time.

PROCREATION CAN BE SUBJECT TO COMMUNAL CONTROL

2   The second independent variable leading to the developments that we are discussing is the total control of human fertility which advances in medical technique have made possible. There is no need here to discuss the pill, intra-uterine device (IUD), and the many other ways that are in use already to separate sex from reproduction, and therefore to free relations between men and women from the fear or risk of begetting children who would be a by-product, an unintended side-effect of fulfilling quite other needs. This control of human fertility means that what procreation does occur in the future is going to be by choice, not by accident. Both illegitimacy and venereal disease will be almost extinct, too, in 20 years. It also means that reproduction and child rearing can henceforth be subjected to communal control, will be potentially regulable by society at large. Without contraception, all the rest of these trends and changes would not be occurring at all.

HUSBAND–WIFE EQUALIZATION IS "INEVITABLE"

3   Women's Liberation, I believe, is not a fad or a current mass hysteria but is here to stay. Once the schools had instituted coeducation, male dominance was doomed. Let us rephrase that term for present purposes, calling it Husband–Wife Equalization, as a general name for certain tendencies that have been evident for many years and are continuing today. We all know that marriage has shifted, to bor-

row a phrase, from institution to companionship. Indeed, through the demystification–sophistication of young women, their employment in full-status work, and because of the control over reproduction that has now become a reality, the equalization (in regard to decision-making) of wives with their husbands has become inevitable. The implications of this are already being voiced, to some extent, in the platforms and proposals of women's rights organizations, and some points will be touched upon herein.

It must be remembered that there will remain, in the foreseeable future, a traditionalist minority even in the most advanced and change-prone societies. This segment will expend much effort to maintain patterns of marriage and family living that they feel are right, and which are consistent with the patterns they experienced when they were children. This traditionalist minority will certainly not be gone, or vanished to insignificant numbers, in the short span of one generation; therefore, any predictions we make must take into account not only what the "new wave" pattern is going to be, but also the fact that there will be a considerable number of people who elect to maintain the familiar value system that they were socialized with, and to which they are deeply committed.

LAW WILL ACCEPT ABORTION AND NEW FORMS OF MARRIAGE

4   Another trend which is already at work and which, we may assume, is going to accelerate in the future is that legislatures no longer attempt to shape or create family behavior by statute, but are, and increasingly will be, prepared to adapt the law to actual practice, so that it accepts the general viewpoint that public opinion has consensus on. I think that ever since Prohibition, legislators have been forced to agree that sooner or later legal reform must narrow the gap between law on the books and what is really happening in society. It is likely that this reforming and correlation is going to be speeded up in the next few decades, so that the extent to which there is an uncomfortable and problematic contradiction between the

law in force and what people are really doing will be virtually eliminated. Thus, all of the ongoing changes with regard to contraception, abortion, new types of marriage contract, etc., will—it is here assumed—be accepted and in a sense ratified by the Law, as the old-style moralists who can still be found in our agencies of social control cease to fight a rear-guard action against the new norms that are, whether they like them or not, emerging. All modes of birth control will become medical problems, free of any statutory limitation.

5 An important consequence of widespread social-science knowledge among young people today, which is coupled with a greater use of principles drawn from sociology and anthropology in the process of law reform, will be the recognition that continuity or consistency for each person or married couple is necessary, in regard to the larger questions at least, for a particular marriage system to work well in the long run. If the agreements entered into, whatever their content, involve major inconsistency, if people seem to be changing the fundamental norms between them in midstream or giving much more than they receive, then obviously the community has unwisely allowed these people to enter a situation which must lead to disorganization and conflict sooner or later. This realization from our functionalist understanding of how marriage—or any continuing relationship— operates, will lead to acceptance of the clear necessity for such predictability and fairness in every particular case.

So much for the preamble. What are the consequences? Two major principles underlying our model of marriage in 1990 emerge from the forces and trends listed above. They are: (a) the freedom to personally and explicitly contract the type of marriage one wishes; and (b) formal public or communal control over parenthood.

What is meant by the word "marriage," here? To include the newer forms, we require a looser, broader definition than would suffice in the 1950s. Marriage should therefore be understood to refer to a publicly-registered, lasting commitment to a particular person, which generally includes certain sexual or other rights and obligations between these people (that would not be recognized by their community without such married status).

Free choice of the sort of marriage one wishes does not mean that a man and woman (or two men or two women?) will write their own original contract incorporating any combination of rules and arrangements that they like. The reason that such freedom would be beyond that envisioned in our thinking, as argued above, is that they would be able to invent a contract that has severe internal inconsistencies or flights of self-delusion, and which therefore sets up strains for their relationship from the outset. The sophistication which anthropological functionalism has brought to us will lead society to channel the choice of marriage into a selection from among a number of recognized types, each of which has been carefully thought through so that it is tenable in the long run. Thus, people will select from among various ways of being married, each of which makes sense by itself and will enable them to function on a long-run basis once they have had this choice. Neither monogamy nor indefinite permanence is important in this respect, so they will not be required. However, the agreed-upon choice will be explicit and recorded so there's no question of deception or misunderstanding, as well as to provide statistical information, and official registration of this choice is an element of marriage which will remain a matter of public concern.

PEOPLE UNFIT TO BE PARENTS
WILL BE SCREENED OUT

The right of society to control parenthood is something that can be predicted from a number of things we already know. For one thing, the rising incidence of battered and neglected children, and our almost total inability to really cope with the battered child's problem except after the fact, will certainly lead legislators to planning how those people who can be discovered, in advance, to be unfit for parenthood may be screened out and prevented from begetting offspring who will be the wretched target of their parents' emotional inadequacies. Furthermore, increasing awareness of the early-childhood roots of serious crime and delinquency will also lead to an attempt to prevent major deviance by seeing to it that early socialization occurs under favorable circumstances. It does not appear that there will be many other really effective ways in which rising crime rates could eventually be reversed. This, however, will again mean that those who raise children will have to be evaluated for this purpose in some way, so that only those parents who are likely to do a respectable job of early socialization will be licensed to release new members of society into the open community. If such testing and selection is not done, we have no way to protect ourselves from large numbers of young people who have been raised in a way that almost inevitably will have them providing the murderers, rapists and robbers of the next generation. Since we now begin to have the technology and the knowledge to prevent this, we may confidently expect that parent-licensing is going to come into force soon.

One other trend, perhaps phrased from the negative side, must also be mentioned here as we try to describe the norms that will probably circumscribe marriage in another generation. This trend is the decline of informal, personal social control over married couples which was formerly exercised by kinsmen and neighbours. It would not make sense to anticipate massive changes in the law and explicit contractual entry into marriage as the normal way to shape married life, if mate selection and the interactions between husband and wife were still under the regulation of custom, vigilantly enforced by aunts, grandfathers or brothers-in-law. It is precisely because the vast mobility of modern living has led, along with other factors, to the isolation of the nuclear family—which is the source of so many problems in the family sphere today—that this new kind of regulation will be called into force and accepted as necessary and proper. The recognition that marriage has left the sphere of *Gemeinschaft* will help to bring about a consensus that the regulation of this area of life will have to be handled like any other kind of socially-important interpersonal behavior in today's *Gesellschaft* civilization.

COURTSHIP MAY BE "DUTCH TREAT"

What will courtship be like in about twenty years? We can assume that courtship will, as it does currently, serve as a testing ground for the kind of marriage that people have in their minds, perhaps even dimly or unconsciously. Thus, insofar as particular young men or women may have begun to feel that the type of marriage they would like is Type A rather than Type B, their courtship would be of the sort that normally leads to Type A, and in a sense tests their readiness to build their relationship along those lines. Only the traditionalist couples will keep up such classic patriarchal customs as the male holding doors, assisting with a coat, or paying for both meals when a couple dines out together. The egalitarians would go "Dutch treat," i.e., each paying for himself, during this spouse research period. Thus, courtship will be of several kinds corresponding to the kinds of marriage that we are about to describe, with the conventional acts and phases in the courtship signalling the present intention of the parties involved to head toward that kind of marriage. Thus, pre-marriage and marriage will exhibit a psycho–social continuity, the early marriage centering on the basic interpersonal stance that is already represented in courtship.

Of course, courtship will serve this testing and assessing function after people have been approximately matched through computer mate-finding methods. Random dating and hopeless courtships will have been largely prevented through the provision of basic categoric information which people can use to screen possible spouses, such as total years of schooling completed, aptitude and IQ scores, major subjects (which are related to intellectual interests in a very direct way), religiosity, leisure and recreation preferences, and similar things.

For remarriage suitors, data on wealth or credit and occupation would also be used, along with some indication of attitudes concerning home life and procreation. Since homogamy (similarity between spouses) is recognized as an important indicator of marital success, such information will be systematically gathered and made available to cut down on the wasteful chance element in mate selection. It is only when people are continuing their search for a spouse within the appropriate "pool," defined in terms of those who are at the right point with regard to these variables, that courtship as a series of informal but direct experiments in relationship-building will come into play.

CELIBACY WILL BE LEGITIMIZED

Explicit choice of the kind of marriage one enters into is, of course, an effect not only of the emancipation of women but of men as well. What will some of the major options be? With the insurance functions that were formerly secured by having children (who would provide during one's old age) being completely taken over by the government (assisted by unions, pension funds and the like), there will be little reason to warn those who choose childlessness against this course. With celibacy no bar to sexual satisfaction, society will accept the idea that some segments of the population can obtain whatever intimate satisfactions they require in a series of casual, short-term "affairs" (as we call them today), and will never enter any publicly-registered marriage. With celibacy or spinsterhood fully legitimized, and with no fear of destitution when one has retired from the labor force, there will undoubtedly be a sizeable number of people who decide not to enter into a marriage of any sort on any terms.

TRIAL MARRIAGE FOR THREE OR FIVE YEARS

Another not-unfamiliar option in this regard will be the renewable trial marriage, in which people explicitly contract for a childless union which is to be comprehensively evaluated after three years or five years, at which point either a completely new decision can be reached or the same arrangement can be renewed for another term of three or five years. This would not be, then, a question of divorce; it is simply a matter of a definite arrangement having expired. The contract having been for a limited term, both parties are perfectly free to decide not to renew it when that term is over. This would be a normal, perhaps minor, part of one's "marital career."

A third option, which introduces very few complications, is the permanent childless marriage; the arrangement between the two adults is of indefinite duration, but they have agreed in advance that there will be no offspring, and of course, there is no question but that medical technology will make it possible for them to live up to that part of the arrangement. Some will choose sterilization, others will use contraceptive methods which can be abandoned if one changes his mind and is authorized to procreate.

Compound marriages will also be allowed, whether they be polygamous, polyandrous or group marriages. However, these communes will not be free of the same obligations that any marriage entails, such as formally registering the terms of the agreement among the members; any significant change in the arrangements among members of such a familial commune will have to be recorded in the appropriate public place in the same way as marriages and divorces which involve only one husband and one wife. There will be great freedom with regard to the number of people in the commune, but internal consistency concerning the give-and-take among the members, their privileges and obligations, will be required. The functional, pragmatic ethics emerging in today's youth culture will be strictly adhered to, some years hence, not as moral absolutes, not because people have come to the belief that these represent the true right and wrong, but in order to prevent serious conflict.

LESS THAN THIRD OF MARRIAGES WILL PRODUCE CHILDREN

With the majority of young people in society choosing one of the foregoing patterns, the number of marriages in which children are expected will be relatively small; perhaps 25% to 30% of the population will be so serious about having children that they will be prepared to undergo the rigorous training and careful evaluation that will be necessary for them to obtain the requisite licenses. The marriages intended to produce children will usually be classic familistic marriages, in which the general pattern of interaction between husband and wife, as well as the relationship between parent and child, may be fairly similar to the contemporary upper middle-class marriage that we know in 1970. However, three-generation households will probably increase. I see no reason to believe that all of child rearing will be done in a collective way, as in an Israeli kibbutz or in the communes which have been set up in some Communist countries; infant care may gravitate in the direction of day nurseries, however, while school children will live at home, as now.

WOULD-BE PARENTS WILL HAVE TO PROVE THEIR SUITABILITY

The familial pattern, then, explicitly chosen by some men and women to perpetuate the classic familistic marriage, will be intended to provide a home atmosphere approximately similar to that which can be found in those middle class families of today's society that have the best socio-emotional climate. The community will be assured that this home atmosphere is, in fact, most probable, since it has been prepared for, rather than left to an accident of kind fate and to happenstance talents that people bring to parenthood nowadays. All those who desire to become parents, and therefore to exercise a public responsibility in an extremely important and sensitive area of personal functioning, will have to prove that they are indeed the right people to serve as society's agents of socialization. Just as those who wish to adopt a child, nowadays, are subjected to intensive interviewing which aims at discovering the healthiness of the relationship between husband and wife and of the motivation for parenthood, the suitability that the man or woman displays for coping with the stresses of parenthood, as well as the physical and material conditions that the adopted child will be enjoying, the evaluation of mother and father applicants in future will be done by a team of professionals who have to reach the judgement that this particular individual or couple have the background to become professionals themselves: that is, recognized and certified parents.

PARENT-TRAINING WILL BE INTENSE

The course of study for parenthood will include such subjects as: human reproduction and gestation; infant care; developmental physiology and psychology; theories of socialization; and educational psychology. Starting with a foundation of systematic but abstract scientific knowledge, the practical and applied courses in hygienic, nutritional, emotional and perceptual-aesthetic care of children will follow, in the same way as training for medicine and other professions. In addition to the subject matter referred to above, prospective parents will be required to achieve some clarity concerning values and philosophy of life, in which they will be guided by humanistic scholars, and will also be required to attain a clear understanding of the mass media, their impact on children, and how to manage mass

> Suitable examinations will be devised, and only those who achieve adequate grades in these areas will be given a parenthood license.

media consumption as an important part of socialization in the modern urban environment. One side effect of such parent training may be a sharp drop in the power of the peer group, as parents do more and with greater self-confidence.

Suitable examinations will be devised, and only those who achieve adequate grades in these areas will be given a parenthood license. Some young men and women are likely to take the parenthood curriculum "just in case"; that is, although they have not yet thought through the type of marriage that they desire or the kind of spouse they are looking for, they may continue their education by entering parenthood studies and obtaining the diploma, should it turn out that they elect a classic, child-rearing marriage later on. Possibly, fathers will be prohibited from full-time employment outside the home while they have pre-school children, or if their children have extra needs shown by poor conduct or other symptoms of psychic distress.

One of the more striking areas of change, which can serve as an indicator of how different things will be then from what they are now, is age. Age of marriage now is in the early 20's, and child bearing typically occurs when women are in their middle twenties. Also, husbands today are usually about three to four years older than their wives. In another generation, the age of child bearing will probably be considerably advanced, as people who have decided upon parenthood will either be enjoying themselves during an extended childless period before they undertake the burdens and responsibilities of child rearing, or completing the course of study for certification to undertake parenthood. It is probable that women will bear children when they are in their middle and late thirties, so that they will have enjoyed a decade or a decade and a half of companionate marriage in which there was full opportunity to travel, to read, or just to relax before they have to spend 24 hours a day caring for a small child. As to the age difference between husbands and wives, which is essentially based on the patriarchal tradition that the man is the "senior" in the home, it will probably disappear in the case of all forms of marriage other than the classic familistic one; there, where people have explicitly decided that the kind of marriage they want is the same as their parents had back in the medievaloid 1970s, or the ancient 1960s, the husband will continue to be a few years older than his wife.

This picture of the marriage situation in 1990 leaves open various questions and problems, which should be touched upon briefly in conclusion. One of the difficulties in this scenario is the question of what authority will make the necessary decisions: What sorts of committees will be in charge of devising the various internally-consistent kinds of marriage, working out the parent education courses and certifying people for parenthood? There are, after all, political implications to controlling marriage and parenthood in this way, and the general public will have to be satisfied that those who exercise authority in this area are, in fact, competent as well as impartial.

Another problem is that of securing complete and valid information: (a) for those who are preparing to locate suitable mates through computer matching, or who are preparing to make a commitment in some specific form of marriage; and (b) concerning those who apply for the parenthood course and later for the license to practice parenthood. Unless we can be sure that the inputs used for making such judgements contain information which is adequate in quantity and true as well, these new systems will not be able to function without a great deal of deviance, and might easily engender problems which are worse than those which we confront today.

WILL CHILDLESSNESS LEAD TO LESS LONG-RANGE INVESTMENT?

A third issue is that of parenthood having tied people to the community, and given them a commitment to the environment: What will childlessness do to one's motivation for planning/preserving; will it de-motivate all long-range investment? Research on this could start now, comparing parents with the childless.

Finally, we have assumed that marriage is going to continue, in some way. That is based on the belief that people will continue to desire a secure partnership with another person or small group, and that youth will feel it is better to institutionally buttress their sharing of life, in general, by setting up a marriage of some kind. This depends, in fact, on the interpersonal climate in communities, and the extent to which people feel isolation and unmet needs that marriage will solve. When marriage is not desired, then we will have discovered new forms of warm, dependable primary association replacing the old institution which has supplied psychological support to people through the millennia.

Part 3

Intimate
perspectives

PART 3 / INTIMATE PERSPECTIVES

This part presents some personal perspectives on human sexuality written very subjectively and without statistical data. The reader is invited to enter the world of these individuals, as a means of learning more about self. What is it like to be Ingrid Bengis, a feminist woman searching for a way to make sense out of love's capacity to destroy or to refresh? Bengis writes of her surprise at finding how sex can create powerful bonds that don't disappear when a relationship ends, and of her ambivalent feelings— desperately wanting love and its energizing power, but strongly fearing that power. She has seen women emerge from a terrible dependence on men to achieve a badly needed autonomy, and yet she mourns the scarcity of men who can match these independent, self-motivating, spontaneous, passionate women. Have men become more oppressed than women—victimized into docility and conformity, and passionless sex? Bengis describes how she and her lover attempted to keep their relationship fresh by a sophisticated arrangement of alternating togetherness and separation for three-month periods, with no long-term commitment—and of her yearning for something more stable. Is it possible for two people to have a long-term commitment to live together, and continue to love? How many couples have survived a twenty-five-year test of such a commitment?

Some of Bengis's concerns are echoed by the four men with whom Simon talks about sexuality. Their diversity of age, profession, and marital status provides a collage of male perspectives, although their viewpoints may not represent typical male attitudes. What important distinctions among these men's thoughts about sexuality can you identify? Do these males represent the "socialized penis" approach to women that Litewka speaks of in the next reading, or do you see their sexuality as strictly related to their individual styles and preferences? Lucy Komisar and others have talked of a "masculine mystique" of aggression, violence, and insensitivity that is exaggeratedly symbolized in war.[1] Is there such a mystique which makes it difficult for a man to be gentle, sensitive, and nonaggressive?

For some time, women have been meeting in consciousness-raising groups, talking with each other about early childhood experiences and concepts, learning to understand and appreciate their own bodies, and finding it possible to support each other rather than to compete. A similar men's movement has begun where men talk to each other about their past and present feelings and problems, and about the effects on them of the women's movement. What is it like to be a man like Jack Litewka, tuned into and conscious of the humiliation many women experience in our ritualized sexual encounters—yet perplexed by his own body's refusal to "perform" as usual in certain sexual situations? Does Litewka's objectify–fixate–conquer socialization formula match your experience? Is male sexuality a self-contained system, focused on its own genital satisfaction—unshared if necessary?

Litewka's female friend analyzed his impotence as a type of sexual withholding verging on punishment of his female partner. Do you agree with her analysis? If men, in order to become genitally aroused, are socialized not to focus on the uniqueness of a particular female but to objectify her and fixate on her sexual apparatus, can they be retrained? Would it be a better sexual world if men were socialized to want and expect total body caressing and touching, with less focus on the penis as the center of their sexuality? Would such socialization "emasculate" men?

What is it like to be Karla Jay, a lesbian living in a continuing relationship despite gay friends' accusations that she is imitating the coupledom of the straight world? Perhaps such criticism among gay sisters is a healthy sign in the gay community, which during the early days of their movement presented a consistently united front to the straight world, evincing no internal disagreement. Must a minority group that is discriminated against hide internal differences in order to survive?

As they talk through their differences, Jay and her lover sound like many heterosexual couples trying to find ways to live together and meet both partners' needs. Are the needs of a gay couple really different from those of a heterosexual couple, except in the gender of the partner? How big an "except" is that? Are the external pressures identified by Jay more difficult for a lesbian couple than the internal pressures? Some people feel that gay couples may lead the way for heterosexual couples to find a new egalitarianism. In the past, there has been sharp role segregation in some gay relationships, but an increasing number of gay couples see their relationship as a place where two human beings can share their unique gifts, skills, and preferences in doing work, assuming responsibilities, and developing a relationship relatively free of role stereotypes.

Mark Freedman asserts that gay people tend to be more expressive and more innovative than straight people in their sexual relationships. He concludes that "many gay people know how to focus on sex as an expression of warmth, tenderness, and sensuality. And at least part of the gay world engages in the sexual variety that many psychologists consider extremely valuable."[2] What evidence do you see in your reading, your observations, or your own experience to support or contradict this statement?

What is it like to be Louie Crew, a gay man refusing to conform to the straight sexuality of his academic community but still surviving—and thriving? What motivated Crew to "come out of the closet" in a rural community and in the teaching profession—traditionally anti-homosexual environments? Why not have the best of both worlds, travel incognito, and avoid the pain and humiliation that sometimes accompanies being known as gay? Many homosexuals insist that the pain is worse when they have to be continually on guard against accidental discovery of their "secret." As long as they are in the closet, the problem is theirs; but when they affirm their identity openly, the "problem" becomes another's because there is no longer a "secret" to be protected but an actuality to be dealt with. Do you agree with this reasoning?

Crew's story seems to substantiate Freedman's view that gay people become more "centered" and clear about their own identity than are straight people because they have discovered their own values and live accordingly. Freedman says,

> An intense quest for identity, purpose, and meaning often begins quite early, certainly by the time young homosexuals begin to appreciate the tremendous social pressures against them. . . . I believe creative opposition has produced not only new social concepts but an increased sensitivity to the value of the individual person in our society.[3]

Do you see evidence for this viewpoint? What can heterosexual people do to open up the possibilities for experiencing themselves and gay people as whole persons? One gay student writes,

> As a straight person, you can help by making sure you never act in a patronizing way to gay people. Maybe you wouldn't want your brother or son to be gay, but chances are someone you know is. If you ever find out that your brother is a homosexual, don't tell him that it's all the same to you. Instead, invite him and his lover to dinner. And don't kiss your wife in front of them unless you are prepared to see them kiss.

Ziva Kwitney or some of the women in the Boston Women's Health Collective affirm the choice of celibacy as a means of clarifying their own sexuality. These women acquired a sense of peace and completeness and became more aware of themselves as unique sexual beings freed from dependence on men. Will celibacy move women toward what Litewka calls a self-contained sexual system? Is the need for clarifying identity away from the complications of genital sexual activity limited to women? Are religious celibates the only men who deliberately choose a celibate life style? Is choosing celibacy motivated by fear of intimacy, or does celibacy deepen the possibilities for intimacy?

Many of the readings in this part highlight the element of choice in sexual interactions and illustrate decisions that have been made after reflecting on a range of options. Do any of the viewpoints presented here represent new options for you?

NOTES

1 Lucy Komisar, "Violence and the Masculine Mystique," *The Washington Monthly*, January 1970.

2 Mark Freedman, "Homosexuals May Be Healthier Than Straights," *Psychology Today*, March 1975, p. 31.

3 Ibid., p. 30.

Love

Ingrid Bengis

I am of that generation which was brought up to believe that
women had very special emotional needs, that love was always, or almost always, a more significant or more encompassing experience for a
woman than for a man, and that because of the dichotomies between men and women it was necessary to protect women against
the ravishments of male sexuality. I was taught: women love, men
screw; save yourself for marriage; taught: don't squander your
inner resources on someone who will only smash them; taught: men
have affairs, women don't (although it was never clear with whom
those men were having affairs if not women, since no one assumed
they were having them with men); taught: men respect a woman
who can say "no"; men want to marry virgins; don't let your passions
(if you have passions) run away with you. It can only lead to a bad
ending.

By the time I reached the age to apply any of these standards, however, the standards had changed. Women were supposed to be

---

"equal" to men. That meant that being a virgin was nonsense, and having affairs wasn't. I was 16 in 1960. My friends were becoming emancipated. Girls in my class at college spent whole evenings talking about whether or not to "give" their virginity to the boy they were going out with. Boys, in the spirit of true equality, offered to take it. By the time a girl was a sophomore, she wasn't supposed to be a virgin any more. True to the tone of the times, I wasn't. But two years later, I had a long talk with a male friend, three years older than I, who was planning to get married. He, as I, had always said that the idea of virginity was anachronistic. Except now, as he talked, he admitted that his prospective wife was a virgin, one of the few he had met, and said that it really meant something to him. I was astonished. And retrenched to think things over.

That was in 1963. A year or two later, I was no longer concerned about whether or not men wanted to marry virgins. What I was more concerned about was that some collision between the past and the present was taking place. "Egalitarianism" notwithstanding, women, including myself, were having a hard time being casual about the relationship between love and sex. Having decided on our own steam that promiscuity wasn't a dirty word any more, our physical needs were still constantly being challenged by our emotional ones. Those of us who were trying to be free and committed at the same time discovered that it was a schizophrenic proposition. So was trying to be both romantic and practical. I attempted the adaptation, coming to the "sensible" and "emancipated" conclusion that dating and Victorianism were idiotic. Daily life and sex, I decided, had to be blended carefully together. "Love" was something that you created and built. It did not just "happen."

Conceptually, of course, that was fine. Except even though it did not "just happen," it kept on happening. Having concluded that trial marriages were the only way to find out whether you could work things out together with a man, it never occurred to me that a trial marriage might not succeed, that affairs might end, that love might die in arguments which were supposed to be settled by making love, or in resolutions about "freedom" and "nonpossessiveness" which tore the very heart out of intimacy. For years I had had an upward and onward view of life, believing that growth inevitably led to more growth. Living with someone, I thought, was supposed to make you love each other even more.

I discovered that I was wrong. There were a number of things which I hadn't counted on, things which none of my friends who wanted to be "free" counted on. The first of these was that my attachments to men usually deepened the longer I knew them, and the more I shared with them, whereas their attachments seemed to lessen. The second was that when love didn't turn out as planned, there was some peculiar pain which I refused to acknowledge, a pain of separation that had not been part of the design. There was love and there was hate. Even though being emancipated meant being willing to take chances with your life, it also meant that you might take chances which sent you reeling when you lost.

The other thing I didn't count on was the power of sex. I didn't realize that sex made a difference, or at least not that *kind* of a difference. What I thought was that sex was an expression of love, a part of love. What I didn't think was that it transformed everything, that for me and for most women, making love with a man several times created unpredictable bonds, bonds which weren't broken by saying: "This Was a Trial Marriage for Which the Contract Has Expired." I didn't realize that intimacy, physical intimacy, had unknown properties, that it created deepening needs, created highly unprogressive bursts of possessiveness and jealousy, created some balance between tension and satisfaction which became the mirror of every other aspect of a relationship; didn't realize that sex deepened love and love deepened sex, even when love was on its way out. I didn't realize that love could reverse itself, could be withdrawn, or that the consequences of such a withdrawal could be so powerful as to crush vast expanses of one's own potential for feeling. I didn't realize that there really was such a thing as falling apart over the loss of love, nor that the difference between waking up next to a man you loved and not waking up next to him could be all the difference in the world.

Nowadays we are cynical about the possible outcome of relationships; we say let's try to have relationships which are free of romantic poison, free of jealousy and possessiveness, which are generous, undemanding, truly open.

What we do not say, however, is that despite our belief in freedom for nations and individuals, we have become so boxed into our circumlocutions about love that we admit only reluctantly the bald fact that whatever it is, we still need it. For when all the remedies and all the rhetorical armor have been dropped, the absence of love in our lives is what makes them seem raw and unfinished. Personal hatred and personal fear destroy our capacities for loving more thoroughly than any social system possibly could. What we do not say is that love brings us face-to-face with the barest of our being. What we do not say is that we are all, every last one of us, scared of love's power to create and destroy.

Most of us at this stage of things aren't even sure of what we mean when we talk about love. If "real love" is simply a matter of contentment, why does the thought of a sexless union chill us to the bone? We want to love people who are "good for us" and find that sometimes we love people who are not. Then we say it probably wasn't love in the first place, but masochism. We want to combine the sensible and the impassioned, but when one or the other is missing (as they so often seem to be), we conclude that this must not be the real thing. The real thing perhaps is something that people who have lived together and compromised together and struggled together for 25 years or more know about, if their sense of affection and respect for each other has endured all that time, if they are still capable of seeing each other freshly. But we have such few examples of that kind of attachment that we can scarcely look to them for help.

As a child in Russia, my mother was considered so fragile that she was expected to spend her days lying in a hammock, resting. As a wife, she was expected to be a beautiful and charming doll. As a mother, she wished for a daughter who would also be a doll. It was expected that in line with middle-class European standards, she would have a governess to take care of the house and the children, that she would never hold a job, and that she would spend her evenings waiting for her husband. What she should *do* with her life was think about the needs of her family, get a lot of sleep, and go to the beauty parlor once a week. Not knowing how else to use up her energies, she became a compulsive shopper, going from one department store to another, buying and exchanging, buying and exchanging, even at those times when she had so little money that almost everything had to be returned. She is exquisitely sensitive, high-strung as a hummingbird, and so insecure that she has to telephone my father five times in the course of a day to resolve the question of what she should prepare for dinner. She possesses an enormous wealth of untapped strength, and, since no one ever provided channels for that strength, she is in a constant state of nervous paralysis . . . terribly afraid of life . . . afraid of our lives as much as for her own. She lies awake at night, transforming our worlds into disaster areas from which she should be clearing the rubble, imagining fatalities at every street crossing, sure that we will not survive from one breath to the next. And yet . . . in a crisis she has more strength than any of us, can cope with gargantuan problems, carry enormous packages up six flights of stairs, understand the subtle problems of my father's business affairs (but only at those times when he can't understand them and literally *has* to be helped), and drive 600 miles in the course of a day to deliver a car for him, and cook in one evening 12 courses to feed 50 people, even though at other times she is so "inefficient" about cleaning the house that the dishes sometimes sit in the sink for 24 hours. She's not really inefficient or incompetent. She's miserably unhappy, and doesn't know that the lack of an independent focus to her life has turned all her best impulses destructively inward. I love her, but I can hardly look to her as an example.

Elsewhere, the prospects are not much more reassuring. I can scrounge around and come up with a handful of antecedents, women writers who spent a good deal of their lives in open revolt against their "condition" . . . George Eliot and Virginia Woolf and Simone de Beauvoir and Sylvia Plath in particular, whose work I admire at least as much as the fact that they are "women writers." But the lives and loves of women writers have not been notoriously successful (writers are a neurotic breed to begin with): Plath and Woolf both committed suicide, although at very different stages of their lives, and Simone de Beauvoir questioned in *The Prime of Life,* when it was too late to change things, whether she hadn't made a crucial mistake in not having had children. George Eliot fared a good deal better.

None of them, however, successfully combined marriage *and* children and working, which is what I and many of my friends would like to do. But even if all of them had led superbly balanced lives, fulfilling every aspect of their personal and biological destinies, three or four literary models are not very much to go by. The result of all this, for me at least, is the reluctant conclusion that whatever I will become and whatever ways of loving I will find, will have to be the product of a union between frequently blind struggle and sheer luck.

There was a time in my life when I swore that I would never get married, never be "chained" to another human being, never allow myself to depend on any person other than myself, never try to inhibit a man in the pursuit of his freedom, never demand anything at all, least of all fidelity. Happiness, I thought, lay in the commitment to freedom. When my mother said, "You can't have love affairs the rest of your life. Look what happens when they end," I answered with "Oh, Mother, don't be ridiculous. I have a life of my own. I have my work, my friends, my freedom."

My plan certainly wasn't a success, for despite the fact that I could live alone for years at a time, support myself in banal as well as curious ways, travel alone all over the world, drive a motorcycle at 70 miles an hour, have sex with whomever I chose . . . I was still capable of sitting by a telephone, unable to think of anything beyond whether or not a man I loved was going to call and feeling the most common hurt and frustration when he didn't. I have known myself to spend hours or even days wandering around my apartment, uninterested in books or even music or friends, days uninterested in going anywhere or doing anything, simply because my imagination had made me believe that some slight quarrel with someone I loved or some excessive or inappropriate demand represented a prelude to the "final separation." I have heard the voice struggling to burst free inside of me, the voice which longs for a condition of life in which my every action and reaction would be regulated by me and no one else, the voice which demands a freedom which all too often seems hollow when it is achieved.

Certainly it was not a question of being liberated enough to make phone calls myself; I had made those calls many times. It was a question of security (a word which I have always looked upon with contempt). No female Bill of Rights could give me that kind of security. For

> Perspective, I soon realized, was a fine commodity, but utterly useless when I was in the thick of things.

what I needed to know at those particular moments was whether it mattered enough to the man for him to do the calling. Yes, of course, I should have had more confidence, should have been able to say, "Well, if he doesn't care that much, the hell with him," or, "Phone calls aren't so important." That is precisely what I *did* say. I grew furious at myself and spoke contemptuously of "neurotic need." I stiffened with resistance, swearing that "never again" would I allow that to happen. Hating myself for retaining these vestiges of insecurity, I struggled to raise my consciousness to such a high level that I might purchase immunity through it. Perspective, I soon realized, was a fine commodity, but utterly useless when I was in the thick of things. My "wisdom" deserted me; a crisis that should not have been a crisis became one anyway. Maybe he didn't want to be with me . . . was it because of me? . . . Did he still love me? . . . Why couldn't I control the terrible trips my imagination went on? The horrifying absurdity of not being in control . . . ever . . . except when I wasn't in love, except when someone didn't really matter . . . it scared me so much, I decided it was better not to love anyone at all. Wasn't it easier in the long run, to simply be alone? Yes it was . . .

sometimes. But then at other times, well . . . something crunched inside of me at the thought. I might wrestle myself to the ground . . . but it was always me who lost.

Of course, I know that the fear of immobilization and the fact of immobilization are not unique to me. I have seen too many men who were as happy or as demoralized as I, depending upon the current status of their intimate relations with women. Men and women usually love differently (and in general I think that women love in a more integrated way), but we all feel the same sense of seemingly excessive consequence when love doesn't turn out as we want it to, or when we are not what we thought we could be or when love is simply absent from our lives.

Still, I have never been able to get over the secret twinges of sympathy, pity, and contempt (fear's disguise) which mingled inside of me whenever I saw a woman suffering over love . . . pity and contempt because she was so exposed, because she made me feel so painfully aware of my own susceptibility to the same kind of exposure . . . sympathy because of the shared knowledge derived from similar experience. I remember one day when I was waiting for a pay telephone hearing the young woman who was talking inside of it say, "Barry, please are you coming? Please just tell me, are you coming?" Barry's answer apparently wasn't affirmative because the woman then said, "Listen, I'll *pay* for the plane. I know it's a long drive. But I have the money. And I want you to come."

I couldn't stay around to hear the rest. Even the fragment of unsatisfied need made me cringe for her. And I wanted to run from the sound of her voice, so unhappy, so dependent, so desperate. For to many women (to me) the desire to reach out toward men, both physically and spiritually, is constantly being sabotaged by the fear of being psychologically mutilated. Many of us, I think, have turned against our own needs mostly because we've seen the price other women have had to pay for them. If it hurt me to see the woman in the phone booth needing "Barry," then damn it, I was never going to need a "Barry." If it hurt me to see my parents' marriage flounder in its own contradictions, then I would never marry. If it hurt me to see women suffering over their husband's infidelities, then I was going to make absolutely sure that fidelity was unimportant. If the thought of living with someone and having them leave me made me physically ill, then I just wouldn't live with someone . . . period. Those "free choices" I had told my mother about, were not, as it turned out, such free choices after all. They were choices made as reaction to a need, not out of the need itself.

I do not know many women who spend their lives waiting for phone calls or cleaning out ashtrays or wondering frantically what they are going to do on a Saturday night. I do, however, know a great many women who are active, sensitive, and intelligent, women for whom the achievement of "liberation" was a goal long before it became part of a crusade, a goal created by inner necessity rather than popular concern. There was no choice for them except to struggle to be themselves, simply because it took too much out of them to go by the rules. It is precisely those women, however, who are currently in the worst predicament, stranded on the outer edges of the Movement, increasingly isolated and frustrated.

In the past several months, four men whom I like and respect, said to me on separate occasions that they missed having a worthwhile male companionship. "The most interesting people around are all women," they said.

It was true, I thought, that there seemed to be a shortage of male counterparts. I, too, was unhappy about the flaccidity, the one-dimensionality, the lack of imagination, the lack of life in most of the men I saw around me. Where was their energy, their activity, their spontaneity? Where was their passion? The women I knew were filled with passion, not only sexual passion, although that too, but the passion for seizing life and shaping it, infusing it with the breath of an expansive humanity, an intelligent vitality. And they were gagging from the effort of repressing their desire for a truly human form of love.

What are we freeing ourselves *for*, I thought, if not to become happier people? What use is it to liberate one's potential if there is no one capable of valuing or matching or responding to that potential?

None of us can go back to the old images of domestic bliss—we were revolting against that long before we had any coherent sense of why we were doing it. We worked to create ourselves, and then looked for male co-creators. We wanted so badly to be "finished women" first. But the struggle to become self-reliant cost us so much, required so much sheer hard labor, and made such tentative gains that it sometimes seemed we would never succeed in overcoming our own psychic entropy, never be complete. Yes, we wanted to sharpen our minds on the daily clashes of alive intellects. Yes, we wanted our days to be rich in exposures to a kaleidoscopic outside world. Yes, we wanted to be proud of our strength. But no, we never wanted to become worthy of the pedestal, the icy heights of achievement. We wanted love that was intense but not consuming. We wanted to be cared for, thought of, and valued, not abstractly as men often value women, but in the accumulation of daily minutiae which make life dense and intricate and worthy of infinite consideration. We were seeking in men what we were seeking in ourselves, a combination of strength, diversity, commitment, passion, and sensitivity—seeking an equivalent humanity.

In the process of attempting to become "separate individuals" many of us have had to anesthetize ourselves to needs which are nonetheless real and deep. We have rationalized our desires for love and affection, permanence and stability, equating those desires with a capitulation to unresolved weakness in ourselves. We have lost touch with much of what we really want. Trying to be undemanding and independent, we discover that we are engaging in a new form of self-sabotage. Concentrating our energies on one person, we're fearful of being overly vulnerable to the effects a single relationship can have on us.

At bottom, though, the need for continuity, for love, for something which has at least the solidity which *might* make permanence possible, even if it usually doesn't come about, persists.

My aunt recently said to me, "You want too much. You aren't willing to compromise. Men will never be as sensitive or aware as women are. It's just not in their natures. So you have to get used to that, and be satisfied with something else."

"What else?"

"Either sexual satisfaction or theoretical intelligence or being loved and *not* understood, or else being left alone to do the things you want to do."

"But those aren't enough."

"They have to be."

"Then I'd rather do without love altogether."

"You'll have to."

My aunt is 55 years old. She has learned the meaning of compromise. But how can I possibly compromise on things like warmth, communication, a passionate sense of life, a healthy capacity for commitment to me as well as to an outside purpose? I don't want to compromise on those things even if my aunt *is* right about the limitations of masculine "nature" (and I think she's wrong). Why should anyone compromise on whatever makes love worthwhile for them in the first place? And yet, even as she was talking, I thought that maybe she was right in this respect, maybe I did expect too much, the chief indicator being that for the present, I was in fact doing without love altogether—although as far as I could tell, that wasn't the reason, since I had, despite all my criteria, always fallen in love with people, not characteristics, people who, although they did in fact possess those traits I wanted, possessed some very contradictory ones as well.

What I wanted finally, or so I thought, was someone whom I could enjoy being with as much as I enjoyed being with myself. A narcissistic notion admittedly, and wide open to criticism, since even if I cannot quite forgive my own weaknesses, I at least know how to live with them and cannot say the same about someone else's weaknesses. All these thoughts succeeded in driving me back in on myself, to a critique of my misplaced idealism, my stubbornness and "inflexibility," my unwillingness to adapt to "reality," the all or nothing quality of my attachments. If my aunt was right though, then why hadn't her life been any happier than mine? The question gave me a headache and I finally left the house.

If Victorian society decreed that sex for women was taboo and enlightened society decreed that women were entitled to as much sex as men were, "liberated" society has decreed that sex and even exclusive love are oppressive to women. Suddenly I want to scream—for God's sake, just *stop*. Let me off this idiot merry-go-round. My psyche is not an ideological playground. My inner feelings, at their most genuine, are not ruled by social decree. You can have a thousand lovers if you want, or have none. You can be a lesbian, a virgin, a career woman, a mother, or all four. But don't tell me who I am, or who it's best for me to be. I recognize parts of myself when you speak of "women," but other parts don't fit the formula. I recognize parts of the males I know when you speak of men, but other parts defy categorization. I can't make the transitions required to fit the current theories of the age, especially since the ages are so telescoped that one barely has time to absorb one set of perspectives before another is all the rage. I don't know who women are. I scarcely even know who I am.

The rational mind is capable of making astounding leaps. I can create and destroy whole new systems of thought, systems of being, systems of living, within the course of a dinner conversation. What I cannot do, however, is *become* the person that every decade newly assumes I ought to be. I cannot be the "completely feminine woman" of the fifties, or the emancipated, sexually free woman of the sixties, or the militant antisexist woman of the seventies. I cannot ignore the fact that my own life has unfolded slowly, that it has been a part of all of those trends and none of them. I cannot ignore the fact that essentially the same me has persisted throughout the upheavals, throughout the analyses of historical circumstances, and evaluations of what a woman's life ought to be.

The woman I've continued to be is a contradictory and uncertain human being. Believing in love, I am also terrified of it. Believing in stability, I live a thoroughly unstable life. Believing in marriage, I have never risked it. I am occasionally attracted to men exclusively on the basis of their sexuality, but am appalled when they are attracted to me on the basis of mine. I care about affection and doubt my capacities for it. I say friendship is superior to passion even as my throat is locking with the effort to suppress the effects of my latest passion. The woman I am knows that when I meet a man who is kind but sexless, my interest ebbs; that when I meet a man who is less than kind but sexually attractive, there is a struggle; that when I meet a man who is kind *and* sexually attractive, I am afraid of falling in love. Difficult problems to resolve. But real nonetheless. My needs, fears, and desires remain as part of my daily life. The liberated woman often fades into obscurity. And I am forced instead to confront a person—merely a person.

For a relatively brief period in my life, I believed as some feminists now do, that selective promiscuity was a means of resolving some of the conflicts of love. It seemed to me then that the best way not to invest too much in a relationship with one man, and the best way to avoid being hurt, was to love a lot of men; if I wished to protect myself against my own intensity, my natural drift toward exclusivity, then I should learn to spread myself around and thus avoid being a burden to myself or anyone else. But I found it confusing, to say the least, to wake up to three different people in the course of a week. I am always astounded when philosophers of the Movement talk blithely about the "ideal of uprootedness"—the freedom to move around—and express contempt for the apparent lack of originality in the lives of people who have struggled for stability and permanence. I am equally astounded when serial relationships are proposed as quick solutions to human misery, as if to suggest that the transition from one relationship to another could be made "naturally."

Recently I had a long talk with my 24-year-old brother who had returned only a few months before from a trip to India, where he had spent five months meditating in a mountain village at the foot of the Himalayas. He was thinking of getting married to a woman he'd known for about three years. My immediate reaction of course was, "But, Steven, how *could* you? You're so young, and marriage is so *permanent*. Why don't you at least wait until you want to have children and just keep on living together?"

"It's so easy to do that," he said. "You can live with someone and move out anytime. . . whenever it gets rough. We already *know* we can live together. I don't see any reason to stay in the same stage all the time, and marriage is another stage. There's a difference."

I was about to say, "Of course there's a difference. . . and that's why you should keep on living together," but then an image passed through my mind, and I realized how quickly one could deny the evidence of one's own experience.

The image was of a hotel near a railroad station in a small town on the Austro–Italian border. I was sitting out on the patio drinking *caffè latte* with a recently divorced painter. We had been living together in Greece for some time and I was on my way back to the States. He was on his way back to his home in Austria. We were spending

> **"Three months together, three months apart," he said. "That will keep things fresh."**

a last weekend together before separating. It was a weekend of being in love and making plans. The plans included his coming to America several months later . . . maybe.

"Three months together, three months apart," he said. "That will keep things fresh. You'll do your work and I'll do mine. The time will go very fast. And then we'll be together again."

"Yes." I said, "I suppose so," and felt something drop inside of me like a stone falling down an elevator shaft.

"One thing is sure. I never want to be married again."

"Never?" I said.

"No, never."

"What about children? Don't you ever want to have children?"

"No."

"Oh."

It had been a long time since the subject had come up. The last time we'd talked about marriage I had agreed with him . . . marriage was a trap . . . it took the spontaneity out of life. Now I wasn't so sure. There was something so final about the word "never." It was like looking down a tunnel that got progressively darker instead of moving up toward the light. It was a dead-end word. But wasn't "marriage," too, a dead-end word? Suddenly it didn't seem to be . . . in an instant, my perspective had shifted almost imperceptibly to the right. A theory had transformed itself into a reality, wedged now between two words.

"How can you say 'never' about something? Life is always changing. You can't know how you're going to feel a year from now about anything."

"I know. I've been through it once and I don't want to go through it again."

"But that's so static. I think maybe some day I would want to be married and have children. I don't know for sure, but I certainly couldn't say 'never.' Why say it? Can't you just leave things open and see what happens?"

"Look," he said, "there isn't any point in talking about it now, is there? We're not thinking of getting married, so why discuss it?"

"We don't have to discuss it. I just don't like the sound of the word 'never.' "

"All right, then," he said. Then he laughed and kissed me. But he didn't retract the "never."

I was 22 then. For the next year and a half we lived out our "arrangement" . . . together three months, apart three months. It was a very contemporary arrangement. We flew back and forth across two continents. For a while I thought it was very romantic. Then I began to think that it really ought to be more romantic than it was. I wasn't feeling spontaneous and fresh because of being apart for so long. In fact, if anything, I was feeling much less spontaneous, since it always took me several weeks to adjust to our being together or being apart. Continuity, it seemed, might be what made spontaneity possible in the first place.

After the year and a half was over, we split up. I didn't understand why we had to do that. I wanted to keep on working at things. He didn't. Suddenly I realized that we had been so concerned with maintaining freshness that we had forgotten about laying foundations and building with cement.

I think about my brother, about how similar words like "never" and "forever" are. And I wonder about having to walk such very thin lines.

Male Views of Sexual Satisfaction

William Simon

What happens when a group of men get together and talk about sex?
How do they feel about themselves, the women in their lives, and
the roles these women play? The answers will vary from one man to the
next—revealing an individuality of need and desire that has long been
obscured by the myth that sex for men was somehow something
that just happened. Granted it is a mythology sustained by some
men. But today it is being slowly dismantled as more people are willing
to talk about sexual joys, uncertainties, and even fears.

Here are four men different in age, occupation, and outlook
who have agreed to a candid discussion of male sexuality. They
draw upon their personal experiences and philosophies, sometimes
agreeing, but often not, as they seek to discover the meaning of
sexual satisfaction in their lives.

Lionel, 51, is a business executive, married 22 years and the father
of four children. Mark, 23, a teacher in an experimental school, is
single and has been living with a young woman for almost a year—it
is his third such relationship. Herbert, 34, and married for 11 years, is a

Reprinted from *Today's Health*, April 1975, with permission of the author and of *Today's Health*, published
by the American Medical Association.

research scientist, and the father of one preschool child. Evan, 28, is divorced and currently going out with several women. He is a graduate school dropout turned successful rock musician.

Dr. Simon: Can we begin by defining what sexual satisfaction means to each of you?

Lionel: For me it goes beyond the immediacy of just physical sex. It is not 20 minutes in bed or 2 hours or the whole day that make sexual relationship satisfying. Good sex can produce a sense of physical satisfaction, but that can't fully compare to the satisfaction that comes with the involvement of the total human being.

Evan: From my experience, I find that I can have a number of kinds of sexual relationships. Some are immediate WHAM! They just happen and they are out of sight. Other sexual liaisons go beyond that.

Herbert: For me, there can't be anything like immediate satisfaction. Nor without a strong sense of emotional involvement. Without that, it's little more than masturbation.

Evan: As long as I feel that I'm connecting to her it can be immediately satisfying and very real.

Mark: I have to like what I am doing and like the person I am doing it with—or at least think that I am going to like her when I get to know her better.

Lionel: If you are talking just about a sexual experience, it can be very satisfying, very intense.

Dr. Simon: Is there really a difference between the satisfaction created from a sexual relationship as against that which might come from a single sex act?

Herbert: I don't think that for me the purely physical can be satisfying outside of a deep personal relationship that extends over time. You have to be secure—secure enough to be yourself and to know that it's you whom she is making love with.

Mark: There were times when I was busy playing the field having sex with a number of different women, and I can't say that it wasn't fun.

But it's only when you go beyond that and really dig into someone that it becomes more than fun and begins to feel like satisfaction. I'm not as hung up on her knowing me. That's her trip. But I want to know her.

Lionel: I have no trouble with that. I've had relations that were 99 per cent pure lust. We met, we enjoyed, we never saw each other afterwards. There was no commitment to love or even communication. The commitment was to some kind of immediacy—some of it frenzied, some of it calculating, some of it testing. And it has been fun! I

> **You seem to be saying that many men are really as romantic as women are purported to be.**

wouldn't say it was more than that, but it was a lot of that, and I wouldn't have given it up for the world. But I always understood that it was just an encounter. It never had the responsibilities of a relationship—never the satisfaction either.

Dr. Simon: If I'm hearing you correctly, I can only conclude that men in general have been getting poor public relations. Men have usually been thought of as being casual about sex, staying very close to the physical level—while it was the women who had to be in love or think they were in love before becoming aroused. You seem to be saying that many men are really as romantic as women are purported to be. Some women, however, are now acknowledging that they can become sexually aroused by the idea of making love to some phantom stranger. How about you? Do you find the idea of making love or having sex with a total stranger attractive? A woman you didn't know before and would never see again?

Evan: That's off the wall. It's crazy. There is no sex without feeling. When I walk down the street, I'm not turned on by every woman I see, not even every attractive one I see. The fact that I get turned on by one person rather than all the others means that at least there has to be the anticipation of something more than two bodies coming together. There has to be some kind of exchange of messages. It may happen very quickly, but it has to be there. And if it was really good, you want to do it again.

Herbert: The one big reason that I don't pursue every female who might turn me on is that I know I will probably never feel anything more intense than just turned on. At least for me, satisfaction has a sense of satiation, of physical release, of psychological pleasure. Just as important to it is the feeling of having produced the same feelings in someone else.

Dr. Simon: But couldn't that happen with a stranger?

Herbert: No, because you don't know enough about her to be comfortable with your own pleasure and you're not sure how to satisfy her.

Mark: If they start as phantoms, they don't stay that way for long. Even in those cases where we didn't really know each other before going to bed, I inevitably worked to create some kind of emotional rapport. Right now I am involved with a young woman I met last fall. We hadn't really known each other, but we got it on, and it quickly became a very tight emotional thing. I guess I'm not content to leave it on a physical level.

Lionel: I must be different. I don't feel that I have to be an integral part of anyone's life in order to enjoy sex with them. You seem to be saying that you have to be an important part of a person's life before it fully works for you. I've had that kind of relationship, but I don't think that it is essential to good and enjoyable sex.

Dr. Simon: But what about the woman's enjoyment of sex? Some have suggested that while orgasm is the natural end of the sex act for men, it is not as important for women. Regardless of how important it may be for her, how important is it to you that she have an orgasm?

Evan: That's one of the most important things. If she has an orgasm, you are inevitably going to have one, too. Two people got together, and something happened that was gratifying to the other person and to you.

Lionel: I really want my own personal pleasure. I invest something in it, including a lot of myself. My ego satisfaction, which is part of sexual satisfaction, depends more on what happens to me than what happens to her. There were times when I had a great sexual experience, and she was bored to tears.

Mark: I just don't see that. I can't see how there can be a relationship without sharing. That way the sex act is no different from any other transaction. I have never had an orgasm when my partner was left cold.

Dr. Simon: You mean to say you don't have orgasms when your partner doesn't?

Mark: No, I guess not. I do it, but mostly because I feel that it is expected. But orgasm in that case becomes a way of ending it, without any kind of real high.

Lionel: Behind all that talk is still a lot of male selfishness. What about her wanting just to satisfy you? She may be working at it harder than you are. I think there is too much emphasis placed upon orgasm. For me it doesn't center exclusively on orgasm for either of us. There are also the pleasures, in their own right, of foreplay and a hell of a lot in the pleasures of afterplay.

Dr. Simon: With all the recent talk about women's orgasm, some "experts" have argued that that is creating an excessive amount of anxiety in men. Has that been true for any of you?

Mark: I have a lot of anxiety about that, particularly during the early part of a relationship. Almost invariably the first one or two encounters with any woman are surrounded by an aura of tension on my part, perhaps on her part as well. I feel a need to respond to her needs and, if I think I have failed, I feel rotten.

Evan: I think that you are missing something important. Anxiety is a critical part of sex—it's part of the hit, part of the groove. I don't want to get rid of it, I dig it. I don't want to start making love if I know in advance how it's going to end.

Mark: No one—not even you, Evan—wants anxiety to the point where you can't have an erection. For me the most fulfilling relationships are those that are devoid of tension and anxiety. When she can't fully respond, it ceases to be making love and for me becomes a duel. That kind of relationship never does last for very long.

Herbert: Speaking from the vantage point of a totally monogamous relationship of over 10 years, I can say that there is very little anxiety left. For me there is a profound sense of being comfortable with someone I know and love, and whom I am sure knows and loves me. We can take it slow and easy, and I say: Thank heavens!

Lionel: Speaking from over 20 years of marriage, we have yet to be without anxiety. Every time you get into bed there is a kind of testing. It's no longer the testing of whether she can turn me on or I can turn her on, because that kind of thing doesn't last for long. You even give up quickly in new relationships. But I've never assumed that I was THE man for THAT woman. Each day we are a little different. Different in mood. Different in the meaning of our day. For all the familiarity, it becomes an occasion for discovery. It also becomes an occasion for revealing yourself.

Dr. Simon: One of the most difficult aspects of sexual relationships appears to be the difficulty many people experience in talking about it. Not talking about it the way we are doing right now, but talking about it with your partner. Speaking about what I would call the "doing of sex": Having discussions before you do it, while you do it, as well as after you've done it. What is the most important advice you would give a partner to help her increase your capacity for sexual satisfaction?

Evan: Be less inhibited by what you think I want. That's very important to me. When I feel that she is trying too hard—I guess it makes me feel uneasy. I become too self-conscious, then I begin to worry about the signals I am sending her or what she thinks my signals are. At the same time, though it may sound contradictory, I do like variety, even if I don't always know how we get together on it. I like being the seducer. But then, sometimes I also like being seduced. What I don't like is having to do the same thing all the time.

Lionel: When you make love you often want different kinds of returns. There is a type of aggressive, direct, and fast love. There is also a slow, passive love. There are times when you want a lot of foreplay of different kinds, times when you want the immediacy of full contact. Maybe I'm fortunate—I have the power of expression, or think I have. I have asked and been given answers. I have been asked and can give answers. There are things that I really enjoy when having sex. I don't kid myself. If I don't get them I feel disappointed. I don't, for example, like women who I feel are rushing me. I mean rushing me in my lovemaking. She is an instrument, and so am I; we are two instruments sharing a bed and enjoying the pleasure. To get the most profound enjoyment you have to learn to express what your needs or preferences are.

Mark: I have often felt that way, but your ability doesn't automatically follow. It is easy to say that we should talk to each other, but I have problems talking about making love. I wish I could say lots of different things—faster, slower, wait, this turns me on, or let's not do that. I can't do it, and neither can she. It's not that we don't care, but that we care too much. There is a shyness we can't seem to escape.

Dr. Simon: Mark has just touched upon something. You have all, more or less, agreed that sex as part of an enduring relationship provides the greatest potential for satisfaction. But, if I hear Mark correctly, he seems to be saying that the very importance of that person, on many levels, is experienced as inhibiting his performance. Perhaps inhibiting him from engaging in the kinds of sexual behaviors that he would otherwise like.

Evan: However tight the relationship might be, no matter how much mutual trust there may be, there are still inhibitions. You still draw your limits—we all have limits that we live within. To be up front, I know there are lots of things I used to think about when I was younger and doing a lot of masturbation. Many of these I still think about. But I know I will never do them.

Dr. Simon: But why not?

Evan: Because they are a part of me and still not part of me. While they still have a capacity to turn me on, I know they are childish—perhaps too theatrical.

Herbert: I am not sure inhibition is the right word. There is always a sense of regret. Regret because your fantasies are always greater than reality. If they weren't, there wouldn't be so many books and magazines that feed this capacity for fantasy.

Dr. Simon: If fantasy—something almost all men develop, if only during masturbation—is always greater than reality, doesn't that somehow serve to impoverish the more real, the more directly physical encounter between a man and a woman?

Lionel: Not for me. When I was young and doing a lot of fantasy, I really didn't know very much. Not as much as there was out in the real world. Later, in doing things with real women, I learned that there were a whole series of acts one could do that I didn't know were possible when I was an adolescent.

Evan: I think that I had and have a richer fantasy life than that. But you have to remember what the fantasy trip is all about. I know—most of us know—the difference between illusion and reality. I think that my fantasies help me to be more sexual, but they don't necessarily affect what I am doing in a real situation. Fantasy is always futile, real sex rarely is. If the imagery becomes that important, then you are really not there with your partner. In fantasy you always have total control. You have to learn to share control. That's part of the excitement of making love.

Herbert: You know, I have fantasies about walking on the moon. But I know I am never going to do it, because I get dizzy just thinking about going up on a ski lift. The same is true of many of my fantasies. It's not my wife's reactions that worry me, it's just that I know that there are some things I either can't do, period, or wouldn't do because I wouldn't like myself for doing them.

Mark: Some of my fantasies are what you might call kinky. But I think I have learned to translate these into more acceptable forms of action. That way I don't feel deprived and, at the same time, I haven't offended myself or my partner. It creates a tenuous balance. But that may be what my sexuality is all about: trying to satisfy the fantastic and the real.

Dr. Simon: For some of you, fantasy clearly serves to create a kind of erotic imagery that facilitates sexual interest. I wonder if you could tell me what those images might be? What are the things that, when you see them in a woman, help to create sexual interest?

Lionel: It's hard to pin down. I think it is the expressions or the gestures that somehow denote a hidden, but present, lustful sensuality. I sometimes see it in a gesture such as the way she might touch herself. Or a turn of the head or the way she looks at your whole body. It has little to do with shapes or sizes—it comes in all shapes and sizes. It's a way of saying without being too explicit: I want to enjoy you.

Evan: For me it is lights and eye contact. Whether I want the experience of both of us giving me the command—controlling, domineering—or, if I'm submissive and responsive, I need eye contact to make it possible. She has to be watching what we do. So many women I have known insist on closing their eyes much of the time; or they prefer the darkness, which amounts to the same thing. When they do that, I feel less erotic. I feel that we are not sharing the same experience.

Herbert: It is not easy for me to say this, but most of the words I first learned in connection with sex were what people might call dirty words. It's not that I think that sex is dirty or anything like that. But using them while we make love somehow seems to add to or heighten a sense of excitement. Possibly because it reminds me on some level that it was once forbidden.

Mark: I don't know why, but one of my two turn-ons is hair. Almost all of the women I have been attracted to had lots of hair, particularly long hair. I'm also attracted to women with hair under their arms. Possibly it makes them appear more earthy, more natural. On the other hand, I find unshaven legs something of a turnoff.

Dr. Simon: To change the subject just a little: We've talked about mutuality in response to having sex, but what about mutuality in interest in having sex. How is your sense of satisfaction affected, say, when you are interested, but your partner is not?

Evan: Then it's even better because she cares enough to be there for you. But that can happen only now and then. I recall one woman I had a relationship with—she seemed to be giving all the time. After a while I felt that I wasn't being loved, I was being indulged.

Herbert: If she isn't interested, we don't. Making love is not always better than not making love. It doesn't always have to be a disappointment, it doesn't always have to be interpreted as a put-down.

Dr. Simon: How about the reverse, when she may want it more than you?

Herbert: It has to go both ways. Unless we both are interested, it's better not to get started. I don't think that this happens very often, particularly in an enduring and strong marriage, because you become sensitive to each other's moods.

Lionel: I don't see why you have to say no. You can define it as a very simple act. You don't have to make a big case out of it. And sometimes it can be very gratifying just because you don't really have a very strong urge, you can respond more fully to your partner's urge. We all meet other people's needs in all different ways. This is just another need.

Mark: I agree. There have been times when I felt I was making love out of a sense of obligation rather than interest. Sometimes, before we finish, my interest is as great as it ever is. Other times I have to work harder at getting and keeping an erection. I may not always have enjoyed the act, but I usually felt glad that I did it. I guess mostly because it made me feel like a competent man—and that is always a considerable part of sex.

Dr. Simon: In these days of many crises, it may be appropriate to ask you to comment on how having to respond to economic worries or pressures at work affects your capacity to enjoy sex.

Mark: If the nature of my funk is real, I am often irritated when my girl friend tries to get me out of it. Sometimes I reach a low level, get very depressed, and I tend to get irritated when someone tries to humor me or trick me out of it—it doesn't matter whether they use sex or not. But when I come back from just an ordinary bad day at school, I often enjoy sex, but not because it is some kind of recompense for my trials.

Herbert: With me and my wife, when one of us is down and the other is up—well, that has produced some of the worst sex. It just seems to underscore how far apart we are at that moment.

Lionel: I don't agree with that at all. When things are bad, this kind of clinging can produce some of the best sex. It's a kind of yearning.

> **A question that frequently occurs in discussions of sex, particularly for those who have been married or in a stable relationship, is that of boredom.**

When my wife is low and I can build her up as a woman, she responds tremendously. It works the same way for me. There is something about helping to build the ego of someone you love and who is important to you. It is a satisfaction of a very special kind. And though it happens through sex, it is not purely sexual.

Dr. Simon: A question that frequently occurs in discussions of sex, particularly for those who have been married or in a stable relationship, is that of boredom. Has this been a problem for you? How do you handle it?

Lionel: I've been married over 20 years, and there are still things that my wife doesn't know about me. You need to have a private self so that you can appear mysterious, complicated, and challenging to your partner. I'm often somebody other than who I am with everyone I'm with, even my wife. It's not that I'm acting; I prefer to think of it as exposing a different aspect of myself and letting it take over for a while.

Herbert: I find the idea of role playing, when the role is not an essential part of your own self, to be a silly game. At the same time, you are not always the same person. We all relate to others through selective revelation—emphasizing one part or another. That's not deception or game playing.

Evan: It is very important to be able to play, particularly when it comes to sex. So much of our uptightness is that it has to be a serious business. The ability to laugh in bed is really where it's at. For me, that has been how some of the best sex went. It should be intense and joyful. But it can't be something just in your head—you have to be there. If people can play any game and still really be there—that's a groove.

Mark: That's like a masquerade. You shuld have the right to experiment with yourself and your partner. To try on a new mask. Otherwise it does get very boring.

Lionel: My feeling generally is that you act out of bed, you act in bed. You end up acting a great deal of the time. It's a game we put on for one another. If we didn't we would be terriby boring—all of us. You act your fantasies in bed as best you can, given your own limitations. My limitation is that I can't do it three or four times a night anymore, so I can't fantasize that anymore. I play act a whole different role to substitute for what I'm lacking. Sometimes I am totally out of myself. One of you said that it has to be a part of yourself. That's nonsense. Sometimes I act like someone else just to see how my partner will respond. That's the way you discover a lot of things about yourself and your partner as well.

Herbert: It comes back to what Evan calls "being there." To me that means being committed to what you are doing. You make it all sound so very grim. I don't think that's necessarily true. I really don't see how you can enjoy something that you are *not* committed to more than you enjoy something to which you *are* committed.

Dr. Simon: Lastly, we are all constantly maturing and growing older. As you have grown, how has your concept of sexual satisfaction changed?

Herbert: Between the time I was in college and now, I have changed profoundly. Then I was closer to where the sexual revolution is supposed to be. I was very interested in making out. It was scoring, and I realize how superficial and unsatisfying that was. Now I see that it was little more than organ grinding connected to some silly status game. Since then, I've found how sustaining a long-term relationship can be. I also have a greater idea of the pleasures of security and comfort with someone to whom I am very committed and who is equally committed.

Lionel: My marriage is a very strong marriage, one based on many things more important than sex. Many of our most intimate moments are over the dinner table when we talk to one another. It is not that sex is unimportant, it's just not what the intimacy is based on. In the last 15 years I have learned a lot more about sex. My outside experiences seem to have helped. I think I have helped my wife be less inhibited. I think I am less intimidated by the conventional rules for what middle-aged, middle-class men should be and do.

Evan: As you grow older, you do mature. At least I hope I have. That means that your sense of a good relationship also deepens. If you don't love, you die. I don't think I understood that when I was younger.

Dr. Simon: I think that the one conclusion I can draw from this discussion is that there are very few generalizations that apply to people's attitudes toward sex. When it comes to what you do and what you feel, books and statistics may help, but not very much. The ultimate conclusion about what we do sexually is a very private decision. The best results may be reached by those who learn to trust their partners and, more importantly, who learn to trust themselves.

The Socialized Penis

Jack Litewka

This is, to a certain degree, a personal story. I felt the need to make it public because I have sensed for a long time, and now see more clearly every day, the disaster of sexuality in its present forms. Some women have been struggling with this reality. They have attempted to expose the male/female myth in the hope of creating a healthier reality. But most men have been (at best) silent or (at worst) dishonest—and often ignorant and defensive. This essay is an attempt to help men begin talking among themselves and hopefully with women.

The people who should have initiated the dialogue are psychoanalysts and psychiatrists: the psycho-healers. But they have failed us. And themselves. By and large, they have concentrated their energies on helping people adapt to the realities of the existing social system rather than examining the foundations of that system. But, like the rest of us, these people are damaged. And being damaged, they are incapable of dealing with their own experience. Have you seen much written or spoken about masturbation? I haven't. The psycho-healers, most of whom are men, always talk about the phenomenon of masturbation as if it was "other," "out there." Have you ever heard a psycho-healer say, "When I masturbate(d) . . ."? Of course not. They are incapable or terrified of dealing with their own experience. So I am attempting to deal with mine, with those of men I know, in an effort to help us begin to deal more honestly with one aspect of male socialization.

Like the psycho-healers, like everyone, I am also damaged. I may be incapable of asking the right questions. I know I'm not able now to supply the "answers" that are needed. Desperately needed. But I'm

> **I was raised in America and learned—as did many other boys in my childhood and men I know now—to perform sexually on desire or request.**

going to try, and I hope that other men will also begin trying. Through persistence and honesty and perhaps by accident, we'll end up asking the right questions and be better able to answer them.

I'm very grateful to a few close friends, male and female, who are involved in this struggle and who have given me support and encouragement and criticism and chunks of their own lives in the writing of this essay. I'm also very happy that the Women's Movement exists and that many women are committed to undoing the damage done to all of us. I am not going to re-discuss what women writers have already explored. The sexual socialization of men in this century is what I want to deal with. More specifically, socialized sexual response. Still more specifically, the socialized penis. My penis, not just those of other men out there.

I was raised in America and learned—as did many other boys in my childhood and men I know now—to perform sexually on desire or request. This performance I think can be considered the norm, an ability that most males wanted to develop or maintain. The males who didn't conform to this norm usually felt incomplete, unskilled, or unmanly. And this insufficiency often resulted in self-damning fear and anxiety, while other "healthy" males who automatically or easily conformed to the norm just cruised along, dropping anchor in this or that port when entertainment's hunger urged.

I think I am typical of most American males when I say that getting aroused, getting an erection, was not a major problem in adolescence. If there was a major problem, it was in not knowing what to do, or not being allowed to do anything, with an erection. So you had to learn how to hide it or deal with the embarrassment of its discovery.

I don't know when I began to be annoyed with the way women and men relate. Like most men, I think, I only dealt with a relationship when I had experienced enough and was troubled enough to look back at a previous relationship. But by the time one seriously begins to examine male/female relationships, it is usually too late. Because one has already been thoroughly socialized. So instead of dealing with male/female relationships, one is incapable of examining them, or refuses to examine them, or represses what one knows, or stands under it intellectually and laughs at the absurdity. Or tragedy.

In the last year and a half, something happened to me on three separate occasions that made me decide to seriously analyze the way I had been sexually socialized. I now understand that the incidents occurred because I was already grappling with the origins of my sexuality.

Incident 1. A woman I liked (and who liked me—"love" may be a mythic word so it is not being used, especially since it has nothing to do with erection) and I were in bed together for the first time. We talked and hugged and played. To my surprise and dismay, I didn't get an erection. At least not at the propitious moment (I did have erections now and then throughout the night). And I didn't know why. Maybe I was just too tired or had been fucking and masturbating too much (though that had never been a problem before). But it didn't disturb me too much because the woman was supportive and we both knew there would be other nights. So we rolled together, smelled each other, heard our breathing, and had a lovely night despite absence of coitus.

In the following year, I had a few relationships and my penis was its old arrogant self, so that one night seemed an unexplained oddity and was pretty much forgotten. My sexual life had the same sexual dynamic as my previous sexual history, so things were back to normal. But then came round two.

Incident 2. Similar in all respects to Incident 1. No erection at the right time. Again, I did have erections now and then throughout the night. Again, I didn't know why. But I knew it wasn't from being too tired or fucking or masturbating too much, since I hadn't slept with a woman in about a month and since I had spent the past week on vacation just reading, resting, doing odd jobs—not masturbating—and enjoying the absence of tension. Again, it wasn't a hassle because the woman knew me and I knew her and we both knew people the other had slept with, so it was chalked off as a freak with neither of us to blame. We touched along the whole length of our bodies and discussed basketball, politics, and our social/sexual histories. She fell asleep. I couldn't, my brain gnawing at me, having scary thoughts about a present (temporary) or impending impotency, and resolving to do something—but not knowing what.

Simplistically, I made an assumption: it has to be me or the woman I was with. But since it had happened with two different women, I figured it was me (though there might have been similarities between the women and the situations). But since I had performed sexually in a normal way many times in the year between these incidents, I assumed that it has to be something about these particular women in combination with me.

My immediate concern was my own fright. The "no erection at the right time" syndrome had happened to me twice. I was scared, very scared. Images of impotence hung in the air and wouldn't disappear. So I got in touch with an old love who I still spend a loving night or two with every five or six months and with whom I had always had good sexual chemistry. We got together two nights later and history prevailed: my penis had its timing back and I performed like the stud I was always meant to be. Which was a tremendous relief.

But I still had no answer to my question: why didn't I get an erection at the right time on two different occasions when I was with women I wanted to be with and who wanted to be with me, when there was mutual attraction and social/political/intellectual compatibility? I had a few clues, a few hunches, a few theories. But at best they were very partial answers. So I started to do a lot of thinking and isolated myself from old loves and potential new ones. I decided to read a lot of 19th-century porno literature, hoping that there might be repeated patterns (and there were) of male/female sexual activities that I could learn something from. (I realize now that this was a cop-out, a refusal or inability to look at my self, my own sexual experience; and that to look at "other" sexuality, to learn from second-hand experience, was a safer path and one of less resistance. And for that reason, too, it may actually have been the only way I could start the examination.) I also read a lot of feminist writings, and continued to have many and long talks with a few close friends, all of whom are intensely involved with the liberation of people. I learned much during this time (a lot of which I already knew but couldn't make cohere), not all of which lends itself to this essay. But it all fed into an increasingly less diffuse puzzle.

Incident 3. This occasion was similar in almost all respects to Incidents 1 and 2, occurring about 18 months after the first incident and 6 months after the second. Between the second and third incidents, my sexual life had again been normal (for me).

This time I wasn't as frightened because I had already begun to figure out what the fuck was going on and had the reassurance that I was determined enough to maybe, just maybe, see it through to solution. Again, the woman was supportive and someone who I had gone through many things with over the years: this was just going to be another thing that we would have to deal with. Also, there was some hope because perceptions were beginning to clump together.

It became increasingly clear to me that in order to find answers to my emerging questions, I would have to go back and retrace the steps that were parts of my sexual history. Simultaneously, I was thinking that if my socialized sexuality was in any way similar to that of other men, then my formulations wouldn't be idiosyncratic to my experience. And as clues found me, I remembered old talks with young male friends and checked them against recent talks with adult male friends. It seemed that we had all gone through a basically similar process (with countless variations). Even those males who had not conformed to the norm, who didn't perform sexually according to the book, were affected by the norm process (sometimes resulting in a devastating social and sexual isolation). So I thought it would be worth the effort to construct a norm, however flawed, to determine what shape that image took. And to see if that image could teach.

The Initiation of a Young Male: In looking back on my sexual experiences and those of male friends, a very definite and sequential pattern was evident. I'm talking about actual (overt) sexual events, not subliminal or imagined or representational sexual experiences. I'm thinking of adolescent times in adolescent terms when males begin to experiment and develop their knowledge and expertise. I'm thinking about things you did sequentially as you got older. With a few total exceptions and an odd irregularity or two (like fucking a "whore" before you'd kissed a "girl") among the many men I have known and talked with, the sequence runs roughly as follows.

You kiss a girl. You kiss a girl a number of times. You kiss a girl continuously (make-out). You kiss a girl continuously and get your tongue into the act. All through this process you learn to use your hands to round out the orchestration, at first with simple clumsy chords and later with complex harmonies (with the woman, of course, being the instrument made to respond to the musician). You, as a young male, are told (or figure out) what sensitive spots you should seek, and learn more as the young female (hopefully) responds to your hands. First you just hug and grasp. Then you make little circles on her shoulders with your fingers. Then you go for the back of the neck, and run your fingers through her hair (music, please), and then over her face and throat. Then the outer ear (lobes especially). And middle ear. Then lower back (at which point your tongue might cover the ear as a stand-in for the absent hand). The the tender sides of the waist above the (maybe-not-yet) hip bones. Then the belly. And after, the upper belly and the rib cage. Here let us take a deep breath before the great leap upward to the breast, which is a bold act broken into a number of ritualistic steps. First the hand over one breast, with blouse and bra between your hand and the female's flesh. This is a move that took special courage (balls?) and was very exciting for it seemed a new level of sensuality (which it was for the female, but for the male? no, only a new level of expectation). Then came a kind of figure-eight roving over the chest from one breast to the other (if your position allowed—how many right-handed lovers out there?). Then a sneaking between buttons (later unbuttoned) so your hand is on the breast with only the bra separating you from flesh. (Or if this procedure was too uncouth or too visible to others in the dusky room or impossible because of a no-button sweater, you worked underneath the garment from a fleshy belly right up to the bra.) Then, by means of gradually developed finger dexterity, you begin to attack the flesh of the breast itself, working down from the top of the bra into the cup. And if you hadn't yet picked up any signs of female complicity in your previous experience, it was often clear here. If she sat and breathed normally, your fingers didn't stand a chance (bras were worn very tightly in my junior high school so that nipples were always pointing up at your eyes). If she wanted to be helpful, she would deeply exhale and move her shoulder forward so there was space between the bra and the breast. (Women's cooperation during all these events is an interesting topic and really should be written about by a woman.) And here came the rainbow's gold—the assault on the nipple. While a kiss was exciting, and cupping a breast breathtaking, the conquest of the nipple was transcendent. Partly because it was the only part of a female's anatomy that we have dealt with so far that isn't normally seen or even partly exposed. Also because you knew that when this was achieved, the girl really liked you, and that getting the bra unhooked and off would not be far away. Maybe as soon as next week. When older, the same night. And you also sensed that you were getting closer to the core of sexuality (excuse the geographically mixed metaphor). Then began the assault on the crotch, in steps similar to those of the battle of the breast. You caressed her hip, worked around to her ass, pulled her close to announce (if it hadn't already been discovered) the existence of your penis and give it some pleasurable friction (and provide the girls with a topic of gossip later? if you were erect). Then you worked down to the side of her leg. Then the front of her thigh. Then with a deep breath, and microscopic steps, you slowly progressed toward the vaginal entrance (how many of you had imagined the entrance 4 inches higher than you found it to be?). Now here there are many variables: was it at a swim party when she only had on the bottom part of a two-piece suit, or was she wearing jeans, or did she have a skirt on? Whatever the case, you usually ended up rubbing her crotch through cloth and then worked down from her belly toward her crotch, getting your hand (as one variation of the phrase goes) in her pants. Then you sort of played around above or on top of her slit and eventually got a finger in it, and by accident or design (depending on your previous intelligence briefings) found the "magic button." And soon (usually), all hell broke loose, and more than ever before, you didn't quite know what to do with yourself if fucking wasn't yet in the script.

And that pretty much covers the pre-coital scenario. Except it was described in a semi-humorous manner and, as a male, many of these events were terrifying. You, most often, had to take the first step. And you could be rejected. Refused. Denied. Cold and flat. And that could hurt. Hurt bad. In your own eyes and in your male friends' eyes. Being scared to try and therefore not trying could just as easily become the subject of psychological self-punishment and social ostracism. So there was always this elementary duality: while apparently the aggressor and conqueror, you were captive to a judgment by the female who would accept or reject you.

Also important to remember is how these events were reported to/discussed with male friends after the party or date. Or gone over in your mind, again and again, detail by detail. How every step along the initiation route was stimulating and could/did cause an erection (remember the 4-hour erections and blue balls?). How we compared notes, made tactical suggestions, commented on important signs—heavier breathing, torso writhing, aggressive hands, a more daring tongue, involvement of teeth, goose bumps, erected nipples, and when menstruation occurred or was expected to occur. Which girls liked what, since in those days "relationships" were short-lived and you never knew which female you might be with another time. And if you were ever in doubt as to what came next in the scenario, your friends informed you of the specifics of the next escalation. And sometimes, if that wasn't possible, the female you were with (em-

barrassingly enough) let you know in any one of a number of subtle (or not-so-subtle) ways what was next on the agenda.

There were, in retrospect, many funny occasions that cropped up in
this initiation process. I don't really need to talk about them because you probably have your own to tell. What stuns me now is
that origins of the tragedy of sex emerge clearly from that process of
socialized sexuality.

Three elements seem to reappear constantly in every step of the development of male sexual stimulus and response: Objectification,
Fixation, and Conquest. (Idealization is a romantic concept that is
both bible and aspirin for the three basic elements and tends to obfus-
cate them.) In any given situation, the order of occurrence and importance of these elements varies, but I believe the order given corre-

> **Part of male sexual initiation is
> learning to fixate on portions of the
> female's anatomy: at first, breasts,
> and later, that hidden unknown
> quantity, the vagina.**

sponds to the chronological reality (most of the time) and is more easily
discussed.

Objectification: From a very young age, males are taught by
everyone to objectify females (except Mom?). They generalize the
female, in an almost platonic sense. This generalized woman is a
concept, a lump sum, a thing, an object, a non-individualized category.
The female is always "other." Against this backdrop males begin,
when society allows, overtly to exercise bits of their sexuality.

Males learn to objectify through a process of "definition." We
identify, and have identified for us, many female attributes. It starts
simply: girls have long hair, wear ribbons in it, have on dresses,
and like pink and yellow things. And, of course, they play with dolls.
Then comes a sexual understanding: females have no penis, bear chil-

dren, have breasts, thinner waists, and hips that swell. Until we realize the vagina's existence, we think females are missing their penis and in its absence is a void (are they incomplete?). As we accrue this knowledge, the female social role has already been defined everywhere for us. If we play hospital, the little girls are, of course, the nurses and we, of course, the doctors. If it's time for exercise at school, they play hopscotch while we play football. When it's time to learn practical living skills, they sew and bake while we use tools and build. They are easily recognized as different. There's them and there's us. And who'd want to do a silly girl's thing anyhow?

Fixation: Part of male sexual initiation is learning to fixate on portions of the female's anatomy: at first, breasts, and later, that hidden unknown quantity, the vagina. Somewhere, in some deep cavern in our brain, before we consciously know about sexuality, it must register on us that we never see males touching the female chest or lower belly. And in movies, on TV, in advertisements, where else can we look when the camera's eye focuses on breasts? So our eye is trained and we fixate. Emotionally, too. We learn that if we do that, we will eventually get pleasure and have fun. And be men. Be seen as male. Be reacted to as male.

Because of the way we are socialized, erection follows fixation or occurs in a situation in which fixation plays a role. We observe this coincidence. We learn we can *will* an erection without a woman being near us. And since it is pleasurable (and, at first, astounding), since it gives us assurance that we are male, we create erections out of our imagination, by merely objectifying a female of our choice, fixating on the parts of her body that excite, and usually manipulating that body (see Conquest, below). By denying this process, by repressing our desire and fantasy, we avoid embarrassing erections in public, which is vital since we are always "seeing" breasts and vaginas, hundreds of them, which have the potential of putting us into gear. So we exercise control over our penis while often saying that our penis has a mind of its own—all of which is true.

Conquest: To conquer is a highly valued skill in our society. We are taught to alter the enemy into nothingness, to convert the bear into a stuffed head and rug, to gain power and rule. It's very much either/or: you're a winner or a loser, a good guy or a bad guy, someone who's made it or hasn't. Male initiation rites and activities always require trophies (e.g., sports) and the more numerous and advanced your "awards," the more of a man you are. In sexual matters, the male conquers when he succeeds in reducing the female from a being into a thing and achieves some level or form of sexual gratification—a kiss, or your hand on her breast, or intercourse, depending on your age, sexual advancement, and surrounding social norms. Conquest logically (ahem) follows Objectification and Fixation. I mean, after all, what the hell's the sense of objectifying and fixating if you're not going to get off your ass and do a little conquering? And when we do conquer, what is the trophy? In the old days it might have been a lock of hair or a garter strap. A ring can also announce your achievement. But always, your own knowledge of what transpired is your reward—being pleased with yourself and being able to say to yourself, "I am a man." And if others have knowledge of your conquest, your knowing that they know is as great an award as any.

That, in brief, is the Objectification/Fixation/Conquest dynamic. The implications and ramifications of these elements of socialized sexual responses are staggering and too numerous to attempt to list and discuss here. But let me offer one implication (as an example) that seems realistic to me: that male sexual responses have little (or nothing) to do with the specific female we are with at any given moment. Any number of lips or breasts or vaginas would do—as long as we can objectify, fixate, and conquer an erection and (provided there is some form of penile friction) ejaculation will occur.

If this example rubs you the wrong way, think about the existence and effectiveness of pornography, both verbal and photographic. What pornography does is create a fertile environment that makes it "natural" for the imagination to objectify, fixate on, and conquer a verbally or photographically depicted female. So without even a female being present in the flesh, the penis grows. Now you may say that the female *is* present, that is, in the male mind. And I'd agree, but the female is not physically there. So in a certain sense, most males become a self-contained sexual system—not homo- or heterosexual, but self-sexual.

This shouldn't surprise anyone: it's based in our physiology and it's based in society's denial of sexual gratification. But, on conscious and unconscious levels, this is threateningly close to homosexuality. Because having a penis and getting erections is equivalent to maleness and ego, it seems that what's important to us as males is the male genitalia, and that might appear suspect to the puritan heterosexual mind-set.

How then do we draw the line between our own penis and all those other penises which are virtually identical to our own? The answer: we do to our penis what we do to females. We objectify it, fixate on it, and conquer it. In that way we "thingify" our penis, make it "other," so that we can talk about "it" and apologize for "its" behavior and laugh at "it" as if it were a child on the rambunctious side whom we can't control. So we have confirmed "its" separateness from us. We can even give our penis a name, like John Thomas or Peter, which states positively to the world that our penis is its own man. (And therefore we are not responsible for its actions?)

Because our penis is central to our own sense of ego and manhood, it is natural that anything that causes erections (with the resulting pleasure and power and self-identification) is to be used. Objectification/Fixation/Conquest of females allows us to function this way. Because we have been socialized to respond that way. So we *do* function that way (nothing succeeds like success, etc.).

Now there is a new female before us. Without really knowing her, without really knowing (or caring?) what she thinks or feels, we "like" her. Because she is female. Because she is "other" and with her you will be your self—a male in a potential relationship that reestablishes, affirms, proves your manhood. Which means that at the moment of meeting, we have already objectified the female. And for our maleness, this is a necessary first step which permits us to fixate and hopefully go on to conquer so that our climax can strengthen our ego and sense of maleness. When you hear a man "complain" that he's slept with his wife "hundreds of times, and each time I have to seduce her as if she was a virgin,'" you observe a woman who has learned her lessons too well and a man who loves responding to them (though I don't mean this to be an example of a typical relationship). Seduction, in its crudest sense and crassest form, is nothing more than Fixation and Conquest made possible because the male has already made a generalized object out of a specific female. (Listen to the language: cunt, tits, pussy, boobs, snatch, jugs . . .) This is the procedure males follow to get their sexual machinery into gear (with many personal idiosyncrasies, which is why prostitutes keep careful notes on the likes and dislikes of their clientele). Again, pornography and its effectiveness is telling us that we needn't have a real, living, breathing female with us to respond sexually. What is needed for a good old healthy erection to occur is the opportunity to objectify, fixate, and conquer.

Well, now we have some clues as to how our penis gets socialized and what it responds to, and there are endless questions to ask. But my first question is: What happened to me on those three occasions when I didn't get it up at the proper time?

Tell me how this sounds. My relationship to the woman and the woman's relationship to me was similar in all three instances. They were

> **The terrifying evidence is that we males never are dealing with the whole female being at the beginning of a relationship.**

women I knew very well. They were people I liked very much. Liked because they were decent, liked because they were loving, liked because they were involved in the struggle (at great risk and cost) to make this world a better place. But with them, though I find them very attractive, I didn't automatically play stud the way I had been socialized to do. Because I knew them as whole beings, I couldn't objectify them, and consequently couldn't fixate on (though I tried) or conquer them. And they didn't put pressure on me to do that (and as women can, and do, for a variety of reasons). So, I didn't play my role and they didn't play theirs. No roles; no seduction, no Objectification/Fixation/Conquest—ergo, no erection (except at those odd, non-propitious times when I was probably unconsciously fixating on a part of their body or fantasizing and got the penis into gear).

We spent, I think, very intimate and sensuous moments together. And since those evenings, we've talked about what happened. And about this essay (each of the women has read it). And we'll spend other evenings together, trying to learn about the damage, the terrible damage, that has been done to all of us. And stopping its continuance. And trying to undo as much of it as we can. Well, that's one possible explanation for the "no erection at the right time" mystery. And I come off looking pretty good. Looking pretty damn egalitarian. At least I did until I talked to a friend who, given the same information, had an entirely different interpretation of what happened. Her version follows.

I have, to a certain degree, re-socialized myself and become liberated because I was able to accept these women on all levels as equals. Except for one level: I was not capable of accepting females as sexual equals. I held onto this last bastion of male supremacy with a death-grip. I was willing to deal with these women on a human (rather than male-to-female) basis, except in relating to them sexually, where I still had to deal with them on an objectify, fixate, and conquer basis. But since I couldn't objectify them, I rejected these women rather than give up my last heirloom of maleness. I totally refused to allow them to sexually stimulate or arouse me. By preventing my penis from getting into gear, I ironically preserved my male superiority in the situation. This is because the women, who also need to be re-socialized, would not understand that my lack of erection was a result of fearing that I was going to lose touch with the last remnant of male socialization. They could not understand that I was in fact forestalling my own liberation because I lacked the courage or the knowledge necessary for the last step. What the women would feel is that I have rejected them, since they knew other women stimulated me sexually. They would feel that there is something wrong with them, some way in which they are lacking, if they can't arouse me. So in refusing to allow myself to be stimulated by them, I have in fact turned the tables and made them feel inadequate in relation to me. In making them feel inadequate, I made them doubt the very thing in themselves that I was doubting in myself—sexuality. And while they are pretty liberated, it is the area of their own sexuality which they still have to deal with more.

Well, there's another explanation for the syndrome. And I don't come off looking so good. In fact, I look rather bad. Even desperate. It's an interpretation that is fairly consistent and contains energy.

When I first heard it, it really threw me, which gives some credence to its validity. Then I thought, although my friend's interpretation is interesting, I really think mine is more accurate. But that may be male equivocation. Also, I'm not sure that the two interpretations are mutually exclusive (to explain that would take another essay). But the important points to remember are that we still have much to learn and that there are alternatives to avoiding, fearing, and ignoring present sexual realities. If we nurture our blindness and cheer our resistance to change, the damage will continue and worsen.

Some of you may be thinking that because all three instances dealt with the first night of a relationship, the analyses are invalid. And some of you may be thinking that even if a relationship begins in a classical sex-role way, the couple can still grow beyond the male/female roles that they embodied when they first met. I agree, but with major qualifications. I have seen relationships that never grow beyond where they began. No comment necessary. I have also seen relationships that have grown, but I think we have to ask: What is the nature of that growth? What do they grow from? I think those are important questions because when the shit hits the fan in a relationship, friends of the couple will often say things like: "After all those years . . ."; "It's hard for me to believe . . ."; "Of all the couples we knew, they seemed . . ."; "It came out of nowhere . . ."; "I just can't understand . . ." Was the couple's break-up really "unexpected"? There are surprises, I think, only if certain basic questions were never asked, existing realities not examined, and alternatives not explored.

The terrifying (to me) evidence is that we males never are dealing with the whole female being at the beginning of a relationship. We have been socialized, on behalf of our penis, to divide a woman's body up. The vernacular of males is usually a dead give-away and varies from slightly crude to incredibly crude. Phrases like "I'm an ass man" or "a breast man" or "a cunt man" or "a leg man" are common self-perceptions and self-descriptions. The street jargon of males watching females stroll by is similar: "Would I like to get my hands on those tits" or "Look at that beaver [cunt]" or "I could suck those sweet nipples for days." The refined professor in the yard gazing at a coed amongst the grass and trees might offer up "a veritable Diana with alabaster orbs" in a non-iambic mode. But the phenomenon is the same. Fixation. That is how we see. We objectify (generalize) the woman and then we fixate on a physical characteristic. And even later in a relationship, when to varying degrees we do deal with the whole female person, very often we snap back into our original sex roles (as if sleeping together for the first time?). We do it because that is how we have been socialized to act and respond. We do it because it is the path of least resistance. We do it. It is the only way we know.

During the past year I have tried to call up and reabsorb conversations I have had with various males over the years concerning females I've also spent a lot of time talking to all kinds of males, working class and professional, young single males and males who are "happily married and have three lovely children." When sexual fantasies were discussed, I found that there are very similar fantasies among most males.

The fantasy is revealing. "The ideal turn-on would be two or three women at once, who are lesbians, and who are of different racial/cultural origins." Why is this the super dream? Simple: it allows for magnified Objectification, Fixation, and Conquest. Two or three women are more than one. Lesbians are by definition the most difficult conquest, so they are potentially the greatest trophy, the strongest vitamin for building health egos and solid definitions of self as powerful male. Differing racial/cultural origins add exotic uniqueness and make one a universal image of manhood. And this, remember, is the common fantasy of what are normally regarded as sexually healthy, well-adjusted males.

So, while many relationships do grow beyond the initial sex-role encounters, I think it becomes increasingly clear that the growth is upon a diseased foundation. And as a result, there are built-in limitations (and too often, built-in tragedies) in relationships as we know them—which means perhaps all relationships we have seen, known, or been personally involved in. And that is why we can no longer feign surprise when a relationship we consider good and mature begins to crumble and the old sex roles come exploding off the blocks like sprint champions. It happens in many forms, depending on the cultural/educational/economic backgrounds of the people involved. But it does happen. Has happened. Will continue to happen—if left unexamined.

I've spoken to a number of friends about this essay and asked them to read it and offer criticisms. They did. Some were nervous, some astounded, some calm, some just smiled. But most of them agreed with the general thrust of the argument (there were disagreements over specifics). And we talked for many hours about sexuality. But our discussions didn't have an immediate or visible effect on our existing realities. Because we have all been thoroughly socialized. We are all trained actors. Character actors. Method actors. And no method actor with 20 years or more experience is going to lose his skill, forget or confuse his role, miss the lines at the right time, unless the script is re-written or eliminated, the sets changed, and the desires and expectations of the cast, stage hands, directors, and audience re-socialized.

I want to ask people to do that, but I can't. Because I don't know what that kind of re-socialization entails. I have some vague ideas, but at this point I'm struggling. I can't offer any simple answers. Obviously, there are many risks involved. Some of my male and female friends, who are pretty open and enlightened people, have said that they would rather keep things the way they are if trying to change them is going to cause doubt, pain, and an awful lot of work. I suspect that those conditions will have to be a step in the transition (although easier than we think); men and women are going to have to be prepared for rough times and be ready to deal with them. But when I look around me and see the alternatives to taking risks and living with uncertainty, those alternatives are so unpalatable that the need to change becomes a command. Even though it's not going to be a rose garden. At least for a while.

I would like to raise a few questions. I think all of them have been asked before. And they have been answered before. But I would like to ask them again and attempt at least partially to answer them in the context of the socialized penis. I'm very aware that these questions don't have simple answers, and I don't want to discount other answers that have been offered. I have read answers to these questions that I have agreed with. But my intention isn't to definitively answer these questions by exploring all info available. My intention is much less ambitious: to see what (if any) new perspectives are available by placing the questions against the backdrop of Objectification/Fixation/Conquest. Some of the "answers" may seem old hat; others may seem substantively different; still others may strike you as foolish. What really matters is that we all understand that there's so much more to learn and so many essays and personal accounts that still need to be written.

My attempted "answers," even within their defined context, aren't sufficiently thorough and aren't intended to be the last word on anything. So consider each "answer" a question, and deal with your own shit.

Why do so many men fear women's liberation? One of the things that terrifies men about the women's movement is that women are talking to each other. About themselves. But also about men. And that as women do this, the man's game is up, his strategy is laid bare, and he feels the threat of becoming objectified. As his machinations, maneuvers, and *modus operandi* become known, he won't be able to perpetrate the fraud that he is something special to his woman (women?), since many women are getting to know that all men do pretty much the same things in striving to empty their sacs. Now, many women have known this all along but have either kept quiet about it or repressed their knowledge of it because they have been socialized to do so and because there are pressures that bear down hard if they don't. And men didn't know, or pretended not to know, that women knew; so they thought they were always successful in convincing their women that they were special and unique (and therefore a valuable commodity). And now that men are being exposed, some of them are cowering in their nudity. As a close woman friend once wrote to me—"Men don't marry harlots; they know too much."

Why do men hate women? Not too many men will admit to this, and I'm not sure what percentage of men actually do hate women. But more than a few women believe men do. And I think a number of men do hate women but aren't aware of it.

To hate someone (because of race, religion, or political belief), you must first de-humanize them, make them sub-human. After you have done this, you can hate them (and even be righteous about it) because they aren't worthy of human regard, consideration, or treatment (e.g., "gooks"). When men objectify (generalize) women, they take the female's human-ness away, making her less than human, non-specific, sub-human. This allows men to carry out their role with women, exert their power over them. But if a man has a bit of decency lurking in his brain (and I like to think most do), he hates himself for having been evil enough to destroy the female: that is, evil enough to have taken a whole breathing thinking feeling human being and to have made something less than human of it. He also dislikes himself for the crude games he plays, the strategies he develops and implements to relieve "the torment of the testicles." And he may even resent the fact that this role is demanded of him and that he is a prisoner to it.

But all this is difficult for a man to realize or admit about himself. And deal with consciously. So he transfers the hate to the woman for making him act in a less than human way and she thereby becomes responsible for his sub-human actions. So she is made sub-human a second time because the man feels she is the one who caused him to be sub-human. So he hates her. Hates her even though he is the one who is the de-humanizer. And because her existence, as a socialized woman, reminds him of this. Constantly. . . .

Why do men get jealous? If a woman rebels (flirts, denies him sex, has an affair), it lets the man know that he has failed to de-humanize his woman, failed to make her his subject. Therefore, he is a failure, less than a whole man, with cracked ego and lost manhood. And this thought doubles back because he feels that that is why his woman prefers other men who are more manly than he. (And what if she's *right?*)

Why do men go to other women? In relationships that grow beyond the initial sex-role-playing, a time often comes when the man can no longer conquer his woman because she is willing and there. But the man has had his penis socialized (and his brain along with it) to feel manly when he is fixating and conquering. And he may by now know her too well even to be able to fixate on her, since he has probably come to realize that her breasts and vagina are connected to the rest of her being. So the old excitement isn't there. "Something" has gone out of the relationship.

Another explanation for why men run to other women is that other women are closer to being whole human beings (like their loves once were). The other woman is by definition more attractive, more interesting, a potential new trophy, while his wife (or lover) is a less-than-whole human whom he has already de-humanized. When (if) he conquers this new other woman, and succeeds in de-humanizing her, the man will tire of her also and look for yet another close-to-whole female being.

Men who are not capable of running around are often considered suspect by men who do run around. Again, the crude male vernacular tells the story: "She's got him by the balls." Or: "He's pussy-whipped."

Why is premature ejaculation a problem? There are three varieties of premature ejaculation. The first is a result of some anthropological studies which suggest that all Western men ejaculate too soon; but since this problem has been discussed elsewhere and is considered the norm, it will not be discussed here.

The second variety of premature ejaculation is described by that great teenage pre-coital phrase—"coming in your pants." Which translates as ejaculating before the reality seems to warrant it. The third variety is ejaculating before the woman has orgasm (what if she doesn't have orgasm?). Both of these latter varieties lead us back to the way the penis is socialized: it responds to Fixation and Conquest. Usually men come too soon because they are having fantasies which include Fixation and Conquest. They are not really sleeping with/involved with the woman in their arms.

When I was in my teens there was a common bit of advice provided by experienced males on the subject of premature ejaculation. It was: "Think of garbage cans" (oh, the power and beauty of language). Which was profound advice although no one knew why. What the advice means is: if you think of garbage cans, that is, if you interrupt your Fixation and Conquest syndrome, you will interrupt your sexual functioning. When the time is right, forget the garbage cans, and you'll ejaculate on schedule. So the problem of premature ejaculation is really rooted in the factors which caused the present kind of penis socialization to develop.

Why are men afraid of "nymphomaniacs"? If you're laughing at this question you'd better figure out why the ideal turn-on of most males is a lesbian and not a "nympho."

"Nymphomaniacs," by definition, can't be conquered. In fact, they may be objectifying/fixating/conquering the man. Instead of using,

> A female homosexual makes a man feel unnecessary, inadequate, and un-manly because she doesn't need men. A male homosexual makes a woman feel unnecessary, inadequate and un-womanly because he doesn't need women.

the man is being used. He is nothing special or unique to this woman—she's had a hundred more like him. So sleeping with her undermines the man's definition of self. Also, because a "nympho" is defined as insatiable, a man (in his heart of hearts) knows his limitations but his ego isn't likely to let him admit this easily. So the "nympho" is feared because she destroys the male role in a very basic way.

Why do some people have an aversion to homosexuality? The simple answer is that all of us have been socialized to fear/hate/scorn homosexuality. For that reason, I may not be capable of dealing with homosexuality in a non-prejudiced manner. The only non-partisan reason I can think of for my aversion to homosexuality is that most homosexuals I have known have not transcended the sexual roles we are all damaged by. They have their male and female too and are playing the same games we play except that they play them with members of their own sex. Which may explain part of our aversion: namely, we dislike homosexuals because they are epitomies of what our roles are, of how we act, as males and females. In that way, they are an insult to us. They mock us, make a joke of us, seem to caricature what we really look and act like if only we had the sufficient distance from ourselves to rationally observe our actions.

There is another obvious, perhaps too obvious, reason for our fear of homosexuals. A female homosexual makes a man feel unnecessary, inadequate, and un-manly because she doesn't need men. A male homosexual makes a woman feel unnecessary, inadequate and un-womanly because he doesn't need women. And nothing in our socialization has prepared us for not being needed by members of the opposite sex.

Why do men masturbate? Because it feels good and it's fun. It may be a natural outgrowth of our unnatural sexual socialization. It provides sexual release and may be the only sane choice (as opposed to abstinence or rape, for example) where there are no other alternatives.

Perhaps we should first ask: how do men successfully masturbate? First, the penis (sensitive thing that it is) responds to friction, if that friction is connected with Fixation and Conquest (that is why underpants and zippers by themselves do not constantly have all men walking around with erections all the time). And secondly, the penis has been socialized to respond to the imaginings of Fixation and Conquest.

So, when men are in a situation or society where social intercourse does not result in genital intercourse, men may masturbate for any one of (or combination of) a number of reasons. It feels good. It's amazing to see what their own body can do. They're "horny." They fear impotence, and masturbation (inadequately) alleviates that fear for a while. They played around with a woman for a few hours but they didn't make it into bed, and their balls hurt, and masturbating is an effective way of relieving that pain or pressure. They don't want to "attack" a woman (let's say, on a first date), so they masturbate to insure their penis won't be in control of their social actions that evening. If they are impotent with women, or if they have no one to sleep with, masturbation provides sensual pleasure. And most important, ejaculation defines one as male: so if you're not "shacked up," or having an affair, or married, masturbation allows a man to continue defining himself as male, as a power, as a conqueror.

I wrote this essay during the summer of 1971. From the beginning I was annoyingly aware of the limitations of what I was doing. I knew it was a narrow exploration, a formulation that would help me deal with one aspect of male sexual socialization. It also had an undercurrent of behaviorism, which I don't like and didn't want; but I just wrote, and what happened is what you read. The essay isn't, and wasn't intended to be, a consistent historical tract or sociological treatise. Nor was its design political, in the worldly sense. I felt the need, and thought I saw the reasons, to stay fairly specific.

Because it's easy to escape. From self and others. It's safer to be all-inclusive in generalized "out there" ways. It's tempting to become resigned to the "realities," to let the definition of the disease become an argument that supports the disease's continuance. To say, "Yes, I'm damaged, but just look around at the whole fucking world and how messed up it is and how the hell can I change until all those things out there change, allow me to change, help me to alter my being?"

I agree: it is near-impossible for any one of us to change the world. I agree: it is difficult to change the self if the world remains a constant (especially since self is contained in the definition of world). But the world doesn't change by itself, and the one place the individual *can* begin is with self, translating self to the world in a personal, rather than grand, political way. (And maybe, at some time, in a grand, political way, too.)

Perhaps the greatest short-coming of the essay is its avoidance of political and societal questions. "Does unalienating work necessarily result in unalienated sexuality?" "In what ways does patriarchy determine social-sexual roles?" "To what extent does our physiology affect our social development?" And many others. All vital questions, but ones which permit the possibility of escaping one's self. And since what I've read is largely political or scientific or psychological, and predominantly academic, I thought it might be meaningful to deal with a specific topic, from a personal and self-specific stance.

Another problem was trying to envision the audience. Males only? Males and females? Whichever individual happens to be reading the words? I didn't have an answer to that, though I tended to conceive of it as a dialogue with men. But what if the essay alienated some men who didn't share my experience of "normal" sexual socialization? I couldn't discover anything close to a perfect solution to the whole question of audience (or voice). So I wrote by feel and instinct. And if I've insulted or harmed anyone, that wasn't the intent.

During the six months I re-read and re-thought what I had written, yet another problem became apparent: the essay raised many questions (direct and indirect) which I didn't deal with. And now that I've done the final re-write, I still haven't dealt with them. Because the discussion is endless and I'm just not up to writing a monstrous tome. So I avoided tangents and detours and tried to exercise self-restraint. And also because many of the questions are questions I can't answer.

Another point of information. Throughout the essay I used the word "socialized" rather than a word like "conditioned." Intentionally. A word like "conditioned" loses sight of who does what to whom. The word "socialized" never lets you forget that there are many things—males, females, cultures, societies, institutions, nations—that do it to all of us. Not the maligned mother or mythified father, but everyone and everything that embodies and fosters sexual role-playing. And I didn't want to lose sight of that larger context, even though my parameters overtly excluded it.

All this as explanation. And premature apology. And maybe self-defense.

Surviving Gay Coupledom

Karla Jay

I. EXTERNAL STRESS

There is a persistent myth among both heterosexuals and homosexuals that long-term relationships are a trait of heterosexuality, whereas social interrelations among homosexuals comprise brief and frequent encounters in dark bars, tea rooms, and bushes in the local park. This so-called "promiscuous" homosexual is the one put forth to the public in novels and movies with rare exceptional "stable" couples shown in movies such as *That Certain Summer*. Undoubtedly, the promiscuous homosexual *does* exist in visible numbers, just as the stereotypical fag hairdresser or designer is also a reality.

However, there are no reliable statistics to show what percentage of gay people do *not* fit this stereotype. Although my contacts are large and international in scope because I do a great amount of traveling and speaking on behalf of gay liberation, even I am relying here on my own sampling, which is naturally biased because one would assume that I associate with those who have something in common with me—that is, other couples.

Despite the unscientific base of my sample, my conclusion is this: the proportion of gay couples is probably almost as large as the percentage of heterosexual couples, and the spectrum of types of relationships is at least as large—that is, gay couples range from those who are completely monogamous to "swingers" and "spouse-swappers," and gay singles range from asexual (but gay-identified) or "one-at-a-time" individuals to numbers-counters who notch their bedposts.

Legally, of course, all gay people are considered "single"—that is, one can't file a joint income tax form with one's lover and one can't

> Heterosexuals have a vested interest in seeing us as "the Other" . . . that is, the more unlike them we are, the more they will be able to point us out and hopefully keep us at a safe distance.

pass on any benefits or rate reductions such as social security or health insurance to a gay spouse, so I'd like to make it clear that I use the words "single" and "couple" only in a social context. I'm sure, however, that no one will argue this point, nor will many people of any sexual orientation deny the wide range of gay sexuality. However, probably many gay liberationists as well as heterosexuals will want to deny for different reasons that a relatively large proportion of gay couples exists.

Naturally heterosexuals have a vested interest in seeing us as "the Other," as Simone de Beauvoir might put it—that is, the more unlike them we are, the more they will be able to point us out and hopefully keep us at a safe distance, for if they can't do that, how will they distinguish us from them? And if we are just like them, a further step might make us them—or worse yet, them us. For homosexuality—unlike blackness or womanhood—is "contagious." A white man won't wake up one morning to find himself black or a woman, but he might become "queer" just as millions in this country are gay without any adequate medical, psychological, or sociological explanation. We are inexplicable, and, ergo, no one has a clue to immunity! We are greatly to be feared. It is thus no mistake that the phrase "Pinko Commie queer" emerged. If we deny the majority's vested sexual interests, we must be "Commies"—against the family, God and Country, haters of Mom and apple pie, and fancy-free, footloose hedonists.

It's all a neat package: Again, some of us fit this description; others don't. Many gay people, including myself, do oppose the nuclear family and with good reason, for it is this neat foursome (Ozzie, Harriet, and two kids) which was always held before us and which was a prime instrument of an oppressive atmosphere which conspired but failed to make us "straight."

Some of the "radicals" go even a step further: They automatically eschew any traditional heterosexual value, just as heterosexuals have condemned in wholesale fashion the lives and loves of gay people. To this way of thinking, since heterosexuals have traditionally lived in couples, such a lifestyle must be pronounced "perverse," and one is told to live in threesomes, foursomes, collectives, and alone—in short, everything but . . .

Of course, monogamy—the preached but rarely practiced virtue of the heterosexual—has got to go, too. In addition to being a trait of those other people, monogamy is flagrant capitalism. The argument, if I can put it succinctly, is that having a "mate" is part of the whole hang-up of having property. Marriage and its ills are even traced back to when the nomads became cultivators and thus the first capitalists.

This argument is also supported along anthropological and biological lines, just as homosexuals have argued (and rightly so) that homosexuality is frequent and "natural" in many animals (such as monkeys) and should therefore not be considered unnatural in humans. This reasoning also rightly points to human cultures in which homosexuality was (ancient Greece) or is almost institutionalized.

When applied to monogamy, the homosexual theorists point to all those animals out there hoofing it with more than one—dogs, elephants, and so on. The trouble with this type of argument is that it tends to neglect those animals that are monogamous, such as the wolf, and many species of birds. In fact, much like the Bible, the animal kingdom can be looked at to support any type of lifestyle: should we applaud harems just because they are supported by the wild stallion with his herd of mares?

Worse yet, such dogmatic attitudes against monogamy and couple-dom, along with downright condemnations of other heterosexual values such as a straight-male-God-the-father, drive people from our midst. Like the preachers who promised Heaven if only we would give up sex, liquor, and all worldly gain, we often promise people the abstract pleasures of liberation and self-love providing they first give up monogamy and coupledom in general, and that male chauvinist God and role-playing in particular. In short, we attempt point-blank to pull their entire value system from under their feet, and the result is that those who don't cherish anomie or who lack the proper spirit of adventure/liberation dash right back into the closet and bolt the door.

Of course, one can point to our gay churches and synagogues replete with marriage ceremonies and say that only "those radicals" are seeking another way of life, but that would deny the reality of the threat of gay liberation to the nuclear family, its traditional role-playing, and even to the nature of God him/herself. This emphasis also neglects the very real waves the radical is making, if only because those homosexuals who look and act just like the heterosexual have been so coopted into the system that they are practically invisible. Ask any newsperson! Only the ugly or different stories make the paper—if 210,000,000 do it daily, that ain't news.

It is ironic, I suppose, that I do not deny the validity of most of the "radical" concepts I have just described, whereas I do object to the usual belligerence and absolute dogmatism of the arguments. Having been told all my pre-liberated life by straights how to catch a man, I resent being told by gays how to order my current sex life. Further-more, we who have been regimented all our lives into one neat hetero box should allow for variety in others. Can't there be both monogamous and polygamous creatures among us as well as in nature?

Of course, we should encourage people to experiment with other ways of life, but let's have an end to this fascistic way of shoving our points of view down the throats of fellow homosexuals. And if we "radicals" have come to the conclusion that monogamy and/or role-playing is "wrong," we have reached that point only after months or perhaps years of raising our own consciousness on a personal/political level. Why do we expect others to grasp in a day what it took us so much blood, sweat, and years to understand? And how can we be so absolutely sure that our way is the "correct" way? We must finally realize that consciousness can be passed onto others only in a general sense (such as the fact that homosexuals are oppressed) but deep individual change comes slowly—especially change in one's whole way of relating sexually—and we must allow others the same time, mistakes, and plateaus of consciousness we ourselves had. If we insist on being dogmatic, we should aim our fierceness at dogmatism.

In addition to the heavy rhetoric driving people away, there is an underlying ambiguity. A few of the people who have the heaviest anti-couple rap have come up to me privately and informed me that they envy my long-standing relationship with my lover but fear that such a destiny is not to be their lot for a wide variety of reasons—usually based on failures of past attempts.

Even more confusing is when some of the people who swear by anti-couple lifestyles come to me for advice on how to keep together in or form new relationships, which they supposedly reject politically and personally. Why do they want me to help them when they continually scorn the nature of my relationship or put me down indirectly—when they speak abstractly of "those couples," I'm part of one too!

I suppose, however, that the ambiguity is preferable to some of the wounding put-downs. One concrete example of this is when I protested the proposed picketing of a movie on the grounds that my lover and I felt it had more merit than fault. In the heat of the discussion, all of another woman's latent hostility toward my relationship emerged. She announced that our opinion only counted as "one opinion" since we "always think alike." I'm sure that if she really knew us, she would have heard of the heated "discussions" we have continually over movies, books, and politics (to name a few areas in which we sometimes disagree), and that idea would have been quelled in a hurry! Perhaps she was implying that we are together because we like to see all our thoughts mirrored or that we naturally have the same thoughts. Sure, people must have something in common to relate, but a continuous echo would be dull and nauseating—for us at least.

More insulting was the trip she way laying on us—a trip laid on heterosexual couples too, I'm sure, especially before the advent of women's liberation; that is, whatever hubby likes, wife will like too. When the wife of this model heterosexual couple finally spoke up, and loudly too, men finally realized that she had her own mind, no matter how close her relationship to her mate. If we haven't learned this lesson from women's liberation, what have we learned?

Finally, this opinion expresses a great fear of the couple: that is, in a society of supposed singles, the couples have two voices and could form in theory a political bloc in decision-making. Again, this type of thinking about couples does not give us the credit of having individual ideas.

Furthermore, anti-couple people insist that as a couple we are unrepresentative of lesbians, without realizing that lesbianism today is predominantly represented by couples, such as Phyllis Lyon and Del Martin, Sidney Abbott and Barbara Love. They lay on us such a set of "couple" stereotypes that I sometimes feel that we should do an "Amos 'n' Andy Show." They insist that we are monogamous, which we are not. They act as if we are physically tied as if by an umbilical cord and show great surprise if I mention I have some friends who are not also friends with my lover. Or if either one of us shows up alone, they suppose the other has malaria. They must think all our mail comes addressed to Ms. and Ms.

Since we are backward enough to be in a couple, they also assume we are into role-playing, and they proceed with great authority to tell us who is who, in case we've forgotten. They forget, I suppose, that a lot of role-playing was and is enacted in the singles set as well as among couples. In any case, since I am a writer, they assume me to be the "butch" and think my lover sits home knitting. They cannot or will not see that we merely have different talents—I am verbal and my lover visually artistic—and some are shocked when they discover that two of my hobbies are cooking and gardening, and hers is ham radio, a supposedly "masculine" hobby. We *do* play roles—but only *survival* roles, and who does what best does it.

If other couples are treated this rudely, it's no wonder couples are not seen nor heard as often as they should be. However, I don't want to leave the impression that the only flack couples get is from the uncoupled. Unfortunately, other couples also oppress us. As soon as a relationship is on thin ice, the couple runs over to us for help. We have been together longer than they, so we must have the magic

> **The specific difficulties that gay couples experience within their relationships are difficult to analyze, because we suffer from many of the same problems that beset heterosexual couples.**

formula. They naively ask us what we do about various matters, as if our solution will automatically apply to them. Since they see us as stable, they lean on us—and lean and lean. To a rocky couple, and to some singles too, our stability makes us parent figures, so they feel safe to come to us to have their nervous breakdowns. You may think it's flattering for people to have so much faith in you, but after the tenth nervous breakdown each month, we disconnect the doorbell. I know of another "stable" couple who got so many advice-seekers they had to set up a special "crisis room" with a ten-day limit to make room for the next impending crisis. Of course, we care about our sisters and brothers, but we have only so much energy and would rather spend what we have on those we feel close to.

Individuals are also oppressive sometimes, making thoughtless remarks they think are compliments. For example, lots of couples and singles think they are flattering us when they tell us how pleased they are that we have managed to stay together so long—as if our function is to be their North Star in an ever-changing world. It's hard enough to have a relationship without all these people following us around with egg timers wondering if and when we will make the *Guinness Book of Records*. For us, our relationship is a matter of quality not quantity, and we stay together because we love one another. Pleasing others is extremely incidental.

Needless to say, but necessary to repeat, all types of gay people have something to contribute to the movement. If love and constructive thinking (i.e., show people alternatives, but leave the choice to them) operate, with any bitterness going to our true oppressors, then couples will feel free to come out more openly among movement people, for certainly the cause is the same one. Of course I don't speak for *all* couples, but I have a feeling that all we really want is to be treated like normal *individuals* (just as singles are treated) with a basic recognition of our lifestyle as couples and a recognition of the unique types of suffering couples undergo in a singles world.

II. INTERNAL PROBLEMS

The preceding analysis of the pressures and difficulties gay couples experience from the gay singles community in no way implies that external problems are the only ones that gay couples have to cope with. In fact, despite all external difficulties, it goes without saying that gay couples most often break up due to *internal* turmoil, although outside social pressures may be a contributing factor.

It is also true that the specific difficulties that gay couples experience within their relationships are more difficult to analyze, because we suffer from many of the same problems that beset heterosexual couples. Like heterosexuals we may fall into sexual or behavioral roles which eventually prove destructive to one or to both members of the couple. We often also suffer economic inequalities in the relationship, with one partner making more money than the other, a disparity which may cause strain in the relationship by making one partner feel "inferior" to the other or in some way inadequate. Finally, each person comes into a relationship bringing her or his own personal and cultural values which may conflict with those held by the other partner.

But while many books have been written for heterosexuals on the problems experienced within relationships, we have very little written directly for us. Often we are forced to read about how some heterosexuals have dealt with their problems and then have to transfer their solutions onto our own relationship. This process may or may not work, but at best it is inadequate. It also seems that it would be inadequate and unfair for me to offer "general" or "total" solutions in an article of this size. Therefore, I have decided that it would be better for me to relate how I have dealt with these problems in my own lesbian relationship; perhaps my own experiences will be useful to others facing the same difficulties.

First there is the problem of roles. Since neither my lover nor I was into butch/femme roles, we only had to combat other kinds of divisions of labor, which had their origins in what we came into the relationship equipped to do. For example, since I had lived by myself for six years, I was able to cook, whereas my lover had lived with her parents and knew only how to thaw food or open cans. For sheer survival I did most of the cooking until I gradually taught her how to cook, and now she does half the cooking. On the other hand, I had never learned to drive a car, and frankly I didn't particularly relish the idea of doing so. However, she taught me how to drive, and now I do half the driving. We divide even the most pleasant and unpleasant tasks equally, and the only role division is based around survival necessities. For example, I get deathly ill if I have to empty the carpet sweeper, as I am very allergic to dust, and so my lover does that task. I do other work to make up for this lopsided division of work.

As for economic differences, luckily we have none. We are both impoverished! However, what money we do have we keep separately, since we each want to feel financially independent. Having our own separate checking accounts allows us to feel free to spend money on whims, such as books or records of no interest to the other person, without feeling guilty about "wasting" communal funds. However, we pay equal amounts for most things (such as rent, food, electricity, etc.), including the car, and each item we purchase together becomes common property. In the event that one of us would make inordinately more than the other, we would divide what we put into rent, food, and so forth on a proportional basis with the larger "breadwinner" paying more.

Differing social values are the hardest to deal with, and we each came into the relationship with opposite views in many important areas. My lover believed in monogamy (although she no longer does), and I don't. She wants to spend more time with me than I care to spend with her, since I have a very strong need for time alone. At times, these differences seemed insurmountable. However, we both have an enormous amount of love for one another and try to understand and relate to the other's views and needs. I am still uncomfortable with her monogamy (since in practice she is still monogamous) as she is with my lack of it, but we have each grown more tolerant of where the other is at. And she respects my time alone, as I have come to an understanding of her need for my time and attention. The struggle has not been an easy one, nor has it ended, but it has not torn us apart either. To expect a relationship with no tension is unrealistic, but it is also impracticable to be completely obdurate about one's own position.

Finally, I would like to write about the one problem which seems to confront most homosexual couples far more than heterosexual couples: jealousy. "The jealous lesbian" seems like a stereotype laid on us by heterosexuals, but there is a lot of truth to this image for a very simple reason, which is that we socialize in groups which are usually all men or all women. In other words, each time I go out to a party or a dance, every woman in that room is a potential sex partner for my lover or me. In a similar heterosexual situation, a man would only have to worry about his female partner being attracted to another man, or vice-versa. We have fifty percent more people to worry about and thus more cause to be jealous!

And because we live in a single-sex environment, a jealousy problem among non-monogamous couples can become much more complex than in a similar heterosexual situation. For example, once my lover was jealous not only because I had another lover, but also because she too wanted to sleep with the woman I was relating to.

In addition to the jealousy problem, we face one other problem in social situations that heterosexuals don't—that is, one partner of a gay couple may be used or played with merely to get to the other partner sexually. For example, my lover was befriended and much sought after by a woman whom she thought was interested in her affection. She was then astonished to discover that the woman was really interested in becoming my lover and was using her for this end. The reverse has also been true. I have even witnessed situations in other couples in which a woman has slept with first one member of a couple and then with the other member of the couple just to separate the couple so that she could retain the first woman!

I don't really know what can be done about this situation, but I suspect that half of the solution lies in a recognition that a lot of paranoia is justified. Every woman in a lesbian community is a potential sex partner, and in many communities of limited number, breaking up another couple is the only way to obtain someone for oneself. Realizing that all involved are oppressed by such a situation, we can perhaps have more tolerance for all involved.

But no matter how many potential sex partners are out there, couples should realize that whether the relationship ultimately stands or falls depends on themselves. We stay together because of our own love or willingness and desire to stay together, and others are actually only a catalyst that may ignite an already troubled situation. For despite all external and internal problems and pressures, only the members of the couple control the course and outcome of the relationship. And that knowledge that we alone have this ultimate authority on the direction of our lives may help us survive and flourish in gay coupledom.

Thriving Decloseted in Rural Academe

Louie Crew

[Author's note: This article was written some four months after my decloseting. Now, almost a year after the letter to my bosses, I can see herein some of the marks of the oppressor still impressed upon me: most notably the erotophobia of the piece. No longer can I say that "the use of class time to talk about personal sexuality is deplorable to me." Today I am disturbed by those who abuse class time by never talking about sexuality. I feel that as gays we have much to give up-tight straight colleagues by our being, once out of the closet, inescapably the teacher as sexual person. Still, the article remains an honest statement and is a moment detached from a continuing process of personal liberation. Any pangs herein are birth pangs.]

Last November a combination of pressures led me to revise dramatically my professional self-concepts. In a letter which I read to my students, I outlined to my administrators these pressures and knowingly, irrevocably charted new directions:

> Gentlepersons:
>   I wish to take this opportunity to speak clearly to explain an unusual action which I have taken in the last five minutes of each of my classes today. I have told my students that I am gay,

---

and I have tried to explain the reasons for my so saying. These reasons are very important to me, and I would like to reiterate them.

First, I can no longer tolerate the mask of having people assume that I am what I am not. I want honesty, with other people, yes, but most essentially with myself. Sexuality is a part of any person's whole personhood, hence a part of his integrity. The use of class time to talk about personal sexuality is deplorable to me; my use of the time is merely to free people from their logical misconception about my identity. My integrity, my wholeness, demands clarity.

Second, all study for serious scholars is a passion, and all passion is in some vague way related to sexual passion. My passion for literature is definitely of one piece with all aspects of my identity. Any literature demands judgment based on human experience. I feel that my students have a right to know the potential biases of my judgments.

Third, I am involved deeply in some . . . important research into homosexuality. . . . I feel that I would be intellectually dishonest if I were to use the pronouns *they, them,* and *their* when I really meant *we, us,* and *our.* I cannot be healthy if, as a scholar, I bring one level of honesty to my research and another level of honesty to my classroom.

Fourth, sexuality is only a minor part of any person's identity. When hidden behavior is discussed, it assumes major proportion through gossip and distortion. I prefer to be open so as to minimize sexuality and to hold myself publicly accountable for my behavior. I can take no responsibility for my affections, but every responsibility for the use to which I put them.

Fifth, my many gay brothers and sisters on this campus and throughout the world need the support that can come only through leadership that is strong and healthy. I am grateful to do whatever I can, and I hope that others will not have to remain afraid and lonely so long as I chose to do. I am sensitive to the fact that the timing of anyone's coming out is immensely complicated. I am grateful that I have all along had the privilege of being of some help to such persons. I have notified campus counselors . . . volunteering my services in any way that they may be useful. I have similarly notified my Bishop and my priest. . . . I suspect that my main services will continue to be through articles and other scholarship.

I wish to make it very clear that this letter and the class statements which prompted it are not intended to be a radical confrontation. I am thoroughly committed to the assignment I have accepted here, and I am giving my fullest energies to the institution, which has my great loyalty and respect. I am not asking for any special treatment, only this brief opportunity to make it quite clear who I am. Most assuredly any dangers rightly or wrongly associated with a gay identity are hereby greatly minimized. I ask only to be judged on the quality of my work, not on factors over which none of us has control.

Finally, I wish to thank all of you for making my stay here thus far one that has been immensely enjoyable and productive. I thank you for the faith that you have shown in me, and I hope through service and work to justify your trust.

Warmly and professionally,
Louie Crew, Associate Professor

This letter was never officially answered. One dean, in confidence, admired my "courage." All others continued to treat me pleasantly, and I have not been notified of being fired, as I would have had to be by the first of February, according to faculty statutes for first-year people without tenure.

It is gratifying to report that the euphoria of that first day of revision has been at least partially sustained in many of the consequences. In my classroom, I speak from a clearer, if narrower base of authority; hence my students more freely negotiate my comments as they pick and choose in the charting of their own literary judgments. For example, I now offer as an insider my critique of Somerset Maugham's preference for heroes and anti-heroes who never share themselves openly, who never decloset, who, like Maugham himself, endure stoically, sterilely. (Cf. Noel Coward's similar gay indictment in *Song at Twilight*.) Likewise, I now possess an outsider's detachment in evaluating literary heterosexual conflicts. I no longer have to translate into my experience and ignore what is lost in translation. All of us who are gay have been living in straight families all along, and we know the truth about loveless families, about unwanted babies, about careless birth control, about a marriage license as an excuse for legalized rape, about a whole host of crimes against the human spirit in which we have not been directly involved, except often as victims. We do not have to go along with straight writers who make special pleadings for straights who are inauthentic.

As a teacher of black literature, I have often been frustrated by my black students when they tell me that they do not need to read most black literature, that a man like James Baldwin, for example, writes only to tell whites about the black experience, an experience they claim already to know all about. When I have told them that Baldwin speaks to me as a man, not as a white man, many students have said that I muddle only from my white experience. Perhaps I do. But now I can say what I really mean, that Baldwin speaks to me as a gay brother, that I read myself more readily into a book like *Go Tell It on the Mountain* than I read my students into it!

The real importance of this revision of my gay identity in the classroom is not any claim to greater accuracy for my judgments, but the claim to making those judgments more negotiable and accessible as buffers for the students' growth. Most of my students will hopefully never again invest me with the undesirable role of being spokesman and deliverer of their cultural values. Rather, my classes become vehicles of healthy suspicion, mandates that they weigh all issues and be prepared to defend their positions.

Student response is always difficult to measure. I have always enjoyed high class attendance without requiring it; yet it has risen even higher since my coming out. The first quarter this year I had several visitors almost daily, in addition to those on roll. My department chairperson, who has never specifically mentioned the letter, has told me that she is pleased with my work, specifically with the good response that she is getting from students. For my part, I know that I continue rarely to lose a pair of eyes in discussions. I know too that I like this attention more than ever now that I am not worried about their finding out about "the real me." Also, I get enough mixed feedback to know that they are neither mesmerized nor otherwise intimidated.

Equally positive has been my continued freedom of mobility on campus. In fact, I am freer. I now fearlessly, even righteously, charge my colleagues—particularly librarians, historians, psychologists, but also fellow teachers of literature—with their blatant neglect of gays, not only of those in their classrooms, but also those who ought to be in their textbooks, or on their committees making decisions affecting sexual understanding, etc. For example, one historian here has written the definitive work on lynching, and yet knows nothing of the historic persecution of gays, whether by Justinian or by Hitler. Silent for thirty-six years, I am now discovering my voice, my identity, my wholeness. In fact, I am not even sure that I would still say, as I did in the original letter, that sexuality is a "minor part of a person's identity." As I have been asked to speak to classes in numerous other departments (including philosophy [ethics], psychology, physical education, and religion) on our campus and elsewhere, I have become

> **Am I talking "too much" when I'm the only openly gay professor most of my present students will ever have, when I give less than five minutes out of every fifty to anything directly relating to the gay experience?**

aware of how major a part sexuality is for all of us in the academy. In these forums I am constantly having to counter the stereotypes that straights have about gay people, primarily because we gays have never been allowed to be visible, or even to write the major accounts of our experience. I have had the pleasure of affirming, celebrating gay diversity. Moreover, I have been free to speak out on behalf of specific gays persecuted by the academy. One gay student dismissed in a witch hunt eight years ago, charged with being "a moral danger," is about to be readmitted because certain administrators would be quite happy if I did not get my right to review his confidential folder so that I can properly advise him. Similar memoranda throughout the bureaucratic land need to be rooted out and all dishonorable discharges need to be reversed. Even closeted faculty here have rejoiced with twinkling eyes to see me bring the aid they were powerless to bring to this student.

Not all results have been positive. Many have been mixed, as in the case of the talented student who dropped my course in creative writing because he said I "talked about gayness too much." How does one measure "too much"? Did my teachers who were parents draw too many literary generalities from their socially acceptable experiences of sexuality? Am I really talking about sexuality merely to mention my "lover" rather than my "friend"? Maybe it is a mark of my oppression that I never questioned the rights of my straight teachers to allude openly to straight roles? Did my literary textbooks through the doctorate—which never gave a positive view to, rarely gave any view to gay experience—cheat me and my straight classmates of an experience of the world as it really is, with one out of every six of us having had homosexual experience? Am I talking "too much" when I'm the only openly gay professor most of my present students will ever have, when I give less than five minutes out of every fifty to anything directly relating to the gay experience? Clearly one student felt this much was "too much." I wonder how much my professors would have respected me had I dropped a course saying that they talked about straight identity too much; yet strangely I do respect this student. He told me to my face what he felt.

Equally mixed has become the "blessing" of being The Campus Homosexual. By the stingiest straight sociological estimate, I have at least 160 brothers and sisters on this campus of close to 2,000 souls. Their tight closet doors are a partial measure of my vulnerability. Being conspicuous is not new to me. In the past I have been highly visible as Louie the Actor, Louie the Writer, Louie the Choir Member, Louie the Seamster, Louie the Jogger. . . . Now, in the public mind these roles have all been subsumed under Louie the Queer. A nice queer, perhaps, but a queer nevertheless. I am often exhausted by taking on this role, by the internalized pressure to feel a credit to my race, my tribe. Still, I consciously fight to preserve, to integrate all other roles and dimensions of my identity while my colleagues and students come to terms with their own homophobia.

Homophobia is indeed the problem. One colleague shared with me the fact that he had overheard some of my students saying that they felt they would be penalized if they told me what they really felt about gay people. This colleague cautiously suggested that their fears were rational. I countered, "Would you think to lower my grade for what I think about heterosexuality?" "Of course not, but that's different!" he exclaimed. Is it? Why? Fortunately I was able to take the matter directly to my classes and reaffirm their freedom. The game they were really playing was projection, in that, doubting their own ability to be fair to sissies, they projected their own inadequacies upon me. "How," they rationalized "can you be fair to us if we can't be fair to you?"

I have had to expose similar homophobia in many academic social contacts with my students. Always a gregarious person, I noticed shortly after coming out that fewer students spoke when greeted in public, that many looked nervously about when I stopped to chat in the student center. I called this behavior to the attention of my classes so that I might explain that I really don't like embarrassing people, that I have no desire to have my students maligned by their peers' thinking that they have something going with the teacher, etc., but also explained that my only alternative is to go to the back of the bus. I refuse. I shall keep on being as friendly as I have always been, even if this means I must sit by those who do not want me, that I must share my oppression until here is indeed no back of the bus.

I have been very fortunate in being loved through all of this by a very great man. I have also been fortunate in having already known a good bit about my strength before I ever dared to make this move of coming out. More than ever I respect my brothers and sisters who have either come out or been forced out without such preparation. Those straights who complain about the gays still hiding, a complaint I hear daily, would better spend their energies making their own families places safe for gay members to come out in. Each person must work on her or his own timetable. To those of you still in the closet, if my experience says anything to me it is the greater awareness I have of how much we have to contribute to this culture. When we come out, we not only start revisions for ourselves, but also for our straight brothers and sisters. If we keep our heads about us, we may yet make the world a safer and happier, healthier and more knowledgeable place in which to live.

One of my student friends who already knew, told me last November that she had heard about my "confession." "But it wasn't a confession," I said; "rather a profession." "But why in Georgia and in 1973?" she asked. "Because I live in central Georgia and in 1973; I have no other time or place in which to work out my own salvation."

Feelings About Celibacy

Sexual relationships often create anxieties and distractions that keep us from getting in closer touch with ourselves. We wonder why we didn't come, or if the other person liked it, or if he or she wouldn't rather be in bed with so-and-so, and so on. This takes up lots of psychic energy that could be used for other thoughts and activities.

Celibacy, for different periods of time—two weeks, a month, a year—allows us to explore ourselves without the problems and power struggles of a sexual relationship. We can begin to define ourselves not just in terms of another person.

Many of us have entered periods of celibacy with apprehension—we have feared the insecurity of being without a partner. Yet often this anxiety diminishes because being alone is a very positive experience. It has given back to us out integrity, our privacy, our pride.

At this point I realized that I had been initially frustrated by not having a man, because I felt incomplete without one: a man meant completion. After several months of celibacy I saw that I could feel whole by myself.

My first reaction to being without a man was frustration and anger. I thought, Well, here I am feeling pretty liberated sexually, and there's no one to sleep with. Over time, I thought less and less about being with a man. I had very relaxed times with my friends, and never had to think twice about making plans with them for dinner. I was not asexual during this time. I was

> **I have been celibate for over a year. . . . I feel happy, independent, and free to figure out my own expectations of me.**

masturbating with much pleasure, having different kinds of orgasms—some long and slow and ripply, others short and jerky and tenser. I explored my sexuality in a way I had not with men. It was also easier to work at what I wanted to, because I was my only obligation.

I have been celibate for over a year, since the beginning of my involvement with the women's movement, which gave me a lot of support. I work very hard and feel good about working. I have created my own physical environment building a house and provided my own psychological space— a good combination. I masturbate a lot and enjoy it. I feel happy, independent, and free to figure out my own expectations of me.

Some of us come out of celibacy deliberately, feeling that we need a primary relationship. Some of us, feeling isolated and outside the norms of society, give up and flee into the arms of the first person to come along. Some of us may find we feel better being more autonomous.

The luxury of this kind of solitude has been very liberating. But for most of us being celibate has not provided a long-term solution to the problems posed by sexual relationships. There are also some very real drawbacks to long periods of celibacy.

Most of us crave physical contact and physical affection. To be alone, or to receive physical affection only from our animals and children, doesn't quite work. We can have fantasies about sleeping with them, but it doesn't feel right to act on them. We need other adult human beings to meet our deeper sexual/sensual needs.

Going without physical affection for long periods can be a kind of starvation. We won't die as we would without food or air, but the effects may still show in our bodies. We may get stiffer and out of touch with our sensuality. Though we can masturbate a lot and enjoy it, masturbation doesn't fill the same need as sex with someone else. When celibacy no longer feels good we should get out of it, but that's easier said than done. And it feels harder the longer we have been celibate. Coming out of celibacy, we may feel awkward or defensive, or we may feel embarrassed by needs that seem insatiable. Sometimes it's easier to start a new relationship with someone else who is also coming out of celibacy.

One unresolved thought: Do we ever choose celibacy out of fear of any kind of physical intimacy? What does this mean?

It's hard to take on the loneliness, the bad parts of being alone as well as the good parts of getting in touch with ourselves. It's also difficult to explore fully what being celibate can mean to us, since society does not generally accept the idea of choosing to refrain from sexual activity.

On Celibacy

Ziva Kwitney

I made the decision to become celibate three years after my divorce. I was 20 when I married and when I got unmarried at 34, I was, in the ways that suddenly mattered, a social retardate. I had not the faintest idea of how to perform or maneuver in that mating dance that is at the core of the contemporary "dating" relationship. How should I respond to sexual advances when I was interested, but had doubts? What was the best way to say no when I wasn't attracted to the man, but didn't want to hurt his feelings? How many men could I have sexual relationships with, without suffering guilt pangs? And what about *afterward?* What should I do when I had had sex with a man and didn't want to again? And, God help me, what did I do with my bruised psyche when it was the other way around?

It all seemed to boil down to expectations: his of me, mine of him, before, during, and after. And it all seemed equally treacherous: one of us invariably expected more than there was and was let down. Or worse yet, having engaged in the most intimate physical encounter there is, I would end by feeling *more* distant, *more* alone, less loved,

---

Reprinted from *Ms* magazine, February 1976, by permission of the author.

and less loving than before. That last horror began happening to me with cruel and increasing regularity. Although I had accepted the fact that I did not have to be "in love" to have intercourse, what I could *not* accept was the lack of closeness I felt once the passion was spent. There were times when the passion was not intense enough to sustain me through half an hour of lovemaking. (Sometimes, in the middle of a sex act, I would fantasy rising from the bed like an apparition, to hover in midair above my partner and ask him, sweetly, if he would mind finishing without me.)

I was, however, raised to be polite; and I trained myself to be realistic: did I expect to wait forever for the perfect lover while my loins ached and my prime passed inexorably by?

Sex, I discovered, was not simple—at least not for me. I expended too much energy tending to my displaced emotions (or his)

> **The longer I was celibate, the more centered I felt.**

and what I got out of it simply wasn't satisfying enough, either to my soul or to my cunt. One night, after making love with a decent man, and lying in his arms quietly for what I thought was a "proper" length of time—I asked him if he would mind going home. He was shocked. "You're the first woman," he told me, "who hasn't wanted me to stay the whole night." I told him that I didn't feel close enough to him to spend the night in the same bed, to go to *sleep* next to him. He left, appalled and hurt, and I felt grotesque—*like the man I had always feared being intimate with*—the one who wants you out of his sight when the sex is over.

Thereafter, it was simple: I decided, despite occasional bursts of lust, to forgo sex with partners. I did not deny myself light, or casual, physical contact with men or women—I simply avoided genital contact. I purchased a vibrator. I found sensual gratification in massage with women and men I cared for. I decided to trust myself to know when to attempt a union again.

I stayed celibate for about a year and a half. Oddly, it was a very sexual period for me. I became sensitive to my body, to its rhythms and contours and textures. It was the same sort of heightened awareness I used to experience during a fast, that (interim) denial of my hunger in service to myself. I even began to enjoy the low-level sexual tension; it had a vitality and excitement of its own.

But the longer I was celibate, the more centered I felt. My celibacy was for me a body-and-psyche meditation, a retreat inward. It made me peaceful, it made me stronger, it expanded my sense of myself as *myself,* without husband or lover or partner. I began to have a sense of myself as a universe, complete, without need of another. Even my desire, when it came, was my own—to contain as a pleasure, or to satisfy by my own hand. *I'm the woman in charge around here,* I would think to myself. And I set about learning who that woman was, and feeling that I was responsible for her life.

Then, one winter evening, I met a man to whom I was strongly drawn, and sensed in his intensity and restraint—so much like my own—that he would be the right partner for my scary journey back. He was. It was possible that I could be free in our lovemaking when we came together because, for the first time in my adult life, I had let myself be free *of* sex. Buoyant with relief, I ventured out again into the world, and found myself different. I'm taking pleasure from the relationships I've chosen now, and I'm no longer deflated by those that don't work out. Yet I know I will periodically return to celibacy—to get back to that territory where I am total center. I see that there is some work on the self that can only be done alone, independent of relationships. That work is the affirmation of one's self. *You are the only one who will never leave you,* someone once told me.

Curiously, it is a thought that reassures me.

Part 4

Some
public
issues

PART 4 / SOME PUBLIC ISSUES

In our pluralistic American society, value conflicts cut across age, sex, color, and socioeconomic lines. These conflicts produce racism, sexism, class imperialism, and the generation gap, and create fear and discord within society as a whole. Solving these problems is not easy. Human sexuality, with its private, taboo-ridden character, is especially vulnerable to emotional rhetoric, which can obscure substantive data supporting any sex-related issue under public debate. Furthermore, contradictory opinions abound concerning every controversial aspect of human sexuality, including extramarital cohabitation, abortion, racism, homosexuality, and pornography. Consensus among adults is lacking; and when we consider how public policy is legally hamstrung by codes that are outmoded, unenforceable, and dysfunctional in terms of contemporary sexual behavior, the obstacles to rational decision-making seem formidable indeed.

The readings in this part speak to a selected few of the issues involving human sexuality that sharply divide and baffle large segments of the populace. We hope the reader will be stimulated to examine his or her own thoughts and feelings and to seek an informed, rational position for personal action on these and other issues.

Greer's essay is a biting commentary on the exploitation,

bigotry, and trauma that are visited on women by men bent on violating women's bodies by rape. She categorizes the crime of rape at several levels. For example, when a man rapes a woman he does not know, he commits "grand rape." If the victim reports the crime to police, she is frequently subjected to further humiliation and embarrassment by demeaning and inept handling of her case by the (male) authorities.

Greer's sharpest barbs, however, are directed at "petty rape," or seduction, which occurs daily in interpersonal contacts between husband and wife, father and daughter, brother and sister, and dater and datee—and in billions of liberties exacted from passive, confused, and lonely women. This kind of rape is sex used as an exploitive tool to maintain women's sexuality as a commodity for male pleasure.

Greer does not explain why men rape women or why the incidence of forcible rape keeps rising. James Prescott, a neuropsychologist, believes that rape results when a mother denies physical affection and fondling to her son, who then grows up to express his hostility by raping other women.[1] Prescott agrees with Greer that

women's increasing freedom threatens male dominance in our society, and rape is one way to show which sex is in control. Does "petty rape" result from men fearing the loss of male privilege and prerogative? Isn't rape of any kind intimidation of a weaker person by a stronger one? Greer says yes, stating that only when "petty rape" no longer occurs, and when women learn to respect themselves and assertively say no to seduction, can meaningful and pleasurable erotic relationships develop between the sexes.

Greer's reading raises some important questions: Why is rape sometimes called a "victimless" crime? Why is it so difficult for women to fight with intent to hurt a would-be rapist in trying to save herself? What would *you* do about a rapist? Would it make any difference if he raped another man?

In February, 1973, a Supreme Court decision legalized abortion in the United States, thereby giving any woman and her physician the right to decide to terminate her pregnancy in its first trimester. In effect, the Court ruling rejected the "right-to-life" thesis that a fetus is a human being with legal rights. Since the ruling, there has been increasing polarization between those who favor the 1973 decision and well-organized, well-financed groups intent on amending the Constitution to prohibit abortion.

What has been lost in the "war" is a consciousness of the personal relationship between the women and the fetus. Lessard keenly feels this lack and is concerned that abortion may become as inconsequential as a tooth extraction. As she describes the ambivalent feelings and doubts that some women suffer, Lessard stresses the need for responsible, personal decision-making, and urges women to gain an understanding of themselves and their motivations for becoming pregnant—and for terminating a pregnancy. Such a personal struggle may well be the first step some young women take toward growing up and gaining some control over their lives.

In his reading from *Sex and Racism in America*, Calvin Hernton vividly describes the "double-bind" lives of black people, especially black males, that still exist in this country. Although it was written in 1965 and the term "Negro" seems archaic to many of us, the causative relationship of sex to racism is a present reality. The inequalities and patterns of racial and sexual subordination forced on blacks by white society have been encouraged by the widespread, sexually tinged hucksterism of the media. The myth of the potent black male with the overly large penis has distorted the perceptions blacks and whites have of each other. According to Hernton, the white community still harbors the nagging fear that blacks have "an uncontrollable urge" to mate with the white man's sisters and daughters.

The research done by Petroni substantiates this fear of interracial sex and has made it difficult for adolescents to integrate socially in desegregated high schools. In a study of interracial dating, Petroni interviewed a representative cross-section of 3,000 students in a desegregated Kansas high school. Both races stated that they felt extreme pressure by parents, peers, teachers, counselors, school administrators, and the community not to date across color lines. Although no interracial dating occurred between white males and black females, some black males with prestige (athletes, school leaders, and so forth) dated white girls, a fact that caused tension between white and black girls. Black girls preached separatism as they watched their chances for dating desirable black males narrow and their chances for dating white boys disappear.

The pressures exerted by their social world prevented nearly all of these teen-agers from dating across color lines, for few wanted to try to cope with the hassles involved.[2]

The changing times are slowly removing social, economic, and political barriers between different races, and as Hernton predicted, sexual liberty has become an increasingly important issue in our society. But has it been achieved?

Weinberg indicts straight society for its phobic attitudes toward the gay community, and states on the basis of his therapeutic practice that the words *healthy* and *homosexual* are not antithetical. Although homosexuality is no longer classified as an illness by the American Psychiatric Association, the strength of *homophobia*, or fear of homosexuality, indicates that the population at large (and males especially) may still be operating on a "contagion" or "illness" theory—fearful that they may have already contracted the "disorder" by some mishap of their parental upbringing and that latent homosexuality is lurking in their psyche ready to emerge. Unfortunately, this repressed fear fosters antagonism and acts of violence, especially against male homosexuals by male heterosexuals, who seem to have the greatest problem accepting gays of either sex.

Since the mass "coming out" of homosexuals in the 1960s, the Gay Liberation Movement and other homosexual organizations have provided support for gays and information for straights. Their attempts to modify the general public's attitude are slowly gaining them some freedom from abuse and discrimination, but securing fair treatment under the law remains a major problem. Aside from antiquated laws that prohibit homosexual acts and allow consequent police harassment, there are no laws that take into account homosexual life styles. Hurley's reading describes some of the difficulties gay lovers have in contracting marriages, establishing families, and owning homes. Well-known test cases have been appealed to the highest courts to no avail: marriage licenses for homosexuals have been denied. Gay lovers must then decide whether to fight the law and face long, drawn-out legal confrontations that will probably be lost, or to circumvent the law and seek "less dramatic but effective solutions." A few of these are described by Hurley, but the basic problem remains unsolved. Should the laws be amended to allow for a wide diversity of life styles, including homosexual marriage, with the same rights and protection under the law accorded heterosexual marriages?

Since the U.S. Commission on Obscenity and Pornography published its fact-finding report in 1970, the storm of controversy over this topic has not appreciably diminished. Although the Commission found that the availability of erotic materials had no apparent harmful effects and that sex offenders had generally less experience with pornographic materials during adolescence than normal control subjects, the report so offended political leaders that then-President Nixon denounced the Commission as "morally bankrupt."

Despite the research data, a sizable minority in this country want pornography controlled by the government, which they expect to uphold the moral standards and values important to our society. In his reading, Wilson claims that to put this kind of power into the political structure is to invite catastrophe, for "moral crusades and political repression often go hand-in-hand."

In his case for controlling pornography, Kristol argues cogently and potently on behalf of censorship. He makes a clear distinction between pornography and erotic art: art touches and excites the complete human being; pornography reduces men (and women, of whom pornography is usually exploitive) to their animal component and dehumanizes them. Kristol finds this dehumanization to be obscene, and he suggests a "little" censorship to protect the young. But how much, exactly, is a "little" censorship? Could it become an unethical vehicle leading to a greater evil that controls thought? There are no simple answers to the questions surrounding pornography and obscenity, and we must weigh carefully all aspects of this complex problem.

NOTES

1 James Prescott, "Body Pleasure and the Origins of Violence," *The Futurist*, April 1975, p. 72

2 Frank A. Petroni, "Teen-age Interracial Dating," in *Love, Marriage, Family—A Developmental Approach,* eds. M. S. Lasswell and T. E. Lasswell, (Glenview, Illinois: Scott, Foresman and Company, 1973), p. 144.

Seduction Is a Four-Letter Word

Germaine Greer

Once in a hot courtroom in New Zealand, I had occasion to ask a lady who was giving evidence against me for saying fuck in a public meeting whether she was as disgusted and offended by hearing the word rape used in a similar context. She wasn't. I asked her why. She thought for a moment and said happily, "Because for rape the woman doesn't give her consent."

My little linguistic inquiry opened a sudden peephole on the labyrinth of crazy sexual attitudes that we have inherited from our polyglot traditions (although it did not prevent my being sentenced to three weeks in jail). The craziness extends into our (mis)understanding of the nature of sexual communication and thereby finds its way back to behavior. Our muddled responses to the word rape have their source in the sexual psychosis that afflicts us all, especially the policemen and judges who are most vindictive in their attitudes toward those few sexual criminals who have sufficient bad luck or bad judgment to fall foul of the law.

Otherwise quite humane people entertain the notion that women subconsciously or even consciously desire to be raped, that rape liberates their basic animality, that, like she-cats, they want to be bloodily subdued and savagely fucked, regardless of their desperate struggles and cries. Women are thought to provoke the sexual rage of men who in turn may need to add blood lust to their sexual desire in order to achieve full potency. Darwin is sometimes quoted as the ideological ally of the rapist and forcible impregnator—how else but by his marauding activities could the survival of the fittest be assured?

Yet many women are afraid of rape as of nothing else. Women who have been raped may, as a consequence, be too terrified to leave their house by day or night or so distressed by male nearness that they cannot take a job or get onto a crowded train. There may be some truth in the notion that the lonely spinster who is terrified of intruders is actually longing to be violated, but her subconscious wish is of the same order as the wish of a mother to destroy her children, which is chiefly expressed in her fantasies that they may have come to violent harm. The fury that a father feels against the man who rapes his daughter might as profitably be construed as jealousy. For all practical purposes what the spinster experiences is a fascinating terror that may become an obsession. The man who actualizes her fantasy is in no way gratifying her or benefiting her, except in his own overweening estimation. The extent to which all men participate in this fantasy of violent largess can be dimly detected in their willingness to laugh at Lenny Bruce's description of his aunt going into Central Park each day for her appointment with the flashers or in the sneering assumption that older women and unattractive women are disappointed if intruders or invading soldiers don't rape them.

Many (men) believe that rape is impossible. The more simple-minded imagine that the vagina cannot be penetrated unless the woman consciously or subconsciously accepts the penetration, and so the necessary condition of rape cannot be fulfilled. The difficulty of getting a fully erect penis into the vagina is in direct proportion to the difficulty of overcoming the woman, either by physical force or by threat or by drugging her or by taking her by surprise.

The idea that rape is impossible may be an invalid extension of the view that all women subconsciously desire or provoke rape. It is certainly true that women do not defend themselves against rapists with any great efficiency. Even though they know that a sharp blow to the groin will incapacitate a man, or that a high heel smashed into the temple will have a certain effect, they seldom take advantage of what forms of self-defense may be accessible to them. The fault lies not in their suppressed lechery or promiscuity but in the induced passivity that is characteristic of women as we have conditioned them. Feminist encounter groups have developed routines in

> **Without special help, most women have no idea how to defend themselves and no concept of themselves as people with a right to resist physical misuse with violence.**

which a woman is encouraged to fight off a would-be rapist. Even strong heavy women have had to struggle to overcome the passivity that impeded the release of energy in self defense: passionate urging from the other members of the group was needed before they could take advantage of their own strength and determination.

Without special help, most women have no idea how to defend themselves and no concept of themselves as people with a right to resist physical misuse with violence. They are like children being beaten by their parents and their teachers, or slaves being brutalized on the plantation. Their physical strength remains unexploited because of the pathology of oppression. Women are poorly motivated to be as aggressive with their assailants as their assailants are with them, and so rape is easier than it should be. But this cannot be held to justify the contemptuous attitude of the rapist. Women's helplessness is itself part of the psychosis that makes rape a national pastime. And even encounter groups have not yet developed the kind of psychic energy that can defeat a gun or a knife or the frenzy of drugs.

The fear of sexual assault is a special fear: Its intensity in women can best be likened to the male fear of castration. As a tiny child I was utterly unafraid of the derelict old men who drooped their pallid tools at my mother and me when we sun-bathed in the beach park, but I remember an occasion when much less sinister behavior provoked wild terror. A young man simply came up to me and offered me a sweet; his kind smile was the most hideous thing I had ever seen. Usually I invoked my parents' rage because I consorted so readily with strangers, but this time I recoiled from the bribe, speechless with fright. Then I was running and running until my lungs were screaming, and I fell down and cowered in the grass, desperate not to look up for fear I would see that indescribable smile. Whenever I saw that man hanging out in the lane below our apartment, looking up my six-inch skirts as I went up or down the stairs, I was terrified. When I tried to explain to the grownups why I loathed that man, I had no words for it, but I knew it was the greatest fear of all, worse than spiders or octopuses or falling off the roof. Devoted sadists might argue that my terror was simply the terror of my own innate femaleness, but it would be bad Freud, because I was presumably in my phallic phase and unaware of my vagina; and if such a view is not to be justified by the great apologist of female masochism, it is not to be justified at all. What I was afraid of was rape as Eldridge Cleaver described it, "bloody, hateful, bitter and malignant," even though I had no clear idea of what it entailed.

Sexual intercourse between grown men and little girls is automatically termed rape under most codes of law. It does not matter whether the child invites it or even whether she seduces the adult; he and he only is guilty of a felony. From the child's point of view and from the common-sense point of view, there is an enormous difference between intercourse with a willing little girl and the forcible penetration of the small vagina of a terrified child. One woman I know enjoyed sex with an uncle all through her childhood, and never realized that anything unusual was toward until she went away to school. What disturbed her then was not what her uncle had done but the attitude of her teachers and the school psychiatrist. They assumed that she must have been traumatized and disgusted and therefore in need of very special help. In order to capitulate to their expectations, she began to fake symptoms that she did not feel, until at length she began to feel truly guilty about not having been guilty. She ended up judging herself very harshly for this innate lechery.

The crucial element in establishing whether or not vaginal penetration is rape is whether or not the penetration was consented to. Consent is itself an intangible mental act: the law cannot be blamed for insisting that evidence of absence of consent be virtually conclusive, so that a woman who has not been savagely beaten or threatened with immediate harm or rendered unconscious has little chance of legally proving that she has been raped. Consent is not a simple procedure: it may be heavily conditional or thoroughly muddled, and the law cannot allow itself to be drawn into ethical conundrums. Most of us do not live according to the bare letter of the law but according to moral criteria of much greater complexity. Morally, those of us who have a high opinion of sex cannot accept the idea that absence of resistance sanctions all kinds of carnal communication: rather than rely on such a negative criterion, we must insist that only evidence of positive desire dignifies sexual intercourse and makes it joyful. From a proud and passionate woman's point of view, anything less is rape.

The law of rape was not made with a woman's pride or passion in mind. The woman is no more and probably even less the focus of the rape statutes than the murder victim is the *raison d être* of the homicide statutes. The crime of rape is rather considered an offense not against the woman herself but against the men who made the law, fathers, husbands and kin. It is a crime against legitimacy of issue and the correct transmission of patrimony. The illegitimate sexual intercourse constitutes the offense; what the woman who complains must do is primarily to dissociate herself from any suspicion of complicity in the outrage against her menfolk. This she must do by making a complaint immediately. She is regarded as the prosecutrix of the rapist and he has all the recourse against her accusation that any defendant has against the state prosecutor, and then some. Only a girl child escapes the ordeal, because she is automatically deemed incapable of consent. An adult woman is actually called upon to prove her own innocence in the course of a rape prosecution, as well as managing to establish that the circumstances of the man's behavior are as she alleges.

A man has to be very unlucky to be convicted of the crime of rape. He has to be stupid enough, or drugged or drunk enough, to leave a mile-wide trail of blood, bruises, threats, semen, screaming and what have you, and he has to have chosen the kind of woman about whom the neighbors have nothing but good to say, who has enough *chutzpah* to get down to the police station at once and file her complaint, and, if it results in a trial, to face down public humiliation, for hearsay evidence about her morals and demeanor is admissible. The most the court will do for her is to rule that evidence emanating from a district other than the one she actually lives in is inadmissible. Then the jury must feel confident that no element of consent entered into the woman's behavior.

Nevertheless, men do go to jail for rape, mostly black men, nearly all of them poor, and neither the judges nor the prosecuting attorneys are hampered in their dealings by the awareness that they are rapists, too, only they have more sophisticated methods of compulsion. A deprived man forces his way into a woman's body by pressing the point of a knife against her throat; a man who owns an automobile may stop on a lonely road and tell his passenger to come across or get out and walk. The hostility of the rapist and the humiliation of the victim are not necessarily different, despite the difference in the circumstances; indeed, they could both be worse in the latter case, and that sort of thing happens every day. Probably the commonest form of noncriminal rape is rape by fraud—by phony tenderness or false promises of an enduring relationship, for example.

The woman who is assaulted and raped by a total stranger may suffer less than the woman who endures constant humiliation at the hands of people she is trying to know and love. The inadequates and psychotics who are arrested for rape have been known to select their victims and lie in wait for them; other criminal rapes may involve women who are known to or even related to their assailants, but for the most part, the selection of the victim is as fortuitous as it might be in an automobile accident. That element of haphazardness can help the woman avoid permanent psychic damage, because she is not compelled to internalize the experience, and so to feel guilty and soiled as a consequence of it.

One of the great injustices that the victims of criminal rape must suffer is the necessity of reliving the experience in minute detail over and over again from the first complaint to the police to the last phase of the trial. By attempting to prosecute the man who has raped her, a woman dissociates herself from the crime and endeavors to reconstitute her self-esteem, but it is a rare woman who is so independent of the evaluation of others that she can survive the contemptuous publicity that her attempt will draw upon her. If she fails to make her accusation stick, so that people assume that she is malicious or hysterical or that she enticed her rapist, she is in more serious psychic trouble than before. The odds against her succeeding in her prosecution, even after the police have reluctantly agreed to charge her assailant, are rather worse than four to one. If a woman's only concern is for herself and her eventual recovery from the experience, then she is much better advised not to prosecute. Rape is a habitual crime, however, and any woman who decides not to prosecute ought to spare a little thought for the women who will be raped as a consequence of her decision.

It is true that women have attempted to frame men for rapes that were never committed. Some have done so out of fear of punishment for an illicit sexual relationship that has been discovered. Others have done so because they needed abortions, others for revenge and other ulterior motives, for politics or policy. Some studies of rape quote a percentage of phony rape charges as high as 20 percent, but it is important to remember that the essence of the frame is that it is public, and that a good deal is left to the discretion of law enforcers in deciding whether or not a woman has been truly offended. There are not too many profeminists in police stations.

Criminologists believe that fewer than one in five rapes are reported, making rape the least reported crime on the books. Those figures are, I believe, conservative, even within the terms of their narrow legalistic definition, which refers to the second gravest crime in the statutes—what we might call grand rape. The punishments for grand rape are very savage, but it was not women who decided long ago that rapists should be blinded and castrated or hanged with benefit of clergy (as they once were) or sentenced to jail for life (as they still are). Nevertheless, even from a woman's point of view there are instances in which rape is an injury just as serious as homicide, and perhaps more so. A black friend of mine spent years of passionate effort to see that the seven white youths who raped her when she was 16 years old and a virgin spent the maximum time in jail, for they ruined her life by cursing her with a child whom she could never leave and never love. (The wonder of it is, of course, that a white jockocratic court convicted on the evidence of a black girl.)

It is in the interests of everyone involved that pregnancy must not be allowed to be a consequence of rape. This means that all women claiming rape must be entitled to abortion, long before the offense can be proved. To wait for any legal process is to increase the degree of physical and mental trauma involved. Nowadays a raped woman has a pretty good chance of getting an abortion, especially if she can supply reasonable circumstantial evidence of the offense. However, the women who are most traumatized by rape are reli-

> **Bored policemen, amusing themselves with girls who come to them to complain of rape, often kick off the proceedings by asking if they have enjoyed it.**

gious and sheltered women who are not likely to get over their experience by the necessity of committing what they devoutly believe to be a mortal sin as a result of an act committed upon their person against their will. In cases of scrupulous religious conscience, religion can be the woman's only consolation, but most cases of normally muddled morality would be best aided by the adoption of a protocol by medical officials confronted with rape cases. One practical solution would be to order the removal of the contents of the womb by aspiration as part of the diagnostic procedure. This would diminish the element of psychic intrusion and relieve the woman of the necessity of making a difficult moral choice arising out of circumstances beyond her control. The procedure is the same as biopsy aspiration, which is commonly practiced and need occasion very little discomfort.

The woman who is not impregnated or physically injured as a result of rape may nevertheless suffer acutely. The idea, so commonly entertained, that women somehow enjoy rape is absolutely unfounded, and a further indication of the contempt that men feel for women and their sexual functions. One might as well argue that because most men have repressed homosexual or feminine elements in their personalities, they enjoy buggery and humiliation. Women are, as a result of their enculturation, masochistic, but this does not mean that they enjoy being treated sadistically, although it may mean that they unconsciously invite it. Because of this masochism, women frequently take the whole burden of horror upon themselves. I know personally of a case in which a woman has been repeatedly raped by her mentally retarded brother for 30 years and has never sought any protection from him because of the distress that the knowledge would cause her parents. Her struggle to cope with the situation alone has had a marked effect on her psychic balance, and yet it is not beyond a law-enforcement officer to argue that she is guilty of collusion, that she is an accomplice, in effect.

Bored policemen, amusing themselves with girls who come to them to complain of rape, often kick off the proceedings by asking if they have enjoyed it. Rapists often claim in their defense that the prosecutrix enjoyed herself, that she showed evidence of physical pleasure or even had an orgasm. Most of them are lying. Some are sincere, but men are notoriously incapable of judging whether or not a woman is feeling pleasure, and women are not so unlike men that terror cannot cause something like the symptoms of erotic excitation in the genitals. Even if a woman were to have an orgasm in the course of a rape, it need not necessarily lessen the severity of the trauma that she suffers. This, it would seem, is quite understandable in the case of men raped by women, which, although not an entity in law, is still a possibility. Malinowski describes with thrills of disgusted horror the rape of a Melanesian male; if the clear evidence of the victim's sexual excitation makes any difference to his sense of outrage, it is to intensify it:

> The man is the fair game of women for all that sexual violence, obscene cruelty, filthy pollution and rough handling can do to him. Thus first they pull off and tear up his pubic leaf, the protection of his modesty, and, to a native, the symbol of his manly dignity. Then, by masturbatory practices and exhibitionism, they try to

produce an erection in their victim and, when their maneuvers have brought about the desired result, one of them squats over him and inserts his penis into her vagina. After the first ejaculation he may be treated in the same manner by another woman. Worse things are to follow. Some of the women will defecate and micturate all over his body, paying special attention to his face, which they pollute as thoroughly as they can. "A man will vomit, and vomit, and vomit," said a sympathetic informant.

For Malinowski the trauma is directly connected with loss of dignity and obliteration of the individual's will, at which his body actually connives. Women, too, have been known to vomit and vomit, to wash themselves compulsively, to burn their clothes, even to attempt suicide, after a rape. Nightmares, depression, pathological shyness, inability to leave the house, terror of darkness, all have been known to develop in otherwise healthy women who have been raped.

Malinowski was writing from the point of view of the rapee. The injury for him lay not in an outrage to his tutors and guardians, nor in injury to his body, nor in an unwanted pregnancy, but somewhere even more fundamental, in his will, and thence in his ego, his dignity. In this perspective the legalistic category of grand rape fades into unimportance. Sexual rip-offs are part of every woman's daily experience; they do not have the graitifying strangeness of disaster, with the special reconstructive energies that disasters call forth. They simply wear down the contours of emotional contacts and gradually brutalize all those who are party to them. Petty rape corrodes a woman's self-esteem so that she grows by degrees not to care too much what happens or how. In her low moments she calls all men bastards; she enters into new relationships with suspicion and a forlorn hope that maybe this time she will get a fair deal. The situation is self-perpetuating. The treatment she most fears she most elicits. The results of this hardening of the heart are eventually much worse than the consequences of fortuitous sexual assault by a stranger, the more so because they are internalized, insidious and imperceptible.

The idea that a woman has merely to consent, or to give in to sexual contact, provides the basic motivation for petty rape. Silence or failure to resist is further misconstrued as consent. Then, by a further ramification of blunder, passive silence is thought to indicate pleasure. The breakdown in sexual communications occasioned by acceptance of these related vulgar errors can be illustrated by an example.

A young Cambridge undergraduate at a party in London missed his last train back to Cambridge and so asked around the party for a bed for the night. A female guest, who lived nearby, said he might use her spare room, unconcerned by the fact that her husband was away, for the young man and all his family were well known to them. She duly drove him to her apartment, where clean towels and pajamas were laid out for him, and he was wished a good night's rest in the spare room. She had had a lot to drink at the party and was feeling giddy and rather ill, so she was grateful to slide between the sheets and pass quietly out.

It was beneath young Lochinvar's dignity to stay in his room, though, and his hostess was just slipping through rather swirling veils of sleep when he climbed into the bed beside her. She resisted, but there was little point in making much to-do; having the police called to the apartment would have made a scandal, upset everybody and left her in a ridiculous situation. The law would take only one view of an unaccompanied married woman's invitation to a young man to stay the night, regardless of the fact that Victorian sexual paranoia is gradually ebbing in other areas. She scolded and pleaded, exaggerated the degree of her drunkenness and even resorted to being sick, but the young man's ego would give no quarter. Like a Fascist guard in Mussolini's Italy, he woke her every time her eyelids began to close. Then he made his little show of force. She offered only passive resistance and so got fucked.

It was, of course, a terrible fuck. She was exhausted, distressed and mutinous; he was deeply inconsiderate and cruel, although he fancied himself a nipple twiddler and general sexual operator and believes to this day that he gave her the fucking of her life. He has boasted of his conquest just often enough so that his talking about it has come to her ears and reduced her to a state of misery. She has never told her husband what happened because of the sheer unlikeliness that he would exonerate her from any taint of desire for the little shit, however nobly he decided to behave. Worst of all, she must see her enemy frequently at dinners and parties in friends' houses and endure his triumph over her time and time again. She has not allowed the circumstances to corrode her self-esteem to any serious extent, but her enemy cannot lay the fact to his credit.

What happened is just one of the zillions of forms of petty rape. There is no punishment and no treatment for offender nor victim in a case like this. It just has to be crossed off as another minor humiliation, another devaluation of the currency of human response. The woman in this instance revenged herself by striking the man from her list of friends, but he hardly noticed. His account of the affair, needless to say, is very different from hers.

The attitude of the rapist in such an example is not hard to interpret in terms of the prevailing sexual ideology, A man, is after all, supposed to seduce, to cajole, persuade, pressurize and eventually overcome. A reasonable man will avoid threats, partly because he has a shrewd idea that they will not produce the desired result. A psychotic rapist is quite likely to desire fright and even panic-stricken resistance and struggle as a prerequisite to his sexual arousal or satisfaction. But not your everyday pusillanimous rapist. He simply takes advantage of any circumstances that are in his favor to override the woman's independence. The man who has it in his power to hire and fire women from an interesting or lucrative position may profit by that factor to extort sexual favors that would not spontaneously be offered him. A man who is famous or charismatic might exploit those advantages to humiliate women in ways that they would otherwise angrily resist. In cases like these, mutual contempt is the eventual outcome, but what the men do not realize is that they are exploiting the oppressed and servile status of women. The women's capitulation might be ignoble, but it is morally more excusable than the cynical manipulation of their susceptibility.

One of the elements that is often abused in the petty-rape situation is the woman's affection for the rapist. This might not even be a completely nonsexual affection: There is a case on record in Denver in which a woman who was brutally raped explained to the judge that she would have been quite happy to ball with her assailant if he had asked her nicely, but as soon as they got into her apartment, he beat her up and raped her. The parallel in petty rape is the exploitation of a woman's tenderness, which would involve eventual sexual compliance, for a loveless momentary conquest. Because a woman likes a man and would like to develop some sort of relationship with him, she is loath to make trouble when he begins to prosecute his intentions in an offensive way. Her enemy takes cold-blooded advantage of that fact. For lots of girls who slide into promiscuity, this is the conflict in which they are defeated time and time again.

In all but the most sophisticated communities, a young woman who wishes to participate in the social life of her generation must do so as a man's guest. Dating is a social and economic imperative for her. This situation is the direct result of her oppressed condition, and however venal her motives may seem to be, she is not totally responsible for them. For her the pressure is disguised as pressure to fall in love and go steady; he may see it as a kind of being on the make, corresponding to his own fairly impersonal desire for sexual gratification. If she gets raped as a result of her dependence upon a man as an escort, neither party thinks that she has anything grave to complain of, and yet a great wrong has been done.

For most young women who set out on the dating road to marriage, petty rape is a constant hazard. The fact that a man pays for the night's entertainment, that he owns and drives the car, that he has initiated all that has happened means by extension that he is also entitled to initiate and to set the pace of the physical intimacies that will occur. She would probably be disappointed if he manifested no desire for her, but she also has the problem of not seeming easy while keeping him interested. His self-esteem prompts him to achieve as much intimacy as he can before she draws the line. The element of petty rape appears when he threatens to throw her over if she doesn't come across or whenever he decides that he does not like her well enough to move gradually through the stages of intimacy as she desires them, but will force the pace to get as much as possible out of an otherwise unsatisfactory encounter. His use of the vocabulary of tenderness becomes fraudulent. He may even fake an excess of sexual desire.

A group of law students at the first university I attended had a competition to see who could fuck the most women in one semester; one ploy that they all had in common was a trick of heavy breathing and groaning, as if they were writhing in torments of desire. As they were after quantity and not quality, this was not often the case. It worked very well, in the main, but partly because they were exercising the class prerogative of the rich bourgeois and wantonly disrupting the lives and expectations of women situated in less fortunate circumstances, like the hero of *My Secret Life*, but more callously.

The man who won that competition was an expert in exploiting women's fantasy and vanity, and their tendency to delude themselves that the contact they were experiencing was a genuine personal encounter and not a crass sexual rip-off. He and his friends were proud of their mastery of the gestures of tenderness, but their use of them was utterly self-centered. They were simply exercising a skill like angling, drawing silly women to their own humiliation. The only way to earn their respect and friendship was to resist them, so they wantonly encouraged toughness and suspicion in this cold world. The girls they had had never realized they'd been victims of petty rape until they grasped the fact that the first time was also the last.

For such rich and handsome young men, petty rape was a sport that by virtue of their privileges they played with great success. There were occasional uglinesses that marred the lightheartedness of their proceedings. One of them was threatened with a paternity suit, but all his friends turned up in court and testified that they had had carnal knowledge of the plaintiff, and so he got off. In fact, they committed perjury, but it did not disturb their sleep.

The group-bonding skills of males will always defeat the interests of isolated women. Men will conspire to see that acts of petty rape are successful. Many women would be appalled to learn just how their most intimate behavior and physical peculiarities are discussed by men, and this supplies a further dimension of petty rape by blackmail. There is no point in resisting a man's advances if he is going to talk about how he had you in any case, especially when your word is generally less respected than his. I was once pestered for three of four days by a detestable male chauvinist who explained my consequent dislike of him as pique because he refused to fuck me. When sex is an ego contest, women get fucked over all the time.

Petty rape is sometimes called seduction, which is not regarded as a contemptible or particularly damaging activity. A woman who capitu-

lates to a seducer is considered to do so because she really wanted
to or because she is too silly or too loose to know how to resist. It
might even be thought to be in her interest to overcome her priggish-
ness about sex. The man who excuses his unloving manipulation
of women's susceptibilities in ways such as these cannot honestly claim
to have the women's interests at heart. His assumption that he knows
what is good for them is overweening even if it is sincere, which it
usually is not.

Some men decide that it is their prerogative to punish a woman in a
sexual encounter, either for her looseness or for teasing or for lying
and evading the issue. The distortion of an erotic response into a chas-
tisement is pathological, but not uncommon. An economics student,
son of a high-ranking public official, boasted to me once that because a girl had lied to him that she was menstruating, he punished
her by raping her, buggering her and throwing her out of his rooms in
Cambridge in the small hours of the morning, knowing that she
would find no kind of transport to take her back to her home in the
country. He had absolutely no understanding of her motives for lying
to him. He believed she was stalling him; in fact, all she needed
was time to build up a desire for intimacy that he was forcing on her.
She could have walked out earlier, or screamed and brought the
housekeeper to her rescue, but that would have meant rustication
for him and a summary end to any developing relationship. Either
course would have required positive hostility, which she simply did
not feel. She had very little understanding of the sexual hostility
that he did feel, which underlay a good deal of his sexual response,
especially in casual affairs.

The men who do cruel things to women are not a class apart;
they are not totally incapable of relating to women. In nearly every case I
have described, the details were told to me by the men, who explained
their comparatively humane attitudes toward me as a result of my
own respect for myself and my own straightforwardness in sexual
matters, both results of my unusually privileged status as a woman; I
was also older than most of them. But I have not entirely emancipated myself from the female legacy of low self-image, self-hatred and
identification with the oppressors, which is part of the pathology of
oppression. The girls who have been mistreated in the ways that I

have described take the fault upon themselves. They think they must have made a mistake somewhere, that their bodies have provoked disgust, that they were too greasy in their conversation. The internalization of the injury is what makes petty rape such an insidiously harmful offense against women. What the men have done is to exploit and so intensify the pathology of oppression.

Many petty rapists do not wittingly dislike women or hate them; they do not revenge themselves upon their mothers through other women's bodies in any conscious way. Group-therapy sessions at treatment centers for sex offenders are producing results that seem to indicate that repressed hostility toward the mother is one of the most common unconscious motivations for violent rape. But these conclusions ought not to be regarded as particularly enlightening; if an analyst is seeking evidence of an infantile trauma involving women, it is almost inevitably going to involve a mother or a mother surrogate. It is small wonder that our civilization manifests a psychotic attitude to women, when children are thrown upon the mercy of one woman almost exclusively during the formative years between one and five. Women's hostility to one another may be explained by the same phenomenon, at least partially. Teachers anywhere, women in authority over men in any capacity attract a good deal of antagonism, some of which masquerades as affection.

There are other discernible motives for active sexual hostility in the male. Religions that rely upon guilt mechanisms for their hold upon the faithful build up an image of the female as an occasion of sin. The nuns at my Catholic primary school prepared the children for raping and being raped by treating even the littlest girls' bodies as dire inducements to lasciviousness, to the point of forbidding us to bare our upper arms or our collarbones, and begging us all not to look at our "private parts" even when we were washing them as perfunctorily as possible in the bath. This wanton stimulation of sexual tension still goes on in religious schools. If scientology and other forms of psychic manipulation for eventual control can be declared illegal, then some attention should be paid to this process, enacted without fear of reprisal upon the very young.

Undue aestheticism in representing sexual behavior can also have harmful effects. The inauthenticity of sexual fantasy as it is

293

stimulated by commercial representations of the woman as sex object leaves many immature men unable to cope with the eventual discovery that women do not feel smooth and velvety all over, that their pubic hair exists and is not swan's down or vine tendrils, that a woman in heat does not smell like a bed of roses. (Most convicted rapists who have been subjected to any degree of analysis have shown an exaggerated dislike of menstruation.) For most men, sexual experience begins and persists throughout the years of most intense libidinous

> **Those who hate women most are often the most successful womanizers.**

activity, the teens, as fantasy and masturbation rather than actual physical confrontation with the object of their desire. It is not surprising, then, that the imagery of their puerile fantasies continues to interpose itself between the ego and the reality long after their active sexual life has begun in earnest. What the permissive society has achieved, in fact, is merely the proliferation of inauthentic sexual fantasy, with virtually no degree of emancipation of the sexes into genuine communication and mutual understanding.

Women are not yet consumers of commercial soft-core pornography; they do not have the same fetishistic attitude toward men's bodies that men have toward women's. Instead they are further alienated from the area of male sexual orientation by their own culture of romantic fantasy. Attempts to duplicate the marketing of images of women's bodies have been made with men's bodies without much success, and similar inauthenticities were represented. When my husband, Paul du Feu, posed for the gatefold in the British edition of *Cosmopolitan*, it was found necessary not only to cover him with body make-up and hide his penis behind his upraised thigh but also to airbrush his navel and wrinkles on his belly clean out of the picture. Men trying to understand feminists' reactions to the commercialized stereotype of women ought to study their own reactions to the degradation and desexualization of Paul du Feu.

Those who hate women most are often the most successful womanizers. The connection used to be recognized in common parlance by the expressions lady-killer and wolf. Sylvia Plath describes a crucial encounter with one such in *The Bell Jar*, leaving it to the reader to estimate the role that this humiliation plays in Esther Greenwood's eventual collapse.

> Marco's small flickering smile reminded me of a snake I'd teased in the Bronx Zoo. When I tapped my finger on the stout cage glass the snake had opened its clockwork jaws and seemed to smile. Then it struck and struck at the invisible pane till I moved off.
>
> I had never met a woman hater before. I could tell Marco was a woman hater, because in spite of all the models and TV starlets in the room that night he paid attention to nobody but me. Not out of kindness or even curiosity, but because I'd happened to be dealt to him, like a playing card in a pack of identical cards.

Young Esther has no hope of beating Marco at the game he has been perfecting most of his adult life. He sweeps aside her tremulous attempts to remain independent. On the dance floor he forces her to give up all idea of independent locomotion:

> "What did I tell you?" Marco's breath scorched my ear. "You're a perfectly respectable dancer."
>
> I began to see why woman haters could make such fools of women. Woman haters were like gods: invulnerable and chock-full of power. They descended and then they disappeared. You could never catch one.

Marco's excuse for treating all women like sluts is an impossible love for his first cousin (probably a narcissistic fantasy), who is to become a nun. After he has assaulted Easther, and she has partly beaten him off and he has partly given up, saying, "Sluts, all sluts . . . yes or no, it's all the same," Esther goes back to her sex-segregated hotel, climbs onto the parapet of the roof and feeds her wardrobe to the night wind. Marco has brought her to the beginning of the end.

In all cases of petty rape, the victim does not figure as a personality, as someone vulnerable and valuable, whose responses must not be cynically tampered with. So great is women's need to believe that men really like them that they are often slow to detect perfunctoriness in proffered caresses or the subtle change in attitude when the Rubicon has been crossed and the softening up of the victim can give way to unilateral gratification. Not all woman haters can belie their feelings of hatred and contempt successfully throughout a sexual encounter. When their situation is secure—say, when they have the victim safe behind the hotel door and know that she is not about to run screaming through the lobby in a torn dress—they may abandon all pretense of tenderness and get down to the business of hate fucking, and yet still the wretched woman attempts to roll with the punches. Her enemy may use physical and verbal abuse, even a degree of force to make her comply with forms of sexual intercourse that she does not desire. Mostly he retreats into an impersonal, masturbatory frame of mind. After the loveless connection is over, he cannot wait to get rid of her, either by giving her cab fare or shutting her out of his mind by going to sleep or pretending to.

Guilt and disgust may follow. The man may be sorry that he went with such an abject creature, but he will not blame himself for the poor quality of the sex he has had, any more than when he finds the woman unresponsive because her sexual submission has been extorted from her. If he is distressed by the crassness and perfunctoriness of the love he has made or embarrassed by the willingness and generosity of the love he has been given, he will abuse the woman in his mind. She is a dog, a pig, goes with anyone, is so dumb she wouldn't know you were up her till you coughed. Like the grand rapist, he excuses his conduct on the grounds that she asked for it, by her lewdness, her willingness to discuss sex, her appetite at dinner, the money she made him spend, the dress she had on, the size of her breasts. If she has enjoyed and responded to caresses up to the point when they became brutal and then struggled to escape, then she is a tease who leads men on and then wants to chicken out when he gets to the nitty-gritty. No punishment is too severe for a tease.

Some men who are very well aware of their own preference for force fucking and their hostility to women may doubt that women's sensibilities are elevated enough to perceive their own humiliation. Feminists are at least beginning to spell it out for them, but too many men do not realize that the slogan "An End to Rape" does not so much refer to grand rapes committed on the crime-ridden streets of the cities as to the daily brutalization of contact between brother and sister, father and daughter, teacher and pupil, doctor and patient, employer and employee, dater and datee, fiancé and fiancée, husband and wife, adulterer and adulteress, the billions of petty liberties exacted from passive and wondering women. The solution is not to be found in the castration or killing of the rare rapists who offend so crazily that they can be caught and punished but in the correction of our distorted notions of the nature of sexual intercourse, which are also the rationale of the law of rape as a felony.

Women are now struggling to discover and develop their own sexuality, to know their own minds and bodies and to improve the bases upon which they can attempt communication with men. The men who continue to assume that women must be treated as creatures who do not know what is good for them, to be cajoled or coerced or punished at the will of a stiff-standing cock, seek to imprison women in the pathology of their oppressed condition. Some women are coquettish, although far fewer than the mythology of rape supposes; the only way to put an end to such fatuous guile is to cease to play the game, simply by taking women at their word. The woman who says no when she means yes and so loses a man she wants will find a way to see him again to tell him that she meant yes all the time—if she really did mean yes, that is. If she didn't really mean yes, then she is better left alone.

Any man who realizes that he likes screwing mutinous women, that he is bored at the prospect of balling only women who want him, had better be aware that he finds resistance and tension essential to his satisfaction: He is a petty rapist and should look to it.

The abandonment of the stereotype of seduction, conquest, the chase and all, increases the number of erotic possibilities rather than diminishing it. Once the rigid course of sexual manipulation is disrupted, the unexpected may occur, some genuine erotic development can take place. Even the rapist author of *My Secret Life*, whose sexual activity was entirely dependent upon the possibilities of exploiting lower-class women, was aware that coercion and insistence were not in his best sexual interests, even when he had paid for the use of a woman's body and was in some sense entitled to it:

A custom of mine then, and always followed since, is putting down my fee—it prevents mistakes, and quarrels. When paid, if a woman will not let me have her, be it so—she has some reason—perhaps a good one for me.

Nothing that I have said should be interpreted to mean that no man should try to make love to a woman unless he is prepared to marry her or to undertake a long and serious affair with her. A one-night stand can be the most perfect and satisfying sexual encounter of all, as long as there is no element of fraud or trickery or rip-off in the way in which it develops. If women are to free themselves from the necessity of deploying their sexuality as a commodity, then men will have to level in their dealings with them, and that is all we ask. There is still room for excitement, uncertainty, even antagonism in the development of sexual friendship, but *if you do not like us, cannot listen to our part of the conversation, if we are only meat to you, then leave us alone.*

As women develop more confidence and more self-esteem, and become as supportive toward one another as they have been to men, they also lose their reluctance to denounce men for petty rape. Where before they respected men's privacy a good deal more than men respected theirs (despite the phony claims of chivalry), they are now beginning to tell it how it is. A theatrical impresario well known for his randiness recently invited a leading women's liberationist to his hotel for a business meeting. To her amazement, for she had thought such gambits long out of style, he leaped on her as soon as he had her fairly inside the room. She held him off until suddenly he ejaculated all over the front of her dress. Gone are the days when she would have slunk out behind a newspaper. Her dress is a museum piece of the women's movement in her country, and the joke will be around for years.

Rape crisis centers are being set up by groups of women more interested in self-help than in vindictiveness. Here a woman who has been traumatized by a sexual experience can come for counsel, for medical and psychiatric help. She is not regarded as a culprit or challenged about the length of her skirts or the thickness of her eye make-up; her word is believed, as the first step to reconstituting an ego damaged by sexual misuse. The victim is encouraged to externalize the experience rather than to entertain feelings of guilt and shame, and she is also taught how to defend herself against future assault and brutalization, even from her husband, who by law has the right of rape over her. Menstrual aspiration will also be practiced as the technique becomes better known and the instruments more widely available. Force fucking is being phased out.

The new feeling of solidarity among women will render petty rape quite futile. Women who used to rejoice to think that their men treated other women badly cannot accept it once their consciousness is raised. A musician returning to his feminist old lady after a protracted tour abroad boasted that he managed to be faithful to her (something she had never demanded) by making the adoring groupies give him blow jobs and then get out. He was proud that he had never even kissed one of them, let alone balled one. To his amazement, his old lady walked out on him.

Women are finding, in the stirring words of women's advocate Florynce Kennedy, that "kickin' ass and takin' names, talkin' loud and drawin' a crowd is better than suckin'." Our weapons may be little more than ridicule and boycott, but we will use them. Women are sick to their souls of being fucked over. Now that sex has become political, the petty rapist had better watch his ass; he won't be getting away with it too much longer. How would you feel if a video tape of your last fuck were playing at the Feminist Guerrilla cinema? We didn't start this war, but we intend to bring it to an honorable settlement, which means we have to make a show of strength sometime. People who are fighting for their lives fight with any weapons that come to hand, so it is foolish to expect a fair fight. Sex behavior is becoming as public as any other expression of political belief: Next time I write an article like this, I'll tell you all the names. So don't say you weren't warned.

Aborting a Fetus: The Legal Right, The Personal Choice

Suzannah Lessard

The belief that abortion must be legally available to those who want
it comes to many of us first as a gut certainty, not that the procedure itself is morally acceptable, but that to deny women the option is intolerable and insane. The intuitive recognition is most likely to spring
either from experience, or having been close to people who have
been through it—from one way or another having gotten into the
shoes of an individual faced with the dilemma of an unwanted
pregnancy. The intimate appreciation of what's involved is why so
many women, sometimes to the jeopardy of the cause, take the issue
so personally. A friend of mine, who has had an abortion and who
considers the moral implications insoluble, described coming out of
a museum into a demonstration against legal abortion. "There they all
were with little children, chanting these slogans, and I just sat
down and cried. I thought they were trying to stamp on me, that if they
had their way I wouldn't have any choice." In print this attitude looks
childishly selfish and petulant, but it is a primal and very honestly

expressed feeling. While it won't get one very far in the attempt to build a philosophical edifice justifying abortion, understanding the strength of that feeling is the key to understanding why so many women appear irrationally certain about a question which is patently conflict-ridden and inescapably charged with ambiguities. The feeling doesn't say "I have a right to an abortion"; it says "you have no right to decide for me one way or the other and your presumption to do so is violently offensive."

> To the rhetorical question put by the Right to Lifers—does the human creature suddenly undergo some absolute transformation in the short passage from the womb to the outside world—the answer is yes, at least people have always behaved as though that is what they believe.

TWILIGHT ZONE

Moving backward from this gut certainty, one blunders into a wilderness of intellectual constructs built in the attempt to either condemn or justify abortion in a rational, consistent manner. Many of them are cockeyed; some, on both sides, are orderly and impressive, but none of them contain the matter satisfactorily because the basic question—what is the value of the life of a fetus—is unanswerable and therefore a matter of faith. The second thing one notices about both sides is that besides being ferociously dogmatic and blind to each other's points, the emotional pitch of the battle is deafeningly high. That, no doubt, is because if it's difficult to discourse with someone you consider a murderer, it's equally, if not more difficult, to be open-minded toward a person who is calling you one.

Looking at the inadequacy of the constructs on either side, there

301

seems little point in trying to erect a more perfect one, since at bottom it is a matter of faith and people who hold the opposite faith are not likely to be persuaded otherwise. At best one can hope that the Right to Lifers will acknowledge that the question is ultimately imponderable, and that those who press the case for abortion have as much right to their belief as their opponents. At most, the fetus exists in a twilight zone of humanity. Despite their repeated use of the word murder, even the most virulent of the abortion opponents aren't arguing that abortionists and consenting mothers be given prison terms remotely like those given murderers. A miscarried fetus is not mourned the way even a one-day-old child would be. So to the rhetorical question put by the Right to Lifers—does the human creature suddenly undergo some absolute transformation in the short passage from the womb to the outside world—the answer is yes, at least people have always behaved as though that is what they believe. According to Kinsey, one out of four American women has privately wrestled with that question in a very immediate sense and has decided to have an abortion. The law which forced them to take the often high physical risk of going to illegal practitioners was passed in the 19th century, not for the protection of the fetus, but, ironically, for the woman's protection, because it was at that time a far more dangerous operation than normal childbirth. The transformation of the legal issue into a debate over the right to life of the fetus as opposed to the safety of the procedure for the woman has occurred not through legal process but in the minds of the latter-day opponents of abortion. Now that abortion is eight times safer than childbirth, the only question that remains is whether a woman has a right to decide on her own what course to take in this intensely personal matter of such far-reaching consequence to herself. . . .

"A MASS OF PROTOPLASM"

The failure of both sides to distinguish between the legal and the personal aspects of the issue has been one of the reasons, I think, for the bad blood and seemingly hopeless division on fundamental principles between the two groups. I don't understand the strident

ferocity of the Right to Lifers, so I can only say that their absolute refusal to even acknowledge that there might be a matter of separation between state and private life indicates that they have con-
founded the two perspectives. I do understand the stridency of the
feminist position. Their doctrinaire intensity is due in part to the
fact that the way the still-fragile crusade ends will vitally, drastically, affect the lives of millions of women, and in part to the rage which an intrusion of the state into this area inspires. But I don't think I'm
alone in being acutely uncomfortable with many of the arguments
and descriptions of the issue as they have evolved on the pro-abortion
side, or in feeling that many of the positions taken serve only to tie
the knot more tightly in the minds of opponents and waverers. I can
best describe the source of that discomfort as the failure of the "movement," not unlike the opposition, to distinguish between abortion
as a legal option and abortion as a personal decision.

For instance, the tenet that the state has no more right to interfere in
an abortion than it does in a tonsillectomy (or any other form of
minor surgery) is often transformed into a description of abortion as the
equivalent of a tonsillectomy. At least for an awful lot of women, their
belief that the state should keep out notwithstanding the
psychological, emotional, and just plain personal elements involved
in deciding to have an abortion make such an equation outlandish.
Another point of wild confusion between personal questions and
political questions has involved the description of the fetus. A fetus,
even at two months, is a good deal more than a "mass of dependent
protoplasm," as Gloria Steinem recently wrote in *Newsweek*. It has
a very well-defined human shape—head, back, legs, arms, sometimes hands and feet. It's growing, and it is highly likely to become a
separate human being if left alone, a fact which certainly can't be
said of just any blob of protoplasm, and which any intelligible description of the fetus would have to be based on. To describe it that way is
either extraordinarily ignorant, as an absurd reduction of all
protoplasmic—i.e. "living"—forms which renders any distinctions
between them impossible, or a blatantly false description of reality in
order to make it conform to ideological lines.

Reaction formation along ideological lines has cropped up in several
areas of the new feminist movement. In the early stages of most re-

volts, the self-overhaul into a catechism of "correct" responses is prevalent, and often for good reasons. I think a lot of women need to go fanatically ideological for a while because they can't in any other way overthrow the insidious sense of themselves as inferior, nor otherwise live with the rage that comes to the surface when they realize how they have been psychically mauled. But I don't think that state of mind—hopefully temporary—is the strength of the movement. It has very little to do with working out a new, undamaging way of living as women. Specifically with regard to abortion, just because it's an essential goal in building a new world for women to convince the state that it has no right to see abortion any differently than a tonsillectomy, it does not mean that whatever feelings a woman having an abortion might experience over and above what she experiences when undergoing a tonsillectomy are counterrevolutionary.

BRAINWASHED PLUMBING

A critically important part of the movement has been the demystification of a woman's sexual and reproductive life and the substitution of scientific education where fear, uncertainty, guilt, and ambivalence existed before. It's been a great help to learn to look at our bodies as plumbing rather than as mysterious, at once glorified and faintly disgusting things, as it's a great help to any human being undergoing a physical-medical operation to overcome fear by thinking of what is going on in those terms. Knowing what's happening scientifically helps put you on top of it. But to carry this revelation to the point where you insist that it's nothing but plumbing, that bearing a child or aborting a fetus are different only in a neutral sense, to me turns what should be a liberation into a denial of the real self as violent and as destructive as the old mystique in its heyday. There is little question that many of our reactions, particularly those relating to sex and reproduction, have been formed by social pressures under which we grew up, and there's little question that many of them are unhealthy and imprisoning. Nevertheless, I am not only affronted when, for example, it's suggested to me that all my feelings about abortion, since they don't conform to ideology, are the result of brainwashing, but I think it's an absurd accusation, which, taken to its logical limits, reduces the human being to a blank.

To dictate how women "should" feel about abortion—to say they "shouldn't" feel it's as inconsequential to their inner life as having a tooth pulled—would be to fall into the same fallacy as the positions under criticism. I will admit, however, that I suspect any grown woman who claims that deciding to have an abortion was a totally neutral act of either being afraid of the truth, of having artificially overhauled her emotions to conform with ideology, or, as Simone de Beauvoir suspected 20 years ago when she wrote *The Second Sex*, of being protected from her true feelings by her political environment. I'm not implying that the experience must be a great agonizing tragedy, just that more is involved than the removal of a blob of protoplasm and that most women know that and react accordingly.

"NOBODY ON THE TABLE WITH YOU"

Since legal abortion is relatively new, the only sources of collected information on how women react to the experience are limited to a few formal studies and the cumulative wisdom of counselors. (Many clinics maintain a large staff of counselors to deal with physical fears and psychological conflicts.) Since counselors are immersed daily in the actuality of going through with an abortion, they tend to be less interested in doctrine and focus instead on trying to understand all the dimensions of an experience which is only beginning to be systematically explored. Conflict, psychological and moral, is what much of their work is about. From their descriptions of what concerns their patients, two categories of conflict emerge. First are conflicts clearly related to the shame attached to illicit sex—in other words, the violation of social mores—in terms of which getting pregnant and having an abortion are more punishment than anything else. The second category concerns the abortion itself, quite separate from guilt about the act which resulted in the predicament. As described by counselors, those battles seem much more prone to line up within the patient herself, rather than as an attempt to come to terms with a gap between private practice and public standards of behavior. This makes good sense, since awareness of abortion has been pushed so far back in the public consciousness that moral repulsion from it isn't likely to have been ingrained very deeply in the average American. The rusty coat hanger and the physical fears it conjures up, not the red letter A, is likely to be the strongest socially-ingrained association. (Catholics are an exception, though there, too, the concern is separate since the relevant teaching relates to abortion itself, not illicit sex, which will be listed under a different heading on Judgment Day.)

The two levels of conflict are often mixed up, as one quickly learns sitting in on a counseling session. Very often, for instance, a young woman has gotten pregnant because she was so ambivalent about her violation of sexual mores that she didn't face up to what she was doing and its possible consequences, and therefore didn't use contraception. For the same reason, she doesn't want to face the fact that she is having an abortion or any other evidence of sex and her sexual nature. The most well-defined object of this kind of counseling is to get patients to confront this lapse and to take responsibility for their actions by using adequate contraception in the future. Sometimes the blocks are formidable, condensing into: "I don't need it. I got caught. I'm taking my punishment, and I'm never going to have sex again." A good counselor works hard on such patients as experience indicates their attitude makes them highly prone to getting into the predicament a second time.

Though frequently entangled with the outside influences of sexual mores, making the decision to have an abortion tends to precipitate a woman into an unusually unencumbered confrontation within herself, because being pregnant isolates a person, particularly if she's single and doesn't want to have a child. If you live in a society where bearing an illegitimate child is something to be ashamed of, and where, on the other hand, abortion is illegal, you are suddenly cut off from all the support, advice, information, and facilities which have diluted the immediacy of previous crises in your life. This compounds the isolation which accompanies pregnancy under any circumstances. Whatever you decide to do, you are ultimately alone. As one young patient put it. "Nobody is going to get on that operating table with you." You have to decide for yourself. This is true of any medical procedure one has to go through, but most of them don't present such a serious and complex choice.

NO HOLD ON HER LIFE

The discomfort with having violated social mores, and a person's consequent ambivalence about her sexual nature in general, if very strong, will probably preclude getting in touch with real self—completely. But insofar as patients do wrestle with questions about

> The average patient who comes through a clinic is under 20, definitely not in command of her life, and the consequence of bearing a child clearly may mean that she will never gain command.

abortion itself, their concerns are often cast precisely in this kind of internal frame of reference and therefore can be especially "pure" or "unsocialized." From descriptions, the issue in such cases takes shape not so much in terms of "murder" (though fetal size and characteristics are points of great interest) but of violating one's maternity (in a very broad sense). Insistence that "I really love children," or "I definitely want to have children," for instance, is a common patient protestation. In other words, the question is often more one of "what am I doing to myself" than consideration of the fetus as an independent entity: the perspective is one from which the fetus is more the fruition of a part of the woman's nature which she values highly and doesn't want to grow calluses over, than it is a creature to be considered separately from herself. Along these lines, it's common for an abortion patient to be in one way deeply pleased at being pregnant, even though the whole business has been a nightmare, even though she definitely doesn't want to bear a child at this point, and fervently wishes the pregnancy had never happened. That contradictory pleasure—surely independent of social mores, independent even of a disastrous, personal predicament—and the fear of frustrating the nature which generates it, is the most explicit expression of irreducible conflict in making the decision to have an abortion which I have come across.

Patients, most of them very young and new to this whole side of themselves, are also not likely to identify their feelings, much less the distinctions I am making here, very clearly. Counselors, however, who usually suffer very little from concern with social mores or aversion to sex, have often thought a lot on this level. "There's a conflict, no question about it, you can't think it away. The best you can do is to face it," said Vicki Simons, head counselor in one of New York's largest clinics.

> Many of the counselors had to deal with their feelings about their own abortions all over again when they first started work here. . . . They might not admit it, but I think many have deep feelings of ambivalence about abortion. . . . We've had some counselors who have had to have abortions while working here and it was a crisis in their lives. At a workshop for abortion counselors, many of them said they would not have abortions now, and a majority said that it would be a very very difficult decision for them . . . because they wanted to have children even though it wouldn't fit very well into their lives right then.

I'm not setting up this particular attitude as a norm beyond which lies only abnormality. Some women are genuinely uninterested in bearing children and others may want children but simply have no problem at all with abortion. My point is that many women, who could not possibly be called reactionary, see the personal decision in very serious terms, and that it's significant that among them are people who have been heavily exposed to the experience and have had occasion to think about it especially hard. Secondly, this attitude doesn't weaken the feminist case. Awareness of an irreducible conflict and personal resistance to having an abortion in no way dilutes these peoples' conviction that abortion must be legal and unconditionally accessible. Following them through a day's work lets you know why.

The frame of mind which considers abortion a morally acceptable option yet would lean heavily towards carrying an unexpected pregnancy to term despite grave difficulties depends on a very important
factor—a sense of being fundamentally in command of personal
destiny so that making way for an unexpected child, however disruptive, is still possible without throwing the mother's life beyond her
control. Women in their mid-twenties and older often have developed that stability and, according to observations, they are the ones
who are most likely to come to a decision to have an abortion with sorrow and difficulty. The average patient who comes through a clinic
is not in this category, however. She is under 20, definitely not in
command of her life, and the consequence of bearing a child clearly
may mean that she will never gain command.

After getting to know, however slightly, a number of teen-age patients, the insanity of compelling them to give birth crashes through
whatever vestiges of doubt one might have harbored. For most of
them "getting pregnant" really is an event that somehow happened
to them. Not having been brought up to look directly at their own sexuality, they seem to have fallen into it sideways, having looked
even less directly at its possible consequences. Abortion counselors talk
about how having an abortion can be a positive experience, which
sounds a little strange at first, but what they mean is that the experience can be more than an ordeal or even the solution to a particular predicament. It can mean facing a crisis, sorting it out, through
the questions that sorting leads one to ask, taking control of one's
own life. It can change a person from being menaced and therefore eva-
sive of this whole side of their nature into someone who willingly takes
responsibility for what previously was shadowed with threat.

In a lecture at Berkeley, Garrett Hardin, a professor of biology,
said:

> Critics of abortion generally see it as an exclusively negative thing,
> a means of nonfulfillment only. What they fail to realize is that
> abortion, like other means of birth control, can lead to fulfillment in
> the life of a woman. A woman who aborts this year because she is
> in poor health, neurotic, economically harassed, unmarried, on the

verge of divorce, or immature may well decide to have some other child five years from now—a wanted child. If her need for abortion is frustrated, she may never know the joy of a wanted child.

IT HAPPENED TO THEM

In *It Happens to Us*, a documentary film by Amalie Rothschild on people who have had abortions (legal and illegal), one interview brings this home especially vividly. A young, unmarried couple talk about what they've been through in these terms. The man tells how sex had always been presented to him as something that was going to get him in trouble—before he went on his first date at fourteen, his parents had warned him, "Now don't get her pregnant." The nightmare having finally come true, confronted, and worked out with an abortion, "my attitude towards marriage, having children, and sex have benefited." These things have become matters of choice, he said, not forces of circumstance. Needless to say, it would be preferable to work these problems out beforehand, thereby greatly reducing the chances that an abortion will be needed. But given the predicament, the sanity of solving it with an abortion cannot be denied. As they themselves said, Betsy and her boyfriend have a much better chance of being good parents some day: not people who feel they have been forced into something, and basically blame a child for it, but people who have freely chosen the responsibilities of parenthood. The forces of desperation which involuntary parenthood can create are starkly documented in that victim who inhabits all levels of the social structure in horrifyingly high numbers, the physically battered child.

The Betsys come to the clinics in hordes, hopefully leaving behind the combination of ignorance and evasion which got them into the predicament. Another kind of patient comes less often but with alarming frequency nonetheless. She's younger and would be even more vulnerable to permanent psychic damage if she bore a child. Unlike the 19- or 20-year-old who generally just wants to stop being pregnant as fast as she can, causing the least possible disruption in her life (the straightforward personal crisis attitude seems to come with maturity), the younger teenager often wants desperately to have the baby. Somebody else has pressed her into the abortion. A theory about this phenomenon, advanced in several studies, is that the subconscious reason she got pregnant was that she felt rejected, and sees in the future baby a substitute for herself on which she will lavish the love she herself needs badly. None of this has the remotest connection with what taking care of a child actually entails, and it's through pushing her to face the gulf between her fantasy and what motherhood would really be like for her that she can be led to understand her motivations. As a young girl said in *It Happens to Us:* "Now I know that I don't want a baby until I'm taking care of myself, until I'm fully responsible for myself," an insight many older women have failed to perceive.

Ulterior motivation behind unwanted pregnancies is not limited to teenagers. The complex forces which motivate a woman who does not have room in her life for a child to become lax about contraception, or fail to use it at all when it is available, are only just beginning to be explored. But even the rudimentary knowledge which has been gained reinforces, as in the case of the rejected teenager, the gut sense that prohibiting abortion does violence to sanity, and, on the other hand, that there's a lot more than plumbing involved. A study was made by Lawrence Downs and David Clayson of abortion patients at New York Hospital after the psychiatric department was called in to help a medical staff beset by this new kind of patient who "presented with tremendous emotionality that ran the gamut from extreme sadness, fear, and guilt through various psychotic and borderline conditions to those patients who demonstrated a bizarre euphoria, making a social event of their hospitalization" (not, in other words, your average tonsillectomy patients). Several characteristics distinguished the test group from the population at large. Sixty-six per cent of them recently had suffered either some kind of traumatic separation, such as termination of a marriage, or a death, recent or anticipated, in the immediate family. Fifty-one per cent had either felt disturbed enough to seek psychiatric help around the period when they conceived, or habitually used hard drugs or tranquilizers. Eighty-five per cent suffered from at least one of these situations. Other patterns emerged, such as a high incidence of women coping with unstable love relationships in which they were extremely dependent. Thirty-seven per cent had been recently troubled by a gynecological abnormality, and more than half of these thought they might be infertile. Seven per cent of the patients were teenagers whose mothers had recently had hysterectomies. The study opens only the tiniest chink towards truly understanding what might be going on in our heads when we ill-advisedly get ourselves pregnant. The glimmer that comes through, however, not only suggests that the points in our life when we make that mistake are likely to be the points when we are least able to cope with a child, but that the pregnancy is likely to be tied up with deep feelings about life, death, and generativity which would have to be dealt with in any healthy decision to end or go ahead with it.

AN ABORTED CALVINIST

Of all the counterarguments made by Right to Lifers, one reaches me with force. You cannot, they say, use social utility as the ultimate criterion in matters which involve life and death and essential liberties. There is one point on which abortion proponents switch from focusing entirely on the mother, take the fetus as a separate entity, and talk about its right not to be subjected to the misery which it is likely to suffer if born unwanted, and here, I think, they get into very deep water. While a huge proportion of the unhappy lives, and a whole network of social ills, can most likely be traced to a common condition, the unwanted child, when you start arguing that the person a fetus is going to become should not exist because he or she will be unhappy and/or will be a trouble to society—because they will be damaged goods—I bale out. Most of us would rather be alive than not, even if being alive also means being deformed, battered, halfcrazy, or poor.

In *Abortion Rap* by Florynce Kennedy and Dianne Schulder, Rabbi David Feldman's testimony in a federal suit challenging the constitutionality of New York's pre-1970 abortion laws is quoted. He makes the distinction between the two ways of thinking very clear.

. . . if the woman were to say that she had taken thalidomide during pregnancy (and the chances of a risk of deformity are very great) and she wanted an abortion, because a deformed life is not very good, the Rabbi would dismiss such talk of the future on grounds of "Well, you don't know what's going to be, whether the child is going to be deformed and whether being deformed is worse or better than not being born."

But if the same woman were to phrase the question differently and say that "the possibility of deformity is driving me to anguish or distraction" then the Rabbi would say: "Well, now, you're talking about someone who is here and alive and real and all of Jewish tradition says . . . if a woman asks for compassion in that respect, then she is entitled to it."

The distinction may seem like a philosophical nicety, but to me if the answer to the two ways of asking the question were "Have an abortion," the difference between those two ostensibly identical answers is a matter of opening the door to a utilitarianism in which the human life is reduced to the value of a machine—how well does it work.

I'm not suggesting that abortion should be accessible to women on a basis of how they answer questions. But these considerations are crucial as we build a case for, and tradition around, abortion, because how we think about its function and the function of other medical advances which introduce previously unimagined subtleties about the borderlines of life, is going to determine in the end how we think about all life.

Rabbi Feldman also said, "One thing emerges from the writings of all rabbis . . . that the welfare of the woman is primary, and that welfare, of course, is not limited to saving of life, but even to saving of mental health and to saving of welfare. It might even be extended to saving her the anguish of shame or embarrassment." Later he quotes a 19th century Hungarian rabbi: "No woman is required to build the world by destroying herself." An understanding of pregnancy, wanted and unwanted, and what it means for a woman to decide whether to go through with it or not, is the proper ground on which to base a case for abortion—not the social value of unwanted children, over-

313

population, or any other overview which is based on conjecture of whether or not the growth of the fetus into a human being ought to be canceled. Aside from opening the door to an abhorrent utilitarianism, such arguments lead as surely as the Right to Lifer position into an intolerable intrusion into the privacy of woman's choice in matters of maternity.

The hypocrisy this civilization has managed to maintain in its attitude towards unwanted pregnancies is unmatched. From the homes for unwed mothers where the inmates have pressed upon them first of all the importance of secrecy—the child will be whisked away at

> It would be sad indeed if in the process of rejecting the notion that abortion is something to be guilty about we substituted the equally un-straightforward mindset that it is something that shouldn't entail any feelings at all.

birth and lucky-lucky you will be able to resume life as though nothing had happened—to the gynecologists who refuse to help a woman who comes to them to get an abortion, yet tells her to come back when it's all over for a checkup, the social duplicity about this age-old, widespread, and drastic predicament is astounding. No less mystifying has been the silence of women; the fact that no bond grew between the millions who journeyed either into those treacherous regions of undefined conscience, illegality, and physical risk, or through the traumatic experience of bearing a child and giving it up. Now that it's all out in the open at last, we are faced with building new attitudes and principles which integrate this experience honestly into the social picture almost from scratch.

The centuries of acquiescence by women to the old attitudes demonstrate that we can dupe ourselves into believing almost anything: it would be sad indeed if in the process of rejecting the notion that abortion is something to be guilty about we substituted the equally unstraightforward mindset that it is something that shouldn't entail any feelings at all. Should I have a daughter, I want a world for her in which abortion is as available to her as a tonsillectomy. But I don't want her to grow up in an atmosphere which propels her into aborting an unwanted pregnancy without considering it a matter for deep and careful thought. To make that reflection truly free of social pressure, I also want the option of having the child, and the help and care she would need, openly presented to her and considered a respected and a viable alternative in the society she lives in. I hope she will reflect, not because I'm a Calvinist and want her to suffer where, if left alone, she would feel perfectly unconcerned about an abortion, but because I think she would otherwise be closing off to a part of herself if she didn't. Women have been closed off to themselves for too long.

The Sexualization of Racism

Calvin Hernton

More than two decades ago, a Swedish social scientist was invited to America for the purpose of conducting perhaps the most thorough study of the race problem ever undertaken. The social scientist was Gunnar Myrdal. As it turned out, he produced a monumental work entitled *An American Dilemma.*

One of the most interesting aspects of the race problem was formulated by Myrdal into a schema which he called "The Rank Order of Discrimination." When Myrdal asked white Southerners to list, in the order of importance, the things they thought Negroes wanted most, here is what he got:

1 Intermarriage and sex intercourse with whites
2 Social equality and etiquette
3 Desegregation of public facilities, buses, churches, etc.
4 Political enfranchisement
5 Fair treatment in the law courts
6 Economic opportunities[1]

The curious thing about this "Rank Order" was that when Myrdal approached the Negroes, they put down the same items as did the whites, but with one major change—they listed them in the direct *reverse* order!

Today the same reverse positions are still maintained with equal vigor by both whites and Negroes. While I am not going to charge either group with being totally dishonest, I am going to assert that neither whites nor Negroes were or are being completely honest with themselves. For, of the various facets of the race problem in America, there is no doubt that the sexual aspect is as much a "thorn in the side" to Negroes as it is to whites. Both groups, for their own special reasons, are hideously concerned about it.

The white man, especially the Southerner, is overtly obsessed by the idea of the Negro desiring sexual relations with whites. The Negro man is secretly tormented every second of his wakeful life by the presence of white women in his midst, whom he cannot or had better not touch. Despite the severe penalties for associating with white women—lynching, castration, electrocution—Negroes risk their lives for white flesh, and an occasional few actually commit rape. On the other hand, the white man, especially in the South, cannot seem to adhere to his own laws and customs prohibiting interracial intercourse—he insults, seduces, and rapes Negro women as if this were what they exist for. A preponderance of racial violence takes the form of sexual atrocities against not only black women but black men as well.

In the North, Midwest, and West, where there are few legal barriers against race mixing, many Negroes and whites suffer social ostracism and castigation for engaging in interracial relations.

What does all of this mean? It means that the race problem is inextricably connected with sex. More and more in America, everything we make, sell, handle, wear, and do takes on a sexual meaning. Matters dealing with race relations are no exception. The Madison Avenue "hidden persuaders" and the "organization men" of the commercial world are functioning now in such an all-pervasive way that virtually no area of social reality, no facet of our psyches, can escape the all but total sexualization of American life. In nearly every television commercial, in every fashion magazine, on the "center pages" of our newspapers, on billboard, bus, and subway ads, in the tabloids of scandal, on the covers and pages of every "cheap" magazine—there is but one incessant symbol: the naked or half-naked white woman. The scantily clad white woman is irresistibly enticing as the ubiquitous sex symbol of our times. Sex pervades everything.

The sexualization of the race problem is a reality, and we are going to have to deal with it even though most of us are, if not unwilling, definitely unprepared.

> **The white man's self-esteem is in a constant state of sexual anxiety in all matters dealing with race relations. So is the Negro's, because his life, too, is enmeshed in the absurd system of racial hatred in America.**

A tall, dark Negro boards the subway at 42nd Street in New York City. He takes a seat in the corner away from everybody. He pulls from his hip pocket a magazine; he looks around carefully, then opens the cover and instantly becomes engrossed. He turns the pages slowly, almost as if transfixed in and by some forbidden drug. There are naked women in various "naughty" poses on every page of the magazine. Their skin is white. A white man enters and stands beside the Negro. Quickly the Negro snaps the magazine shut, tucks it into his pocket, lays his head back and closes his eyes, probably to dream or to have a nightmare.

"I can't hardly sit by a Negro woman," said a white man who served as an informant for this book. "I can't be comfortable in their presence. I mean I get excited. They don't even have to be good-looking. I can't help but get erect no matter what kind of looking Negro she is."

I have before me the October (1963) issue of the *Science Digest*.

There is a picture of a Negro on the cover. The caption reads:

The Negro
HOW HE'S
DIFFERENT
WHY
WHITES
FEAR HIM[2]

Inside, on one of the pages, it says that the thing whites fear most about Negroes is that Negroes have an uncontrollable urge to mate with the sisters and daughters of white men. White men, especially Southerners, are afraid of the so-called superior, savage sexuality of the Negro male, and they are dead set against any measures that will lift the Negro's status, because they are certain that such measures will bring the Negro one step nearer to the white woman's bedroom. Meanwhile it is a common saying in the South among white males that "a man is not a man until he has slept with a nigger."

Listen to the advice a Negro woman in Mississippi gave reporter John Griffin, who she thought was a stranger to the way of white folks in the South.

> . . . well, you know you don't want to even look at a white woman. In fact, you look down at the ground or the other way . . . you may not know you're looking in a white woman's direction but they'll try to make something out of it. . . . If you pass by a picture show, and they've got women on the posters outside, don't look at them either . . . . Somebody's sure to say, "Hey, boy—what are you looking at that white gal like *that* for?"[3]

The white man's self-esteem is in a constant state of sexual anxiety in all matters dealing with race relations. So is the Negro's, because his life, too, is enmeshed in the absurd system of racial hatred in America. Since racism is centered in and revolves around sex, the Negro cannot help but see himself as at once sexually affirmed and negated. While the Negro is portrayed as a great "walking phallus" with satyr-like potency, he is denied the execution of that potency, he is denied the most precious sexual image which surrounds him—the white woman. The myth of the sanctity of "white womenhood" is nothing more than a myth, but because this myth is acted upon *as if* it were real by blacks and whites alike, then it *becomes* real as far as the behavior and sensitivities of those who must encounter it are concerned.

The sexualization of racism in the United States is a unique phenomenon in the history of mankind; it is an anomaly of the first order. In fact, there is a sexual involvement, at once real and vicarious, connecting white and black people in America that spans the history of this country from the era of slavery to the present, an involvement so immaculate and yet so perverse, so ethereal and yet so concrete, that all race relations tend to be, however subtle, *sex* relations.

It is important to see how the racism of sex in America has affected the sexual behavior of blacks and whites toward one another, and how black and white people perceive each other and themselves sexually as a result of living in a world of segregation and racial bigotry. As Negro and Caucasian, male and female, what do we mean to each other as sexual beings?

I am reminded of the way the policemen, during the historic march on Washington in 1963, constricted their eyes, tightened their faces, and fondled their sticks every time an interracial couple passed them in that mammoth parade. I am further reminded that when the marchers were yelling for F-R-E-E-E-DOM, for jobs, civil rights, equality of education, and the rest, a young Negro leaped in the air and shouted out—"S-E-X!" Perhaps he was a "crackpot." Even so, can one be certain that he was not an omen for our times? I am not certain, for I submit that, secretly, for many Negroes and whites, sexual liberty is as precious and sought-after as any other freedom. As the other barriers to freedom fall down, sexual liberty will become increasingly important in our society.

NOTES

1 Gunnar Myrdal, *An American Dilemma*, 7th ed. (New York: Harper and Row, 1962), Vol. 1, pp. 60–61.

2 My italics.

3 John Griffin, *Black Like Me* (New York: Signet Books, 1963), p. 60.

Homophobia

George Weinberg

. . . What causes homophobia—the dread of being in close quarters with homosexuals—and in the case of homosexuals themselves, self-loathing? Volumes have been written—by psychologists, sexologists, anthropologists, sociologists, and physiologists—on homosexuality, its origins and its development. This is because in most western civilizations, homosexuality is itself considered a problem; our unwarranted distress over homosexuality is not classified as a problem because it is still a majority point of view. Homophobia is still part of the conventional American attitude.

Despite massive evidence that homosexuals are as various in their personalities as anyone else, the public at this time still holds many misconceptions which in some cases are thought to justify our discriminatory practices. Among these misconceptions are the belief that homosexuals seduce young children (child molestation is preponderantly a heterosexual practice); the belief that homosexuals are untrustworthy; that homosexual men hate women; that homosexual

From *Society and the Healthy Homosexual* by George Weinberg. Reprinted by permission of the author and the publisher, St. Martin's Press, Inc.

women hate men—all beliefs unsupported by evidence, but held unquestioningly by millions.

If there is any doubt of the existence of homophobia, consider that in England and the U.S., for hundreds of years, homosexuality was unmentionable. In the courts, homosexual crimes were alluded to in Latin, or implied by circuitous language, and judges have sentenced people to languish in jail for acts considered so vile that they should not be talked about. For this reason, homosexuality has sometimes been called "the crime without a name."

There is a certain cost in suffering from any phobia, and that is that the inhibition spreads to a whole circle of acts related to the feared activity, in reality or symbolically. In this case, acts imagined to be conducive to homosexual feelings, or that are reminiscent of homosexual acts, are shunned. Since homosexuality is more feared by men than women, this results in marked differences in permissiveness toward the sexes. For instance, a great many men refrain from embracing each other or kissing each other, and women do not. Moreover, men do not as a rule express fondness for each other, or longing for each other's company, as openly as women do. Men tend not to permit themselves to see beauty in the physical forms of other men, or enjoy it; whereas women may openly express admiration for the beauty of other women. Men, even lifetime friends, will not sit as close together on a couch while talking earnestly as women may; they will not look into each other's faces as steadily or as fondly. Ramifications of this phobic fear extend even to parent-child relationships. Millions of fathers feel that it would not befit them to kiss their sons affectionately or embrace them, whereas mothers can kiss and embrace their daughters as well as their sons. . . .

When a phobia incapacitates a person from engaging in activities considered decent by a society, the person himself is the sufferer. He loses out on the chance to go skiing perhaps, if it is acrophobia, or the chance to take the elevator to the street each day if it is claustrophobia. But here the phobia appears as antagonism directed toward a particular group of people. Inevitably, it leads to disdain of those people, and to mistreatment of them. This phobia in operation is a prejudice, which means that we can widen our understanding of it by considering the phobia from the point of view of its being a prejudice and uncovering its chief motives.

Here are the chief ones that I have been able to identify. There are five of them.

THE RELIGIOUS MOTIVE

. . . Much of our present tradition around homosexuality, and sexuality generally, goes back to the Judaeo–Christian code. The Biblical stricture against "spilling the seed" covered homosexuality too, and there are explicit prohibitions against homsexuality in the Bible. Oppression of homosexuals became most atrocious when

> **Some leaders of the homophile movement believe that the most vociferous enemies of homosexuals are combatting homosexual urges in themselves.**

ecclesiastic powers brought their backing to it. As part of its wider campaign against pleasure, the Church evolved an enormously strict system. The Christian ideal was complete celibacy—accompanied by a craving for asceticism, purity and poverty. For hundreds of years Christianity set itself to distinguishing possible sources of pleasure and prohibiting them.

Not even sexual intercourse between husband and wife for procreation was fully above reproach. The Church catalogued variants of that act too, and banned most of them in belief that they involved choices aimed at enjoyment. It banned nudity, and the sexual intercourse position using entry from the rear, because this position was thought unduly pleasurable. . . .

As an obvious seeker for sexual pleasure without the excuse of child-getting, the homosexual came to seem a living rebuke to

Christianity. Under its influence, emperors borrowed the tactic of putting homosexuals to death, and the public embraced this view of homosexuals as heretics and sinners. . . .

The influence of ecclesiastical thinking is still to be found, not just among Christians but everywhere among us. Sometimes the Bible itself is blamed for this. But, as the Reverend Troy Perry notes in public appearances, those who base their condemnation of homosexuality on Biblical admonitions are exercising considerable personal judgment over which Biblical teachings to accept and which to disregard. Perry often refers to Leviticus, where the recommendation is made that two men who engage in a homosexual act should be stoned. He observes that in the same book of the Bible, it is said to be wrong for a woman to wear a scarlet dress or for anyone to eat shrimp. And yet people who wear scarlet and eat shrimp continue to cite Leviticus as their authority for condemning homosexuality.

Reverend Perry, who is pastor of the Metropolitan Community Church in Los Angeles, is the best known of an increasing number of religious leaders who give services for homosexuals. In only two years Perry won a following of 16,000 homosexuals in eleven major cities in the United States. The main issue for these men and women is not whether one believes in God, but whether belief in God is incompatible with homosexuality. Reverend Perry's own answer is repeated as a chant by those who attend his services: "The Lord is my Shepherd and He knows I'm gay." To blame the Church alone for the phobic attitude toward sexuality held today is to overlook ongoing dynamic attitudes, which must always be present in a population when a prejudice persists.

THE SECRET FEAR OF BEING HOMOSEXUAL

A second motive for the homophobic reaction is the fear of being homosexual oneself.

When Dick Leitsch, who was then head of the New York Mattachine Society for the rights of homosexuals, was on a speaking tour of the colleges, he would sometimes encounter opposition in an unexpected form. At Ohio University in Athens, a man stood up out of the audience and roared at him after his speech: "But you see, Mr. Leitsch, if you take the laws away, and the social stigmas too, against homosexuals, then everyone will be homosexual." Apparently, the man perceived the law as a vital help in deterring him from becoming homosexual himself.

Similarly, in discussing a file clerk who, for homosexual acts committed as a minor, had been fired from his job as an adult and was later reinstated, Presidential Assistant Walter W. Jenkins gave assurance in 1964 that the man "would not actually control air traffic." Months later, this very man who had tacitly granted the irresponsibility of homosexuals left the government after being discovered in a homosexual act.

In both cases we see what Freud called *reaction formation*, the mechanism of defending against an impulse in oneself by taking a stand against its expression by others.

There are many cases of prejudice as part of reaction formation. In fact, some leaders of the homophile movement believe that the most vociferous enemies of homosexuals are combatting homosexual urges in themselves. However, my own study suggests that the motives are usually more complicated than the mere concern with being homosexual.

REPRESSED ENVY

The third motive for homophobia is repressed envy. "An outstanding result of studies of bigoted personalities seems to be the discovery of a sharp cleavage between conscious and unconscious layers" (Allport). The prejudiced person harbors ideas about himself that he does not express. The dangerous constellation is of the form, *I am successful because I am thought to possess some particular attribute, but I fear I am deficient in it.*

Two kinds of vulnerability are possible here. The person may see someone who shakes his confidence regarding how much of the attribute he possesses. A would-be competitor looms in front of him. Threat of this form has been discussed occasionally in connection with the prejudice against blacks. The argument is made that some white men rest their sense of security on the belief that they are supreme as lovers; believing that blacks have special sexual prowess, they downgrade black men in order to deny them the right to competition.

But the imagined vulnerability is of a different form where homosexuals are feared. *The homosexual is felt to belie the importance of the attributes themselves.* The homosexual man does not seem to be saying, "I can do better with women than you." He seems to be saying, "Your success with women isn't nearly so important for happiness as you imagine. And look at all you've sacrificed for it." Of "masculinity" he seems to be saying, "That attribute of yours means nothing! Here I am with no desire to possess it."

The homosexual man is much more apt to be regarded as threatening on this score than the homosexual woman. Most men are taught from early childhood that to engage in homosexual acts would be to surrender their "masculine identity." Women are not, by analogy, imagined to be less feminine if they engage in homosexual love-making, and moreover, they do not learn to fear the loss of their identity as much. After years of struggle to achieve a precarious masculine identity, many heterosexual men feel threatened by the sight of homosexuals, who appear to them to be disdainful of the basic requirements of manhood.

To these men, personal success appears to demand that they go on conveying an impression of themselves which is so far from the fact that they cannot possibly manage it perfectly. There appear to be numerous requirements. For instance, they envision the successful man as perennially confident, as dressing well and appropriately at all times, as making a good living, as commanding respect from his wife, and as in command of "where he is going." Without respite, this would-be ideal American man must toil to appear as what he knows he is not; and since he is apt to believe that lapses *should disqualify* him from enjoying the culture's rewards and even from love, he is particularly disturbed by the sight of someone who apparently feels no need to assert himself in the same ways. Puritanism was once defined by H. L. Mencken as "the lurking fear that someone somewhere is happy"; and surprising as it sounds, this fear often operates in the heterosexual's view of the homosexual.

Despite their social role as outcasts, homosexual men, and often homosexual women too, are thought by a surprising number of people to have it *easier* than others and become the objects of suppressed envy. In cases where being a responsible head of a household is thought of as a requisite for sex or family pleasures, where courtship is thought of as the minimum payment for sex, and where sex itself is sanctioned only as a means of propagating the race, it vexes people to see others apparently matching the profits without having to pay as

> **The notion that there are homosexuals distresses some people because the thought of persons without children reawakens their fear of death.**

dearly for them. The laws branding homosexuality a crime are felt to restore the balance somewhat, but not enough for some people.

Homosexual women appear to suffer less from this sort of envy than homosexual men do. Perhaps this is because "many men regard the lesbian choice as that of a lesser for a lesser," as feminist leader Dr. Catharine Stimpson put it.

Besides, the machinery of discrimination against lesbians has been able to grind quietly. By granting numerous social privileges and responsibilities to women only if they married, societies have uniformly punished lesbians without even having to acknowledge that they existed. In addition, many men, and perhaps those who tend to dislike lesbians most, pride themselves on being charitable toward women. For ages, homage to women has been serving men as a sign of their own decency, and has often been used to justify ruthlessness elsewhere. One doesn't punch lesbians with impunity for the same reason one doesn't kill women and children, according to the rules of war. Probably for this reason more than others, lesbians have been spared the more pointed and brutal kinds of attacks that have been made on homosexual men. On the whole, repressed

327

envy operates more as a motive for the abuse of homosexual men than of homosexual women.

THE THREAT TO VALUES

Another motive for resentment toward homosexuals is that they are seen as constituting a threat to one's values.

Anyone who does not adopt a society's usual value system runs the risk of being seen as undermining the society. Because the person does not share the interests and goals of the majority, there is suspicion of him. This remains so, even if the person produces as much as others and works as hard over a lifetime. . . .

The rift between homosexuals and others in this respect bears close analogy to certain aspects of the so-called generation gap. Underlying it is a severe clash of values, with resultant rage toward those considered nonconformist. . . .

EXISTENCE WITHOUT VICARIOUS IMMORTALITY

Finally, by getting patients to free-associate at length, I have discovered a strange and poignant reason for the phobia.

The notion that there are homosexuals distresses some people because the thought of persons without children reawakens their fear of death. Today in the larger population, vicarious immortality through having children and grandchildren assuages the spirit of millions and blunts the edge of mortality for them. Our great glorification of reproduction, with all the customs and modes that advance it, serves in part as a ceremony to circumvent death as if by magic. The decision by a person not to have children opens up the concern in many minds, "What about death? How can he live with the knowledge that he is going to leave no one behind?" It jars these people to think that the homosexual may not be concerned with leaving "his own flesh and blood" after him. Whether or not the homosexual man or woman has had children in a particular case, the person's very existence becomes a fearful reminder to people of what life would be like without children. . . .

Observe how preoccupation with the nuclear family, and the blind faith in reproduction as the standard for sexuality, and the religious motive, tie together. Reproduction and children and the promise of an afterlife are utilized by some as magical devices to cope with the fear of death. To many, the homosexual, who does not appear to be wearing these amulets, evokes this fear.

Those who shun homosexuals tend to share a number of unstated assumptions, of which the most important is that something is frighteningly wrong when a human being diverges from the standardized pattern of existence. Some, especially the uneducated, are still apt to express their attitude with open, ugly hostility: by jibes and insults, or by actually beating up homosexuals. More insidious in its way is the disguised hostility of many who consider themselves enlightened and educated; this hostility is often concealed by the device of shifting the irrational fear to an intellectual level and presenting it as if it were rational. Perhaps the most usual expression of this is an endless absorption with the question: How did the homosexual get that way? This ostensibly valid intellectual inquiry is frequently an expression of hostilities or fears, which become presented as if they were part of a serious intellectual exploration.

The fact is that the combination of physiological readiness and social experience resulting in the development of *any* erotic preference—homosexual or heterosexual—is so intricate that science has not been able to fathom it as yet. No group of experts in any field can predict who will be homosexual, though after the fact, psychologists of nearly every school stand ready to pontificate to individuals about how they became homosexual. The homosexual man or woman who goes to psychologists using six different approaches will hear six different explanations of how he or she became homosexual.

It is noteworthy that we seldom hear the question: How did a person become heterosexual? Probably we shall discover the answers to the two questions at the same time, if we ever do, since the real issue is: How does one learn sexual preference? The origin of homosexuality comes into question because it is considered a deviant course.

What pebble diverted the stream? As if without proof it were assumed that the capacity to reproduce sets the standard in sexual conduct from which one should not deviate—that, therefore, heterosexuality must in some profound sense be in the mainstream of thought and activity in the life of every individual and homosexuality a sign of interference. The truth is that reproduction is seldom the motive for sexual activity and that the human range of sexual possibilities develops independently of the desire to reproduce. . . .

Implicit in all this is the unwarranted assumption that at bottom we all crave the same ends and advantages. In the last analysis, the homophobic reaction I have been describing is a form of acute conventionality. Ultimately, it condemns because of difference. It has every basic attribute of an irrational social prejudice.

Gay Couples and Straight Law

Tom Hurley

A man and a woman fall in love. They get married, have children. The husband and wife take care of their children, feeding, clothing, educating them, loving them. The relationship is so familiar we hardly stop to notice it.

Another relationship is more noticeable: two women or two men fall in love. They get married, adopt children or retain custody of their own from previous marriages, feeding, clothing, educating them, loving them. This relationship gives pause to most people, gay or straight. Such relationships do, however, occur—now—in this society.

But if gay couples, with or without children, want the protection of the law over their unions, they have to perform legal acrobatics straight couples never dream of. No marriage statute in this country forbids the marriage of two people of the same sex, but legal custom and usage have held that the intent of the law is for marriage to be a contract between two people of the opposite sex. The Washington State Court of Appeals, for example, upheld in 1974 a lower court decision that denial of a marriage license to two gays is neither unconstitutional nor discriminatory. The Court's opinion was based on the argument that marriage is primarily for the procreation and education of children. Apparently the judges weren't aware of the fact that many straight couples marry without the intention of having children. Or that gay couples can raise children as well as the straight family next door.

In spite of what the courts have said, gay couples are still seeking to have their unions ratified by law. The first such marriage took place on June 12, 1970, when the Rev. Troy D. Perry married two Los Angeles women who had a *de facto* common-law marriage. Under

> **Many gay couples feel a need to solemnize their relationships with legal contracts.**

California law, a religious ceremony alone and not a license is needed to validate a common-law marriage.

Consider also the case of Jack Baker and Mike McConnell, who began fighting for gay civil rights several years ago when Baker became president of the student body at the University of Minnesota. Baker and McConnell applied for a marriage license in 1970, but authorities denied the application. Appeals through the state court system were defeated, and a final appeal was dismissed by the Supreme Court. The couple finally solved their problem with the law by a two-step process. Making use of the relatively uncomplicated Minnesota adoption laws, McConnell first adopted Baker, thus binding the two legally. Baker took as his new name Pat Lyn McConnell. Then Mike McConnell drove to a Minnesota town well out of the range of the Minneapolis media and took out a marriage license. In one space he filled in his own name; in the only other space left—that for the woman—he wrote down the name of his spouse: Pat Lyn McConnell. And so they were legally married. Local authorities now recognize the marriage as valid, but both the Veterans' Administration, to whom Baker applied for a change in status on account of his spouse, and the Internal Revenue Service are challenging the union. According to Baker, he and his lover are eagerly awaiting the new court contests. They are also presently seeking to become foster parents.

Baker, now a lawyer, and McConnell possessed the energy and determination to enter test cases that would radically alter the law. Baker sums up their approach this way: "If you're concerned about the movement—whatever that is—there's a duty to get yourself into the most controversial position you can, and then put out a press release. You get things changed very quickly that way." Baker has little patience with lawyers who counsel their clients to seek ways *around* the law.

Not all gay couples feel up to putting their lives under the legal spotlight, but many gay couples still feel a need to solemnize their relationships with legal contracts. A Boston couple, for example, wrote a chapter in the history of gay life versus straight law, a chapter that involved a circumvention of the law rather than a head-on collision.

Bob Jones and Harry Freeman presented themselves to Richard Rubino, the Boston lawyer who has made a name for himself by defending gay people. What they wanted was a legal relationship that would bind them together as an ordinary marriage does, but would allow them to avoid a confrontation with city hall. Rubino did three things: (1) He drew up a mutual contract combining a partnership agreement and an ante-nuptial agreement (the latter making stipulations about what would happen if the pair were to desire a "divorce"). The mutual contract made each partner liable for the other's debts and dealt very specifically with the property they shared; (2) He drew up manual wills, making each the other's executor and sole heirs; and (3) He arranged for a legal name change that involved a hyphenation of their last names.

To be sure, there are some differences between this arrangement and the usual marriage contract: the legal relationship was tailored to Jones and Freeman's particular needs; they could end their contract easily while the divorce of a straight couple would require lengthy legal procedures. But, explains Rubino, the contract gives the pair what they asked for: legal as well as moral obligations. "It's not quite the same as marriage, but it's as close to the same as we can get now," Rubino comments.

Whether a gay couple are legally bound together or not, other legal problems, depending on the nature of their relationship, may arise. Wills and insurance policies, for example. While talking with Rubino about wills, for example, the specter of Alice B. Toklas arose in my mind. She was left destitute because the family of Gertrude Stein prevented her from sharing in her lover's estate by contesting Stein's will. But Rubino's attitude in dealing with a family challenge to a gay person's will is optimistic. The basic legal argument in the contest of a will is that the person was not "of sound mind" when making out the will. If a family could not prove this, they could not successfully challenge the document. Rubino feels that the will he drew up for the Freeman-Jones would withstand a family challenge. A couple's homosexuality, he would argue, is certainly not evidence of mental instability and is simply not relevant to a case of this kind. More importantly, says Rubino, objecting to the introduction of a client's sexual preferences into a civil case has worked for him: the courts have refused to consider the matter relevant.

Books about gay life often present us with one story after another about the legal hassles of couples: Look, for example, at the chapter on "Lifestyle" in Del Martin and Phyllis Lyon's *Lesbian/Woman* (Bantam, 1972). These disturbing stories are culled from the authors' own experiences and those of their sisters. But while the horror stories are true, Richard Rubino emphasizes that in many cases they need not have occurred. Civil cases involving gay couples, if handled by a sympathetic lawyer and tactfully presented, can be successful. The rule is to be pragmatic, to determine what strategy to use in each particular case.

Claire Shanahan of Boston agrees. Most gay couples, she feels, stop short of legal confrontation anyway. If they do go ahead, they proceed carefully and slowly, and they get what they want. Claire had her insurance policies made out to her lover, Linda Lachman, describing her relationship to Linda simply as "friend." The insurance company did not object and even stated specifically that the policy was hers and she could name whomever she pleased as beneficiary. The company might have been a little uneasy had it known that the policy holder and beneficiary were gay lovers, but Claire feels Linda and she got exactly what they wanted without a lot of fuss. Her medical coverage, however, specifies familial relationships, thus providing for her children but excluding her lover. This bothers Claire for obvious reasons, but she remains philosophical while keeping her eye on the Massachusetts State House for legal changes favorable to gays. Her approach, in the meantime, is to "walk very softly, and don't carry too big a stick."

Hospital rules do not have the force of law, but if a lover becomes seriously ill and enters a hospital, doctors may restrict visits to members of the immediate family. This separates lovers at a crucial time. An *ad hoc* group of the Homophile Community Health Service of Boston, according to Paula Bennett of Lesbian Mothers, is now talking about getting lovers spouses' rights. But while awaiting changes of this kind, people solve the problem in various ways. Rubino says one solution is to have the sick lover grant "power of attorney" to the other. This tactic, of course, depends on the condition of the patient—he or she must be able to write—but if the power is granted, no hospital authority can deny access to the sickroom. Claire Shanahan's approach was a bit more direct: when Linda was in the hospital, Claire simply explained to the nurses that she was Linda's "sister." It worked.

So this much becomes clear. If two women or two men desire to live together as a couple, the legal aspects of their action—whether they involve marriage, wills, name changes (or other legal questions like property and taxation not touched on here)—can be handled in either of two ways: the couple, as openly gay people, can fight a long, difficult war that may involve many defeats before it produces a victory; or they can avoid directly confronting the law and seek less dramatic but effective solutions. In either case, people should consult a sympathetic lawyer who will fight what fights are needed, make what arrangements are necessary, in the manner most appropriate to the desired ends. In fact, says Rubino, more and more gay people are coming to him about civil questions rather than criminal cases: "It's a healthy sign of the gay community getting its head together."

On his part, Rubino vows that when a case must go to court, he will "educate the courts about individual clients and what is going on in the world today, especially with gay people in the United States." The courts, as legal arms of straight society, certainly need that education.

The American Civil Liberties Union is also trying to educate the courts. The ACLU's, "National Project on Sexual Privacy" declares as its purpose "to coordinate a national effort to remove all laws which proscribe private consensual sexual activity among adults and to eliminate discriminatory practices which flow from the existence of such laws." A legal docket prepared by the project shows that a good number of cases completed or in progress during 1974 pertained to the lives of gay couples. The docket should thicken as more gay couples attempt to make the law serve their own needs.

A larger question, however, is whether gays should be getting involved in the institution of marriage at all. Reverend Don McGaw, director of Boston's Homophile Community Health Service, thinks that "gay marriage is beating a dead horse." He argues that "if we have to [have gay marriage], it's because we haven't yet figured out other ways to get what we want legally." But the fact remains that at this stage in gay history, many gay people believe that a marriage relationship is the best way for two people in love to build a life together.

The law, reflecting the society that creates it, does not approve of gay love. The courts have usually found a gay household, whether male or female, unsuitable for raising children. Martin and Lyon's *Lesbian/Woman* pointed out the difficulties gay women, particularly women who live with their lovers, have had in maintaining custody of their children from previous marriages. In one case, a woman was denied custody and allowed visitation rights only in the presence of her child's father—this on the basis of a psychiatrist's testimony that although the woman was a stable, sensitive person, a heterosexual environment was preferable for a growing child. But *Lesbian/Woman* records another case: a woman openly declared her love for another woman; the husband's lawyer could find nothing in her background to prove her unsuitable as a parent; the woman won unrestricted custody of her children.

Martin and Lyon were quick to point out that the first case was far more the rule than the second, but the situation just a few years after the publication of their book appears to be changing. Women in Transition, a Philadelphia group that helps divorced and separated women, is currently investigating custody and visitation rights of gay mothers. Favorable precedents are hard to come by, but a 1974 Washington state decision may give the group the argument they need. A Tacoma judge not only granted a lesbian permanent custody of her three children but did so without preventing her from living with her lover. The court's decision was based on testimony by a

> Adoption agencies are seeking gay parents for the large number of gay children who have severe problems living with their straight families.

sociologist, on the viewing of a movie called "Sandy and Madeleine's Family"* and on a social worker's investigation of the family environment. Nothing in the woman's background, the judge declared, made her unfit to have custody of her children.

But one legal precedent does not mean a sudden change in the attitudes of society. The courts need to be educated, case by case, before they will reject the widespread view that homosexuality is a necessary bar to child custody. Richard Rubino explains that although a woman in a child custody case is usually presumed to be fit, the presumption reverses itself when the mother is a lesbian. But Rubino would argue in court (armed with statistics) that gay people who bring up children no more affect the sexual preference of their offspring than do straight parents. From that point, Rubino moves to the question of what is best for the child, given the individual circumstances of each case. He also asks questions like: Do the parents want a court fight? How sympathetic has the judge been in the past? Usually, Rubino notes, custody cases can be worked out before the formal court

---

*Available from Multi-Media Resource Center, 1523 Franklin St., San Francisco, California 94109.

appearance. In any case, he recommends that a client neither confirm nor deny his or her gayness. If the non-gay party raises the issue, Rubino feels confident he can persuade the court of its irrelevance.

Gay couples are also adopting children with increasing frequency. In fact, adoption agencies are seeking gay parents for the large number of gay children who have severe problems living with their straight families. Of course, not all the authorities have hopped on the bandwagon; some have even tried to pull its wheels off. In the state of Washington, the head of the Department of Social and Health Services tried in 1974 to prevent gays from becoming foster parents by changing adoption regulations. The proposed rules specified, among other things, that "foster parents shall be persons who have satisfactory, stable interpersonal relationships, free of chronic conflict both within and without the family group and who are without severe problems in their sexual orientation." After continued pressure from gay groups, the wording was modified, omitting "severe problems in their sexual orientation" but retaining phrases that could be used against gay people. Gay Oregonians have run into similar problems with that state's Department of Human Resources.

But there have been victories, too. A Philadelphia lesbian couple are now foster parents for a fifteen-year-old transvestite boy. The boy had been shunted from the streets to straight foster families and back again. Although the judge was not aware of the couple's sexual preference, the adoption agency knew that the two women were gay and found them fully qualified to care for the youth. In Minnesota, Jack Baker and Mike McConnell, those indefatigable gay challengers of the law, have applied with several agencies to adopt a child. In New York City, the National Gay Task Force announced, in June 1974, a program to find homes for gay children. NGTF will search out mature gay people who want to help troubled younger gays and will then recommend the prospective parents to cooperating local agencies.

Boston's Homophile Community Health Service experimented with such a program but abandoned the effort in 1973. Director Don McGaw explains that the service had trouble finding couples who were: (1) financially sound; (2) together a long time; (3) not up-tight about dealing with a gay teen-ager; and (4) aware that they would not be "parents"—since McGraw feels that the parent-child relationship is inappropriate to adolescence. Unhappy with the idea of the nuclear family, McGaw would prefer a foster house made up of several gay adolescents, two gay adult men, and two gay adult women. Significantly, however, he found no problem with the state agencies, who were very willing to place gay young people with gay foster parents.

Whatever their life plans, gay people are now demanding that the law serve *their* needs as it does straights. Gay couples who want marriages and children are figuring out ways to change the law or get around it. The efforts of gay couples help themselves and other gay couples, but they also make it easier for all gays to obtain equal justice under law. The courts, like society itself, must realize that we are here, and we are not going to be adjudicated away.

Facts Versus Fears: Why Should We Worry About Pornography?

W. Cody Wilson

The publication and distribution of salacious materials is a peculiarly vicious evil; the destruction of moral character caused by it among young people cannot be overestimated. The circulation of periodicals containing such materials plays an important part in the development of crime among youth of our country.[1]

> If a case is to be made against "pornography" in 1970, it will have to be made on grounds other than demonstrated effects of a damaging personal or social nature. Empirical research designed to clarify the question has found no reliable evidence to date that exposure to explicit sexual materials plays a significant role in the causation of delinquent or criminal sexual behavior among youth or adults.[2]

Thus is the issue drawn: popular rhetoric versus the findings of empirical science—fears versus facts. This issue is, of course, much larger by far than the issue of pornography. But the issue of pornography may serve as a case study which illuminates the larger

Reprinted from *The Annals of the American Academy of Political and Social Science*, September, 1971, Volume 397. Reprinted by permission of publisher.

issue—and, indeed, pornography is an issue of considerable interest in itself.

This paper will review the "facts" about pornography as they are revealed by empirical research in the social, behavioral, and medical sciences, and then explore some of the implications of these "facts" for our society.

Many of the data that exist at the present regarding pornography are either the direct or indirect products of the needs and interests of the U.S. Commission on Obscenity and Pornography which began its work in 1968 and made its report in 1970.[3] The Commission, created by Congress, was assigned four specific tasks: (1) to analyze existing laws, (2) to ascertain the volume of traffic and patterns of distribution for obscene and pornographic materials, (3) to study the effects of these materials on the public, and (4) to recommend policy. A review of the existing empirical literature in 1968 concluded that

> we still have precious little information from studies of humans on the questions of primary import to the law. . . . the data "stop short at the critical point." Definitive answers on the determinants and effects of pornography are not yet available.[4]

The Commission spent two years and nearly one million dollars in research on these tasks. The result was not a "definitive answer"—but there are, now, a few facts with which to think about the issues.

PATTERNS OF EXPERIENCE WITH EXPLICIT SEXUAL MATERIAL

Extent of Exposure

In retrospect it may seem incredible that in 1968 there were no "facts" about people's experience with erotic materials. Alfred C. Kinsey and his associates had collected information on this topic, but it had never been adequately analyzed and reported. Any estimate was necessarily a projection of one's own personal experience or one's own private fears and fantasies. Each individual was a repository of information about such experiences, but this experience had never been collated to provide a description of the typical experience in our society.

In 1969 several investigators began to ask selected individuals about their experiences with pornography or explicit sexual materials.

Approximately 20,000 readers of *Psychology Today* responded to the question, "Have you voluntarily obtained or seen erotic or pornographic books, movies, etc?" In this sample (obviously not representative of the general population since 77 percent were less than 35 years old and 89 percent had some college experience), 92 percent of the males and 72 percent of the females said, "Yes."[5]

> **Younger adults are more likely to have been exposed to erotic materials than are older adults; and the more education one has, the more likely one is to have been exposed to such materials.**

The same question was asked of 450 members of professional and community service groups in metropolitan Detroit, and 80 percent indicated that they had voluntarily obtained erotic materials.[6]

A questionnaire submitted to several hundred predominantly middle-class men and women members of social, professional, service, and church groups in Denver revealed that 83 percent had seen at some time in their lives depictions of people engaged in a sex act.[7]

Intensive clinical interviews regarding experience with a variety of sexual materials were conducted with predominantly lower middle-class, black and white, normal males in the age range 20–40 in Los Angeles. Over 90 percent of the group reported that they had seen photographs of fully nude females, and 86 percent of the whites and 76 percent of the blacks reported having been exposed to photographic depictions of sexual intercourse.[8]

These several studies of selected samples are quite consistent in their results and suggest that experience with explicit sexual materials sometimes called pornography is rather widespread in our society.

This hypothesis was tested by conducting face-to-face interviews with approximately 2,500 adults selected in such a way that their responses could be generalized to the total adult population of the United States. This survey asked questions about seeing pictorial depictions and reading verbal depictions of the following five types: emphasizing the sex organs of a man or woman; mouth-sex organ contact between a man and woman; a man and woman having sexual intercourse; sexual activities between people of the same sex; and sex activities which included whips, belts, or spankings. Eighty-four percent of the men and 69 percent of the women in this representative national sample reported having been exposed to at least one of these kinds of depictions.[9]

Experience in the United States is very similar to that in Denmark. In a survey of a representative sample of 398 men and women in Copenhagen, 87 percent of men and 73 percent of women reported that they had "consumed" at least one "pornographic" book, and similar percentages had "consumed" at least one "pornographic" magazine.[10]

Correlates of Exposure

Experience with explicit sexual materials varies according to the characteristics of both the material and the person.

People are more likely to have experience with depictions of sexual activity which conform to our society's general cultural norms than with portrayals of sexual activity which deviate from these norms.[11] The rank ordering of depictions in terms of their likelihood of being seen in our society is: full nudity, heterosexual intercourse, oral sex, homosexual activity, and sado-masochistic activity. Portrayals of combinations of sex and violence are relatively rare in the experience of normal adults in our society.

People with different characteristics have differential experience with explicit sexual material. It was reported above that men are more likely to have had experience with sexual materials than are women. Younger adults are more likely to have been exposed to erotic materials than are older adults; and the more education one has, the more likely one is to have been exposed to such materials. These two relations hold for both men and women. For men, but not for women, those who live in large metropolitan areas are more likely than those who do not to have had experience with explicit sexual materials People who read general books, magazines, and newspapers more and who see general movies more, also see more erotic stimuli. People who are socially and politically active are exposed to more erotic material. Both these latter two findings hold for both men and women. People who attend religious services more often are somewhat less likely to be exposed to erotica.[12]

These differences in experience with sexual materials may be summarized by the following profiles. Persons who have had greater amounts of experience with erotic materials tend to be younger, better educated, better read, urban males who are socially and politically active, but less involved in religious affairs. Those who have had less experience with erotic materials tend to be older, less educated and less well read females who live in smaller communities and are more isolated socially, less politically active, but more active in religious affairs.

Similar profiles have been reported for Sweden.[13]

Although some experience with explicit sexual materials is almost universal among males in our society, only about one-fifth to one-quarter of the population have somewhat regular experience as adults with materials as explicit as heterosexual intercourse.[14]

Age of First Experience

The representative sample of American adults was also asked to try to recall the age at which they had first been exposed to explicit sexual materials. Roughly three-quarters of the males reported having been exposed before age 21, one-half before age 18, and one-third before age 15; females report being exposed to these materials about two years later than do males. These figures may report later exposure than actually occurred, however, because it may be difficult for older people to make differentiations of a few years when recalling teenage experience. For example, although 19 percent of all male adults report first exposure at 12 years of age or younger, 34 percent of men age 21-29 report first exposure at age 12 or younger. This difference in reporting may reflect errors in recall among older respondents, or it may reflect actual changes in experience in more recent decades.[15]

The clinical interviews with normal subjects in Los Angeles confirm these findings that adult males report considerable experience with explicit sexual materials in adolescence. Three-quarters of the subjects reported having seen photos of heterosexual intercourse in adolescence, and two-thirds reported having seen photos of mouth-genital activity in adolescence.[16]

Three studies of college students indicate a greater degree of exposure to explicit sexual materials during adolescence than do retrospective reports of older adults. Again, it is not clear whether this reflects more precise recall or a change in cultural experience over time.

A report of a survey of a national random sample of the college students conducted in 1967 concluded that over 90 percent of college students have exposure to explicit sexual materials before reaching college.[17]

Another study found that over two-thirds of students in five different universities in New York, Providence, and Boston reported first exposure to "pornography" in any form by age 13.[18]

The third study found that 49 percent of male students in 8 colleges in Westchester County, New York, report having been exposed to "pornography" before age 13, and 50 percent of the females report having been exposed before age 15.[19]

Three sets of investigators have inquired into the experience of adolescents with explicit sexual materials using selected convenient samples.

One researcher submitted a questionnaire to more than 300 eleventh and twelfth grade students in a public school in a working-class suburb of Chicago. The respondents were nearly all white and Christian, with slightly more than half belonging to the Roman Catholic Church. Eighty-one percent of the boys and 43 percent of the girls reported having seen photographs of nude males and females engaging in sexual behavior, and 95 percent of the boys and 72 percent of the girls reported having been exposed to printed material describing sexual intercourse.[20]

A study of 473 working-class, white, predominantly Roman Catholic adolescents aged 13 to 18 obtained similar results. Seventy-seven percent of the boys and 35 percent of the girls (the girls in this study were on the average a couple of years younger than the boys) had seen pictures of sexual intercourse, and 79 percent of the boys and 78 percent of the girls had been exposed to books describing sexual activities in slang terms.[21]

The third investigator studied inmates of a youth reformatory in a Northeastern city; the subjects were males ages 17 to 20 and predominantly from minority ethnic groups (67 percent black and 21 percent Puerto Rican). Eighty-four percent had seen pictures of heterosexual intercourse.[22]

The national survey described earlier also included a sample of more than 750 adolescents age 15 to 20 who were living at home. This group, while more representative than the other groups of adolescents reported on above, is not representative of all adolescents in the United States this age, because it leaves out those who were not living at home, such as those who were away at school or in the armed services. Ninety-one percent of the males and 88 percent of the females reported having been exposed to depictions of sex at least as explicit as nudity with genitals exposed and emphasized.[23]

These various studies are quite consistent among themselves in finding that there is considerable exposure to explicit sexual materials on the part of minors. One may rather conservatively estimate from all these figures that 85 percent of boys and 70 percent of girls have seen visual depictions or read textual descriptions of heterosexual intercourse by the time they finish high school, or reach the age of 18. Substantial proportions of adolescents have had more than an isolated experience or two, although the rates of exposure do not indicate an obsession with erotic materials. A great deal of exposure to explicit sexual materials occurs in the pre-adolescent and early adolescent years. More than half the boys would appear to have some exposure to depictions of sexual intercourse by age 15. Exposure on the part of girls lags behind that of boys by a year or two. Exposure to depictions of nudity with genitals occurs earlier and more often. Exposure to oral-genital and homosexual materials occurs later and less frequently. Experience with depictions of sadomasochistic material is much rarer, although it does occur.[24]

The most common source of exposure to sexual materials is a friend; and this exposure appears to be a part of the "normal" social activity centered around home and school. [25] Young people rarely purchase explicit sexual materials; most of their exposure occurs in a social situation where materials are freely passed around among friends.

Few adults report that they buy erotic materials, also. In the national survey only 5 percent of the men report having brought the pictorial depiction they most recently had seen, and 26 percent of men

> **Opinions that sexual materials excite people, provide information about sex, provide entertainment, and improve sex relations of some married couples seem to be grounded in experience. . . . Opinions that sexual materials lead to rape, or to a breakdown in morals, seem to be based more on hearsay.**

report having bought the most recent textual depiction that they read; most report having obtained these from someone else (it was shown or given to them by a friend) at no cost. [26] The study of social, professional, service and church groups in Denver found that only 26 percent of those who had seen depictions of sex acts with full exposure of sex organs had also bought these materials at some time. The principal source was a friend or acquaintance. [27]

Patrons of "Adult" Bookstores

Although a small proportion of people buy sexual materials, nevertheless, customers of "adult" bookstores and movie theaters probably constitute a sizable absolute number of people. Several studies have attempted to document the characteristics of these people.[28]

In these studies nearly 14,000 "customers" were observed in 12 different cities. The profile that emerges from all these observations is: middle-aged, middle-class, married, white, male, dressed in business suit or neat casual attire, shopping alone. More intentsive studies using questionnaires and interviews with smaller groups confirm the characterizations of patrons derived from external observation.[29]

People in pornography shops in Denmark were found to be very similar in characteristics to customers of adult book stores in the United States.[30]

EFFECTS OF EXPLICIT SEXUAL MATERIALS

In 1968, the state of our factual knowledge about the consequences of exposure to explicit sexual materials was quite circumscribed; the existing empirical knowledge generally was limited to sexual arousal responses. Briefly, pictures and words depicting various aspects of human sexuality produce sexual arousal in a considerable proportion of the adult population; the amount of arousal is a joint function of the characteristics of the stimulus, the characteristics of the viewer, and the context in which the viewing occurs. There was no empirical information concerning the duration of the arousal or how this stimulation might affect overt behavior, attitudes governing behavior, or such things as mental health.[31]

Opinions

Lack of empirical information often encourages people to speculate and project their own fears to fill the void. The Commission on Obscenity and Pornography reviewed the popular literature concerning pornography and collected a variety of presumed consequences of exposure to explicit sexual materials such as: sexually aggressive acts of a criminal nature, unlawful sexual practices, sexually perverse behavior, adultery, deadly serious pursuit of sexual satisfaction, obsession with sex, moral breakdown, homicide, suicide, delinquency, indecent personal habits, unhealthy thoughts, ennui, information, attitudes, draining off of illegitimate sexual desires, release of strong sexual urges without harming others, pleasure, and assistance in consummation of legitimate sexual responsibilities.[32]

Many of these presumed consequences of exposure to explicit sexual materials receive rather widespread acceptance among the public. The earlier cited survey of a representative sample of American adults asked for "opinions about the effects of looking at or reading sexual materials." The most widely held opinion about effects, subscribed to by two-thirds of the adults in the United States, is one supported by empirical research, namely, that these materials excite people sexually. Three-fifths of those asked feel that these materials provide information about sex. Approximately half the sample are of the opinion that sexual materials provide entertainment, lead to rape, lead to a breakdown in morals, and improve sex relations of some married couples.[33] The same 50 percent do not necessarily subscribe to all these opinions!

The opinions that sexual materials excite people, provide information about sex, provide entertainment, and improve sex relations of some married couples seem to be grounded in experience; that is, people who hold opinions that these are consequences of exposure to such materials tend to report that the materials have had this effect on them or on someone they know personally, and they also report more experience with such materials in the past two years. On the other hand, the opinions that sexual materials lead to rape, or to a breakdown in morals, seem to be based more on hearsay, since the people who hold these opinions tend to report that these effects have not occurred to them nor to anyone they know personally, and also report less experience with such materials.[34]

Empirical Studies of Adult Sex Criminals

Although there has been for some time a considerable amount of concern about possible harmful and anti-social consequences of exposure to explicit sexual materials, almost no controlled empirical studies had been carried out until relatively recently.

In 1964, one study reported no significant differences between matched groups of delinquent and nondelinquent youth in the number of "sensational" books they had read.[35] In 1965, a book from the Kinsey Institute reported no significant differences in exposure to sexual materials among white male sex offenders, males who were not sex offenders, and volunteer non-offender males from the general population.[36]

More recent research provides elaboration on these findings.

Long intensive clinical interviews regarding sexual history were conducted with sex offenders in a California state hospital for the criminally insane and with a group from the general population which was similar in age, ethnic group membership, and socio-economic status. Particular attention was paid to experience with explicit sexual materials during adolescence and pre-adolescence, with the aim of checking out the idea that early exposure to sexual materials produces sexual deviance and sexual criminals. The investigators did find a correlation between exposure to sexual materials in adolescence and pre-adolescence and the committing of sexual offenses—but it was in a direction opposite to that embodied in our cultural myths. Sex offenders (rapists and pedophiles) had had significantly *less* experience with explicit sexual materials in adolescence and pre-adolescence than had the normal control subjects from the general population![37]

Similar results were obtained independently by investigators in other geographical regions using other research methods: one group compared offenders and non-offenders in the prison system of Wisconsin using a brief face-to-face interview;[38] a second study compared sex offenders with non-offenders, college students, and business men's service club members in Texas;[39] a third compared probationed sex offenders in Pennsylvania with a national sample of men of similar age and socio-economic status using survey interviews.[40] All these studies indicate that sex offenders have somewhat later and relatively less experience with explicit sexual materials than do people who have not committed sex offenses.

The California study also included groups of homosexuals, trans-sexuals, and customers of adult bookstores and movie theaters. These groups also reported less experience with explicit sexual materials in adolescence and pre-adolescence than did the control subjects.[41]

These several investigators also inquired about more recent experience, as adults, with sexual materials. In general, the results indicate that the recent experience of sex offenders and other population subgroups with depictions of sex is very similar. When differences are observed they are usually in the direction of the sex offender having less experience.

Sex Crime Statistics

Additional data regarding the relationship between explicit sex materials and sex crimes come from a "natural field experiment" that occurred in Denmark as a result of recent changes in the law. The Danish Parliament voted to remove erotic literature from its obscenity statute in June, 1967, and then two years later, in 1969, repealed the statute entirely. It is now legal in Denmark to disseminate sexually explicit materials to persons sixteen years of age or older. An analysis of sex crimes reported to the police in Copenhagen over a 12-year period, 1958 to 1969, was undertaken at the request of the U.S. Commission on Obscenity and Pornography. This time period included nine years prior to the change in the law, two years subsequent to the first change, and one year subsequent to the second change. The statistics indicate that the number of sex crimes decreased by 40 percent in the two years following the first liberalization of the availability of pornography as compared with the relatively stable average of the previous nine years; the number of sex crimes reported to the police decreased 30 percent further in the year in which the second liberalization of the pornography law occurred.[42]

This decrease in reported sex crimes did not include obscenity offenses, and cannot be attributed to changes in police procedures in recording nor to changes in legal definitions of crimes. Indeed, each separate type of sex crime (rape, intercourse on threat of violence, sexual interference with adult women, sexual interference with minor girls, coitus with minors, exhibitionism, peeping, verbal indecency, and homosexual offenses) decreased by more than 30 percent over the interval from 1958 to 1969.

A Danish criminologist conducted a survey of a random sample of Copenhagen residents in order to try to explain the dynamics of this change in the number of reported sex crimes.[43] Some, but not all, of the change *may* be attributable to changes in public attitudes about sex crimes and the willingness to report such events to the police. However, there does seem to be a real decrease in the number of occurrences of certain of the acts, such as peeping and sexual interference with minor females.

At the very least, the data from Denmark contradict the widely held assumption that explicit sexual materials *cause* sex crimes.

Juvenile Crime

Reliable information regarding the relationship between exposure to explicit sexual materials and crime on the part of non-adults is more difficult to find. A review of available social indicator statistics provides some indirect evidence on this topic. Although the availability of sexual materials increased severalfold over the period 1960-1969 in the United States, the number of juvenile arrests for sex crimes decreased.[44] This study also reports that the rate of increase of illegitimate births among adolescent females aged 15 to 19 years was considerably less, over the period 1960-1965, than the rate for unmarried women aged 19 to 44 years.

Another group attempted to study the relationship between experience with explicit sexual materials and various types of delinquency among the juveniles seen by the juvenile court of a large Eastern city. The research was stymied, however, when an examination of approximately 800 records, selected at random from the files for one recent year, revealed no information from police, psychiatric, or social work records regarding sexual material.[45]

A third study collected data on the experience of 476 incarcerated delinquent juvenile males with explicit sexual materials.[46] Although this study did not collect similar data on nondelinquents for comparison, the data on the delinquents are comparable to data collected by other investigators of nondelinquents.[47] The amount of exposure to sexual materials on the part of the delinquents is generally not distinguishable from that of nondelinquents.

Other Antisocial Consequences

Two other "antisocial orientations" have been studied in terms of their relationship to exposure to explicit sexual material: "bad moral character" and "calloused sexual attitudes toward women."

Psychologists found a moderate correlation between exposure to explicit sexual materials and "bad moral character," but pointed out that the raw correlation tells nothing about the direction of causation. After a further complicated causal analysis they concluded that bad moral character "causes" exposure to explicit sexual materials—not that exposure to sexual materials leads to development of bad moral character![48]

An experimental investigation tested the hypothesis that "calloused" sexual attitudes in males would increase after exposure to explicit sexual stimuli. Results showed that exposure to two erotic films did not increase already established frequencies of exploitive sexual behavior; and "calloused" sexual attitudes toward women *decreased* immediately after viewing the erotic films, and continued to decrease slightly 24 hours and two weeks later![49]

Other Consequences

A number of experimental studies have been conducted recently to investigate the effects of exposure to explicit sexual materials.[50]

As a group of these studies indicate: (1) exposure to explicit sexual stimuli produces sexual arousal in most people; (2) there is no general increase in sexual behavior following exposure to sexual stimuli; (3) there is no change in the type of sexual behavior one engages in as a result of exposure to sexual materials; (4) there is no change in attitudes regarding what is acceptable sexual behavior; (5) there is a marked increase in the likelihood of individuals talking about sex in the 24-hour period following exposure to explicit sexual materials—many subjects, especially married people, rate this a highly desirable consequence, since it often results in a breakdown of communication barriers that have retarded the solving of marital conflicts; and (6) attempts to censor by cutting out more explicit depictions tend to increase the arousal value of sex-related materials.

Finally, a representative sample of American adults reports that, on the basis of their own knowledge regarding the consequences of exposure to explicit sexual materials, these consequences tend to be positive or harmless rather than harmful. For example, approximately 40 percent report that such materials have provided information about sex to themselves or someone they know personally; roughly 35 percent report on the basis of their own knowledge that these materials excite people sexually, and a similar number say they provide entertainment; and approximately 25 percent report that these materials improve the sex relations of some married couples, and a similar number report that exposure to sex materials produces boredom with such materials. On the other hand, few people report first-hand knowledge of harmful consequences such as breakdown of morals, rape, or driving people sex crazy.[51]

Conclusions

The facts that have been summarized here would appear to be sufficient to begin to reassure and calm most reasonable and rational people regarding the threat and danger of pornography. Mr. Hoover's fears may now be replaced by empirical facts. Indeed, the majority of the members of the Commission on Obscenity and Pornography

> **There is a "hard-core" minority of adults in our society . . . which is opposed to the existence of explicit sexual materials even if these materials are shown to have no harmful effects.**

concluded that explicit sexual materials could not be considered to play a significant role in the causation of delinquent or criminal behavior among youth or adults. Rather, they concluded that much of the "problem" regarding materials which depict explicit sexual activity stems from the inability or reluctance of people in our society to be open and direct in dealing with sexual matters.[52]

The response of the Commission on Obscenity and Pornography was in many respects a conservative one. In the past half decade, five other nations have had official commissions study and make recommendations in this area: Denmark, Sweden, West Germany, Great Britain, and Israel. Each of these commissions had many fewer empirical facts to guide their considerations than did the United States Commission. Yet each of these commissions arrived at essentially similar conclusions and recommendations: there is no evidence that explicit sexual materials are harmful, and legal restrictions which inhibit freedom of the press and of speech should be repealed.[53]

THE IRRELEVANCE OF FACTS

Why, then, should we worry about pornography?

We should worry about pornography because there is a segment of our society for whom facts are not relevant and who cling, for some reason or other, to fears.

Facts and Attitudes toward Restriction

The national survey that has been cited previously asked a series of questions about attitudes toward the control of availability of explicit sexual materials.[54] The authors report that there is a "hard-core" minority of adults in our society, amounting to roughly one-third of the adult population, which is opposed to the existence of explicit sexual materials—even if these materials are shown to have no harmful effects and the availability is limited to being looked at or read by adults in their own homes!

Political Response to the Commission's Facts

The above group is, perhaps, the constituency to which the President and the U.S. Senate were addressing themselves in October 1970 in response to the *Report* of the Commission on Obscenity and Pornography, which contained a more detailed presentation of facts similar to those briefly reviewed in this paper and a set of recommendations consistent with these facts.

Mr. Nixon called the Commission "morally bankrupt" and promised to ignore its findings and recommendations.[55] The Senate passed by a vote of 60 to 5 "a resolution declaring that the Senate rejects the findings and recommendations of the Commission on Obscenity and Pornography."[56]

Three of the eighteen members of the Commission also felt that empirical facts are irrelevant to the discussion, and issued vigorous dissents to the majority report with its emphasis on facts.

The fundamental "finding" on which the entire report is based is: that "empirical research" has come up with "no reliable evidence to indicate that exposure to explicit sexual materials plays a significant role in the causation of delinquent or criminal behavior among youth or adults. . . . [but] The basic question is whether and to what extent society may establish and maintain certain moral standards. If it is conceded that society has a legitimate concern in maintaining moral standards, it follows logically that government has a legitimate interest which threatens them.[57]

For those who believe in God, in His absolute supremacy as the Creator and Lawgiver of life, in the dignity and destiny which He has conferred upon the human person, in the moral code that governs sexual activity—for those who believe in these "things," no argument against pornography should be necessary.[58]

Characteristics of Those for Whom Facts May Be Irrelevant

Three empirical studies provide some data on the characteristics of the constituency for whom facts appear to be irrelevant.

In the U.S. national adult population, people who are more restrictive in their orientation to explicit sexual materials are significantly more likely to be: older, less educated, female, frequent churchgoers, and conservative (in their own opinion) on other issues. They are less supportive of free expression in terms of the First Amendment: for example, they are more likely to reject the idea that newspapers have the right to print articles which criticize the police, or that people should be allowed to make speeches against God, or that people should be allowed to publish books which attack our system of government. They also tend to perceive widespread support within the public for their own position; that is, the majority think that other people in the community want either about the same amount or more restriction on sexual materials than they themselves do.[59]

Sociologists have studied intensively two ad hoc anti-pornography organizations, one in the Midwest and the other in the Southwest. The characteristics of the participants and the dynamics of the operation of these two organizations were very similar. In comparison with individuals who opposed these organizations' activities, the members were: more likely to be raised in rural communities, older, more active religiously, family oriented, politically conservative, traditional, and restrictive in their sexual attitudes. They were also more likely to score higher on scales of authoritarianism and dogmatism, and to be intolerant of individuals whose political views differed from their own. They tended to feel that there was widespread community support for their position, and to dismiss people who did not agree with them as not representative of the real community. [60]

A national survey of prosecuting attorneys indicates that these law enforcement officials are quite divided in their opinions regarding the helpfulness of citizen action groups to law enforcement in the area of obscenity and pornography, with roughly half feeling that such groups are not helpful. The key to this opinion seems to be the representativeness of the group in terms of the total community. The more representative the group is of the total community the more likely it is to be judged helpful. Unfortunately, the prosecuting attorneys do not report such groups as being very representative of their communities. [61]

In the analysis of the two ad hoc anti-pornography organizations, the authors interpret the actions of these groups and the motives of their members as an attempt to reinforce and reinstate value systems and behavioral norms which are perceived to be in danger of eroding away. Because a number of people will no longer conform to the norms, an attempt is made to arouse the community to a reaffirmation of its values and impose these on the straying ones. Thus, pornography becomes a lightning rod which attracts a variety of not very well defined status anxieties, and its control provides the hope of a simple and sovereign solution to a variety of social ills. The authors draw a number of parallels between the anti-smut movement and the Prohibition movement of the early part of this century. [62]

Conclusion

In the appeals of the politicians and the characteristics of that "hard-core" constituency for whom facts are not relevant, one may perceive the ingredients of a moral crusade. Moral crusades and political repression often go hand-in-hand.

And that is the reason why we, perhaps, should worry about pornography.

NOTES

1 J. Edgar Hoover, Statement, in Interim Report of the Committee on the Judiciary, *Obscene and pornographic literature and juvenile delinquency.* 84th Congress, 2nd Session. June 28, 1956.

2 O. N. Larsen, G. W. Jones, J. T. Klapper, M. A. Lipton, and M. E. Wolfgang, "The impact of erotica: report of the effects panel," in Commission on Obscenity and Pornography, *The Report of the Commission* (Washington, D.C.: U.S. Government Printing Office, 1970).

3 Ibid.

4 R. B. Cairns, "Psychological assumptions in sex censorship: an evaluative preview of recent (1961–68) research," in Commission on Obscenity and Pornography, *Technical Reports,* vol. 1 (Washington, D.C.: U. S. Government Printing Office, 1971).

5 R. Athanasiou, P. Shaver, and C. Tavis, "Sex," *Psychology Today,* July, 1970, pp. 39–52.

6 D. Wallace and G. Wehmer, "Contemporary standards of visual erotica," in *Technical Reports,* vol. 6.

7 M. E. Massey, "A market analysis of sex-oriented materials in Denver, Colorado, August, 1969—a pilot study," in *Technical Reports,* vol. 7.

8 M. J. Goldstein and H. Kant, "Exposure to pornography and sexual behavior in deviant and normal groups," in *Technical Reports,* vol. 4.

9 H. Abelson, R. Cohen, E. Heaton, and C. Slider, "Public attitudes toward and experience with erotic materials," in *Technical Reports,* vol. 3.

10 B. Kutschinsky, "Pornography in Denmark: Studies on producers, sellers, and users," in *Technical Reports,* vol. 7.

11 Abelson et al., op. cit.; Goldstein and Kant, op. cit.; Massey, op. cit.

12 Abelson et al., op. cit.; Wallace and Wehmer, op. cit.

13 H. L. Zetterberg, "The consumers of pornography where it is easily available; the Swedish experience," in *Technical Reports,* vol.7.

14 Abelson et al., op. cit.; Goldstein and Kant, op. cit.

15 Abelson et al., op. cit.

16 Goldstein and Kant, op. cit.

17 A. Berger, J. Gagnon, and W. Simon, "Pornography: high school and college years," *Technical Reports,* vol. 4.

18 D. M. White, "College students' experience with erotica," in *Technical Reports,* vol. 1.

19 W. J. Roach and L. Kreisberg, "Westchester college students' views on pornography," in *Technical Reports,* vol. 1.

20 J. Elias, "Exposure to erotic materials in adolescence," in *Technical Reports,* vol. 4.

21 A. Berger, J. Gagnon, and W. Simon, "Urban working-class adolescents and sexually explicit media," in *Technical Reports,* vol. 4.

22 M. Propper, "Exposure to sexually oriented materials among young male prison offenders," in *Technical Reports*, vol. 4.

23 Abelson et al., op. cit.

24 Abelson et al., ibid.

25 Abelson et al, ibid; Berger et al., op. cit; Elias, op. cit.; Propper, op. cit.

26 Abelson et al., ibid.

27 Massey, op. cit.

28 M. M. Finkelstein, "Traffic in sex oriented materials: adult bookstores in Boston, Massachusetts," in *Technical Reports*, vol. 7; Massey, op. cit.; H. Nawy, "The San Francisco erotic marketplace," in *Technical Reports*, vol. 7; C. Winick, "Some observations of patrons of adult theaters and bookstores," in *Technical Reports*, vol. 7.

29 Massey, op. cit.; Nawy, op. cit.; Winick, op. cit.

30 Kutschinsky, op. cit.

31 Cairns, op. cit.; R. B. Cairns, J. C. N. Paul, and J. Wishner, "Sex censorship: the assumptions of anti-obscenity laws and the empirical evidence," *Minnesota Law Review*, vol. 46 (1962), pp. 1009–1041.

32 W. T. Johnson, L. R. Kupperstein, W. C. Wilson, O. N. Larsen, G. W. Jones, J. T. Klapper, M. A. Lipton, M. E. Wolfgang, and W. B. Lockhart, "The impact of erotica; report of the effects panel," op. cit., p. 144.

33 Abelson et al., op. cit.

34 Abelson et al., ibid.

35 D. K. Berninghausen and R. W. Faunce, "An exploratory study of juvenile delinquency and the reading of sensational books," *Journal of Experimental Education*, vol. 33 (1964), pp. 161–168.

36 P. H. Gebhard, J. H. Gagnon, W. B. Pomeroy, and C. V. Christenson, *Sex Offenders: An Analysis of Types* (New York: Harper & Row, 1965).

37 Goldstein and Kant, op. cit.

38 R. F. Cook and R. H. Fosen, "Pornography and the sex offender; patterns of exposure and immediate arousal effects of pornographic stimuli," in *Technical Reports*, vol. 4.

39 C. F. Walker, "Erotic stimuli and the aggressive sexual offender," in *Technical Reports*, vol. 4.

40 W. T. Johnson, L. Kupperstein, and J. Peters, "Sex offenders' experience with erotica," in *Technical Reports*, vol. 4.

41 Goldstein and Kant, op. cit.

42 R. Ben–Veniste, "Pornography and sex crime—the Danish experience," in *Technical Reports*, vol. 6.

43 B. Kutschinsky, "Sex Crimes and pornography in Copenhagen: a survey of attitudes," in *Technical Reports*, vol. 3.

44 L. Kupperstein and W. C. Wilson, "Erotica and anti-social behavior; an analysis of selected social indicator statistics," in *Technical Reports*, vol. 5.

45 T. P. Thornberry and R. A. Silverman, "The relationship between exposure to pornography and juvenile delinquency as indicated by juvenile court records," in *Technical Reports*, vol. 5.

46 Propper, op. cit.

47 Abelson et al., op. cit.; Berger et al., op. cit.; Elias, op. cit.; Goldstein and Kant, op. cit.

48 K. E. Davis and G. N. Braucht, "Exposure to pornography, character, and sexual deviance: a retrospective survey," in *Technical Reports*, vol. 4.

49 D. L. Mosher, "Sex callousness toward women," in *Technical Reports*, vol. 6.

50 D. M. Amoroso, M. Brown, M. Preusse, E. E. Ware, and D. W. Pilkey, "An investigation of behavioral, psychological, and physiological reactions to pornographic stimuli," in *Technical Reports*, vol. 6; D. Byrne and J. Lamberth, "The effect of erotic stimuli on sex arousal, evaluative responses, and subsequent behavior," in *Technical Reports*, vol. 6; Cook and Fosen, op. cit.; K. E. Davis and G. N. Braucht, "Reactions to viewing films of erotically realistic heterosexual behavior," in *Technical Reports*, vol. 6; J. L. Howard, C. B. Reifler, and M. B. Liptzin, "Effects of exposure to pornography," in *Technical Reports*, vol. 6; B. Kutschinsky, "The effect of pornography—an experiment in perception, attitudes, and behavior," in *Technical Reports*, vol 6; J. Mann, J. Sidman, and S. Starr, "Effects of erotic films on sexual behaviors of married couples," in *Technical Reports*, vol. 6; D. L. Mosher, "Psychological reactions to pornographic films," in *Technical Reports*, vol. 6; V. Sigusch, G. Schmidt, R. Reinfeld, and I. Sutor, "Psychosexual stimulation: sex differences," *The Journal of Sex Research*, vol. 6 (1970), pp. 10–24. P. H. Tannenbaum, "Emotional arousal as a mediator of communication effects, in *Technical Reports*, vol. 6.

51 Abelson et al., op. cit.

52 The Commission on Obscenity and Pornography, op. cit.

53 T. D. Gill, M. A. Hill, B. Scott, W. B. Lockhart, P. Bender, J. M. Friedman and W. C. Wilson, "Legal considerations relating to erotica: report of the legal panel," in *The Reportt of the Commission*, op. cit.

54 Abelson et al., op. cit.

55 *The Washington Post*, October 26, 1970.

56 *The Congressional Record*, October 13, 1970, pp. 17903–17922.

57 M. A. Hill and W. C. Link, Separate statement, in *The Report of the Commission*, p. 385.

58 C. H. Keating, Jr., Separate statement, in *The Report of the Commission*, p. 515.

59 Abelson et al., op. cit.

60 L. A. Zurcher and R. G. Cushing, "Some individual characteristics of participants in *ad hoc* anti-pornography organizations," in *Technical Reports*, vol. 8; L. A.

Zurcher and R. G. Kirkpatrick, "Collective dynamics of *ad hoc* anti-pornography organizations," in *Technical Reports*, vol. 8.

61 W. C. Wilson, B. Horowitz, and J. Friedman, "The gravity of the pornography situation and the problems of control," in *Technical Reports*, vol. 3.

62 L. A. Zurcher and R. G. Kirkpatrick, op. cit.

Pornography, Obscenity, and the Case for Censorship

Irving Kristol

Being frustrated is disagreeable, but the real disasters in life begin when you get what you want. For almost a century now, a great many intelligent, well-meaning and articulate people—of a kind generally called liberal or intellectual, or both—have argued eloquently against any kind of censorship of art and/or entertainment. And within the past ten years, the courts and the legislatures of most Western nations have found these arguments persuasive—so persuasive that hardly a man is now alive who clearly remembers what the answers to these arguments were. Today, in the United States and other democracies, censorship has to all intents and purposes ceased to exist.

Is there a sense of triumphant exhilaration in the land? Hardly. There is, on the contrary, a rapidly growing unease and disquiet. Somehow, things have not worked out as they were supposed to, and many notable civil libertarians have gone on record as saying this was not what they meant at all. They wanted a world in which *Desire*

Under the Elms could be produced, or *Ulysses* published, without interference by philistine busybodies holding public office. They have got that, of course; but they have also got a world in which homosexual rape takes place on the stage, in which the public flocks during lunch hours to witness varieties of professional fornication, in which Times Square has become little more than a hideous market for the sale and distribution of printed filth that panders to all known (and some fanciful) sexual perversions.

> **If you believe that no one was ever corrupted by a book, you have also to believe that no one was ever improved by a book (or a play or a movie.)**

But disagreeable as this may be, does it really matter? Might not our unease and disquiet be merely a cultural hangover—a "hangup," as they say? What reason is there to think that anyone was ever corrupted by a book?

This last question, oddly enough, is asked by the very same people who seem convinced that advertisements in magazines or displays of violence on television do indeed have the power to corrupt. It is also asked, incredibly enough and in all sincerity, by people—e.g., university professors and schoolteachers—whose very lives provide all the answers one could want. After all, if you believe that no one was ever corrupted by a book, you have also to believe that no one was ever improved by a book (or a play or a movie). You have to believe, in other words, that all art is morally trivial and that, consequently, all education is morally irrelevant. No one, not even a university professor, really believes that.

To be sure, it is extremely difficult, as social scientists tell us, to trace the effects of a single book (or play or movie) on an individual reader or any class of readers. But we all know, and social scientists know it too, that the ways in which we use our minds and imaginations do shape our characters and help define us as persons. That those who certainly know this are nevertheless moved to deny it merely indicates how a dogmatic resistance to the idea of censorship can—like most dogmatism—result in a mindless insistence on the absurd.

I have used these harsh terms—"dogmatism" and "mindless"—advisedly. I might also have added "hypocritical." For the plain fact is that none of us is a complete civil libertarian. We all believe that there is some point at which the public authorities ought to step in to limit the "self expression" of an individual or a group, even where this might be seriously intended as a form of artistic expression, and even where the artistic transaction is between consenting adults. A playwright or theatrical director might, in this crazy world of ours, find someone willing to commit suicide on the stage, as called for by the script. We would not allow that—any more than we would permit scenes of real physical torture on the stage, even if the victim were a willing masochist. And I know of no one, no matter how free in spirit, who argues that we ought to permit gladiatorial contests in Yankee Stadium, similar to those once performed in the Colosseum at Rome—even if only consenting adults were involved.

The basic point that emerges is one that Prof. Walter Berns has powerfully argued: no society can be utterly indifferent to the ways its citizens publicly entertain themselves.[1] Bearbaiting and cockfighting are prohibited only in part out of compassion for the suffering animals; the main reason they were abolished was because it was felt that they debased and brutalized the citizenry who flocked to witness such spectacles. And the question we face with regard to pornography and obscenity is whether, now that they have such strong legal protection from the Supreme Court, they can or will brutalize and debase our citizenry. We are, after all, not dealing with one passing incident—one book, or one play, or one movie. We are dealing with a general tendency that is suffusing our entire culture.

I say pornography *and* obscenity because, though they have different dictionary definitions and are frequently distinguishable as artistic genres, they are nevertheless in the end identical in effect. Pornography is not objectionable simply because it arouses sexual desire or lust or prurience in the mind of the reader or spectator; this is a silly Victorian notion. A great many nonpornographic works—

including some parts of the Bible—excite sexual desire very successfully. What is distinctive about pornography is that, in the words of D. H. Lawrence, it attempts "to do dirt on [sex] . . . [It is an] insult to a vital human relationship."

In other words, pornography differs from erotic art in that its whole purpose is to treat human beings obscenely, to deprive human beings of their specifically human dimension. That is what obscenity is all about. It is light years removed from any kind of carefree sensuality—there is no continuum between Fielding's *Tom Jones* and the Marquis de Sade's *Justine*. These works have quite opposite intentions. To quote Susan Sontag: "What pornographic literature does is precisely to drive a wedge between one's existence as a full human being and one's existence as a sexual being—while in ordinary life a healthy person is one who prevents such a gap from opening up." This definition occurs in an essay defending pornography—Miss Sontag is a candid as well as gifted critic—so the definition, which I accept, is neither tendentious nor censorious.

Along these same lines, one can point out—as C. S. Lewis pointed out some years back—that it is no accident that in the history of all literatures obscene words, the so-called "four-letter words," have always been the vocabulary of farce or vituperation. The reason is clear; they reduce men and women to some of their mere bodily functions—they reduce man to his animal component, and such a reduction is an essential purpose of farce or vituperation.

Similarly, Lewis also suggested that it is not an accident that we have no offhand, colloquial, neutral terms—not in any Western European language at any rate—for our most private parts. The words we do use are either (a) nursery terms, (b) archaisms, (c) scientific terms, or (d) a term from the gutter (i.e., a demeaning term). Here I think the genius of language is telling us something important about man. It is telling us that man is an animal with a difference: he has a unique sense of privacy, and a unique capacity for shame when this privacy is violated. Our "private parts" are indeed private, and not merely because convention prescribes it. This particular convention is indigenous to the human race. In practically all primitive tribes, men and women cover their private parts; and in practically all primitive tribes, men and women do not copulate in public.

It may well be that Western society, in the latter half of the twentieth century, is experiencing a drastic change in sexual mores and sexual relationships. We have had many such "sexual revolutions" in the past—the bourgeois family and bourgeois ideas of sexual propriety were themselves established in the course of a revolution against eighteenth-century "licentiousness"—and we shall doubtless have others in the future. It is, however, highly improbable (to put it mildly) that what we are witnessing is the Final Revolution which will make sexual relations utterly unproblematic, permit us to dispense with any kind of ordered relationships between the sexes, and allow us freely to redefine the human condition. And so long as humanity has not reached that utopia, obscenity will remain a problem.

II

One of the reasons it will remain a problem is that obscenity is not merely about sex, any more than science fiction is about science. Science fiction, as every student of the genre knows, is a peculiar vision of power: what it is really about is politics. And obscenity is a peculiar vision of humanity: what it is really about is ethics and metaphysics.

Imagine a man—a well-known man, much in the public eye—in a hospital ward, dying an agonizing death. He is not in control of his bodily functions, so that his bladder and his bowels empty themselves of their own accord. His consciousness is overwhelmed and extinguished by pain, so that he cannot communicate with us, nor we with him. Now, it would be, technically, the easiest thing in the world to put a television camera in his hospital room and let the whole world witness this spectacle. We don't do it—at least we don't do it as yet—because we regard this as an *obscene* invasion of privacy. And what would make the spectacle obscene is that we would be witnessing the extinguishing of humanity in a human animal.

Incidentally, in the past our humanitarian crusaders against capital punishment understood this point very well. The abolitionist literatures goes into great physical detail about what happens to a man when he is hanged or electrocuted or gassed. And their argument was—and is—that what happens is shockingly obscene, and that no civilized society should be responsible for perpetrating such obscenities, particularly since in the nature of the case there must be spectators to ascertain that this horror was indeed perpetrated in fulfillment of the law.

Sex—like death—is an activity that is both animal and human. There are human sentiments and human ideals involved in this animal activity. But when sex is public, the viewer does not see—cannot see—the sentiments and the ideals. He can only see the animal coupling. And that is why, when men and women make love, as we say, they prefer to be alone—because it is only when you are alone that you can make love, as distinct from merely copulating in an animal and casual way. And that, too, is why those who are voyeurs, if they are not irredeemably sick, also feel ashamed at what they are witnessing. When sex is a public spectacle, a human relationship has been debased into a mere animal connection.

> There can be no question that pornography is a form of "sexism."

It is also worth noting that this making of sex into an obscenity is not a mutual and equal transaction but rather an act of exploitation by one of the partners—the male partner. I do not wish to get into the complicated question as to what, if any, are the essential differences— as distinct from conventional and cultural differences—between male and female. I do not claim to know the answer to that. But I do know—and I take it as a sign that has meaning—that pornography is, and always has been, a man's work; that women rarely write pornography; and that women tend to be indifferent consumers of pornography.[2] My own guess, by way of explanation, is that a woman's sexual experience is ordinarily more suffused with human emotion than is man's, that men are more easily satisfied with autoerotic activities, and that men can therefore more easily take a more "technocratic" view of sex and its pleasures. Perhaps this is not correct. But whatever the explanation, there can be no question that pornography is a form of "sexism," as the women's liberation movement calls it, and that the instinct of women's liberation has been unerring in perceiving that when pornography is perpetrated against them, as part of a conspiracy to deprive them of their full humanity.

But even if all this is granted, it might be said—and doubtless will be said—that I really ought not to be unduly concerned. Free competition in the cultural marketplace—is is argued by people who have never otherwise had a kind word to say for laissez-faire—will automatically dispose of the problem. The present fad for pornography and obscenity, it will be asserted, is just that, a fad. It will spend itself in the course of time; people will get bored with it, will be able to take it or leave it alone in a casual way, in a "mature way," and, in sum, I am being unnecessarily distressed about the whole business. *The New York Times,* in an editorial, concludes hopefully in this vein.

> In the end . . . the insensate pursuit of the urge to shock, carried from one excess to a more abysmal one, is bound to achieve its own antidote in total boredom. When there is no lower depth to descend to, ennui will erase the problem.

I would like to be able to go along with this line of reasoning, but I cannot. I think it is false, and for two reasons, the first psychological, the second political.

The basic psychological fact about pornography and obscenity is that it appeals to and provokes a kind of sexual regression. The sexual pleasure one gets from pornography and obscenity is autoerotic and infantile; put bluntly, it is a masturbatory exercise of the imagination, when it is not masturbation pure and simple. Now, people who masturbate do not get bored with masturbation, just as sadists don't get bored with sadism, and voyeurs don't get bored with voyeurism.

In other words, infantile sexuality is not only a permanent temptation for the adolescent or even the adult—it can quite easily become a permanent, self-reinforcing neurosis. It is because of an awareness of this possibility of regression toward the infantile condition, a regression which is always open to us, that all the codes of sexual conduct ever devised by the human race take such a dim view of autoerotic activities and try to discourage autoerotic fantasies. Masturbation is indeed a perfectly natural autoerotic activity, as so many sexologists blandly assure us today. And it is precisely because it is so perfectly natural that it can be so dangerous to the mature or maturing person, if it is not controlled or sublimated in some way. That is the true meaning of Portnoy's complaint. Portnoy, you will recall, grows up to be a man who is incapable of having an adult sexual relationship with a woman; his sexuality remains fixed in an infantile mode, the prisoner of his autoerotic fantasies. Inevitably, Portnoy comes to think, in a perfectly *infantile* way, that it was all his mother's fault.

It is true that, in our time, some quite brilliant minds have come to the conclusion that a reversion to infantile sexuality is the ultimate mission and secret destiny of the human race. I am thinking in particular of Norman O. Brown, for whose writings I have the deepest respect. One of the reasons I respect them so deeply is that Mr. Brown is a serious thinker who is unafraid to face up to the radical consequences of his radical theories. Thus, Mr. Brown knows and says that for his kind of salvation to be achieved, humanity must annul the civilization it has created—not merely the civilization we have today, but all civilization—so as to be able to make the long descent backward into animal innocence.

And that is the point. What is at stake is civilization and humanity, nothing less. The idea that "everything is permitted," as Nietzsche put it, rests on the premise of nihilism and has nihilistic implications. I will not pretend that the case against nihilism and for civilization is an easy one to make. We are here confronting the most fundamental of philosophical questions, on the deepest levels. In short, the matter of pornography and obscenity is not a trivial one, and only superficial minds can take a bland and untroubled view of it.

In this connection, I must also point out those who are primarily against censorship on liberal grounds tell us not to take pornography or obscenity seriously, while those who are for pornography and obscenity on radical grounds take it very seriously indeed. I believe the radicals—writers like Susan Sontag, Herbert Marcuse, Norman O. Brown, and even Jerry Rubin—are right, and the liberals are wrong. I also believe that those young radicals at Berkeley, some . . . years ago, who provoked a major confrontation over the public use of obscene words, showed a brilliant political instinct. And once Mark Rudd could publicly ascribe to the president of Columbia a notoriously obscene relationship to his mother, without provoking any kind of reaction, the S.D.S. had already won the day. The occupation of Columbia's buildings merely ratified their victory. Men who show themselves unwilling to defend civilization against nihilism are not going to be either resolute or effective in defending the university against anything.

III

I am already touching upon a political aspect of pornography when I suggest that it is inherently and purposefully subversive of civilization and its institutions. But there is another and more specifically political aspect, which has to do with the relationship of pornography and/or obscenity to democracy, and especially to the quality of public life on which democratic government ultimately rests.

Though the phrase "the quality of life" trips easily from so many lips these days, it tends to be one of those clichés with many trivial meanings and no large, serious one. Sometimes it merely refers to such externals as the enjoyment of cleaner air, cleaner water, cleaner streets. At other times it refers to the merely private enjoyment of music, painting, or literature. Rarely does it have anything to do with the way the citizen in a democracy views himself—his obligations, his intentions, his ultimate self-definition.

Instead, what I would call the "managerial" conception of democracy is the predominant opinion among political scientists, sociologists, and economists, and has, through the untiring efforts of these scholars, become the conventional journalistic opinion as well. The root idea behind this "managerial" conception is that democracy is a "political system" (as they say) which can be adequately defined in terms of—can be fulled reduced to—its mechanical arrangements. Democracy is then seen as a set of rules and procedures, and *nothing but* a set of rules and procedures, whereby majority rule and minority rights are reconciled into a state of equilibrium. If everyone follows these rules and procedures, then a democracy is in working order. I think this is a fair description of the democratic idea that currently prevails in academia. One can also fairly say that it is now the liberal idea of democracy par excellence.

I cannot help but feel that there is something ridiculous about being this kind of a democrat, and I must further confess to having a sneaking sympathy for those of our young radicals who also find it ridiculous. The absurdity is the absurdity of idolatry—of taking the symbolic for the real, the means for the end. The purpose of democracy cannot possibly be the endless functioning of its own political machinery. The purpose of any political regime is to achieve some version of the good life and the good society. It is not at all difficult to imagine a perfectly functioning democracy which answers all questions except one—namely, why should anyone of intelligence and spirit care a fig for it?

There is, however, an older idea of democracy—one which was fairly common until about the beginning of this century—for which the conception of the quality of public life is absolutely crucial. This idea starts from the proposition that democracy is a form of self-government, and that if you want it to be a meritorious polity, you have to care about what kind of people govern it. Indeed, it puts the matter more strongly and declares that if you want self-government, you are only entitled to it if that "self" is worthy of governing. There is no inherent right to self-government if it means that such government is vicious, mean, squalid, and debased. Only a dogmatist and a fanatic, an idolater of democratic machinery, could approve of self-government under such conditions.

And because the desirability of self-government depends on the character of the people who govern, the older idea of democracy was very solicitous of the condition of this character. It was solicitous of the individual self, and felt an obligation to educate it into what used to be called "republican virtue." And it was solicitous of that collective self which we call public opinion and which, in a democracy, governs us collectively. Perhaps in some respects it was nervously oversolicitous—that would not be surprising. But the main thing is that it cared, cared not merely about the machinery of democracy but about the quality of life that this machinery might generate.

And because it cared, this older idea of democracy had no problem in principle with pornography and/or obscenity. It censored them—and it did so with a perfect clarity of mind and a perfectly clear conscience. It was not about to permit people capriciously to corrupt themselves. Or, to put it more precisely: in this version of democracy, the people took some care not to let themselves be governed by the more infantile and irrational parts of themselves.

I have, it may be noticed, uttered that dreadful word "censorship." And I am not about to back away from it. If you think pornography and/or obscenity is a serious problem, you have to be for censorship. I'll go even further and say that if you want to prevent pornography and/or obscenity from becoming a problem, you have to be for censorship. And lest there be any misunderstanding as to what I am saying, I'll put it as bluntly as possible: if you care for the quality of life in our American democracy, then you have to be for censorship.

IV

But can a liberal be for censorship? Unless one assumes that being a liberal *must* mean being indifferent to the quality of American life, then the answer has to be: yes, a liberal can be for censorship—but he ought to favor a liberal form of censorship.

Is that a contradiction in terms? I don't think so. We have no problem in contrasting *repressive* laws governing alcohol and drugs and tobacco with laws *regulating* (i.e., discouraging the sale of) alcohol and drugs and tobacco. Laws encouraging temperance are not the same thing as laws that have as their goal prohibition or abolition. We have not made the smoking of cigarettes a criminal offense. We have, however, and with good liberal conscience, prohibited cigarette advertising on television, and may yet, again with good liberal conscience, prohibit it in newspapers and magazines. The idea of restricting individual freedom, in a liberal way, is not at all unfamiliar to us.

I therefore see no reason why we should not be able to distinguish repressive censorship from liberal censorship of the written and spoken word. In Britain, until a few years ago, you could perform almost any play you wished, but certain plays, judged to be obscene, had to be performed in private theatrical clubs which were deemed to have a "serious" interest in theater. In the United States, all of us who grew up using public libraries are familiar with the circumstances under which certain books could be circulated only to adults, while still other books had to be read in the library reading room, under the librarian's skeptical eye. In both cases, a small minority that was willing to make a serious effort to see an obscene play or read an obscene book could do so. But the impact of obscenity was circumscribed and the quality of public life was only marginally affected.[3]

I am not saying it is easy in practice to sustain a distinction between liberal and repressive censorship, especially in the public realm of a democracy, where popular opinion is so vulnerable to demagoguery. Moreover, an acceptable system of liberal censorship is likely to be exceedingly difficult to devise in the United States today, because our educated classes, upon whose judgment a liberal censorship must rest, are so convinced that there is no such thing as a problem of obscenity, or even that there is no such thing as obscenity at all. But, to counterbalance this, there is the further, fortunate truth that the tolerable margin for error is quite large, and single mistakes or single injustices are not all that important.

This possibility of error, of course, occasions much distress among artists and academics. It is a fact, one that cannot and should not be denied, that any system of censorship is bound, upon occasion, to treat unjustly a particular work of art—to find pornography where there is only gentle eroticism, to find obscenity where none really exists, or to find both where its existence ought to be tolerated because it serves a larger moral purpose. Though most works of art are not obscene, and though most obscenity has nothing to with art, there are some few works of art that are, at least in part, pornographic and/or obscene. There are also some few works of art that are in the special category of the comic-ironic "bawdy" (Boccaccio, Rabelais). It is such works of art that are likely to suffer at the hands of the censor. That is the price one has to be prepared to pay for censorship—even liberal censorship.

But just how high is this price? If you believe, as so many artists seem to believe today, that art is the only sacrosanct activity in our profane and vulgar world—that any man who designates himself an artist thereby acquires a sacred office—then obviously censorship is an intolerable form of sacrilege. But for those of us who do not subscribe to this religion of art, the costs of censorship do not seem so high at all.

If you look at the history of American or English literature, there is precious little damage you can point to as a consequence of the

> I have not noticed, now that censorship of the written word has to all intents and purposes ceased in this country, that hitherto suppressed or repressed masterpieces are flooding the market.

censorship that prevailed throughout most of that history. Very few works of literature—of real literary merit, I mean—ever were suppressed; and those that were, were not suppressed for long. Nor have I noticed, now that censorship of the written word has to all intents and purposes ceased in this country, that hitherto suppressed or repressed masterpieces are flooding the market. Yes, we can now read *Fanny Hill* and the Marquis de Sade. Or, to be more exact, we can now openly purchase them, since many people were able to read them even though they were publicly banned, which is as it should be under a liberal censorship. So how much have literature and the arts gained from the fact that we can all now buy them over the counter, that, indeed, we are all now encouraged to buy them over the counter? They have not gained much that I can see.

And one might also ask a question that is almost never raised: how much has literature lost from the fact that everything is now permitted? It has lost quite a bit, I should say. In a free market, Gresham's

Law can work for books or theater as efficiently as it does for coinage—driving out the good, establishing the debased. The cultural market in the United States today is being pre-empted by dirty books, dirty movies, dirty theater. A pornographic novel has a far better chance of being published today than a nonpornographic one, and quite a few pretty good novels are not being published at all simply because they are not pornographic, and are therefore less likely to sell. Our cultural condition has not improved as a result of the new freedom. American cultural life wasn't much to brag about twenty years ago; today one feels ashamed for it.

Just one last point which I dare not leave untouched. If we start censoring pornography or obscenity, shall we not inevitably end up censoring political opinion? A lot of people seem to think this would be the case—which only shows the power of doctrinaire thinking over reality. We had censorship of pornography and obscenity for 150 years, until almost yesterday, and I am not aware that freedom of opinion in this country was in any way diminished as a consequence of this fact. Fortunately for those of us who are liberal, freedom is not indivisible. If it were, the case for liberalism would be indistinguishable from the case for anarchy; and they are two very different things.

But I must repeat and emphasize: what kind of laws we pass governing pornography and obscenity, what kind of censorship—or, since we are still a federal nation, what kinds of censorship—we institute in our various localities may indeed be difficult matters to cope with; nevertheless the real issue is one of principle. I myself subscribe to a liberal view of the enforcement problem: I think that pornography should be illegal *and* available to anyone who wants it so badly as to make a pretty strenuous effort to get it. We have lived with under-the-counter pornography for centuries now, in a fairly comfortable way. But the issue of principle, of whether it should be over or under the counter, has to be settled before we can reflect on the advantages and disadvantages of alternative modes of censorship. I think the settlement we are living under now, in which obscenity and democracy are regarded as equals, is wrong; I believe it is inherently unstable; I think it will, in the long run, be incompatible with any authentic concern for the quality of life in our democracy.

NOTES

1 This is as good a place as any to express my profound indebtedness to Walter Bern's superb essay, "Pornography vs. Democracy," in the winter, 1971 issue of *The Public Interest.*

2 There are, of course, a few exceptions—but of a kind that prove the rule. *L'Histoire d'O,* for instance, written by a woman, is unquestionably the most *melancholy* work of pornography ever written. And its theme is precisely the dehumanization accomplished by obscenity.

3 It is fairly predictable that some one is going to object that this point of view is "elitist"—that, under a system of liberal censorship, the rich will have privileged access to pornography and obscenity. Yes, of course they will—just as, at present, the rich have privileged access to heroin if they want it. But one would have to be an egalitarian maniac to object to this state of affairs on the grounds of equality.

Part 5

Toward
a new
sexuality

PART 5 / TOWARD A NEW SEXUALITY

The "new" sexuality that is described in this part is not made up of fantastically novel erotic activities or life styles, nor is it analogous to old detergent powders that are suddenly revolutionized by a special added ingredient. What is new is that the readings represent a departure from: (1) a double-standard sexuality where one person assumes the responsibility for another's sexual activity; (2) a "doing what comes naturally" sexuality where concern for feelings or consequences is missing; (3) equating sensuality with sexual intercourse; and (4) the formula that sexual activity equals coitus equals orgasm (the bigger and more simultaneous the better).

The authors in this section question some time-honored values and viewpoints about sexuality. They deal with a number of factors in defining some "new" dimensions of sexuality: adequacy, communication, decision, intentionality, intimacy, love, orgasm, passion, pleasure, sensuality, and talk.

"*Adequacy* in sexual functioning" has recently become a descriptive phrase in human sexuality literature, reflecting the use of sexual performance as a criterion for evaluating our adequacy as men, women, partners, or human beings. Slater strongly protests this performance–adequacy linkage and objects to our goal-oriented approach to human sexual activity. Both he and May identify a compulsive attitude in our society that focuses on orgasm and sexual activity as ends in themselves, irrespective of personal feelings. We worry if we are not "doing it" as frequently, as exotically, as early, as quickly, or with as many people as "everyone else." According to May, passion in the sense of vivid personal involvement gets lost in mechanical concerns such as "Will I make it?" or "Did she come?" Each sexual encounter is evaluated in terms of achievement or nonachievement of orgasm by one or both partners. May asserts that we have made the body into a kind of sexual machine and have left out the feeling dimension. Do you see any validity to the contention that people's sexual activity is strongly influenced by pressure to "perform"? Do you find yourself thinking of yourself as "inadequate" sexually if you or your partner fails to reach climax during sexual activity? Slater claims that it is primarily men who make orgasm the goal of sexual activity. If this statement is true, how would you change the socialization of boys now entering manhood so as to alter this viewpoint?

Pleasure associated with their own bodies is an aspect of sexuality that young children often discover very early in their lives. Such a discovery is seldom used as a basis for teaching the child about human sexuality; instead, pleasurable exploration of our bodies is usually ignored, if not condemned by parents, school, or church. It is ironic that an article such as the one by McCarthy, Ryan, and Johnson needs to be included in a reader on human sexuality. It would seem that all human beings would be naturally aware of the pleasurable possibilities inherent in their own bodies and of nondemanding ways of giving sensual bodily pleasure to each other, but judgmental attitudes toward pleasure and an orgasm-oriented attitude toward sexual activity have blunted the capacity of many people to enjoy sheer sensuality and pleasuring.

Both Slater and McCarthy *et al* emphasize leisurely lovemaking and caressing that may or may not include intercourse. Many people may have to learn or relearn how to be aware of sensual bodily pleasure, and how to give and receive such pleasure in a leisurely way, without anxiety about whether orgasm will result. Many have to reverse early messages that say it is selfish and narcissistic to focus on the pleasure associated with bodies and genitals. Many are learning to "allow" themselves this enjoyment of their own bodies and their partner's body.

At what point in a child's development do you think it appropriate for parents to talk about the pleasure associated with sexuality, as well as its reproductive aspects? Would you, encourage young teenagers to pet and explore each others' bodies as an alternative to intercourse?

Talking or *communicating verbally* about sex is the primary focus of Brenton's article, but it is also important in the readings by Oden, McCarthy *et al,* Menninger, and Daniels and Horowitz. Sexual activity may be the most silent human activity, where participants usually depend on ambiguous nonverbal communication to convey feelings. A noted semanticist said, "Good communication is at the heart of good sexuality."[1] Many people would say instead, "Good sexuality is good communication." Can we continue to rely on nonverbal cues to communicate our sexual feelings, or must we be more talkative and open with each other? In much current sex therapy, couples are taught to talk about their sexual likes and dislikes and, as Brenton suggests, to verbalize before, during, and after intercourse about what was good and what could have been better. For some people, such conversation takes away the charm and mystique of sexual activity and makes it ordinary and pedestrian: "If I have to *tell* him what to do and where to touch me, I'd rather not have sex." Do you feel this way?

One important aspect of talking about sexual interaction is that the partners no longer need to "divine" or intuit what the other person wants or doesn't want. Sometimes our assumptions are incorrect: "I thought you waited so long because you weren't really turned on by me tonight"; the

---

1   S. I. Hayawaka, "Semantics and Sexuality," *Etc.,* 25:2.

partner responds, "That's not it at all—I thought you were bored, and I didn't want to push you." A verbal check-out, although not so "romantic" as the feel-and-error approach, provides a more direct means for partners to express their concerns, doubts, and delights, and to confront their fears and disappointments rather than storing them up wordlessly. The "romance" and "mysticism" of silent sexuality may indeed be removed, but the possibility is there for a deeper romance and mysticism based on direct and open responsiveness. The art of mind-reading is then no longer a necessary part of love-making.

Love is the subject of readings by May, Ellis, Lederer and Jackson, and Daniels and Horowitz. May is concerned about the increasing separation he sees between love and sex—a reversal of the Victorian emphasis on love without sex to an emphasis on sex without love. Ellis invites consideration of his thesis that love is not necessary for the enjoyment of sex. May and Ellis present divergent views on the relationship between sex and love. With which do you identify? Why?

Lederer and Jackson postulate that love is a rare and unnecessary ingredient in a happy and satisfying marriage. They question the traditional link between sex and love, and between love and marriage. Is that link important for you personally? What viewpoint do you value for your children? for society in the present or future?

Daniels and Horowitz examine various kinds of love and place them in a four-level hierarchy— the first (*object-centered*) being the least fulfilling, and the last (*agape*) being the most mature and fulfilling. Erich Fromm identified *caring*, *responding*, *respecting*, and *knowing* as the essential ingredients of mature love. How do these classifications accord with Daniels and Horowitz's? with your own catalogue of the essentials of love? Is classifying components of love and establishing criteria for loving as potentially destructive of spontaneous responding as is the "tyranny of the orgasm"? How does one evaluate the validity and meaning of love in one's own life?

Oden explores intimacy as a function of sexual interaction and as an entity in itself. Can some approaches to sexual activity destroy rather than enhance intimacy? Can sexual activity be used to increase intimacy? Is it possible to become increasingly intimate with someone in the absence of any sexual activity? Sometimes intimacy is shunned, avoided, or diluted because of the fear, threat, or anxiety implicit in an intimate relationship. Do you agree that intimacy can be threatening?

Some of Daniels and Horowitz's styles of loving do not deepen intimacy. Are there styles of intimacy that do not deepen love? When sex and love coincide, will intimacy always be there?

Intentionality about sexual activity, sexual choices, and sexual life style is an implicit theme pervading this textbook and especially the readings in this part; in Menninger's reading, the theme of intentionality is explicit. Menninger emphasizes that personal decision-making is at the heart of mature sexuality. He identifies a number of nonsexual uses of sex that are both immature and indirect, and sees "doing what comes naturally" and getting "carried away" as irresponsible sexuality devoid of choice. What is your reaction to Menninger's characterization of sexual activity as "biological discharge" that is intense but *ephemeral* (lasting a very short time)?

Menninger's focus on intentionality corroborates McCarthy *et al* and Brenton's emphasis on the importance of communication in sexual activity. If a man and woman develop ways of talking about their sexual activity, they will be more reflective about their desires and less likely to be "swept away" by the "passion of the moment" and its frequent consequences: unwanted pregnancy or unintentional involvement. Menninger asserts that "one act need not lead thoughtlessly to the next with no means for contemplation between. . . . How is one to use these moments of reflection, if one can, in fact, catch hold of them?" His prescription is "both simple and difficult: to find the means and the opportunity to talk."

What does talking do to passion, to spontaneity, to involvement, to mutuality, to decision-making? Can sexual decisions be made in the absence of verbal communication?

What, for you, is human sexuality? Is there such a thing as a new sexuality for you? What are its important dimensions ("old" or "new")?

Sexual Adequacy in America

Philip E. Slater

The use of an engineering term like "adequacy" in relation to an
act of pleasure exemplifies the American gift for turning everything into
a task. Even more curious is that the criteria of adequacy are not the
same for men and women. For men, adequacy is usually focused
on erection; for women, on orgasm. A man tends to be defined as
"adequate" to the degree that he is able to bring a woman to orgasm,
preferably through the use of his penis ("Look, Ma, no hands!"). A
woman, however, tends to be defined as adequate to the degree to
which she is able to "achieve" orgasm rapidly through the same
method. A woman gets defined as sexually adequate only insofar
as she can make the man feel that *he* is sexually adequate. Note that
by these definitions a man is considered adequate when he can delay
climax, while a woman is considered adequate when she can accelerate it. Why isn't the same standard of adequacy applied to both sexes?

Some might argue that women have a different timing pattern than
men and that the goal of these definitions is to bring men and
women into synchrony. We live, after all, in a highly scheduled,

Reprinted from *Intellectual Digest*, November, 1973. Reprinted by permission of the publisher and the
author.

clock-oriented society, and it is important that people arrive at the same place at the same time. But who can say whether these much-discussed timing differences are biological or cultural? The implicit attitude behind most discussions of female orgasm is that the longer time period preceding it is an unfortunate defect of feminine physiology. But why wouldn't it be just as appropriate to say that the shorter time period before the typical male orgasm is due to a defect in men? Don't men say that brevity equals "inadequacy" among men? Then why not say that brevity equals inadequacy for men *in relation to women?* That, in other words, men as a sex are less adequate than women.

Suppose we were to say not that "it takes a woman longer to reach orgasm than a man" but rather that a woman can delay orgasm longer than a man. If we are going to use terms as absurd as "adequacy" in relation to pleasure at all this seems to me the more reasonable statement. We are talking about the "ability" to tolerate and sustain pleasurable stimulation without release: the simple fact is that women can absorb and tolerate more pleasure than men can and hence are more adequate to the "business" of enjoyment.

I have always been fascinated that women seem to be far more capable of being attracted to a homely male than vice versa. Why is it that a homely woman, or an older one, is so much more likely to be disqualified as a sexual partner? Many men in our society are attracted only to women who are young, thin, long legged, large breasted, made-up, depilated and deodorized. Does the fact that men are so easily turned off—by age, weight, and sundry other departures from some narrow *Playboy* ideal—mean that they really don't like women much? Is their heterosexual desire so weak that only some weirdly specialized feminine image can flog it into being? Why is it that women can be turned on by men who are old or ugly? Are they sexier than men? Less squeamish and fastidious? Or do they really like men more than men like women?

Psychiatrists tend to respond to such observations by talking vaguely about latent homosexuality. Yet a large proportion of male homosexuals can be aroused only by *men* who are young or exceptionally good-looking. Reaching the age of 40 can be as great a disaster for a gay male as for a heterosexual woman. In fact, men, whether homosexual or heterosexual, seem far more exacting in their standards of attractiveness than are females of either persuasion. This is another way of saying that women are more easily turned on than men— that they can take their sex with fewer condiments.

This statement flies in the face of the old-fashioned idea that men were "more sexual" than women, but this idea has had a relatively brief history and has been largely limited to the Western world. Historically and cross-culturally it has more often been women who are portrayed as the sexual, earthy beings, with men viewed as more restrained, controlled, spiritual and less susceptible to demands of the flesh. Women, usually seen as the source of evil, have appeared frequently in folklore and literature as sexually insatiable creatures, undermining the efforts of men to pursue chaste and lofty enterprises.

Men throughout history have devoted a surprising amount of energy to the construction of a Feminine Ideal. These ideals have varied from culture to culture, but they share a large area of agreement. Women should be sexually accessible, but not sexually demanding, docile and servile but yet not totally uninteresting. The contradictions are worked out in different ways, usually by emphasizing the passivity of the feminine role (always willing but never asking). The Ideal Woman is sometimes encouraged to develop pleasing little skills that will make her interesting to the male without threatening his vanity. In other instances it is stated flatly that the Ideal Woman should be an ignorant booby. On one point all writers are in complete agreement: the Ideal Woman exists only for men.

It is difficult to read this literature—whether English, Greek, Chinese, Modern or American—without sensing the profound pathology that lies beneath them: the obsessional detail; the writer's exhausting struggle to resolve his ambivalence by controlling and constricting another person's behaviour; the zealous effort to pretend that the problem lies outside the author's perverse brain; the inability to recognize that a completely accommodating individual can be only a nonperson, a robot. One suspects that these lectures are really misdirected. Intended perhaps for the frantic, seductive, demanding and overpowering mothers of their authors, they are delivered instead to their wives, who, thereby constricted and constrained, transfer all their frantic, seductive and overpowering needs onto their sons, thus continuing the cycle.

Women rarely write such documents, perhaps because fathers, as a rule, are less omnipresent in the life of a small child than are mothers. In any case, women seem to have been able to take men pretty much as they found them. They may have tried to make improvements on a given man, and they may have longed for some perfect Prince Charming, but by and large they have not wasted paper writing

> **A man, it seems, has difficulty feeling like a man if a woman approaches him as a free, independent, fully sexual being.**

treatises on how the Ideal Male should behave in the daily fulfillment of his role.

All this suggests that men feel at a severe sexual disadvantage with women. They want them passive, docile, exciting yet undemanding. They continually argue that if only women could walk this or that psychological tightrope, *then* men would feel safe and be attracted to them. A man, it seems, has difficulty feeling like a man if a woman approaches him as a free, independent, fully sexual being. It is as if he feels handicapped in sexual encounters and needs to create a comparable handicap for the woman.

Perhaps men *have* become sexually handicapped relative to women—not just in the physiological sense of having a more finite capacity for repetition, but culturally, in the sense of having evolved a social role that limits their capacity for physical pleasure. In all civilized societies men have sacrificed a part of their eroticism to the pursuit of wealth, status, power and political dominance over women. They have then harassed their womenfolk in a variety of ways to compensate for the feelings of sexual inferiority that this sacrifice engendered.

Work and sex are natural enemies, and the more personal commitment the work generates, the more inroads it makes into erotic life. For the ambitious careerist, as John Cuber and Peggy Harroff found in their study of successful executives, government officials and professionals (*Sex and the Significant Americans*), eroticism tends to become perfunctory—a release rather than a pastime. Clearly if pleasure is something to be caught on the fly in the interstices of effortful striving, than the quicker it is done with, the better. Men tend to define themselves by their professions—a man is a banker or a lawyer first, a person second, and it is difficult for one who thinks this way to invest himself totally in a love relationship or spend days in leisurely lovemaking.

It is often said that love is only a part of a man's life, the whole of woman's. Although the intent of this sentiment is to keep women in their place, it expresses a historical reality. Men have invested in professions a part of the energy and interest that women devote to relationships. Eroticism thereby became woman's domain, into which men enter as dilettantes in some sense.

The history of sexual mores in civilized societies is a chronicle of the efforts of men to use their political advantage to rectify the sexual disadvantage. The most common form of harassment has been through sexual restrictions, such as premarital virginity and marital fidelity. These restrictions have usually been applied exclusively to women and have succeeded to some extent in warping, crippling and blocking their sexual spontaneity. Nineteenth-century Europe produced a more subtle and insidious form of sexual control. Men began to impose upon women a feminine ideal stripped of sexual impulse. Reversing the usual idea of the spiritual male opposed to the carnal female, they made allowances for the "animal nature" of men and denied that any respectable woman had such a thing. This was a more powerful device since it crippled feminine sexuality at the core. Its transparent absurdity, however, made it vulnerable to social reform.

Ironically, the efforts of psychoanalysts to achieve such reform produced what was by far the most powerful technique yet devised for giving women a sexual handicap comparable to that borne by men. This was the dictum that mature female sexuality should center in the vagina and should de-emphasize the clitoris—a brilliant gambit inasmuch as the clitoris is the center of erotic sensation. Before the researches of Masters and Johnson undermined this dogma, two generations of women had felt guilty and inadequate because of a man's fantasy about how their bodies should function. Thus the psychiatric profession was for some years able to achieve psychically the same goal sought by certain primitive tribes, who limit the sexuality of their women by cutting away the clitoris at puberty.

Whoever makes the labels holds the power, and all these devices have been invented by men. Each has served in one way or another to cause women to doubt their natural sexual impulses, and this limitation on feminine sexuality has in turn served to make men feel more competent in the sexual sphere.

Discussions of sexuality in America have always centered on the orgasm rather than on pleasure in general. This seems to be another example of our tendency to focus on the *product* of any activity at the expense of the *process*. It may seem odd to refer to an orgasm as a product, but this is the tone taken in such discussions. Most sex manuals give the impression that the partners in love-making are performing some sort of task; by dint of a great cooperative effort and technical skill (primarily the man's), an orgasm (primarily the woman's, which masculine mystification has made problematic) is ultimately produced. The bigger the orgasm, the more "successful" the task performance.

This thought pattern owes much to the masculine preoccupation with technical mastery. Women in popular sexual literature become manipulable mechanical objects—like pianos ("It's amazing what sounds he can get out of that instrument"). Even more pronounced is the competitive note in writers such as D.H. Lawrence and Norman Mailer, who often make it seem as if lovemaking were a game in which the first person to reach a climax loses.

The emphasis on orgasm also reveals, paradoxically, a vestigial puritanism. The term "climax" expresses not only the idea of a peak or zenith but also the idea of termination or completion. Discussions of the sexual act in our society are thus primarily concerned with how it *ends*. Leisurely pleasure-seeking is brushed aside, as all acts and all thoughts are directed toward the creation of a successful finale. The better the orgasm, the more enjoyable the whole encounter is retrospectively defined as having been. This insures against too much pleasure obtained in the here and now, since one is always concentrating on the future goal. In such a system you can find out how much you're enjoying yourself only after it's all over, just as many Americans traveling abroad don't know what they've experienced until they've had their films developed.

Eastern love manuals, although rather mechanical and obsessional in their own ways, direct far more attention to the sensations of the moment. The preoccupation in Western sexual literature with orgasm seems to be a natural extension of the Protestant work ethic in which nothing is to be enjoyed for its own sake except striving.

The antithetical attitude would be to view orgasm as a delightful interruption in an otherwise continuous process of generating pleasurable sensations. This would transform our ways of thinking about sex—we would no longer use the orgasm as a kind of unit of lovemaking, as in "we made love three times that day" (. . . "I have two cars," "I played nine holes of golf," "He's worth five million dollars"). The impulse to quantify sex would be sharply diminished, and along with it the tendency to infuse pleasure-seeking with ideas of achievement and competition. Affectionate caresses exchanged in passing would not be so rigidly differentiated from those interludes culminating in orgasm.

Women already espouse this view to a greater degree than men; witness the complaint of many women that their husbands never caress them except in bed. The reason they assign to this behavior, however—"He's only interested in sex, in my body, not in me"— misses the point. A man who behaves in this way is not interested in sex, either—he is interested only in releasing tension. Far from enjoying pleasurable stimulation, he cannot tolerate it beyond a minimum level and wants it to end as rapidly as possible within the limits of sexual etiquette and competent "performance."

This desire for release from tension, for escape from stimulation, lies at the root of our cultural preoccupation with orgasm. In a society like ours, which perpetually bombards its participants with bizarre and dissonant stimuli—both sexual and nonsexual— tension release is at a premium. It is this confused and jangling stimulation, together with the absence of simple and meaningful rhythms in our daily lives, that makes Americans long for orgasmic release and shun any casual pleasure-seeking that does not culminate in rapid tension discharge.

It is men who suffer most from this need for tension release, since it is men who have specialized most acutely in sacrificing feelings in the service of ambition—in postponing gratification, in maintaining a stiff upper lip, in avoiding body contact, in emotional coldness. Women often express the feeling in the midst of intense lovemaking that they want it never to end. I wonder how many men are capable of sustaining such a sentiment—are able to imagine themselves enjoying endless inputs of acute pleasurable stimulation?

The emphasis in popular sexual literature on the ecstatic agony thus caters primarily to men. A favorite theme, for example, is that of the inhibited or resistant woman forced by overwhelming sexual arousal into unexpected and explosive orgasm. This sadomasochistic fantasy has two roots. First, it expresses the common masculine wish for some kind of superpotency—one glance and she falls writhing to the ground; one stroke and she explodes in ecstasy. Second, it involves an identification with the woman herself. For it is *men* who have bottled up feelings and long to burst their controls. But since this yearning endangers the whole edifice of our culture, it cannot be allowed direct expression and is projected onto women. Women are the emotional specialists in our society—they are supposed to do the crying, screaming, clinging and so on, not only for themselves, but for the man as well ("It would break your mother's heart if you went away").

The fantasy of the woman propelled into orgasm against her will is just another expression of the general tendency of men to give women the job of releasing masculine tensions vicariously. Indeed, part of the sexual hang-ups suffered by women spring from having to play out this fantasy for men. Many women feel inadequate when they are not consumed with passion at the first approach of their lover and guilty that they have thereby injured his vanity.

It seems to me that when sexual gratification is plentiful, orgasm is not the goal of every erotic encounter from the start but is a possible outcome arising naturally as the lovemaking proceeds. In a comfortable sexual setting, in other words, some lovemaking is nonorgasmic.

This observation should not be considered some sort of ideal. The last thing I want to do is to add another "should" to our already overburdened sexual mores. The notion of sexual "adequacy" seems to have had as poisonous an effect on the American psyche as did simple Puritan prohibitions or Victorian restraints, and the contributions of psychiatry, however well intended and often insightful, have merely added to the confusion. Psychoanalysts have demanded "vaginal" orgasms, have ranked orgasms by degree of total bodily involvement, have demanded fantasy-free sex (which has the amusing effect of consigning all sexual intercourse performed with procreation in mind to the realm of perversion). All these efforts to establish medical grading systems for sexual behavior seem to have had the unfortunate effect of increasing the sexual pathology against which they were directed.

From a cold, detached physiological viewpoint, the "goal" of the human orgasm is to maintain some kind of balance in the sphere of pleasurable stimulation. A degree of tension and excitement is prerequisite to life, and a degree of release is necessary for internal order and serenity. The fantasy of complete discharge—of the perfect, ultimate orgasm—is fundamentally a death fantasy. People we view as particularly alive are those capable of sustaining a lot of pleasurable stimulation without discharging it or blunting their senses, but a person *unable* to discharge often seems nervous and jumpy. These styles are sometimes difficult to distinguish in practice, and, by the same token, a person with a low level of tolerance for stimulation may appear either serene or dead. It is most important to recognize that this balance differs for each person, and no one else can decide for that person the appropriate balance to be maintained or the best way of obtaining it.

But this is, as I said, a cold physiological view of the matter. From a merely human viewpoint an orgasm is simply something that happens involuntarily when pleasure peaks, and probably the less cognitive messing about with it we do, the better.

What Is Our Problem?

Rollo May

Our problem today is set by several strange and interesting dilemmas in which we find ourselves with respect to sex in our society. When psychoanalysis began in Victorian times half a century ago, repression of sexual impulses, feelings, interests, and drives was the accepted situation. It was not nice to feel sexual, one would not talk about sex in polite company and an aura of sanctifying repulsiveness surrounded the whole topic, so that males and females dealt with each other as though neither possessed sex organs. Freud was right in his clinical assessment of this repression of sex with its allied hysterical symptoms.

Then in the 1920s it became widely believed in liberal circles that the opposite to repression—namely, sex education, freedom of talking, feeling, and expression—would have healthy effects, and was obviously the only stand for the enlightened person. An amazingly radical change occurred in four decades: our society shifted from acting

Reprinted from *Review of Existential Psychology and Psychiatry*, Volume III (July 7, 1963), with the permission of the author.

as though sex did not exist to placing the most emphasis on sex of any society, according to Max Lerner, since the Roman. Far from not talking about sex, we might seem, if a visitor from Mars came to Times Square, to have no other topic. It reminds me of the lady from Boston who, on visiting her elderly friends in Chicago, said, "Back East we place much emphasis on breeding." The ladies from Chicago answered, "We like it too, but we also have other interests."

Partly as a result of this radical change, many of us therapists rarely get in our consulting offices any more patients who exhibit repression of sex in the pre-World War I sense. In fact we find just the opposite: a great deal of talk about sex, a great deal of sexual activity, practically no one complaining of any cultural prohibitions over his

> **Whereas the Victorian person didn't want anyone to know that he or she had sexual feelings, now we are ashamed if we do not.**

going to bed as often or with as many partners as he wishes. But our patients do complain of lack of feeling and passion; so much sex and so little meaning or even fun in it. Whereas the Victorian person didn't want anyone to know that he or she had sexual feelings, now we are ashamed if we do not. Patients may have problems of impotence or frigidity, but they struggle desperately not to let anyone know they don't feel sexually. The Victorian nice man or woman was guilty if he or she did perform sexually; now we are guilty if we don't.

Our first dilemma is, therefore, that enlightenment has not at all solved the sexual problems in our culture. Some problems are eased: sexual knowledge is available in any bookstore, contraception is available . . . , external social anxiety is lessened. But *internalized anxiety and guilt have increased,* and in some ways these are more morbid, harder to handle, and impose a heavier burden than external anxiety and guilt.

A second dilemma is that the new emphasis on technique in sex and love-making backfires. It often seems to me that there is an inverse relationship between the number of how-to-do-it books perused by a person or rolling off the presses in a country, and the amount of sexual passion or even pleasure experienced. Nothing is wrong certainly with technique as such, in playing golf or acting or making love. But the emphasis beyond a certain point on technique in sex makes for a mechanistic attitude toward love-making, and goes along with alienation, feelings of loneliness, and depersonalization.

The third dilemma is that our highly vaunted sexual freedom is, in my judgment, simply a new form of Puritanism. I define Puritanism as a state of alienation from the body, separation of emotion from reason, and use of the body as a machine. This was moralistic Puritanism in Victorian times; industrialism expressed these characteristics of Puritanism in economic guise. Our modern sexual attitudes have a new content, namely, full sexual expression, but in the same old Puritan form—alienation from the body and feeling, and exploitation of the body as though it were a machine. In our new Puritanism bad health is equated with sin. Sin used to be "to give in to one's sexual desires"; now it is "not to have full sexual expression." It is immoral not to express your libido. A woman used to be guilty if she went to bed with a man; now she feels vaguely guilty if after two or three dates she still refrains from going to bed; and the partner, who is always completely enlightened (or at least plays the role) refuses to allay her guilt by getting overtly angry at her sin of "morbid repression," refusing to "give." And this, of course, makes her "no" all the more guilt-producing for her.

This all means, of course, that people must learn to perform sexually, but have to make sure they can do so without getting involved, without letting themselves go in passion or unseemly commitment, which latter may be interpreted as exerting an unhealthy demand on the partner. *The Victorian person sought to have love without falling into sex; the modern person seeks to have sex without falling into love.*

Some time ago I amused myself by drawing an impressionistic picture of the attitude of the contemporary enlightened person toward sex and love. I would like to share with you this picture of what I call the new intellectual:

The new intellectual is not castrated by society, but like Origen, is self-castrated. Sex and the body are for him not something to be and live out, but tools to be cultivated like a T.V. announcer's voice. And like all genuine Puritans (very passionate underneath) the new intellectual does it by devoting himself passionately to the moral principle of dispersing all passion, loving everybody until love has no power left to scare anyone. He is deathly afraid of his passions unless they are kept under leash, and the theory of total expression is precisely his leash. His dogma of liberty is his repression; and his principle of full libidinal health, full sexual satisfaction, are his Puritanism and amount to be the same thing as his New England forefathers' denial of sex. The first Puritans repressed sex and were passionate; our new man represses passion and is sexual. Both have the purpose of holding back the body, both are ways of trying to make nature a slave. The modern man's rigid principle of full freedom is not freedom at all but a new straitjacket as compulsive as the old. He does all this because he is afraid of his body and compassionate roots in nature, afraid of the soil and his procreative power. He is our latter day Baconian deviated to gaining power *over* nature, gaining knowledge in order to get more power. And you gain power over sexuality (like working the slave until all zest for revolt is squeezed out of him) precisely by the role of full expression. Sex becomes our tool like the caveman's wheel, crowbar, or adz. Sex, the new machine, *Machina Ultima*.

Fortunately I do not have to solve all these dilemmas. I only want to point out that the existential approach is very much concerned with sex and love. There are several reasons for this concern. The first is that existentialism has always stood strongly against the dehumanizing trends in our society—indeed, the contemporary form of existentialism may be said to have been born in the revolt against dehumanization in our Western society, and the movement takes its decisive form therefrom. It stands against depersonalizing tendencies in all forms, making man into a machine in industrialism or making him into a technical tool in sex.

Second, the existential approach sees the body as an inseparable aspect of being-in-the-world. Thus the body is not a machine but a relatedness, a communion, a participation with and in nature and other persons. The body is one expression of being.

Third, the existential approach places a new emphasis upon passion and feeling. Not passion in the sense of being compulsively driven by sex or eroticism but passion as commitment and involvement of one's total (I speak *qualitatively, not quantitatively* here) centered self.

Fourthly, this approach brings a new dimension of depth and dynamism to the understanding of sex and love. We have tended particularly in America to over-simplify sex and love; one way of our doing this has been to let our too-easy view of *agape* cover up and rationalize the demonic aspects of *eros*. Like most of us, I find my own "definitions" of love written some years ago too superficial, and not giving enough recognition to the powerful nonrational forces of sex and love—powerful with both destructive and uniting possibilities. Freud certainly helped us greatly in appreciating the varied and almost omnipresent channels by which powerful erotic drives express themselves. But I think Freudianism was bound to over-simplify sex and love because it had no norm of I–Thou relationship, or norm of *agape*, which is not sublimation of *eros* but a transcendence of it. We need a new appreciation of the demonic aspects of sex and love, particularly of *eros*. The tragic emphasis present in existentialism also makes a contribution at this point: tragic as meaning not only the negative possibilities but the positive, creative, ennobling possibilities of sex and love as well.

397

Increasing Comfort with Non-Demand Pleasuring

Barry W. McCarthy, Mary Ryan, and Fred A. Johnson

One of the most widely believed and harmful myths that keeps a couple from achieving tenderness and spontaneous feeling for each other is the belief that every touching or other affectionate experience must and should end in intercourse. One of the most crippling aspects of marital sex is the notion that the couple cannot just tease or be affectionate or be close, but that any physical intimacy is an invitation to intercourse. This notion makes spontaneous feelings of touching and pleasure into a demand for a more intimate experience.

It is our feeling that spontaneity and sharing would increase if partners were free to share their feelings and touch without an expectancy and demand being placed on them for a payoff (i.e., orgasm) other than simply the enjoyment of being together. In other words, you as a couple can and should be able to enjoy touching and pleasuring in a non-demanding atmosphere.

Our feeling is that sensual and sexual pleasure and experience are

---

Reprinted from *Sexual Awareness, A Practical Approach* by Barry McCarthy, Mary Ryan, and Fred A. Johnson, by permission of the publishers, Boyd & Fraser Publishing Company, San Francisco, and Scrimshaw Press, Oakland, Copyright 1975, pp. 153 –163.

enhanced if partners can be free and comfortable in their expression, without feeling that each contact must end in intercourse or
orgasm. In fact, we suggest that whenever they feel a need to be close
to their partner, a couple could engage in pleasuring which is sensual but does not end in intercourse.

SHARING PLEASING THOUGHTS

Most of the demands in a sexual experience exist because people
do not share with each other how they feel about being together—
how much they enjoy just being close and affectionate when they just
want to be playful and nothing more. If the sexual interaction is
based on the myth that in order for the experience to be satisfying the
couple both must have an orgasm, or the even more harmful myth that
simultaneous orgasm should be the goal, then the relationship will
probably be much poorer because of these beliefs. It is fine to be orgasmic or even orgasmic simultaneously, but to overemphasize the
idea the orgasms *must* happen is dangerous because it negates
spontaneous responses and puts stringent demands on what should be
an enjoyable, free-flowing sexual experience.

What the couple is forgetting about and losing is the sense of
sharing and intimacy. The couple which is able to feel comfortable in
giving and receiving pleasure and sharing a sense of intimacy in a
non-demanding context will be a sexually well-functioning couple.
When the couple makes intercourse or orgasm the criterion for their success and measures their roles as lovers and the worth of the experience
by this criterion, they lose the sense of sharing and intimacy. A
much better viewpoint is that a feeling of mutual sharing and satisfaction is a better criterion for the couple's feelings about the sexual experience. It is important to be aware that every couple can enjoy a
non-orgasmic experience, and that a fulfilling intimacy can be shared
just by being together. To set a demand on the situation leads to concentrating on the goal and neglecting the main reason one is
there—simply to share and enjoy. The unique aspect of this approach is that with a pleasant, sharing experience you both win; it is
not a competition in which one partner wins and one loses.

TOUCHING

One of the best aspects of a relationship is touching. If the touching is pleasant and creates no anxiety in one's partner, it frees both of the partners to remain much closer to their own feelings of warmth and togetherness. In non-demand positions and situations, a couple can feel close and intimate in a stress-free atmosphere. There should be spontaneous, enjoyable touching and body contact without an expectancy or demand that sexual intercourse *must* follow. If one partner or the couple decides to proceed to sexual intercourse, the decision should be spontaneous, cued by an enjoyment of the situation rather than the feeling typified in the following expression: "We've gone this far—we might as well go all the way."

> Non-demanding touching experiences can do much to keep the sense of spontaneity, experimentation, and communication alive in a relationship.

One of the most important things to be aware of is that the non-demanding touching does not have to occur only in the bed or even in the bedroom. In fact, one of the things which keeps a relationship fresh and spontaneous is the willingness to experiment with a variety of situations. Although most people would consider it improper or uncomfortable to engage in affectionate and sexually arousing touching in a public place, it might be easier to be affectionate on a lonely beach, while walking in a wooded area, or in a car parked by a lake. Even more appropriate is the privacy of your own house— using all the rooms, including some unusual places like the rug in front of the fireplace, the big chair in the den, the dining room table, or even the kitchen floor.

Another important variation upon which to experiment is the amount of clothing. When sexual interaction is discussed, many couples immediately think of nudity. Although this is fine and can be enjoyable, it is not the only way. The female appearing wearing only the male's shirt can be quite enticing, as can the male wearing only his pants without shoes or shirt.

Perhaps the most interesting of all variations concerns positioning. Again, there is no right or normal position to be used in non-demand exercises. The position suggestions below as well as previous suggestions are made to facilitate your exploration of non-demand situations and experiences. The concept of non-demanding touching experiences can do much to keep the sense of spontaneity, experimentation, and communication alive in a relationship. The couple who continually enjoy basic human interactions like kissing, holding hands, and hugging each other are a couple who will continue to enjoy their sensual and sexual functioning.

First Set of Exercises

First sit and discuss your feelings about the use of non-demanding touching and experiences. Be aware of when and how you feel pressure to perform sexually; this is a trap which can serve to take the spontaneity and mutuality out of your sensual and sexual interactions. In these exercises, there will be no demand except your desires and choices. Talk about setting up and refining a communication "signal system" which will tell your partner if you desire to continue on to intercourse or not. This signal system can be verbal, i.e., "I really want to make love," "Let's have intercourse," "I don't want to go on to intercourse; let me just hold you," "I've enjoyed this, but let's stop now" or non-verbal, i.e., massaging the partner's genitals and switching to an intercourse position, using eye contact to say yes or no, moving your partner's hands from your genitals, etc. Also, your partner should have a signal that says "O.K." or "Not tonight—let's do something else instead." A behavioral guideline is that you should not just say no, but rather suggest something else: a backrub, holding each other, using oral sex or any other suitable alternative.

For this first exercise, be in the bedroom and in the nude. Lying on the bed, the female should position herself close behind her partner, with their entire body lengths touching, her chest to his back, with her knees bent inside his. She should have her arms surrounding his body, and thus he can make contact with her arms and can hold hands with her. . . . This is a most effective position for just lying together and feeling warmth and closeness. The male is in a more protected and passive position than usual, and he should be aware of his feelings about this, and allow himself to enjoy the feelings of being cared for. In this exercise, it is the female's prerogative to indicate whether or not she wants to carry this contact on to sexual intercourse. She can use any signal system she wants, verbal or nonverbal; the only criterion of the effectiveness of the system is whether her partner clearly receives and understands the communication. If the signal is positive, the male should also be able to signal clearly and directly whether or not he desires to have intercourse. Couples make a mistake in assuming that the male always desires intercourse and they must accede to the female's request for intercourse. To do so sets unrealistic and demanding expectations and pressures. If the male does not desire intercourse, he is advised not simply to say no, but to suggest an alternative positive way to end the experience. One possibility would be just holding his partner. Another might be manually stimulating her to orgasm. Another might be engaging in wholebody touching with both partners' eyes closed, or doing something else which is mutually pleasurable. If the female signals she does not desire intercourse, she should suggest another way to end the experience. One possibility would be to go to sleep . . . . Another would be to stimulate her partner orally; another to give a whole-body massage. Either partner should accept the initiative or suggest his or her own; neither should press for intercourse or feel rejected. Remember, the idea is to enjoy a non-demanding sensual and sexual experience.

Second Set of Exercises

Discuss how the signalling system operated in the last set of exercises. Are you able to feel just as comfortable in initiating intercourse as in just continuing with the pleasuring and ending the experience with no demand for intercourse? Is your partner able to accept your request or to change it to something more enjoyable for him or her? If you decide not to continue to intercourse are there bad feelings, or feelings of pressure or rejection? If there are difficulties, feel free to repeat the first exercise or to use the same roles (female initiate, male respond) with the second set of exercises. If things have gone well, let the male decide whether or not to continue to intercourse this time.

This time choose a place other than the bedroom to interact with each other. It can be the living room, den, basement, or any room you choose. This exercise is best done in the nude so that you can be comfortable with nudity outside the bedroom. Be sure that you won't be disturbed by children. (Being affectionate in front of children is positive for them to see, so that they may be aware that affection and sensuality are a good aspect of people. However, engaging in sexual activity in front of children is sexually healthy neither for the adults nor for the children.)

For these exercises, the male lies on his stomach, arms extended over his head. Even if you are not in bed, you can use throw pillows or pillows from the bedroom. If pillows are being used, his arms can be resting on the pillows. Lying on her side, the female covers his arms, with one hand holding his. Her other arm is free to caress his back, and one leg can be placed over his for even more contact. This position allows the female access to touching and caressing her partner's body, and the male can either be passive or can return the caresses. However, since males have the tendency to become overly active and initiating, he should remember that this is a non-demand position where much of the pleasuring and caressing comes from the female. Of course, this position—as all non-demand positions—can be reversed with the male covering, holding, and caressing the female.

In this position, it is the male's prerogative to decide whether or not he wants to carry the contact on to sexual intercourse. He can use a signal system, verbal or non-verbal, to communicate to his partner whether he wants to end the experience on a touching, nondemanding note or to continue to intercourse. The male needs to be especially attentive to his own feelings and desires, and he also needs to signal for intercourse not because he "should" or is "expected to" but because he really would rather have intercourse than continue with non-demanding touching. Likewise, the female responds with what she really wants to do rather than what she "should" do, not fearing disapproval or repercussions from her partner. Remember, the best way to improve a couple's sexual functioning and communication is to have both partners aware of their feelings and desires and to communicate them clearly and directly to each other. If the desires are different, it is easiest to resolve by doing a positive sensual or sexual activity, rather than one partner simply saying no. You will find that you can communicate and usually can come up with something that is good for both of you.

Third Set of Exercises

At this point you as a couple are probably aware of the positive aspects of non-demanding touching. You know how it can enhance sexuality and sexual intercourse when you decide to continue to intercourse, and where it can be a positive, affectionate affirmation of you as a couple when you decide not to continue to intercourse. To make non-demand touching more like your real-life sexual functioning, it may be worthwhile to experiment with the amount of clothing you wear and your location somewhere other than the bedroom for this set of exercises.

You might begin the exercise by slowly or teasingly disrobing your partner to a level of undress (other than nudity) in which you find him or her to be the most sexually appealing. Everyone is unique in this respect, and you might test out your feelings. Some females find their partners most enticing when they have only underpants on. Others like them fully clothed on top and nude on the bottom. Do what you like. Some males like their partners best in bra and panties, or with pants and bra hanging, or nude on the bottom with a shirt and a headband; again, your unique tastes are important here.

In continuing the exercise, a male sits propped on pillows comfortably with his legs spread. Facing him, the female lies between his spread legs, with her knees near the side of his body. She also will have pillows behind the lower part of her back so that she is in a good position both to touch and to see her partner. Rather than one partner being primary initiator, this non-demand position allows and encourages both partners to give and receive affection. The couple should be especially aware of using eye contact to facilitate each other's positive feelings about this non-demanding experience. Remember that the most positive aspects of the pleasuring and touching experience are the enjoyment and responsivity.

In the same manner, let the decision whether or not to proceed to intercourse be mutual. Follow your own feelings instead of doing what you think your partner expects. Continue to work toward a clear, honest, and mutual communication system.

Fourth Set of Exercises

Before beginning, discuss what you have learned from these exercises so far and whether you have fallen into any traps, such as having intercourse every time, not establishing a positive, non-intercourse way of ending an exercise, or one partner always pushing for intercourse. If you have fallen into a trap, discuss what you need to do to work out a really non-demanding aspect of your affectional and sexual relationship. Knowing your trap allows you as a couple to monitor it and not to have it continue to affect your relationship negatively.

Approach the last non-demand position with the atmosphere and amount of clothing that you as a couple have decided are most conducive to non-demanding exchanges of affection. Begin the exercise in the male superior position, where the male is lying on top of his partner. The male then moves slowly down his partner's body until his head is resting on the soft stomach area beneath her rib cage. He puts his arms around her body, with her hands being free to caress his head and shoulder area. This position can be particularly arousing because it positions the male where he can easily caress the genital area of the female's body. There is little eye contact, but positionings where there is little eye contact can sometimes be among the most arousing of all. The decision whether to continue with non-demanding touch or to switch to intercourse should be mutual. This experience will provide an opportunity to test your signalling system, since you will not be using eye contact. You can be aware of your own needs and be in tune with your partner's feelings and responses so that the decision simply to enjoy the non-demanding touching or to switch to having sexual intercourse will lead to a smooth transition where both partners feel their needs and desires have been understood and accepted.

AFTERWORD

Feeling comfortable with non-demanding touching and pleasuring is an integral part of a successful sexual relationship. It enhances feelings of affection and sexual interest with the knowledge that not all touching is goal-directed and intercourse-directed. A good guideline to use as a couple is that at least once every two months you reserve an evening for non-demanding touch which does not end in intercourse. This non-demanding touch should also be extended to a variety of non-bedroom situations. To be affectionate with each other is good for your relationship; it provides a positive model for your children. Perhaps the best sex education a child can have is to see his parents hugging, kissing, and demonstrating affection. The message to the child is that you feel good about your bodies, your sensual expression, and yourselves as a couple.

You should also be aware that these non-demand positions are only four of the many that can be used. All can be reversed and can be fun to test out for different feelings when they are reversed. In order to feel more comfortable with non-demand positions and to refine your signal system on whether to proceed to intercourse or not, you will need to continue to be open to experimentation and spontaneity. It is most important to tell your partner your feelings and desires clearly and directly.

Sex Talk

Myron Brenton

HOW TO TALK TO YOUR PARTNER ABOUT SEX PROBLEMS

Tone and Timing

Sylvia is troubled about herself and her husband, Fred. The sexual
verve that characterized the first few years of their marriage is
missing now. And she misses it. She resolves to have a candid talk
with Fred and does so one evening after they've had a good meal and
are relaxing on pillows by the fireplace. Fred tells Sylvia that he,
too, has felt something lacking in their sex life and guesses it's because
he has become preoccupied with business matters. They agree to take a
short trip by themselves soon, a sexy weekend, leaving their children with relatives.

Clara and Don are similarly troubled; their sex life is also marked by
the blahs. But whenever Clara tries to talk to Don about it he balks.
She can't get through. Tension rises and they never really get anywhere.

Same problem, opposite results. Why? Because Sylvia's and Clara's

---

approaches were markedly different. Sylvia chose a time when she and her husband were relaxed, warmed by a good meal, at ease with each other. Clara never chose the time; the time chose her. She plunged right in when the problem was uppermost in her mind—that is, when she was especially disappointed and resentful. Inevitably, then, her approach was accusatory rather than conciliatory. She was far readier to serve ultimatums than to explore the problem non-judgmentally. So Don was always put on the defensive and reacted in kind.

Sex talk, especially sex talk that centers on a problem, is potentially very explosive for couples. Inevitably, the man's reaction is, "What does this say about my masculinity?" Inevitably, the woman has feelings about herself and her femininity. The temptation is to ward off a real talk, to refuse to engage in the discussion, to argue, to deflect any possible accusation by casting blame first.

Don't start a talk when your anger is riding high; in spite of your best intentions that anger will take over and the talk become an exercise in aggression rather than a search for solutions. Don't talk when either of you is tired, preoccupied, or in a hurry to get somewhere, or has had too much to drink. Pick a relaxed moment, one in which you have plenty of time and there are feelings of affection between you.

Picking the right moment doesn't mean nobody will get hurt. But the hurt feelings will be less intense because what's said is said in a way that's less hurting.

Some people invariably choose the *wrong* time; when that happens what they want, wittingly or unwittingly, is for the talk not to come off. Because deep down they want to dodge the basic issues surrounding the problem, or for whatever other reason, they preordain failure.

Before starting to talk to your partner about a sex problem, ask yourself:

1   Is this the right time?
2   Is this the right place?
3   Am I—are we—really in the right mood to begin?
4   What am I really after?

Breaking the Ice

Even in the best of circumstances you may still find it difficult to get that talk going. Maybe the words don't come out the way you want them to; maybe your partner tries to vanish or pleads a headache or attempts to joke out of it—or simply, frankly, refuses to talk.

One of these three techniques may help to break the ice:

1   Use sex manuals   They're handy devices for people who find it easier to read than to talk about sex. Many sex manuals are fairly comprehensive in their treatment of the subject; you shouldn't have trouble finding one that touches on the issue you have in mind. But don't use the book (or pamphlet or magazine article) as a rule book

> **Sharing of feelings ought to evolve from the most easily shared ones to the most difficult.**

for sexual conduct; use it as a tool for facilitating discussion. It may be easier to say, "Honey, there's something that might be useful for us to read," than, "Honey, there's something I want to talk to you about."

The material can be read separately and then discussed together, or read and discussed together, however suits you best. Once you've begun talking about what the book says it should be easier to slide into your own feelings and concerns.

Some provisos, however: a sex manual can work against you if you choose the wrong one, one that's offensive or otherwise vexing to you or your partner. A more inhibited person, for instance, might well be revolted by one of the very graphic new sex manuals like *The Sensuous Woman* or *The Sensuous Couple*. Also, don't be overly impressed with the specific advice given in any of the books. The advice applies generally; you and your partner are individuals, with your own unique physiological and psychological workings. Sexual advice is helpful only when you can fit it in with your temperament, never when you try to fit yourself (or your partner) into the advice.

Above all, don't use a marriage manual as a club to pound home your point of view. Even if the book factually proves you right and your partner wrong, it doesn't take into account your partner's feelings about the issue at hand. When a book on sex is used as a sexual weapon, useful communication becomes the first victim.

2   *Metacommunicate*   That's a common term in communications theory; it simply means "talk about talking." The technique can be very helpful to get a sex talk off the ground because it gets you into a discussion of why you're having problems discussing the subject. In effect, you're saying, "Look, we can't really seem to get started talking seriously and sensibly about sex. Every time we begin, something happens. So let's not talk about sex. Let's talk about why we're having so much trouble talking about sex."

If the problem is one of acute embarrassment, talk about why you're embarrassed (merely bringing the fact of embarrassment out in the open does a lot to lessen it). If quarrels always erupt, maybe your timing is off or you two fall into other communication traps we'll be exploring. The more you talk about talking sex, the more likely it is you'll eventually shift to the crucial issue you actually want to talk about.

3   *Practice gradualism*   Instead of starting in talking about the big problem, the one that seems to generate so much tension, build up to it gradually. Start in talking about sex in general—be it your reaction to the latest raunchy movie playing at the local cinema, or a sex-related newspaper item, whatever. Slowly, maybe over a period of time, work into your personal problems. The idea is first to get used to talking about sex generally; then it becomes easier to get specific.

Gradualism is especially appropriate if you and your partner aren't really used to sharing deeply felt emotions. To make a sudden plunge into this kind of intimacy isn't likely to work out very well; it's unsettling or confusing to everybody concerned.

"You can't impose feelings by an act of will," the Marriage Council's Dr. Philip Feldman points out. He suggests that the sharing of feelings ought to evolve from the most easily shared ones to the most difficult.

The Family and Children's Service of Minneapolis offers a very helpful, broad-based communications course named UNITE to engaged and married couples; the course is particularly appropriate to a topic as sensitive as sex. Throughout much emphasis is given to the styles of talk which people use to communicate, the idea being that the style has to fit the occasion or communication breaks down. According to the program, which was developed at the University of Minnesota, there are four styles to choose from:

Conventional   Superficial. Party chit-chat, matter-of-fact comments, anything that leaves out your feelings, is conventional. In the context of sex, a noncommittal remark along the lines of, "It's Wednesday, this is our usual night," would be conventional. It's really not for facing issues or otherwise talking about sensitive matters.

Assertive   When you're being pushy, demanding, dictatorial, manipulative, belittling. Assertive talk is attacking talk. It can lead to arguments—and it's certainly okay to argue at times—but this style isn't recommended for problem-solving.

Speculative   Wishy-washy talk, a way of getting at a problem by gnawing at the edges. You don't really put much of yourself into it. For instance:
  "Are you in the mood?"
  "Guess so."
  Advice, both in terms of giving and receiving, is often speculative:
  "Well, I really think you'd feel a lot better if you loosened up more."
  "Maybe you're right."
  Questions, especially when they become a habitual pattern of communication, are speculative:
  "Do you think our sex life is all it should be?"
  "Do you?"
  "I asked you first."

The speculative style can sometimes ease you into a meaningful talk but it doesn't get much accomplished in its own right because you put so little of yourself into it.

Confronting   This is the style that requires you to confront yourself and your own feelings, and your partner and your partner's feelings. That makes it the most appropriate system when you truly want to reach someone, solve problems, discuss a sensitive issue. When you talk confrontingly you must conform to three specific rules of communication:

- 1 You speak only for yourself, not for your partner. This means that what you say inevitably has a good deal of "I" in it.
- 2 You "document"—back up—what you say with examples and illustrations. This again brings you into the picture because you're demonstrating *why* you feel the way you do.
- 3 You try to *get* some feedback from your partner, on the order of, "Do you read me?" or, "How do you feel about what I've said?"—and you *give* feedback to your partner, on the order of, "Do I read you correctly?" or, "This is how I read you."

In the confronting kind of communication, therefore, you have to be open and revealing, you have to face issues and the emotions they spark.

In essence, each of you says to the other, "I'm not asking you for your feelings until I tell you what mine are. Until I tell you what my worries and concerns and needs are. I'm going to share *myself* with you first and then ask you to tell me where *you* are."

Both of you, then, give each other permission to reveal yourselves and to explore issues on a very basic level of honesty, clarity, and directness.

Using Confrontation

It's evident that confronting talk is risky talk, the riskiest you can engage in. It's risky when both of you engage in it equally; it's riskier still when you're the one who begins using it or uses it unilaterally.

(Well, someone has to start.) Will your partner be as open as you are? Will your partner somehow use your openness against you? Will your partner scoff or sneer or become angry?

There's an ultimate risk—that once you open up the subject it rebounds on you. This often happens, since sex problems generally are neither partner's "fault" so much as they are a combination of circumstances to which both partners contribute.

A case from the Marriage Council's files will illustrate. A married couple sought help because of the wife's inability to reach orgasm. Both partners saw it as "her" problem. But as they began to open up in counseling sessions the husband admitted something for the first time: he had his own doubts, doubts about his sexual adequacy, about his ability to stimulate a woman and make her responsive. Once this came to light he began to see his wife in a much more sympathetic light than before. And once he began to assume some of the responsibility for their sexual problems the two were able to work on them mutually. In time the wife did become more responsive.

Although this incident took place in a clinical setting, the point applies generally. You don't know where a talk will lead. If you're really intent on reaching the other person and solving problems, you must accept this risk.

What's more, when you engage in a confronting kind of talk you can't take responsibility for your partner's reaction or for the eventual outcome of the talk. What will happen will happen. You can only take responsibility for yourself, for your own involvement in the communication.

All this presupposes a measure of self-confidence; it's an essential when you're being confronting. As Ron Brazman, who co-leads a UNITE group at the Family and Children's Service, aptly puts it, "You really have to trust yourself, that what you're feeling and thinking is okay, before you can let anybody in on it."

But then, why shouldn't you be self-confident? Those are *your* thoughts, *your feelings,* that you want to express. You have a perfect right to them. Of course they're okay!

Its very humanness is what gives confronting talk its power; properly used, it can actually break down strong resistance.

Example You want to have a serious talk but your partner artfully dodges it by being flip. You might say, confrontingly, "This is really important to me, and when you joke about it I feel hurt because it doesn't seem as important to you. I know you're not really hearing me."

A few confronting remarks like that and it becomes very difficult for the jokester to keep on joking.

Example You want to have a calm sex talk but your partner always reacts by attacking you. You might say, "When you start to attack me I really get upset. I find it harder to talk, I feel blamed, scared of you."

Let's suppose your partner replies, "Well, maybe you feel blamed because you feel guilty."

Then you could retort, "When you say something like that I really feel like pulling back and not talking at all about it. I don't know what to do when you make a remark like that."

Again, it's hard for the other person to keep on attacking you when you avoid retaliating but simply express how those attacks make you feel. Your partner's eventual response may not be a warm embrace, but even a noticeable lessening of aggressiveness can lead to a more constructive exchange.

Confrontation and Criticism

What confronting talk does is to create an atmosphere that allows for "open" rather than "closed" (hostile) dialogue. This is especially useful when the talk is of a sensitive or critical nature. Let's take a representative situation of this kind and work with it.

Vicky, let's say, wants Bill to be more aggressive in his lovemaking. There are a number of ways she could approach this problem.

"Sure would be nice, Bill, if you'd work up a little enthusiasm when we have sex."

Poor, poor approach. She's being snide, bitchy, really out to wound Bill. Most likely his reaction will be either to withdraw or to try to wound her in turn. What he's least likely to do is to address himself to her central concern.

"Bill, why don't you loosen up more, be more energetic, when we make love?"

Softer, but starting in with "Why don't you . . ." already makes for heavy criticism. The implication is, "As things are now, you don't measure up." It invites defensiveness on Bill's part.

"You're an excellent lover, Bill, but I do wish you'd be more vigorous when we're making love."

Cagey. Vicky wants to blunt criticism with praise, but this is confusing. If he's so excellent, how come the criticism? His options are: to view the praise as phony, to concentrate on the praise and blot out the criticism, to let the two parts of the message cancel each other out. There's little encouragement for a genuine dialogue to develop.

"I love you very much and I love being close to you when we're making love, Bill. But you're so gentle I don't feel as much as I might if you were more vigorous. I wonder how it strikes you?"

It's all there. Vicky spoke for herself, backed up what she had to say, asked for feedback. Criticism is implied, but she has really put herself into the statement, suffused it with her own warmth and humanity. Naturally, there's no law that says Bill can't still take it amiss, but it's her best chance of reaching him especially if she persists on being confronting. Let's follow through a bit on the way the dialogue could evolve:

Vicky: I love you very much and I love being close to you when we're making love, Bill. But you're so gentle I don't feel as much as I might if you were more vigorous. I wonder how it strikes you?

Bill: Funny you should be complaining about that. A lot of women complain that the men they're having sex with are much too rough.

Vicky: Well, I'm hardly one of them.

And that's hardly being confronting. If she wanted to keep the dialogue open, instead of closing it off like that, she might have said:

Vicky: I think I've made you angry. I hear it in your tone. And I really feel badly about that. I just want us to be as happy in all ways as we can.

Bill: I thought we were happy.

Vicky: Oh dear, when you get that look on your face and that tone in your voice, I feel so helpless, you know?

Bill: Well, you sprang this on me so suddenly. I thought everything was okay.

Vicky: I should have spoken up sooner, but this kind of conversation isn't easy for me so I kept postponing it. I hope you understand that.

Bill (grudgingly): Well, it isn't easy for me, either.

Bill isn't exactly being confronting yet, but he has come a long way from his initial closed-off stance. Actually, he has been putting more and more of himself into his retorts; so, almost in spite of himself, he's being drawn into a sympathetic and exploratory talk. Even though he's still hurt, in effect he's saying, "I share this feeling with you."

It's a big step in the direction of problem-solving.

> **Even some persons who would ordinarily champion another's right to say no somehow put sex in a special category and become furious at being denied what they want.**

CARRYING ON A SEXUAL NEGOTIATION

How Not to Negotiate

To negotiate, the dictionary says, is "to treat with another . . . in order to come to terms or reach an agreement." It's self-evident that "treating" can be a highly useful tool in several kinds of situations common to the sex lives of many couples, namely:

—Where one partner wants to try a specific sexual position and the other doesn't.

—Where one partner wants to try a specific sexual technique and the other doesn't.

—Where one partner wants the other to perform a specific sexual act and the other refuses.

Any such situation is ready-made for arguments and tears, for each partner can easily become outraged by the other's attitude, feel put upon, and build up resentments that are destructive to the relationship.

People who want something in the sexual area but are denied by their partners often go on to act in ways that may, to them, have the look of negotiation but are actually self-defeating patterns of behavior:

They become accusing   Like children who can't get their own way, many men and women (men especially) flare up when they learn that their lovers or spouses won't grant them their wishes. Even some persons who would ordinarily champion another's right to say no somehow put sex in a special category and become furious at being denied what they want. This prompts them to make a personal attack, usually something like, "You're inadequate," or, "You're frigid," or, "You're a lousy lay"—a remark that denigrates the other's sexuality.

This is nasty. It's also unproductive, because it simply invites the other to be vituperative in turn. To have shot back at one, "You're a lousy lay, too!" can be as disconcerting to oneself as the original indignity was to the other.

They become legalistic   This pattern usually begins with the partner whose sexual request has been denied saying, "I have a right to it," or, "I have a right to it because you're my spouse." The other responds with, "I have just as much right to say no."

It's the legalistic approach to a relationship, each partner measuring out "rights" like so many dispensations being issued at the bar of justice. Not only is this antithetical to intimacy and openness, nothing gets accomplished: both partners have "rights" so the two rights cancel each other out.

They use sheer persuasion   Also a very poor tactic. "Convincing" somebody to do something usually is tantamount to coercing him. And coercion leads to reprisals and has the potential of damaging the couple's overall relationship. For example, a husband wants to be fellated once a week. His wife says no. He works on her and works on her until finally, wearily, she gives in. She fellates him but hates it and boils over with resentment toward him because she feels she's being used. Eventually she retaliates: by "forgetting" things, nagging him,

417

belittling him in front of company, or taking unto herself a sympathetic lover who doesn't make her do such (to her) nasty things.

So much for the partner who wants to try something new and is turned down. The partner to whom the request is made also has a responsibility not to communicate destructively. If you've been asked to go along with a sexual technique you find unappealing or even repugnant, keep these pointers in mind:

1. Don't be mad at your partner for asking; asking's not a crime.

2. Don't just say no and expect the matter to be dropped. The logical rejoinder to "no" is "why not?" Any request merits discussion.

3. Don't show contempt or ridicule for the proposed idea; just because it's not your cup of tea doesn't mean thousands of others aren't drinking it.

4. Don't snap, "That's abnormal!" In large measure sexual abnormality, like beauty, is in the eye of the beholder. (From a mental-health point of view only the more extreme sadomasochistic exercises, fetishes, and forcible rape are likely to be called abnormal these days.)

For both the partner who seeks new delights and the one who doesn't think they're so delightful, the confronting approach is the one that can bridge their differences. Forcing both partners to be open rather than judgmental, to explore their own feelings rather than psych each other, to negotiate rather than argue, it can generate the understanding and sympathy that are vital elements to a successful resolution.

Using Confrontation to Negotiate

Let's take a fairly common marital conflict: Husband and wife have been married a few years and they're getting along all right, but now the husband wants them to really do something they've only made half-hearted stabs at in the past. He wants them to add to their repertoire what's currently very much in vogue, mutual oral-genital sex. She says nothing doing, she doesn't like it. He stews about it silently for a few days, then decides to have a talk with her. He's going to try to negotiate.

Here's the way a first confronting talk might go:

Husband: I'm really upset that you're so dead set against it. I wish we could be so free with each other that we could do anything. Do you know what I mean?

Wife: Yes, but when you say that you want me to do *that* with you—well, it makes me feel you don't have any respect for me. And when I think you don't have any respect for me I really get angry at you.

Husband: Well, it could seem like a lack of respect. But I want it to be mutual.

Wife: But I don't enjoy it.

Husband: All right, I'll talk just about my side of it. What it really means to me doesn't have anything to do with respect. I would enjoy it, but also, it would mean to me that you really care for me, that my penis is important to you—

Wife: It is important to me but I just can't understand why that's the way I have to prove it. I don't understand why doing that is so important for you.

Husband: Like I said, I get a lot of pleasure out of it. And when you don't want to do it, it makes me feel you're rejecting me.

Wife: I don't mean to reject you, that's not my intention at all. But I just can't do it, it repulses me.

And that's about where, for the moment, the talk should probably end. Otherwise they're apt to go around in circles. Actually, much more has been accomplished than it might seem on the surface. Both have tried to be open and to relate the talk to their inner feelings. Both have avoided being aggressive and have really tried to explain themselves to and understand each other. The husband especially has put himself on the line. The wife hasn't been able to be that open yet. But that she hasn't, and that this talk hasn't resolved anything, is unimportant. They've spotlighted a sensitive issue and shown trust and concern in dealing with it.

So where are they in the negotiation? Both have difficult tasks ahead. The wife has the task of truly reaching into her emotions for the reasons why she can't participate in oral sex with her husband. The husband has the task of accepting things as they are for the time being. He may, of course, be very impatient to get the thing settled. As social worker Ron Brazman points out, people have a tendency to want sexual desires gratified at once, in contrast to other desires they're willing to defer.

"It's as though sexual feelings are more special than other feelings, and that's because those feelings are concretely tied to being a man or a woman," he says.

But in actuality sexual feelings aren't more special and the man has to wait to give his wife a chance to come to grips with the problem his request has created for her. Of course, the longer he's kept dangling the more likely it is he'll begin to feel somehow cheated. Soon they'll have to talk again. The situation being what it is, he'll probably have to initiate that second talk.

In the confronting spirit he might say:

Husband: I've been doing a lot of thinking about this. I know how difficult it is for you, and if it weren't so important to me I'd drop it right away. But I do feel rejected when you say you're repulsed by it because I guess I feel very strongly that my penis *is* me, in a way. So somehow what I'm left with is that you're repulsed by me.

Wife: I wish I could convince you that the one thing has nothing to do with the other. You're not repulsive to me, not in any way. I love you. I want and need you. Will you believe that?

Husband: I do—but there's that other feeling, too. And there's something else. We've begun talking about this thing now. It's out in the open and I think we should deal with it. When we don't it's like unfinished business to me. Like I'm being left hanging, waiting. I really would like to have us talk seriously about this. I really want to understand why you feel the way you do. Do you understand what's going on with me?

She does, but whether she can explore her own emotions with him now is another question. However, if he keeps on being open, understanding, and supportive, chances are good that during either this talk or another she'll really open up.

Resolution

The essence of confronting communication is a striving for growth and change, a striving for greater intimacy. But one person can't change another. The best either can do is to generate the kind of atmosphere in which they may express themselves freely and mutually. Sometimes an exploration of attitudes really does lead a resistant partner to have a change of heart. When it happens it usually does so because this partner gradually learns, "I don't have to be afraid. Nobody is judging me. I don't have to feel guilty about doing this."

When it occurs this way, a happy ending for everybody concerned, it's wonderful—and the confronting kind of approach gives it the best chance of happening. But neither that approach nor any other can guarantee its happening. The resistant partner may be unable to

> **It's a fallacy to assume that even the most honest and feeling kind of talk will necessarily lead to changed behavior.**

hurdle the emotional blocks that keep him or her from agreeing to the other's request. Sometimes not even complete openness and candidness on the one hand, and utter gentleness and understanding and support on the other, are enough to do away with those blocks. Shocking, traumatic early life experiences may be responsible; some women who can't bear to engage in fellatio, for instance, recall having been forced during childhood to fellate a man.

So an impasse may be reached. What then? It's a fallacy to assume that talk—even the most honest and feeling kind of talk—will necessarily lead to changed behavior. When they start out talking, one partner often wrongly assumes a change will eventually occur in the thinking of the other—and feel hurt and let down if it doesn't. Be fair. Be realistic. Be open-minded about the outcome.

And where does that leave the person who wants to try something new but even after negotiation is left with the answer "no"?

Well, if I want to engage in a particular technique, say, and you simply can't go for that one, I have some choices. I can try to force you, nourish a grudge, seek someone else to have that pleasure with—or evaluate the situation in terms of you and me.

If our overall relationship is a good one and I decide upon evaluation, then I must weigh whether it means more to me to engage in the technique than to acquiesce to the force of your need not to engage in it. If I conclude that it doesn't mean as much to me—then that's it, the matter's dropped, let's come up with something else that we can both enjoy together. I accept your need to refuse because I accept your right to your own likes and dislikes, your right to be different from me.

But if despite the intensity of your feelings mine are equally intense and I just have to engage in that technique, then I'm faced with a new issue—myself. There's a considerable repertoire of sexual activities available to us; why then am I so hung up on this one? What does this one really mean to me, aside from erotic pleasure? Am I involved in a power struggle with you? Does this technique have a special significance to me that I haven't fully acknowledged or recognized? Wherever that line of questioning takes me, if I'm ruthlessly honest with myself, I'll discover something new about myself. And whatever it is I discover is apt to lessen my need for the technique in question.

Paradoxically, a sexual negotiation that is worked out through confrontation can have a positive resolution for both partners even if one is denied a wish. They've discussed a sensitive subject frankly and warmly (albeit with a little heat, too); they've gotten more inside themselves and each other. So the talk is a success in this sense: it has raised the level of intimacy between them.

Four Ways of Loving

Victor Daniels and Laurence Horowitz

Drawing on the ideas of [Erich] Fromm and of Miller and Siegel[1] and our own observations and experiences, we distinguish four kinds of love: object-centered love, projective love, conscious love, and agape (ah-gah-*pay*). Each of these often partakes in some way of the others. Like any concept, the categories lie within lines we've drawn.

1 Object-centered love

Love that is based on the concrete satisfactions that come with loving and being loved is object-centered.

We all know object-centered love from the moment of our birth. This is the love an infant has for his or her mother and her breast. The infant *wants* her, and misses her when she's gone.

Think of a child's love for a teddy bear. The child has a real emotional involvement, wants to be close to the teddy bear as much as possible, and likes the physical joy of its touch and smell.

Most of our object-centered love relationships involve not just

---

From *Being and Caring*, © 1976 by Victor Daniels and Laurence J. Horowitz. San Francisco: San Francisco Book Company, 1976. Reprinted with permission of the publisher. Textbook edition published by Mayfield Publishing Company, 1976.

teddy bears, but other people. If our physical satisfactions remain the only source of our feelings for each other, we're apt to be less than satisfied in our love relationship. But hopefully, as we grow, object-centered love can begin to involve other ways of loving.

The trouble with object-centered love is that I can get so caught up in my craving for emotional or physical satisfaction that I don't care for the other person as another conscious being with his or her own needs and feelings.

The classic "male chauvinist pig" or "macho" attitude is an example of object-centered love. The priority in our relationship is sexual, and I want you to do what I want you to do. If we're making love, I'm likely to forget to stay in touch with where you are, and there's no real relationship, no interchange of consciousness, and little interplay of loving and caressing.

If I want a caring relationship, I don't have to stay in that "me first" place with you. I may want the fullness of our joy and laughter, and also of the quiet, gentle touching that we have for each other. I have to be aware that you have needs and directions of your own, and make space for what you want in our relationship as well as what I want.

2 Projective love

This kind of love plays a large part in what we call "romantic love." In the Middle East, Europe, and the Americas, romantic love is a strong tradition. In certain other parts of the world, it's less common.

I've "fallen in love" so many times! When I "fall in love," I feel the longing and wanting-to-be-with of object-centered love, and I also see you in a highly idealized way. To some degree, I transfer my image of what I want in another person onto you, and then love the image, thinking that I'm loving you. Probably, without realizing it, I see in you some of the things I loved in my parent or other adult who cared for me when I was small.

I may behave toward you in ways I behaved toward others whose qualities I see in you, instead of behaving toward you in ways that fit the unique person you are. To the degree that I do this, you and I miss making contact in ways that could be important to us.

In projective love, I often see qualities in you that are missing in me. You may really possess these qualities, or I may build some way you are into an elaborate fantasy that fits what I want to see.

Todd had a lot of hostility toward his mother that he was never willing to express directly to her. The woman he married was strong and assertive. Todd expected that she would give his mother hell for him and stop her from pushing him around.

When, out of her strong and knowing place, Todd's wife refused to take care of Todd's problems with his mother, the relationship came close to falling apart. Ultimately Todd began to realize that he had to find that kind of power in himself.

> **In a healthy love relationship with you, I keep my sense of myself.**

When I project onto you, wanting you to have characteristics that I need for me, I'm apt to be most disappointed in you when I find out that you don't have some characteristic I thought I saw in you, or that you do have it but don't use it the way I wanted you to. This can be confusing to you and frustrating to me.

When I'm aware of my projected needs, I no longer need to ask you to be a certain way to fill my empty places.

Through our sharing and being with each other, I can learn from you about the qualities that are well developed in you but less developed in myself, and you can learn from me in a similar way. Projective love is a way I keep myself dependent. It lets me avoid dealing with my fears about being inadequate in certain ways. It also stops me from moving ahead in my growth.

Rosie uses love relationships with people as an escape from herself, the way some people use drugs or alcohol. She becomes completely merged in the other person's identity and forgets who she is.

Throughout her childhood, Rosie had been told she was no good as a person, and had finally begun to believe it. Whenever she lost herself in romantic love, she forgot her feelings of worthlessness for a few weeks or months. The man she loved was good in every way she was no good, but she was *still no good, still unworthy.*

In a healthy love relationship with you, I keep my sense of myself. I give you myself as I am, and am with you as you are. In projective love, I may feel I can't make it without you. That feeling is a tipoff that I'm giving away my strength, projecting what I need to do for myself onto you and asking you to fulfill those needs for me. In such a relationship, psychologist John Alan Lee points out, I'm likely to be often yearning and unhappy, anxious about the slightest lack of enthusiasm from my lover, and easily crushed by disappointment. All-consuming thoughts of my beloved, furious jealousy, and tragic endings are the stuff of this kind of loving.

Eventually a relationship based solely on projective love begins to come apart. The burdens on us become too heavy, as I carry your image of me on my shoulders, and you carry my image of you on yours. The images start to crumble as we see each other as we are. This is where many marriages get into trouble. We begin to resent each other for being different from "what was promised," usually more by our projections than by our persons. I want desperately to have you accept me as I am, but you're too disappointed by your unfulfilled illusions, and don't even know them as such.

At this point, any of several things can happen.

One or both of us might be ready to end our relationship. Out of guilt (which may be induced by the other person's manipulations) or for whatever other reason, we feel afraid to say so out front. Instead, we poison each other more and more, making things so bad that eventually there's no way we'd be willing to stay together any longer. A good poison package involves destructive projections that portray the other as no good in many ways.

Alternately, we might recognize what's happening, share our feelings about that as fully as possible, and decide that we've come to a parting place. Under these circumstances, we can separate but still appreciate each other and share a lot of love and caring.

Another alternative is that we may both find that we're willing to do what we have to do to work things out. As we explore and change, we find nourishing ways of relating to each other out of who we really are, and no longer need our distorted images of each other.

As this happens, projective love becomes transformed into "conscious love."

3 Conscious love

When I love consciously, I remember who I am, and I love you as you are. I see and hear myself clearly and I see and hear you clearly. Conscious love is loving you not only for how special you can be, but also for how plain. There comes an ease between us then, as we realize that neither of us has to pretend to be different than we are.

Awareness, caring, and trust are important elements of conscious love. I want to feel your caring in concrete ways that nourish me, and to show my caring in concrete ways that nourish you.

Habit can kill conscious love. Through habit I learn to react to you without being aware of you. At those times when I only go through the motions of loving, love is absent.

The more I can love myself, the more I can love you. The more I take care of my own hang-ups and conflicts, the more energy I have available for loving others.

Walter Rinder, in *Love Is an Attitude*, provides a sensitive description of conscious love:

> If you build an archway for your heart, with neither lock nor door, life will pass freely in harmony with your senses.
> TOUCH . . . your friends, your lover; a stranger, then they are a stranger no more. Hold them, feel the beauty of their skin, their face, their hair. . . .
> LISTEN . . . to their words, their breathing, their heartbeat, their footsteps. . . .
> SEE . . . the expressions on their faces of their different moods. . . . See their hands create their being. . . .
> When you have experienced these things you will know your heart . . . follow it.[2]

In our loving, we need closeness and we need space. If I impose more closeness on you than you want or need, you're apt to feel crowded, resentful, dependent. If you pull me too close too long, I likewise have mixed feelings: How good it is that you want me so much; how stifling it is to be held so tightly.

When I experience your holding me as clutching me, I may be afraid to ask for the space I need, for fear that you'll feel rejected. Yet, when you ask me to be your whole world, you're asking me to be more than I can be.

When I ask you to be my whole world, at some point my dependence on you turns into fear of losing you. That's the point where I stop holding you and start clutching you. Then I may insist on being your whole world, and stifle you.

In his chapter on marriage in *The Prophet*, Gibran writes,

> . . . Let there be spaces in your togetherness,
> And let the winds of the heavens dance between you.
> Love one another, but make not a bond of love. . . .
> Sing and dance together and be joyous, but let each of you be
>   alone,
> Even as the strings of a lute are alone though they quiver with the
>   same music.[3]

Styles of loving　　In our love relationships, misunderstandings often occur when we forget that others' *styles* of loving may be different than our own.

One person may easily *act* in loving ways toward others, but have a hard time putting his or her feelings into words. Another person may have no trouble saying, "I feel very loving toward you right now," but feel ill at ease reaching out to hold or hug.

We can ask each other for the kinds of expression of love we want. We can initiate actions that are hard for the other to initiate, like holding out our arms to someone who has a hard time reaching out to us. Yet, we can also be sensitive to others' ways of showing love, and appreciate the expressions of caring that come easily to them.

J.A. Lee describes some of the different styles of loving that are common in man–woman relationships. Some people plunge immediately and intensely into love relationships, while others share time and space together until love "just comes naturally," preferring a reasonable, predictable relationship that lacks the complications of intense passion.

Some are given to candlelight and roses and laying the world at the feet of the beloved, making every new relationship a Great Romance, while others more often love in the style of "a peaceful and enchanting affection . . . without fever, tumult, or folly."

Some people typically have only one lover at a time, while others tend to be involved in several relationships at once, and avoid becoming too tied to any of them. "When you're not with the one you love, love the one you're with" is their theme song.

Some people typically make love soon after meeting, while others view sex as a deeply intimate self-revelation, and often postpone it until they know each other well in other ways.

And while some people consciously balance the payoffs from various relationships, and pay careful attention to signs of compatibility or incompatibility, others would never conceive of such a calculating approach, and operate much more intuitively.[4]

You can imagine the trouble that two lovers with very different styles might have in trying to work out a relationship that suits them both. We can use our knowledge of different styles of loving to find people whose styles fit with our own, and to get along better when our styles differ. And of course, as we grow and change, our styles of loving too can and often do change.

4 Agape

There's a stage in loving beyond conscious love. It has different names in different parts of the world. In the West, it's called agape, or *loving-kindness*.

Probably you know it. Probably you have had flashes of it that lasted for an instant, an hour, a day, or even longer.

When I am in this "mystical" state of consciousness, I experience my life on this earth as very good and very beautiful. I express a deep caring in my acts and attitudes.

I would like to know that egoless place, *where I am loving rather than lover*, more often. Coming to know who I am, and appreciating the places where I and others are beautiful, helps me find that place. Meditative practices . . . can create states of consciousness from which I'm more apt to move into that very special kind of consciousness.

On the other hand, if that state becomes a "goal to achieve," I'm keeping my ego involved, and I'm less likely to find it.

NOTES

1 Howard L. Miller and Paul Siegel, *Loving: A Psychological Analysis* (New York: Wiley, 1972).

2 Walter Rinder, *Love Is an Attitude* (Millbrae, CA: Celestial Arts, 1970).

3 Kahlil Gibran, *The Prophet* (New York: Knopf, 1966), pp. 15–16.

4 J. A. Lee, "The Styles of Loving," *Psychology Today*, October 1974, pp. 43–51.

The Justification of Sex Without Love

Albert Ellis

A scientific colleague of mine, who holds a professorial post in the department of sociology and anthropology at one of our leading universities, recently asked me about my stand on the question of human beings having sex relations without love. Although I have taken something of a position on this issue in my book, *The American Sexual Tragedy*, I have never quite considered the problem in sufficient detail. So here goes.

In general, I feel that affectional, as against non-affectional, sex relations are *desirable* but not *necessary*. It is usually desirable that an association between coitus and affection exist—particularly in marriage, because it is often difficult for two individuals to keep finely tuned to each other over a period of years, and if there is not a good deal of love between them, one may tend to feel sexually imposed upon by the other.

The fact, however, that the co-existence of sex and love may be desirable does not, to my mind, make it necessary. My reasons for this view are several:

---

1   Many individuals—including, even, many married couples—*do* find great satisfaction in having sex relations without love. I do not consider it fair to label these individuals as criminal just because they may be in the minority.

Moreover, even if they are in the minority (as may well *not* be the case), I am sure that they number literally millions of men and women. If so, they constitute a sizeable subgroup of humans whose rights to sex satisfaction should be fully acknowledged and protected.

2   Even if we consider the supposed majority of individuals who find greater satisfaction in sex-love than in sex-sans-love relations, it is doubtful if all or most of them do so for *all* their lives. During much of their existence, especially their younger years, these people tend to find sex-without-love quite satisfying, and even prefer it to affectional sex.

When they become older, and their sex drives tend to wane, they may well emphasize coitus with rather than without affection. But why should we condemn them *while* they still prefer sex to sex-love affairs?

3   Many individuals, especially females in our culture, who say that they only enjoy sex with it is accompanied by affection are actually being unthinkingly conformist and unconsciously hypocritical. If they were able to contemplate themselves objectively, and had the courage of their inner convictions, they would find sex without love eminently gratifying.

This is not to say that they would *only* enjoy non-affectional coitus, nor that they would always find it *more* satisfying than affectional sex. But, in the depths of their psyche and soma, they would deem sex without love pleasurable *too*.

And why should they not? And why should we, by our puritanical know-nothingness, force these individuals to drive a considerable portion of their sex feelings and potential satisfactions underground?

If, in other words, we view sexuo-amative relations as desirable rather than necessary, we sanction the innermost thoughts and drives of many of our fellowmen and fellowwomen to have sex *and* sex-love relations. If we take the opposing view, we hardly destroy these innermost thoughts and drives, but frequently tend to intensify them while denying them open and honest outlet. This, as Freud pointed out, is one of the main (though by no means the only) source of rampant neurosis.

4 I firmly believe that sex is a biological, as well as a social, drive, and that in its biological phases it is essentially non-affectional. If this is so, then we can expect that, however we try to civilize the sex drives—and civilize them to *some* degree we certainly must—there will always be an underlying tendency for them to escape from our society-inculcated shackles and to be still partly felt in the raw.

When so felt, when our biosocial sex urges lead us to desire and enjoy sex without (as well as with), love, I do not see why we should make their experiences feel needlessly guilty.

5 Many individuals—many millions in our society, I am afraid—have little or no capacity for affection or love. The majority of these individuals, perhaps, are emotionally disturbed, and should preferably be helped to increase their affectional propensities. But a large number are not particularly disturbed, and instead are neurologically or cerebrally deficient.

Mentally deficient persons, for example, as well as many dull normals (who, together, include several million citizens of our nation) are notoriously shallow in their feelings, and probably intrinsically so. Since these kinds of individuals—like the neurotic and the organically deficient—are for the most part, in our day and age, *not* going to be properly treated and *not* going to overcome their deficiencies, and since most of them definitely *do* have sex desires, I again see no point in making them guilty when they have non-loving sex relations.

Surely these unfortunate individuals are sufficiently handicapped by their disturbances or impairments without our adding to their woes by anathematizing them when they manage to achieve some non-amative sexual release.

6 Under some circumstances—though these, I admit, may be rare—some people find more satisfaction in non-loving coitus even though, under other circumstances, these *same* people may find more satisfaction in sex-love affairs. Thus, the man who *normally* enjoys being

with his girlfriend because he loves as well as is sexually attracted to her, may occasionally find immense satisfaction in being with another girl with whom he has distinctly non-loving relations.

Granting that this may be (or is it?) unusual, I do not see why it should be condemnable.

7 If many people get along excellently and most cooperatively with business partners, employees, professors, laboratory associates, acquaintances, and even spouses for whom they have little or no love or affection, but with whom they have certain specific things in common, I do not see why there cannot be individuals who get along excellently and most cooperatively with sex mates with whom they may have little else in common.

> **Although it is usually—if not always—***desirable* **for human beings to have sex relations with those they love rather than with those they do not love, it is by no means** *necessary* **that they do so.**

I personally can easily see the tragic plight of a man who spends much time with a girl with whom he has nothing in common but sex: since I believe that life is too short to be well consumed in relatively one-track or intellectually low-level pursuits. I would also think it rather unrewarding for a girl to spend much time with a male with whom she had mutually satisfying sex, friendship, and cultural interests but no love involvement. This is because I would like to see people in their 70-odd years of life, have maximum rather than minimum satsifactions with individuals of the other sex with whom they spend considerable time.

I can easily see, however, even the most intelligent and highly cultured individuals spending a *little* time with members of the other sex with whom they have common sex and cultural but no real love interests. And I feel that, for the time expended in this manner, their lives may be immeasurably enriched.

Moreover, when I encounter friends or psychotherapy clients who become enamored and spend considerable time and effort thinking about and being with a member of the other sex with whom they are largely sexually obsessed, and for whom they have little or no love, I mainly view these sexual infatuations as one of the penalties of their being human. For humans are the kind of animals who are easily disposed to this type of behavior.

I believe that one of the distinct inconveniences or tragedies of human sexuality is that it endows us, and perhaps particularly the males among us, with a propensity to become exceptionally involved and infatuated with members of the other sex whom, had we no sex urges, we would hardly notice. That is too bad; and it might well be a better world if it were otherwise. But it is *not* otherwise, and I think it is silly and pernicious for us to condemn ourselves because we are the way that we are in this respect.

We had better *accept* our biosocial tendencies, or our fallible humanity—instead of constantly blaming ourselves and futilely trying to change certain of its relatively harmless, though still somewhat tragic, aspects.

For reasons such as these, I feel that although it is usually—if not always—*desirable* for human beings to have sex relations with those they love rather than with those they do not love, it is by no means *necessary* that they do so. When we teach that it *is* necessary, we only needlessly condemn millions of our citizens to self-blame and atonement.

The position which I take—that there are several good reasons why affectional, as against non-affectional, sex relations are desirable but not necessary—can be assailed on several counts. I shall now consider some of the objections to this position to see if they cannot be effectively answered.

It may be said that an individual who has non-loving instead of loving sex relations is not necessarily wicked but that he is self-defeating because, while going for immediate gratification, he will miss out on even greater enjoyments. But this would only be true if such an individual (whom we shall assume, for the sake of discussion, *would* get greater enjoyment from affectional sex relations than from non-affectional ones) were *usually or always* having non-affectionate coitus. If he were *occasionally* or *sometimes* having love with sex, and the rest of the time having sex without love, he would be missing out on very little, if any, enjoyment.

Under these circumstances, in fact, he would normally get *more* pleasure from *sometimes* having sex without love. For the fact remains, and must not be unrealistically ignored, that in our present-day society sex without love is *much more frequently* available than sex with love.

Consequently, to ignore non-affectional coitus when affectional coitus is not available would, from the standpoint of enlightened self-interest, be sheer folly. In relation to both immediate *and* greater enjoyment, the individual would thereby be losing out.

The claim can be made of course that if an individual sacrifices sex without love *now* he will experience more pleasure by having sex with love in the future. This is an interesting claim; but I find no empirical evidence to sustain it. In fact, on theoretical grounds it seems most unlikely that it will be sustained. It is akin to the claim that if an individual starves himself for several days in a row he will greatly enjoy eating a meal at the end of a week or a month. I am sure he will—provided that he is then not too sick or debilitated to enjoy anything! But, even assuming that such an individual derives enormous satisfaction from his one meal a week or a month, is his *total* satisfaction greater than it would have been had he enjoyed three good meals a day for that same period of time? I doubt it.

So with sex. Anyone who starves himself sexually for a long period of time—as virtually everyone who rigidly sticks to the sex with love doctrine must—will (perhaps) *utimately* achieve greater satisfaction when he does find sex with love than he would have had, had he been sexually freer. But, even assuming that this is so, will his *total* satisfaction be greater?

It may be held that if both sex with and without love are permitted in any society, the non-affectional sex will drive out affectional sex, somewhat in accordance with Gresham's laws of currency. On the contrary, however, there is much reason to believe that just because an individual has sex relations, for quite a period, on a non-affectional basis, he will be more than eager to replace it, eventually, with sex with love.

From my clinical experience, I have often found that males who most want to settle down to having a single mistress or wife are those who have tried numerous lighter affairs and found them wanting. The view that sex without love eradicates the need for affectional sex relationships is somewhat akin to the ignorance is bliss theory. For it virtually says that if people never experienced sex with love they would never realize how good it was and therefore would never strive for it.

Or else the proponents of this theory seem to be saying that sex without love is so greatly satisfying, and sex with love so intrinsically difficult and disadvantageous to attain, that given the choice between the two, most people would pick the former. If this is so, then by all means let them pick the former: with which, in terms of their greater and total happiness, they would presumably be better off.

I doubt, however, that this hypothesis *is* factually sustainable. From clinical experience, again, I can say that individuals who are capable of sex with love usually seek and find it; while those who remain non-affectional in their sex affairs generally are not particularly capable of sex with love and need psychotherapeutic help before they can become thus capable.

False Assumption 3: That Love Is Necessary for a Satisfactory Marriage

William J. Lederer and Don D. Jackson

Even though people are reluctant to admit it, most husbands and wives are disappointed in their marriages. There is overwhelming evidence to confirm this.

At least one person out of every three who gets married will be divorced within about ten years. Many of these will indulge in legal polygamy—that is, they will marry and divorce several times. All told, the divorce rate in the United States is 41 per cent.

Marriage is so turbulent an institution that articles on how to patch up disintegrating marriages can be found in almost every issue of our family magazines and daily newspapers, with titles such as "How to Keep Your Husband Happy," "How to Make Your Wife Feel Loved." Surveys show that this sort of article frequently attracts more readers than anything else in the publication. It appears because of public demand, a demand which must originate from millions of unhappy, confused, and dissatisfied couples. Evidently the dreamed-of marriage often does not materialize. There are unexpected shortcomings,

---

bickerings, misunderstandings. Most spouses to varying degrees are frustrated, confused, belligerent, and disappointed.

Almost every expression of our culture, including advertisements, has something to say about how to improve female-male relationships. Motion pictures, plays, television, radio, feature the friction between wife and husband more than any other subject.

The offices of marriage counselors, psychologists, and psychiatrists are crowded with clients who are concerned over problems which mainly involve marriage, and who pay from twenty-five dollars to fifty dollars an hour for assistance. But these troubled people usually cannot identify their problems; even worse, they usually do not sincerely seek solutions. What each one wants is confirmation that he is correct and good, and that his spouse is the one at fault!

One reason for this marital disenchantment is the prevalence of the mistaken belief that "love" is necessary for a satsifying and workable marriage. Usually when the word "love" is used, reference is actually being made to romance—that hypnotic, ecstatic condition enjoyed during courtship. Romance and love are different. Romance is based usually on minimum knowledge of the other person (restricted frequently to the fact that being around him is a wonderful, beatific, stimulating experience). Romance is built on a foundation of quicksilver nonlogic. It consists of attributing to the other person— blindly, hopefully, but without much basis in fact—the qualities one *wishes* him to have, though they may not even be desirable, in actuality. Most people who select mates on the basis of imputed qualities later find themselves disappointed, if the qualities are not present in fact, or discover that they are unable to tolerate the implication of the longed-for qualities in actual life. For example, the man who is attracted by his fiancée's cuteness and sexiness may spend tormented hours after they are married worrying about the effect of these very characteristics on other men. It is a dream relationship, an unrealistic relationship with a dream person imagined in terms of one's own needs.

Romance is essentially selfish, though it is expressed in terms of glittering sentiment and generous promises, which usually cannot be fulfilled. ("I'll be the happiest man in the world for the rest of my life." "I'll make you the best wife any man ever had.")

Romance—*which most spouses mistake for love*—is not necessary for a good marriage. The sparkle some couples manage to preserve in a satisfying marriage—based on genuine pleasure in one another's company, affection and sexual attraction for the spouse as he really is—can be called love.

If romance is different than love, then what *is* love? We do best to return to the definition of Harry Stack Sullivan: "When the satisfaction or the security of another person becomes as significant to

> **People usually marry on a wave of romance having nothing to do with love.**

one as is one's own satisfaction or security, then the state of love exists." In this sense, love consists of a devotion and respect for the spouse that is equal to one's own self-love.

We have already shown that people usually marry on a wave of romance having nothing to do with love. When the average American (not long from the altar) lives with the spouse in the intimacy of morning bad breath from too much smoking, of annoying habits previously not known, when he is hampered by the limitations of a small income (compared with the lavishness of the honeymoon), or encounters the unexpected irritability of premenstrual tension or of business frustration and fatigue, a change in attitude begins to occur. The previously romantic person begins to have doubts about the wonderful attributes with which his spouse has been so blindly credited.

These doubts are particularly disturbing at the start. Not very long ago, after all, the spouse believed that "love" (romance) was heavenly, all-consuming, immutable, and that beautiful relationships and behavior were *voluntary* and *spontaneous*. Now, if doubts and criticism are permitted to intrude upon this perfect dream, the foundations begin to shake in a giddy manner. To the husband or wife the doubts seem to be evidence that one of them is inadequate or not to be trusted. The doubts imply that the relationship is suffering from an unsuspected malignancy.

To live with another in a state of love (as defined by Sullivan) is a different experience from whirling around in a tornado of romance. A loving union is perhaps best seen in elderly couples who have been married for a long time. Their children have grown, the pressure of business had been relieved, and the specter of death is not far away. By now, they have achieved a set of realistic values. These elderly spouses respect each other's idiosyncracies. They need and treasure companionship. Differences between them have been either accepted or worked out; they are no longer destructive elements. In such instances each has as much interest in the well-being and security of the other as he has in himself. Here is true symbiosis: a union where each admittedly feeds off the other. Those who give together really live together!

But it is possible to have a productive and workable marriage without love (although love is desirable) as well as without romance. One can have a functioning marriage which includes doubts and criticisms of the spouse and occasional inclinations toward divorce. The husband or wife may even think about how much fun it might be to flirt with an attractive neighbor. Such thoughts can occur without being disastrous to the marriage. *In many workable marriages both spouses get a good deal of mileage out of fantasy.*

How, then, can we describe this functional union which can bring reasonable satisfaction and well-being to both partners? It has four major elements: tolerance, respect, honesty, and the desire to stay together for mutual advantage. One can prefer the spouse's company to all others', and even be lonely in his absence, without experiencing either the wild passion inherent in romance, or the totally unselfish, unswerving devotion that is basic in true love.

In a workable marriage both parties may be better off together than they would have been on their own. They may not be ecstatically happy because of their union, and they may not be "in love," but they are not lonely and they have areas of shared contentment. They feel reasonably satisfied with their levels of personal and interpersonal functioning. They can count their blessings and, like a sage, philosophically realize that nothing is perfect.

We must return once again to the meaning of the word "love," for no other word in English carries more misleading connotations. The following is an actual example of how distorted the thinking of an individual may become when he believes he is in love.

A young woman and her fiancé visiting a marriage counselor had completed an interpersonal test which told much about their behavior and how they viewed each other. The counselor, after studying the data, asked why the woman wished to marry this man, who was an admitted alcoholic. She said she had sought the counselor's help because she did have some doubts. Her previous husband, from whom she had recently been divorced, was weak and passive. Now she was looking for a man strong enough to take care of her.

The marriage counselor explained that he could not understand why she has picked an alcoholic—obviously a weak man who could not possibly look after her. She would have to look after *him*.

Her fiancé sat passively by and did not enter the conversation.

The counselor asked again, "Why do you want to marry this man who appears to be just the opposite of the spouse you say you need?"

The young woman shrugged her shoulders, smiled happily, and said, with dogmatic conviction, "Because I love him."

Her fiancé smiled and nodded in support of her unsupportable statement.

It is obvious that this woman did not know what she meant by "I love him." She did not even know how she felt about him. Because of her complex neurotic needs she had a desire for this man—and it could probably be shown that this was a unilateral and totally selfish desire. Her choice of someone to "love" had nothing to do with her prospects for having a workable or satisfying marriage. The word "love" was a cover-up for an emotional mix-up which she did not understand.

Often "I love you" is an unconscious excuse for some form of emotional destructiveness. Sometimes it is a camouflage for a status struggle, which may continue even after a couple has separated. A spouse who has been deserted (especially for another) may covertly or unconsciously wish to be identified and applauded as the good and loyal partner. The jilted spouse assumes a saintly, pious behavior—especially in public—and makes certain everyone knows he still "loves" the other and will lovingly and patiently wait forever until the other comes to his senses. This can be accomplished with operatic flamboyance while the individual simultaneously has a well-hidden affair with someone else's husband or wife; and the apparent inconsistency later can be rationalized away: "After John's [or Mary's] departure there was such a hole in my life I *had* to do something to stay on an even keel. If I had had a breakdown it would have hurt the children. But my behavior didn't alter the fact that I loved him."

This type of "love" is especially likely to manifest itself when one spouse believes he received ill-treatment from the other for some years prior to the final desertion. The "injured" spouse (for so he regards himself no matter what he did to hurt and destroy the other) will loudly maintain with grief: "But I still love him." It takes little clinical experience or psychological brilliance to recognize that usually this person really is exhibiting hurt pride and rage at being the one who was left, rather than the one who did the leaving.

"Love" may also be used as an excuse for domination and control. The expression "I love you" has such an immutable place in our traditions that it can serve as an excuse for anything, even for selfishness and evil. Who can protest against something done "because I love you," especially if the assertion is made with histrionic skill and in a tone of sincerity? The victim—the one on the receiving end—may intuitively realize that he is being misused. Yet he often finds it impossible to remonstrate.

Sullivan's definition of love is important. It describes not a unilateral process, but a two-way street, a bilateral process in which two individuals function in relation to each other as equals. Their shared behavior interlocks to form a compages[1] that represent *mutual* respect and devotion. One spouse alone cannot achieve this relationship. Both must participate to the same degree. The necessity for both spouses to "give" equally is one of the reasons that a marriage built upon mutual love is so rare.

People naturally wish to have a happy marriage to a loving spouse. But such a union is hard to come by without knowledge of the anatomy of marriage, plus much patience, work—and luck. Many people fail to face the fact that if their parents' marriage was unhappy or their childhood was neurotic, they do not possess the prerequisite experience for choosing the correct mate. Where have they observed a good model for marriage? How can they possibly know what a loving marriage is like—and what elements must be *put into* it?

Most Americans enter marriage expecting to have love without having asked themselves the question, Am I lovable? Following close behind is another question: If I am not lovable, is it not likely that I have married an unloving person?

There is another misuse of the word "love." Some people believe that they can love generously even if doing so requires behaving like a martyr. They believe their rewards will come not on earth but in heaven, or at least in some mystical, unusual way. Therefore they seem able to love unilaterally and want nothing for themselves. They suffer happily and enjoy making sacrifices while pouring their love out on another. The more undeserving the other is, the more of this love there is to be poured.

This situation is deceptive. Martyrdom is actually one of the most blatant types of self-centeredness. No one can be more difficult to deal with than the one-way benevolent person who frantically, zealously, and flamboyantly tries to help someone else, and apparently seeks nothing for himself.

Nathan Epstein, William Westley, Murray Bowen, John Workentin, Don Jackson, and others who have conducted research on couples who are content with their marriages and have reared apparently healthy, successful children, agree that *companionability* and *respect* are the key words in the lexicon these couples use to describe their marriages. A husband interviewed in one study stated: "In love? Well, I guess so—haven't really thought about it. I suppose I would, though, if Martha and I were having troubles. The Chinese have a saying, 'One hand washes the other.' That sort of describes us, but I don't know if that's what you mean by love."

The happy, workable, productive marriage does not require love as defined [here], or even the practice of the Golden Rule. To maintain continuously a union based on love is not feasible for most people. Nor is it possible to live in a permanent state of romance. Normal people should not be frustrated or disappointed if they are not in a *constant* state of love. If they experience the joy of love (or imagine they do) for ten per cent of the time they are married, attempt to treat each other with as much courtesy as they do distinguished strangers, and attempt to make the marriage a workable affair—one where there are some practical advantages and satisfactions for each—the chances are that the marriage will endure longer and with more strength that the so-called love matches.

NOTE

1 "A whole formed by the compaction or juncture of parts, a framework or system of conjoined parts, a complex structure."—*O.E.D.*

Intimacy: A Definition

Thomas C. Oden

In searching for a working definition of intimacy, the first tasks are:

(1) to track some of the intriguing images of the language of intimacy; (2) to present a collage of impressionistic descriptions of how persons have felt in moments of intense personal closeness; and (3) to thread our way through some of the potential contradictions and internal tensions present in the concept of intimacy.

THE *INTIMUS* SPHERE

I will be arguing that there is a relationship in which persons are in fact closer to each other than in genital sexuality. It can occur with or without sexuality. It is a relationship in which two persons, even at great physical distance, may be deeply responsive to the inner reality of each other. It is called intimacy.

    Much sexuality, to be sure, has the quality of intimacy. But genital orgasm can and often does occur without intimacy, and even as an offense against it.

While intimacy can emerge within the framework of sexuality, intimacy is never adequately defined by sexuality. To view intimacy only as an aspect of sexuality is a peculiar misjudgment of popular modern consciousness.

Not everyone, of course, is desperately looking for intimacy. Although for some this search takes an urgent and overt form, for most it takes a quiet form of waiting and yearning to receive. Yet it re-

> **The Latin word for inner or innermost is** *intimus*. **If one knows, grasps, the internal reality of someone he grasps the** *intimus*, **the inmost character of the person.**

mains a basic question for most persons in our society: How can I come close to others without risking something essential to myself?

What do we want when we want intimacy? Intimacy, according to its dictionary definition, is the quality or condition of being close to another, a warmly personal being-together characterized by self-disclosure and affection. It is the experience of close, sustained familiarity with another's inner life.[1]

Intimacy has long been a euphemism for sexual closeness, but it can also refer to the closeness of friends, family, neighbors, close associates. It deepens when sustained over a duration of time. Insofar as one experiences an intimate relation he experiences a beholding of another person in his or her essential depth; he knows the other person from the inside out, deeply, internally.

The Latin word for inner or innermost is *intimus*. If one knows, grasps, the internal reality of someone he grasps the *intimus*, the inmost character of the person.[2] Similarly, in many other languages the root word for intimacy refers to this "most internal" quality. The German word for intimacy, *Innigkeit*, especially conveys this quality

447

of inwardness or internal awareness. If something is *innig* it is inward, heartfelt, sincere, responsive, deep—in short, intimate. To the degree that one experiences the *intimum* of another, or feels another's *Innigkeit,* he is aware of the internal sphere, the most inward reality of the other.

Influenced by this nuance of innermost, our English word *intimate* points to a particular kind of knowing, a knowledge of the core of something, an understanding of the inmost parts, that which is indicative of one's deepest nature and marked by close physical, mental, or social association. The biblical word for sexual closeness is this sort of knowing: "Adam knew Eve." When I am in touch with the *intimum* of another, I know that which is ordinarily hidden from public view yet revealed in the closeness and vulnerability of the relationship. When I am aware that someone else is in touch with my own *intimum* I know I have been reached at the deeper levels of my consciousness. One does not often reveal or open up one's *intimum* to another. It does not occur easily or readily, even though a certain outward appearance of intimacy may be easy for some to project.[3]

The English word *intimacy* has also taken on the nuance of being a complete intermixture, a compounding or interweaving of things.[4] The closeness is such that "it would call for some effort to disentangle a relationship of things marked by such intimacy."[5]

Although we may speak of intimacy in connection with objects, it more properly refers to persons. One is not intimate *with* things, but may have an intimate knowledge *of* things. In this case the focus is on the closeness and depth of empathic understanding and experiencing of something. One may have an intimate knowledge of an automobile, a garden, a space guidance system, or an eighteenth-century town, and in each case we are speaking of close, detailed inward knowledge of that thing. We are pointing to a sustained experiential knowledge of something in which one has participated and knows "from the inside."

Since the essence of an intimate personal relation is shared experience of each other's interior life, any description that might tend to perceive intimacy as an event in *individual* consciousness would be defective. Whatever it is we mean when we speak of personal intimacy, at least it is something that occurs only in the emotive flow and resonance *between* two persons. The locus is precisely the *relation*, [6] not individual consciousness, although one may experience its flow in individual consciousness.

Thus it is not possible to be intimate with one who does not want to be intimate. Intimacy exists only by mutual consent, never by unilateral desire. If one person wants closeness with another who does not want closeness, then the relation is not intimate. It may be described as a unilateral affection, but not intimacy, where the emotive flow moves both ways.

Furthermore, it is a misundersttanding of intimacy to conceive of it purely as an active relationship of knowing. For there is also the receptive side of one's experiencing oneself as being known by another. It is in the twofold flow of caring and being cared about, of loving and being loved, of knowing and being known, that intimacy occurs. [7]

The study of marital intimacy by Howard and Charlotte Clinebell[8] usefully distinguished twelve different types or strata of intimacy that apply to many close relationships. These twelve types can serve as a beginning point for our exploration of the wide range of intimate relationships. Intimacy is not just one thing, but many, and these twelve strata, however briefly described, show its multiform character:

Sexual intimacy (erotic or orgasmic closeness)
Emotional intimacy (being tuned to each other's wavelength)
Intellectual intimacy (closeness in the world of ideas)
Aesthetic intimacy (sharing experiences of beauty)
Creative intimacy (sharing in acts of creating together)
Recreational intimacy (relating in experiences of fun and play)
Work intimacy (the closeness of sharing common tasks)
Crisis intimacy (closeness in coping with problems and pain)
Conflict intimacy (facing and struggling with differences)
Commitment intimacy (mutuality derived from common self-
    investment)
Spiritual intimacy (the we-ness in sharing ultimate concerns)
Communication intimacy (the source of all types of true intimacy)

These twelve strata of intimacy have been used by the Clinebells as the basis of an action-meditation for marital intimates. I present them early in our discussion without comment as a potential meditation on the varieties of intimacy and as a transition into our next section, which will explore some of these varieties.

THE INTIMATE EXPERIENCE: A COLLAGE OF DESCRIPTIONS

The nature and dynamics of intimacy have received only scant attention by researchers. Not much data has been accumulated by the behavioral sciences on the phenomenon of intimacy. Although many writers (Bach, Berne, Schutz, Lowen, Goodman, Mazur)[9] make frequent use of the concept, few have attempted to define clearly what they mean by it. To my knowledge there is no definitive study of intimacy available in any language.

In order to begin to build a body of descriptive data on the nature and dynamics of intimacy, I have asked groups of persons with whom I have been working to recall in fantasy a moment of intense closeness or warm personal fulfillment with another person, to behold in imagination a specific time of genuine, fulfilling intimacy, to remember the colors, shapes, sounds, and feelings of that relationship, to stay with the fantasy long enough to savor it, so as to be there with the other in memory and imagination. Then I have asked them to write down in clear, descriptive language what it is they have experienced.[10]

I have collected and studied a considerable number of these remembered experiences of intimacy, resulting in a remarkable correlation of factors that recur when people describe intimate experiencing. From these experiential accounts it has become clear that there are many different forms, settings, and qualities of intimacy, yet some characteristic features pervade the descriptions repeatedly. What follows is an attempt to summarize some of these correlations.

Although such varied experiencing is difficult to reduce to categories,[11] the descriptions seem to fall generally into two distinguishable, though inseparable, levels of awareness: the interpersonal and the transpersonal. By interpersonal I mean that which is happening between the persons. By transpersonal I refer to that which transcends the persons, the awareness of awe, mystery, and gift, the sense that the relationship reflects the inner meaning of history that transcends the particular persons.[12]

Rather than belaboring a statistical correlation of the variables of these data, I would prefer to deal with them in a more impressionistic fashion. Using Abraham Maslow's method[13] in reporting peak experiences, I will present the correlated accounts in the form of a collage or impressionistic portraiture of recurrent ways in which persons experience close relationships.

Interpersonal Awareness

How do intimates describe moments of fulfillment? Here is a sampling.

Spontaneity, feeling-flow, openness   Many intimates remember feeling exceptionally in touch with their own here-and-now experiencing in moments of personal intimacy. They are relaxed, spontaneous, and willing to trust their own feelings. They are not internally blocked.

Many speak of an extradorinarily high degree of self-awareness and lucidity in the experience of intimacy. They speak of self-acceptance, inner harmony, feeling "the freedom to be me," feeling confident in the unfolding of their experiencing process, trusting that unfolding; feeling integrated, understanding oneself, discovering insights about oneself. All of these hinge on the experience of heightened self-awareness in the context of an intimate relationship.

Some felt able to unload their feelings toward each other, even if negative. They felt able to get things off their chest. They experienced a relationship of uncommon trust, where the other person was perceived as radically trustworhty.

Some reported a previously undiscovered capacity for honesty and deep leveling with the other, even if it meant facing anger or rejection. They found themselves able to risk conflict and work through it together. They were nondefensive and unashamed. Some described the experience as one of emotive nakedness with no defenses between them.[14]

Closeness, presence, availability   Common to most descriptions is an intense closeness with the other. Some described this as a kind of at-oneness or communion with the other person, even in some cases to the extent of feeling that they are as a single organism, so that the two become "one flesh."[15]

The intimate experience is described by some as one of sheer joy in the mere presence of the other; as being for the other, being in touch with the other's feelings, being aware of the profound goodness of the other; being willing to let the other be himself and experiencing the permission of the other to be oneself.

Some speak of the decisive importance to them of simple presence to another. For them the simple beholding of the partner is the most memorable aspect of the intimate moment. The mere being with another, the feeling that one is fully with the other, is the fundament of the experience of intimacy.[16]

Some speak of the radical availability of the partner. The partner is fully there with no blockages—open, warm, attentive, accepting. The attention and care flows both ways.

More frequently the intimate relationship is described quite simply as one of being loved and loving. It is the awareness that one is cared for, appreciated, desired, and that the care, appreciation, and desire are mutual, even in spite of imperfection and inadequacies.

Sharing, renewing, beholding   Others remember their intimate experiencing as one of sacrificing together amid arduous tasks. They knew the sense of belonging that comes from shared experiencing. Some described a moment of recommitment to an important task as a moment of intense intimacy, wherein both persons were mutually grasped by the excitement or gravity of a commitment to a long-range fate-laden decision. They felt very close to their partner at the moment when the commitment was decided or redecided.

Some experienced a special intimacy in being with an intimate in the context of having lost another intimate through alienation or death. The depth of one relationship illuminated and bestowed meaning on the other. Repeatedly persons reported exceptional lucidity in the presence of the death of an intimate, where the meaning of a person's life, previously undisclosed, seemed to become clear. Intimates often felt needed, wanted, or accepted, particularly in situations where urgent or desperate need was evident.

Some describe the intimate experience in aesthetic terms, as a mutual beholding of unspeakable beauty. Others experience intimacy as a time of shared creativity, of the release of constructive energies, or as the mutual shaping of something together.

Ecstasy, freedom, levity   Intensely intimate experiencing is sometimes described as an ecstasy, an overflow of feelings, beyond words. One cannot contain the joy; it is too much to express; one feels inexpressibly happy, soaring, elated, high, tingles, chills, exhilarated, expansive. "I wanted to dance, shout and yell forever," one wrote.

Many viewed intimate experiencing under an orgasmic analogy:

> **A surprising number of descriptions speak of intimate experiencing in the language of awe. . . . They find themselves surprised to discover that "I am really here with you and really alive."**

the ecstatic explosion of feelings of love in full bodily and spiritual presence and unity with the other.

Others did not experience a highly ecstatic intimacy, but instead reported a varied range of close experiencing over a longer period of time, where closeness at various strata illuminated or radiated into closeness at other strata.

Intimacy is often described in relation to *freedom*, both as a moment in which one feels freedom *for* the other and freedom *from* anxiety, guilt, or boredom in the presence of another.

Similarly some describe intimate experiencing as a sense of release, as if a weight were lifted, the weight of loneliness; or as a victory, as if one had come currently to experience precisely that for which one

453

had hoped, sometimes accompanied by a sense of lightness, giddiness, or levity.

Transpersonal Awareness

Awe, cohesion, letting-be A surprising number of descriptions speak of intimate experiencing in the language of awe, such as the awe one experiences at the presence of birth or death, or in the presence of the struggle of another person through crisis.

In the intimate experience some became aware of the intrinsic value of life, the intense prizing of simple being, the sense that life is profoundly meaningful beyond its seeming incongruities. Some experienced life as a unity, as if that moment all things seemed "put together." They celebrated their aliveness. They found themselves surprised to discover that "I am really here with you and really alive."

Giftlike quality, surprise Many experience intimacy as a profound gift. There is an unearned, undeserved dimension, an aura of sheer grace in the relationship. Persons experience the presence of another in a very close relationship as something they cannot control or manipulate but a presence that comes to them, a relation that is bestowed. They may have to struggle for it, and work to achieve the conditions in which intimacy might occur, but is not controlled or determined by these conditions. One must wait for it to occur, and when it does it is experienced as a profound gift.

Consequently many felt a profound sense of gratitude. They felt deeply privileged to be there. Others felt deeply humbled in the presence of that gift, and sensed the fragility and finitude of human relationships this side of death.[17]

One woman wrote, "Suddenly we looked at each other and asked how long it had been that we were together. Surprisingly fifteen years. We laughed and said, 'Well, I guess the trial period is over!' It was a wonderful warm feeling. Her friends had become mine—mine had become hers. Many things we had enjoyed together—concerts, theater, friends, and families; but we were not dependent on doing things always together. We experienced an enlargement of interest and a deepening of the joys of life in each other's presence—also a sharing of difficulties and sorrows. Sounds like a Pollyanna story, doesn't it? But the enjoyment and mutual appreciativeness was really just that. Mutual trust, I believe, was at the core of the relationship, broken by her death, but still alive."

Mystery, timelessness, wholeness   Many descriptions pointed to the mystery in interpersonal communion, the sense of wonder in the presence of an immensely valued human being who is capable of love, amazed that "it could happen to me." A significant number spoke of intimacy as a moment of eternal awareness, or one in which the eternal now is present, where time loses its movement and one is wholly there with the inner meaning of the cosmos in and through the here-and-now relationship.[18]

Finally, many experienced a sense of purposefulness in history that became intuitively clear through the relation with the partner. Whereas prior to the intimate moment things may have felt dislocated, fragmented, disordered, and broken up, in the moment of intimacy things seemed to cohere in a meaningful gestalt beyond all the tragedies of human existence.[19] This is expressed by some as a sense of wholeness or completion. It is a perspective on history that is focused and integrated through a relationship with another person, in which one feels a cosmic embrace through the embrace of the other.

This variety of intimate experiences may help us grasp something of the scope of intimacy. The purpose is not to pinpoint a definition of intimacy, but to paint an impressionistic portrait or put together a mosaic of moments of personal closeness. From here we proceed to explore some of the seeming paradoxes of the intimate relationship, in search of its basic definition.

THE INTIMATE RELATIONSHIP: SIX IRONIES

The six potential contradictions of the intimate relationship may be stated in terms of six questions.

1   What is the relation of intimacy to time? Is it sustained through time, or is it a moment of ecstatic closeness that transcends time?

2   Is the covenant relationship fixed and without terminus, or is it continually renegotiated?
3   If the relationship is to a high degree empathic and self-giving, does not one risk the loss of self-identity and individuation?
4   If the relation is essentially warm and affirming, how does it deal with legitimate conflicts of interest? Must intimacy necessarily be forced into conflict-avoidance?
5   Can we assume truthfulness as an absolute norm of the intimate relationship without coercively requiring compulsive self-disclosure?
6   Is intimacy subject to or does it transcend death?

Each of the six answers will begin with a thesis statement (italicized) that will focus on essential points in tension and internal stresses that are at work in relationships of intimacy.

In two columns we can visualize the twelve basic dialectical points that grapple with the six questions and thus feed into a full definition of intimacy as follows:

Duration	Ecstasy
Accountability	Negotiability
Empathy	Congruence
Emotive Warmth	Conflict-capability
Self-disclosure	Letting-be
Finitude	Transcendence

No one of these twelve elements of the definition should be considered as artificially separable parts of the total gestalt of intimacy, but rather as dimensions of intimacy that exist in creative tension. Even though they do not all invariably occur with the same force in every intimate moment, they will in time emerge over the course of a sustained intimate relationship.

Duration and Ecstasy

An intimate relationship is ordinarily sustained over a period of time with a shared interpersonal memory, yet it may intensify in ecstatic moments of experiencing that render the other times relatively less vivid. The ecstatic moments, nonetheless, depend on the sustained history of personal covenant for their meaning. Thus there is a dialectical relation between duration and ecstasy.

The crucial distinction here is that between the sustained intimate relationship and the ecstatic intimate moment. Some confuse the two, assuming that when one experiences a brief moment of intense closeness with another, there exists consequently an intimate relationship. Our common language, however, understands the intimate relationship as one that endures, persists, and survives over a period of time. It must have a history. To the degree that it is not sustained in time, it has less chance of developing the profound sort of internal knowledge that we assume in our ordinary language about intimacy.

There is no instant intimacy,[20] even though the encounter culture appears to be trying to facilitate it on a brief basis. It succeeds to some extent, but the short-term relationships often yearn for sustenance in time, and thus for the conditions of true intimacy.

A sustained intimate relationship may suffer long periods of drought without an ecstatic moment. Yet when that moment occurs, it seems to feed the roots of the relationship and bring it new life, like a shower on tenacious plants in arid soil.

An essential dimension of deepening intimacy is shared memory. Persons who have been through conflict together and have understood each other's struggle often grow to be more profoundly intimate, since they are able to be more deeply aware of the *intimum* of the partner. The dispossessed, who have shared a common experience of suffering and subjugation, may have a greater capacity for certain kinds of intimacy with each other than with those who have not shared such experiences. Persons of wide differences, however, can through exceptional empathy develop intimate relationships.

There is a sense among intimates that they share something that is unique to them and them alone. This is why excessively generalized descriptions of intimacy remain unconvincing. Only those who have shared those particular ecstasies or struggles have the innermost knowledge of each other that intimacy apparently requires. . . .

The term ecstasy may be too intense to describe the levels of feeling that many experience in intimate relationships. Friendships do not demand overflowing feelings of ecstasy in order to be deep and

intimate. They may have moments of intensification, of beholding,
of deep belly laughter, of moving affection, but that does not imply that
the value of the relation is judged exclusively by its occasional ecstasy.

Accountability and Negotiability

Is the covenant relationship fixed and without terminus, or is it continually renegotiated?

The ironic hypothesis that follows is that *intimate relationships are
characterized by contractual clarity and enduring commitment on the assumption that mutual accountability is without a fixed terminus, and yet within
that frame of reference they are forever being refashioned and renegotiated
in their specific forms.*

> In an intimate relationship, partners
> are singularly able to share each
> other's consciousness without
> loss of self-identity.

Most contracts have a specific terminus. In a contract to deliver
goods, for example, the moment the goods are delivered the contract is fulfilled. Intimate covenants are never "concluded" in that sense.
The intimate relationship would be offended by the thought that it
should have a designated end. Even though intimates are often
separated by time and distance, still they resume the postures of
closeness when they return, as if time and space could not overcome
their covenant memory and hope.

The intimate relation is sustained in time as an act of covenant fidelity. It is a relation to which one commits oneself, as the service of matrimony says, "for better or for worse . . . in sickness and in
health . . . till death us do part."[21] Thus when intimates confront
obstacles such as dislocation, suffering, and frustration, these are not
necessarily regarded as a threat to intimacy, but rather a healthy intimacy is seen as supportive of the attempt to deal constructively with
these limitations.

While specific expectations are constantly being readjusted, intimates find themselves committed to each other in such a way that the presumption is on the side of the hope of continuance, so that whatever problems or obstacles arise, the assumption is that they will be worked out with mutual trust and accountability. This is one reason why the disruption or termination of relationships that were assumed to be intimate is shocking and painful both to intimates and to third-party observers.

Yet, however bound together covenant partners may feel themselves to be, their continuing relationship requires that specific understandings be continuously open to restatement and sharpening. When the objective situation changes, or when consciousness changes, the expectations of partners change. Thus contract clarification is perennial expression of covenant bonding. Such renegotiations take place, however, within the larger frame of reference of enduring covenant fidelity.

To the degree that both persons find themselves accountable to clear and just covenants, the possibility of intimacy is intensified. The relation functions best when each intimate knows fairly accurately what the other wants and expects from the relationship, and when both are willing to call each other accountable to whatever covenants they have made.[22]

Empathy and Congruence

If the relationship is to a high degree empathic, self-giving, and symbiotic, does not one risk the loss of self-identity and individuation?

In an intimate relationship, partners are singularly able to share each other's consciousness without loss of self-identity, since it is precisely amid the increased flow of empathy that one's individual self-awareness and identity is facilitated and intensified. In sum, intimacy enhances individual identity in the midst of deeping interpersonal encounter.

The same point can be stated differently: Through empathy, intimacy grows into a symbiosis (literally a "living together") of interdependent functions, and yet it is most intimate precisely at the point at which it enables partners to become more individuated, more fully their own unique selves.[23]

Still another attempt to state the same dialectic: Precisely to the degree that one is in touch with his feelings, to that degree he is able to facilitate his partner's empathy toward him. This point can be illuminated by exploring the relation between two crucial components of intimacy: empathy and congruence.[24] I am sufficiently convinced of the importance of empathy and congruence in the formation of intimacy that I will argue strongly that without certain levels of each the intimate relationship has little chance of surviving.

Since this may be *the* most crucial of the six dialectical issues, I will clarify it step by step, delineating first the way in which empathy enables intimacy, and second, the way in which congruence facilitates empathy.

Empathy is the process of placing oneself in the frame of reference of another, feeling the world as he feels it, sharing his world with him.[25] Insofar as intimates are able to feel their way accurately into the affect levels of their partner, intimacy is enhanced. The most descriptive colloquial phrase that expresses this notion is to "stand in his shoes," which means to project oneself imaginatively into how it feels to be him, standing there in his place, his situation. . . .

Empathy is capacity for one person to enter imaginatively into the sphere of consciousness of another, to feel the specific contours of another's experience, to allow one's imagination to risk entering the inner experiencing process (*intimus*) of another.

Some people have a readily recognizable capacity for empathy. When you meet such a person you know intuitively: This person understands. Others listen only to a very small part of you. They do not hear you at the feeling level and are less intimate-capable. For intimacy is relatively more possible to the degree that empathy is possible. A mutual flow of empathic understanding moves between the partners. Conversely, the promise of intimacy is relatively reduced to the degree that partners are not capable of accurately intuiting each other's feelings.

To the degree that I am able to experience myself as understood by my partner, and my partner experiences himself as understood by me, intimacy is possible. This is very near the essential definition of intimacy, since in a mutual flow of empathic understanding we are both giving each other the opportunity to see what is inside us, what is most inward (*intimus*).[26]

Let us suppose, however, that there is a part of me that I would prefer *not* to be known by my partner. I put up blocks and resistances to prevent him or her from grasping and understanding that part of me. That would obviously reduce the level and promise of intimacy. There is a part of my inner reality *(intimum)* that I prevent the other from seeing, and in fact I must search for strategies and security operations to prevent my partner from knowing that part of me. . . .

Congruence   The next aspect of intimacy is closely related to empathy. It has to do with each partner's capacity to feel *his own* feelings The technical term for this is congruence, which means that I am in touch with my own experiencing process, full self-aware. To the degree that I experience my own feelings as they actually are and do

> **Genuinely intimate partners are more than less likely to fight.**

not protect myself against having them, intimacy will be increased. Let us suppose that I have learned to block not only from my partner's awareness but from my own awareness certain uncomfortable experiences. . . . It will make it all the more difficult for my partner to understand them empathetically. If I am so out of touch with myself that important experiences are not accessible even to me, then it will not be easy for my inner life to be shared, and thus will block intimacy.

Trained as we are by lengthy acculturation *not* to feel certain negative feelings, notably anger, many persons in our culture find that it is difficult to open their experiencing process to another. Persons who have difficulty coming close to themselves have difficulty coming close to others.

Congruence is defined by Rogers as a condition in which "self-experiences are accurately symbolized, and are included in the self-concept in this accurately symbolized form."[27] The intimate is congruent when he feels his feelings clearly, is fully aware of his present experiencing, and symbolizes his feelings adequately.

Emotive Warmth and Conflict Capability

If the relationship is essentially warm and affirming, must not it necessarily be forced into conflict-avoidance?

I answer with our fourth irony: It is precisely the intimacy most deeply nourished by affection that is most capable of constructive conflict or "fair fighting."[28] Stated concisely, *the intimate relationship is emotively warm, yet conflict-capable.*

Surely the most recognizable aspect of intimacy is emotive warmth. The fact that such warmth can sometimes get "hot" amid conflicting interests constitutes a special problem of the intimate relationship. Here the work of George Bach[29] has been most useful. He rightly notes that hostility is a closer relationship than indifference. An angry scene may be much more intimate than one characterized by boredom or innocuousness.

Bach correctly reminds us that genuinely intimate partners are more than less likely to fight. Bach tries to teach partners to fight fair instead of dirty. The assumption is that any close relationship is going to be conflicted from time to time, and that if you can teach partners to fight openly, candidly, and without manipulative ploys, then the chances are increased that intimacy will not only survive but deepen through the conflict.[30]

Thus while it is true that acceptance and affection are essential ingredients in intimacy, it is not necessary for them to be constant or syrupy. Deep intimacy can break into open hostility provided partners are able to look honestly at conflicted interests and frustrations, and work through them together with confidence in each other's basic trustworthiness.[31]

A relationship wholly devoid of any warm flow of positive affect or affirmation would hardly be called intimate. Intimacy is, according to the arcane language of transactional analysis, the "best way to get strokes," the ultimately satisfying form of stroking, beyond games and pastimes.[32]

Intimates sometimes report experiencing what seems to be an unconditional positive regard precisely amid their inconsistencies and compulsions, so as to liberate them to feel more fully their actual feelings in the presence of the other. Although the partner's positive regard is never finally unconditional, in the most serious sense, nevertheless at times the intimate experiences it as unconditional. . . .

Readers familiar with the psychotherapeutic tradition will notice that I have just used another therapeutic term (or construct employed by certain therapists) to describe intimacy, namely, unconditional positive regard (or UPR). Rogers describes UPR as "a warm caring . . . which is not possessive, which demands no personal gratification. It is an atmosphere which simply demonstrates 'I care'; not 'I care for you *if* you behave thus and so.'"[33] It is a "prizing" which functions without "conditions of worth."

No one can achieve such an attitude simply by willing it or wishing it were so. The profound prizing of the other without conditions is not readily manufacturable, and must emerge somehow from the wellsprings of one's philosophical orientation and character structure.[34] But at least the recipient of UPR knows, when he experiences it, that it opens up the door internally for greater risk, wider openness, clearer congruence, deeper self-disclosure, and consequently greater intimacy. Why? Because when I experience myself in the presence of one who truly prizes my very being without placing conditions on me, I experience a new freedom to feel those feelings that would be far too dangerous in a more conditional setting.[35]

Thus persons in such intimate relationships often report feeling relatively *safe* with the other. They do not feel that they need to defend themselves. There may be continuing needs for security operations, but in the intimate moment the demand for them is sharply reduced.

A related characteristic of intimacy is tactile or bodily closeness. From time to time the affectionate relationship wishes to manifest itself in touching. The spirit relation or psychological closeness of persons becomes naturally embodied in a touch relationship.[36]

We do well not to stress this point so compulsively as to appear to make it necessary at all or most times for intimacies to be body transactions. But while it is not a necessary condition, tactile intimacy may be at times the most fitting expression of close companionship. Friends embrace, even though an embrace does not constitute friendship. Lovers make love, even though orgasm does not constitute intimacy. The significance of touch relationships differ widely, of course, from culture to culture.

Self-Disclosure and Letting-Be

Can we assume honesty as an absolute norm of the intimate relationship without coercively requiring self-disclosure?

The hypothesis that holds together this fifth tension or irony is: *An intimate relationship is honest, open, nondeceptive, game-free, nonmanipulative, and self-disclosing, and yet it does not compulsively require of the partner self-disclosure and petty acts of confession and compulsive honesty. It allows the partner, when appropriate, distance, solitude, autonomy, and self-direction.*[37]. . .

Emphasis on intimacy as nonmanipulative calls to mind the special definition of intimacy proposed by the transactional analysts; namely, that intimacy is a "game-free relationship." Berne defines intimacy as "a game free exchange of emotional expression without exploitation."[38] Intimacy, according to James and Jongeward, is "free of games and free of exploitation."[39] Although this may at first appear to be merely defining intimacy negatively in terms of something that is absent from it, nonetheless when one remembers the exceptional specificity given to the notion of games by the transactional analysts, the definition takes on more substance.

It is in this frame of reference that we note another condition or characteristic of intimacy: the capacity for self-disclosure. It is the willingness to reveal oneself, to open one's internal knowledge to the view of the other. Jourard[40] has paid special attention to the function of self-disclosure in therapeutic growth. Whereas behaviorist and Freudian psychologies had presupposed that persons resist self-disclosure, and thus devise deceptive experiments and stratagems to break through resistance, Jourard's studies found to the contrary that persons in an accepting environment positively *desire* self-disclosure. Thus therapy is not merely a matter of coercively breaking through resistances, but rather allowing the conditions that permit individuals to reveal what is within. Such conditions facilitate intimacy.

Since the quality of emotive communication is so decisive for intimacy, further attention needs to be given to defining just what we mean by it. The intimate relationship is characterized by an emotive resonance, the nuances of which are admirably evoked in the colloquial image of "good vibes." Intimates experience many subtle energy vibrations between each other, i.e., many signals both verbal and nonverbal that the partner picks up quickly and unmistakably. Just because there are so many transmissions of this sort, both sensory and parasensory, it is virtually impossible for intimates to lie to each other, since their body language and aura perceptions tell the truth, as studies of affairs have shown.[41] Persons having affairs have unaccustomed difficulty telling lies to intimates. The person with whom one is or has long been intimate picks up the nonverbal and etheric signals beyond all verbal concealments.

Even though honesty is a crucial virtue of intimates, they nonetheless find it prudent not to coerce honesty, nor to compel each other to be compulsively self-disclosing. Intimacy must give room for being oneself. It must allow distance, when distance means growth or survival. Intimacy is not an undermining of individuality but an enchancement of it.[42] If the relation is compulsively controlling and the companion is not allowed to shape his own direction, then the mutual respect that intimacy requires is inhibited.[43]

It may seem paradoxical to suggest that intimacy and solitude are mutually supportive, since solitude may at first glance appear to be the mirror opposite of intimacy. Yet, as our discussion of empathy and congruence has shown, one can be more free to be in touch with others if he is in touch with himself. Thus a rhythm of intimacy and solitude appears to be supportive to both.[44]

Finitude and Transcendence

Is intimacy subject to death, or does it transcend death? . . .

Finitude   Since intimacy is a relationship that exists in history and thus within the context of human finitude, it is subject to death. It is a misunderstanding of the intimate relationship to pretend that it lacks limits. For each time I commit myself to a relation of closeness to another person I take the risk of losing it. It is only wise to realize that any human bonding is vulnerable to deterioration, sickness, loss, and finally death.

Although one might suppose that modern scientific empiricism would have little difficulty in grasping and affirming this thesis, that is not so evident. For there appears to be just as strong a temptation among modern men to make an idolatry of the interpersonal as in more primitive cultures, to treat the finite relationship as if it were absolute or not subject to time and death. This is a basic dilemma in all human existence: the temptation to take a finite good and deal with it as if it were the whole good, to absolutize the relative.[45]

To the extent that we idolize finite intimacy, we make ourselves vulnerable to the pain over its loss. The nature of intimacy is best served not by idolizing the intimate partner, but by dealing with the intimate realistically as a person subject to death, so that the relation can develop with an awareness of its actual fragility and lack of absoluteness in time.

Transcendence   The other side of the dialectic that deepens the irony is that interpersonal communion characteristically understands itself (when it understands itself deeply) as transcending the finite sphere, and as touching or being touched by the eternal Other through interpersonal meeting.[46] Interpersonal existence is from time to time sharply aware of itself as rooted in the inner meaning of the cosmos. This widely known experience leads us to hypothesize that intimacy, though gravely subject to finitude and death, nonetheless transcends it in mysterious ways that are not fully capable at this time of empirical verification. . . .

Intimates are aware that their most significant exchanges are not merely body transactions, but as persons in encounter, or the meeting of spirit with spirit. What really happens in intimacy has to do with spirit-spirit communion or interpersonal communion, two persons experiencing their beings poignantly united. When they are most together they are most aware of that which transcends their togetherness. Their oneness reflects a deeper capacity for coherence in the universe. Their interpersonal communion echoes some abyssal capacity given in and with reality itself for communion.

It may be more useful to summarize these twelve points by stating them negatively, rather than positively.

1   Intimate relationships do not grow if not given time.
2   Intimate bonding is less palpable if it never has ways of becoming intensified into ecstatic moments of intimate sharing.
3   If relationships lack contractual clarity, or if the contracts are easily terminable, then to that degree the relationship is less intimate-capable.
4   If within the framework of sustained accountability the relationship is not able to be renegotiated in the light of specific new demands and occasions, then it is less likely to be intimate.
5   If partners are unable to empathize with each other's feelings, intimacy is inhibited.
6   If persons are unable to feel their own feelings clearly and fully, then the empathy that intimacy requires is constricted.
7   If emotive warmth is absent consistently, one is not likely to call the relation intimate.
8   Relationships that are unable to face conflicts are less likely to develop intimacy.
9   Insofar as partners need to resort to deceptive and manipulative behaviors, or lack honest self-disclosure, the relationship is to that degree probably less intimate.
10   To the extent that the relationship requires the constant monitoring of one party and thus inhibits the self-direction of the other, intimacy is decreased.
11   Insofar as the relationship is not recognized as finite and therefore vulnerable to death, it is less likely to achieve genuine intimacy, since it will be prone to idolize the partner.
12   And yet intimates know that when they are most together they are most aware of that which transcends their togetherness, echoing the abysmal capacity given in and with reality itself for communion. It is this experience that energizes the hope that intimacy, in some mysterious way not fully explainable at this time, transcends death.

This attempt at a conceptual clarification of the notion of intimacy has one special difficulty. As we proceed to define intimacy we easily tend to become burdened by a highly idealized picture of the intimate relationship, so that it seems increasingly abstract and impossible to grasp as an actual or even potential reality. It is not necessary for all factors to be present in their absolute form in order for a relation to be intimate. Any one of these factors may have its ebbs and flows. But over a period of time if these conditions tend to persist in a relation between two persons, then they experience that special relation to which our common language points when it uses the term intimacy.

Having discussed the language, the collage of descriptions and the ironies of the intimate relationship, I am now ready to offer a definition of intimacy. *Intimacy is an intensely personal relationship of sustained closeness in which the intimus sphere of each partner is affectionately known and beheld by the other through congruent, empathic understanding, mutual accountability, and contextual negotiability, durable in time, subject to ecstatic intensification, emotively warm and conflict-capable, self-disclosing and distance-respecting, subject to death and yet in the form of hope reaching beyond death.*

NOTES

1 *Oxford Universal English Dictionary*, C. T. Onions, ed., Oxford University Press, 1937, 5: 1034.

2 Albert Blaise, ed., *Dictionnaire Latin Français des Auteurs Chrétiens*, Librairie des Meridiens, 1954, 468. C. T. Lewis and C. Short, *A Latin Dictionary*, Oxford University Press, 1955. R. E. Latham, *Revised Medieval Latin Word List*, Oxford University Press, 1965.

3 Erving Goffman, *The Presentation Self in Everyday Life*, Doubleday, 1959, 208 ff.

4 "This condition may be denoted *crasis*, a genuine interlocking of personalities; or more colloquially, it may be called *intimacy*." Eric Berne, *Transactional Analysis in Psychotherapy*, Grove Press, 1961.

5 *Webster's Third New International Dictionary*, unabridged, G & C. Merriam, 1961.

6 Martin Buber, *I and Thou*, trans. Walter Kaufmann, Scribner's, 1970, 55; *Between Man and Man*, Beacon Press, 1955 (hereafter *BMM*).

7 Ross Snyder, *On Becoming Human*, Abingdon Press, 1967, 54 ff.; Reuel L. Howe, *The Miracle of Dialogue*, Seabury, 1963.

8 Howard J. Clinebell, Jr., and Charlotte H. Clinebell, *The Intimate Marriage*, Harper & Row, 1970, 37 ff.

9 George R. Bach and Peter Wyden, *The Intimate Enemy: How to Fight Fair in Love and Marriage*, Avon, 1968; Eric Berne, *Games People Play*, Grove Press, 1964 (hereafter *GPP*); William Schutz, *Joy: Expanding Human Awareness*, Grove Press, 1967; Alexander Lowen, *Love and Orgasm*, Macmillan, 1965, *Pleasure*, Coward-McCann, 1970; Gerald Goodman, *Companionship Therapy*, Jossey-Bass, 1972; R. M. Mazur, *The New Intimacy*, Beacon Press, 1973.

10 Specifically the instructions were: "Think of a particular relation of genuine intimacy with another person. Call to mind a good friend, close associate, childhood companion, or your spouse—one with whom you have experienced intense emotive reasonance and fulfilling closeness, whose internal reality you have in some sense come to know and love. Let your imagination flow with the experience. Make yourself comfortable; breathe deeply; as you exhale let your muscles relax—around your eyes, mouth, neck, back, arms, pelvis, legs, toes. Experience in memory and imagination what it is like to be there with that person in a moment of warmth and affection. Let that person's facial features appear in your awareness. Recall the particular place, the context in which you felt closest. Be there with your partner. Let that environment frame the face of your partner. Let the feelings flow between you and your partner—whatever feelings are there—do not block them, stay with them. Rehearse in fantasy whatever activity or event you are sharing with your partner. (Pause.) At times there are moments of ecstasy or overflowing feelings with persons with whom we are very close. If you felt such a moment with this person, savor that moment. (Pause.) Now it is time to come back to this group. When you feel like it, open your eyes, and come back and be fully present to this group here and now."

11 For a theoretical discussion of these difficulties, see H. A. Murray, "Toward a Classification of Interaction," in T. Parsons and E. A. Shils, eds., *Toward a General Theory of Action*, Harvard University Press., 1951, 434–464.

12 I have developed this category in *The Structure of Awareness*, Abingdon Press, 1968 (hereafter *SA*), 16 ff., 232 ff.

13 A. H. Maslow, *Toward a Psychology of Being*, Van Nostrand, 1962; *Religions, Values and Peak Experiences*, Viking Press, 1970 (hereafter *RVP*).

14 Cf. Martin Buber, *I and Thou; BMM*, Part I.

15 Genesis 2:234.

16 In this connection see Gabriel Marcel's profound essay, "Presence as a Mystery," in *The Mystery of Being*, Henry Regnery Co., 1950, 1: 242 ff.

17 See Marc Oraison, *Being Together*, Doubleday, 1971, 139 ff; Buber, *The Knowledge of Man*, Harper Torchbooks, 1965, 72 ff.

18 Maslow, *RVP*, 63.

19 See Wayne E. Oates, *Protestant Pastoral Counseling*, Westminster Press, 1962, 75 ff.

20 Contra Berne, who speaks of his " 'intimacy experiment' in which two people sit close to each other 'eyeball to eyeball' and keep eye contact while talking straight to each other . . . it demonstrates that any two people of either sex, starting as strangers or mere acquantances, can attain intimacy in fifteen minutes or so under proper conditions." *Sex in Human Loving*, Simon and Schuster, 1970, 117–118.

21   "The Form of Solemnization of Matrimony," *The Book of Common Prayer*, SPCK, n.d., 217.

22   Virginia Satir, *Conjoint Family Therapy*, Science and Behavior Books, 1967. See "Communication: A Verbal and Nonverbal Process of Making Requests of the Receiver," 75 ff. Cf. my essay, "Optimal Conditions for Learning—Toward a Clarification of the Learning Contract," *Religious Education*, March–April 1972.

23   Howe, *Herein Is Love*, Judson Press, 1961.

24   Carl R. Rogers, *Client-Centered Therapy*, Houghton Mifflin, 1951.

25   Robert L. Katz, *Empathy: Its Nature and Uses*, Collier-Macmillan, 1963.

26   Cf. Max Scheler, *The Nature of Sympathy*, Yale University Press, 1954.

27   Rogers, "A Theory of Therapy, Personality, and Interpersonal Relationships, as Developed in the Client-Centered Framework," in *Psychology: A study of a Science*, ed. Sigmund Koch, McGraw-Hill, 1959, 206.

28   George R. Bach, "A Theory of Intimate Aggression," *Psychological Report*, 1965, *18*, 449–450.

29   Bach and Wyden, *The Intimate Enemy*, 17-95. Cf. Buber, *I and Thou*, 68.

30   George R. Bach and R. M. Deutsch, *Pairing*, Avon, 1970, 153 ff. Cf. Anthony Storr, *Human Aggression*, Atheneum, 1968.

31   S. Schacter, *The Psychology of Affiliation*, Stanford University Press, 1959.

32   Leonard Campos and Paul McCormick, *Introduce Yourself to Transactional Analysis*, San Joaquin TA Institute, 1969, 18; Eric Berne, *GPP*, 180 ff.

33   Rogers, *On Becoming a Person*, Houghton Mifflin, 1961, 283.

34   Rogers, *Client-Centered Therapy*.

35   Jack Gibb, "Climate for Trust Formation," in L. P. Bradford, J. R. Gibb, K. E. Benne, eds., *T-Group Theory and Laboratory Method*, John Wiley, 1964; Everett L. Shostrom, *Man, the Manipulator*, Abingdon Press, 1967.

36   Julius Fast, *Body Language*, M. Evans, 1970; Jane Howard, *Please Touch*, McGraw-Hill, 1970.

37   Buber, *Knowledge of Man*, 59 ff. Cf. F. E. Fiedler, "The Psychological-Distance Dimension in Interpersonal Relations," *Journal of Personality*, 1953, 22, 142–150.

38   Berne, *What Do You Say After You Say Hello?: The Psychology of Human Destiny*, Grove Press, 1972, 444.

39   Muriel James and Dorothy Jongeward, *Born to Win: Transactional Analysis with Gestalt Experiments*, Addison-Wesley, 1971, 58.

40   Sidney M. Jourard, *The Transparent Self: Self-disclosure and Well-being*, Van Nostrand, 1964.

41   Morton Hunt, *The Affair*, New American Library, 1969.

42   Oraison, *Being Together*, 191 ff.; E. Brunner, *The Divine Imperative*, Westminster Press, 1947, Part 3.

43   Erich Fromm, *The Art of Loving*, Harper & Row, 1962.

44 This point has been perceptively developed by Elizabeth O'Conner, *Journey Inward, Journey Outward*, Harper & Row, 1968. See also Dietrich Bonhoeffer, *Life Together*, Harper & Bros., 1954, 40 ff.

45 H. Richard Niebuhr, *Radical Monotheism and Western Culture*, Harper & Bros., 1960. See Oden, *SA*, Part I.

46 Buber, *The Way of Man*, Wilcox and Follett, 1951; *I and Thou*, 123 ff.; *Believing Humanism*, Simon and Schuster, 1969.

Decisions in Sexuality: An Act of Impulse, Conscience, or Society?

Roy W. Menninger

The revolution in sexual attitudes, with a concomitant increase in the freedom to talk about sex, think about it, and even experiment with it, confronts many of us with a need for personal decisions about sexual activity, the kind and the amount, that those who knew a simpler, earlier mode of living did not have to face. The pressure for action is enormous. Daily, those in our environment barrage us with sexual imagery in the service of selling everything from cars to deodorants, from books to a sure-fire method of becoming popular. This latent interest in things sexual is vigorously mobilized by appeals to one's sense of adequacy, capacity, importance, and even one's sense of worth. Sex becomes a means of persuading, demanding, exploiting, motivating. Such widespread consumption of sexual imagery and ideas has effectively promoted the more subtle, general view that sexual experimentation is now more acceptable and justifiable than ever before. Even more insidiously, however, it has begun to imply that those who do *not* participate in this sexual freedom are the deviants.

These pleasures, these invitations, blandishments, and opportunities, all have one element in common: they appear to arise in the environment, from some source external to the self. By offering, encouraging, and persuading, they nullify the questioning doubts that arise from within and may seriously obscure other pressing personal concerns and anxieties by recasting them in the disguise of sexuality.

Particularly for the adolescent and young adult, sexual activity is available both to express and to escape from compelling personal

> **Sexual activity, rationalized as an end in itself, is easily corrupted by internal conflicts and becomes a means to other ends that may be painful, costly, and even self-destructive.**

problems. It becomes a means, for example, that enables the dissident or angry or unhappy individual to reject the "morality of the establishment" by a sexual act. He (or she) may consider that he is "searching for his real self" through sex. Or he may become convinced that sex is the true route to "authentic relationships," that it will disclose personal reality by literally stripping away the covers that conceal; or he may believe that only through a sexual relationship will he find at last a long-sought sense of worth. Sexual activity, rationalized as an end in itself, is thus easily corrupted by internal conflicts and becomes a means to other ends that may be painful, costly, and even self-destructive.

These internal and external forces are enormously complex and operate on us in ways we do not always recognize. Without consciously deciding to do so, we may nevertheless find ourselves involved in complicated and painful situations that include sexual activity; and these "nondecisions" are made by default in response to pressures we did not understand. Even a conscious plan to embark on a sexual affair may contain the seeds of destruction if it masks elements of unsettled internal conflict.

We can therefore profitably explore the field of forces in which a decision, or nondecision, about sexuality comes to be made. This kind of analysis can offer a broader perspective of our own behavior for the tough business of managing one's life.

The first force to which I will refer is that force or a combination of forces that arises from something we call the id. It is a mythical place, but as a word it effectively captures the notion of biologically based drives or pressures that seek discharge. These inborn forces are a part of the biological given of the individual; they seek expression in whatever ways and through whatever routes may be open. This sequence is, at one and the same time, a problem for the individual to manage and an opportunity, for these forces constitute basic energies the individual harnesses to accomplish his personal goals and objectives. What the individual utilizes from the id is the energy and its propensity to seek discharge. It constitutes the fire, the steam; it keeps the personality engine going.

We group these two id forces into dichotomies variously called "love and hate," "sex and aggression," "creation and destruction," "life and death." These are words intended merely to represent ideas, not things, but here we use them to characterize the polar qualities of the instinctual forces that drive the individual's behavior. Contained and properly channeled by the mature personality, they enable us to work, love, and live in effective and mutually satisfying ways.

When neurosis, circumstance, or stress weakens the mature controls of the personality, these forces threaten to break into consciousness and produce an internal experience of great discomfort to which we give the name "anxiety." In defense against this very unpleasant emotion, we are often driven to behave in ways that are in turn potentially destructive or self-defeating. A young man, made anxious by the closeness that an intimate affair has produced, may react with a devil-may-care denial and press impulsively into a sexual experience that leads to guilt, estrangement from the girl, and even more anxiety.

A second pressure that we must take into account is one derived from another part of the personality called the superego. This portion of the personality cannot be localized anatomically; it is not palpable, although it sometimes feels as real as if it were. Rather, the term is a helpful way of grouping together some functions and some forces that we observe to have powerful effects upon a person. In nonmedical terms, the superego is the conscience, or internal policeman. It is the still, small voice inside us that says "no" as we reach for something we should not have. It is also a repository for the values we have acquired from our parents and from the socialization processes of school and society.

The superego also contains the ego-ideal, that image of perfection that guides our behavior by espousing all the values and standards to which we aspire. Violation of these internal standards produces the pang of conscience we label "guilt." By its capacity to evoke guilty feelings, our superego insures compliance to certain preset standards that, like laws passed by an earlier generation, seem immutable and unavoidable. Since the standards and values that both guide and control us are incorporated at a very young age, they are in fact relatively unchangeable and operate in subtle but compelling ways that are often beneath our conscious awareness.

Environment is the third locus of forces that act upon the individual. From the moment of birth to this present moment, each one of us is continually required to take environmental demands into account. We are aware of the many forms that they may take, but two need mention here: productivity and conformity. These things our environment expects—indeed demands them of us—and in return gives us nurture, intimacy, support, approbation, and the opportunity for participation. There is promise of status and worth—values that are important to us—but only if we cooperate.

These three forces—the id, the superego, and the environment—combine and recombine to confront the individual with a continuing need to weigh this advantage against that cost, this opportunity against that consequence. Each individual personality has evolved an executive structure that weighs these risks, chooses, and thereby maintains a balance among these myriad forces. This executive body is called the ego. In common parlance the word has selfish and narcissistic connotations, but its technical meaning refers to the "personality management" functions performed by the individual. Maintaining this vital balance is the ego's main task. To the extent that it is successful, what we see is growth, development, maturity, and a gradual mastery of the inner and outer environments. We see all the qualities of vigor and effectiveness that we call "health." Degrees of failure by the ego to manage the many demands upon it lead to the various disablements we call disease or malfunction: the neuroses

> Conflict is so elemental a part of the human condition that there can be no question of avoiding it. . . . The question is not [its] elimination, but its management.

and the psychoses. But short of such seriously imbalanced states, quite normal people all have days when their balancing functions are less than adequate. At those times they experience feelings indicative of ego failure: depression, anxiety, and uneasiness. These are common feelings and are characteristic of the situation that arises when pressures from within or without are more intense than one can manage.

From this brief survey of the world of personality, we should be left with a new awareness of the incredible burdens of management that our personality executive, the ego, must carry, and perhaps even some amazement at the degree of success that most of us show most of the time. But for each of us, the ego is less successful in its functions in certain areas and under certain circumstances than in others. The more stable and the more supportive our family background, the fewer are these areas of trouble and the less destructive are our bouts with imbalance. Even for the stable, and certainly for the less secure among us, growth itself, and the passage through adolescence into young adulthood, is rocky, and intensifications of the pressures on the executive ego are sharp. Several observations about the problems of decision-making during this period are in order.

First, no decision occurs in the absence of conflict, and, indeed, conflict is so elemental a part of the human condition that there can be no question of avoiding it, whether we actively make decisions about ourselves or try to ignore the need for them and allow circumstances to make "nondecisions" for us. The question is not the elimination of conflict within and around us, but its management. What strategies we develop, what allies, what sources of understanding, what kinds of external supports and strengths—these will determine how successful we are and thus how well adjusted we remain.

Second, conflict, whether internal or external, invariably carries an emotional quality with it: anguish, pain, anxiety—even fear and despair. Indeed, the presence of these feelings is *prima facie* evidence of the presence of conflict, recognized or not, and their persistence or deepening is unarguable evidence of conflict denied, avoided, disguised, and unresolved. They should signal—in ourselves and in those we are concerned about—a need for additional strategies for conflict resolution and, particularly, help from someone else.

Third, it should be clear that everything we do, think, say, or feel contains elements of each of these personality and environmental forces. *No* bit of behavior can be atributed solely to the conscience, or the id, or even the environment. This position will confound those of us who insist that they are (and therefore their behavior is) solely a product of the environment—and that is where the responsibility, the fault, and the cause all lie. They fail to see the parts of themselves that also contribute to the problem, they fail to see what they do that makes matters worse, and they fail to understand their part in finding a solution or a better compromise. These displacements to others and to the environment are an easy cop-out, a serious lapse of personal responsibility.

Fourth, effective decision-making by the executive ego depends in the last analysis on our capacity for thought. Man is a problem-solving animal, and this capability is expressed in his use of the mental activity called thought. Like many obvious statements, this one seems trivial and hardly worth mention, let alone emphasis. But the sad fact is that effective thought is often absent from the scene of conflict, and the means of resolving the pressures of the ego are thereby seriously reduced or even altogether lacking.

Under certain conditions of overwhelming anxiety or confusion, and in people whose style is to act first and think second (if at all), action itself may serve to short-circuit the thinking process. Impulsive behavior then becomes a device by which to escape, not simply to avoid thinking out a better plan, but to avoid the anxiety, the intense discomfort that would accompany a confrontation with the problem and a thoughtful search for the understanding that would solve it. In this context, action to evade thought seldom solves the underlying issue, because it represents a flight from it that leaves the conflict essentially unaltered and potentially able to re-create the problem again and again.

Fifth, as with any executive decision, the better the facts are understood, the better the decision is likely to be. Unfortunately for the ego, the "facts" it needs to understand are at best only dimly seen, for the ego is often only barely conscious of many of the pressures from the id, from the superego, and even from the environment. Some of these forces are quite simply unconscious, but even others, which we may be able to perceive, are badly misrepresented by that mental process of self-deceit most of us know quite well: rationalization. It is an unfortunate fact that most people are exceptionally skillful in concealing important psychological facts from themselves— even frankly denying the existence of the obvious. Observers, even relatively unsophisticated ones, are seldom as easily fooled by us as we are by ourselves. This state of affairs points to the critical importance of using the intelligence and perceptions of others to help us better understand ourselves. I will refer to this strategy again later.

How then does all this bear upon issues of sex, our focus here? Primarily in that sexual behaviors are simultaneously much more highly motivated (by the id drive), much more socially loaded (producing severe environmental pressures), and much more prone to provoke internal conflict with one's conscience than almost any other kind of behavior. Consequently, many problems involving self-esteem and value, personal judgment and feelings of fear, guilt, or anxiety are brought into sharp relief by the prospect or experience of sexual behavior. In the white-hot focus of so many colliding forces from superego, id, and environment, the ego finds decision about sexual activity considerably more difficult, and considerably more liable to defect, than most other usual daily decisions. The five characteristics of the executive ego's decisions are particularly apparent when the decisions are about sexual behavior. They are typically conflictual and emotion-laden, expressive of internal forces of personality as well as the environment, action-provoking and thought-avoiding, and full of self-deception. It is this latter point especially that requires emphasis, for the failure of the ego to discern clearly the forces of conscience and inner conflict will inevitably lead to potentially destructive decisions based on self-deceiving rationalizations, or equally destructive "nondecisions" based on denial and impulsive, thought-free action.

The very plasticity of the sexual drive contributes to the potential for failing to recognize the inner conflicts or anxieties that may be present and critically important. The impulse of which overt sexual activity is presumably an ultimate expression is capable of protean forms. It is generally appreciated that man may express sexual feelings through art, music, or literature, in forms that reveal nothing obviously sexual.

We seem much less aware of the converse fact: that sexual behavior is a ready vehicle for the expression of feelings or concerns that are not in any sense sexual, and it is very commonly used unwittingly as a means for managing (usually poorly) personal problems that are not the slightest bit sexual in nature. Thus used, sexual activity is in no way a constructive, creative expression of love, but a repetitious, destructive expression of unresolved conflict that makes the personal problems worse and irreparably distorts one's capacity for loving sexual relationships.

Sex sometimes masquerades as love. It is sometimes an antidote for loneliness, taken as evidence of personal worth and value, or proof of existence: "If I can engage in the sexual act I must be alive." For some it is a demonstration of potency and masculine adequacy. However, the issue is not that any sexual act does indeed do some of these things; in the context of a loving relationship, it does do all of them. Rather, the issue is recognizing that we are frequently quite unaware of the extent to which illegitimate or inappropriate needs may actually piggy-back their way to expression or solution through sexual activity.

Let us consider what some of these illegitimate needs may be. First, from the environment. There is a widespread belief, reinforced by the pseudo-philosophy of *Playboy* magazine, that the "Big Orgasm" is an adequate definition of potency and a mature relationship. Its presence is a kind of *summum bonum*. This absurd criterion of maturity has created a new guilt that throws consternation into all. We may now feel guilty if we do *not* experience orgasm. Indeed, it reflects a more general view that one needs to engage in sexual activity to maintain good health. Utter nonsense! This is part of a hedonistic mythology that creeps in upon us and applies social pressure to conform. For example, the pre-eminence of the intensely focused, self-indulgent, narcissistic pleasure, which the *Playboy* concept of sex epitomizes, produces an assumption in the young inexperienced person that this is the manner in which 97 percent of the people behave. In truth, the statistics are nothing of the sort, but the unsophisticated does not know that, for he reads *Playboy* and feels compelled to behave in that way too, if he is not to suffer the pains of poor health and social ostracism. The environment thus perpetuates the mythical view that the intensity of the sexual experience has everything to say about truth, existence, and reality.

Equally vigorously perpetuated is the myth that a successful marriage depends on a successful sex life. People who are in love usually do not complain of sexual difficulties. Those who do complain about sexual difficulties do so because they lack the warm qualities that hold a marriage together, and the sexual relationship serves to focus attention on this deficiency.

These exemplify typical current environmental pressures; there are many others with which we are familiar: such beliefs as "everybody is doing it now" or "this is the way to become a man (or a woman)." These are malicious pressures because they are hard to recognize for what they are and even harder to defeat, since they may be actively advocated by the peer culture. They comprise an important part of the external forces pressing upon an individual.

Now let us consider some of the pressures from within. Contesting the biological urge are the forces of conscience, demanding continence and restraint. At times they are consciously identified with one's parents and enhance the conflict by making sex a test of one's liberation from the family and a measure of his or her independence. Aware of a sense of dependent needs left over from childhood, an individual may use sexual behavior as a route to throw off these longings for a simple, protected past—only to select a partner who mothers him!

Even as this example suggests, sexual relationships typically embody much of one's ideas about himself and what kind of person he thinks he is or is not. Close relationships may then express a wish for a manner of being, sought but not achieved; or they may be expressive of parts of himself that he regards as highly undesirable. It is in this way that personal concerns may sneak into expression through sexual decisions, confuse both the individual and his partner about the meaning of the experience, and provoke a whole spectrum of feelings and reactions that can complicate one's emotional life and

> **People may use sexual attractiveness as an evidence of personal worth. "If somebody will love me, then I must be worth something."**

health beyond measure. In particular, these reactions often develop a compelling momentum of their own and drive the individual deeper and deeper into a relationship or a state of mind that nothing short of radical intervention will interrupt.

The sexual act sometimes becomes an arena for the expression of a neurotic need to possess, to own, to keep, to control, to dominate. Again, these are infantile needs, unresolved hang-overs from one's childhood years, and pushed toward solution through the sexual experience. Unrecognized and unfaced, they may subvert the potential for a loving relationship and precipitate a series of unfortunate and destructive decisions. Jealousy, for example, is a reflection of an intense need to own, to possess, and to keep, and it may often be

481

underscored by a demand for sexual experience as a form of proof.

Unrequited self-needs must be considered, too. People may use sexual attractiveness as an evidence of personal worth. "If somebody will love me, then I must be worth something." The tragedy in this piggy-backed solution to the problem is that it is an unreal, temporary respite from self-doubt that leaves the basic problems untouched and creates a secondary upsurge of self-hate after the fact; for the superego then extracts its price: one feels even more unworthy, irritable, and depressed. In an effort to dilute these feelings of self-hate, one nurtures the hope that next time true love will triumph and those feelings of guilt and unworthiness will be washed away. But this hope is a vain one, for repetition only sets off the destructive cycle once again. Unrecognized needs for identity often are apparent in young boys as they engage in and boast about impulsive sexual activity to disguise a diffused, fragmented, and immature masculinity. This behavior is again reinforced by the environment and amplified by the expectations of the group, and it produces potentially difficult consequences.

Let me give you a couple of cases to illustrate some of these points.

Eileen was an attractive, young college sophomore whose attitudes of bravado and certainty contrasted sharply with her haggard and anxious appearance. She made quite a point of her extensive sexual experience and rather aggressively argued that her attitudes about free love were evidence that she rejected her parents' traditional values as phony, superficial, and utterly middle class.

She sought psychiatric help the morning after her affair with the eighth different boy in eight months. She reported that she was not able to study and her school performance had fallen so far that she was on the point of leaving before she was thrown out. She denied any particular feelings of depression, self-preoccupation, or doubt and vociferously rejected any suggestion that her promiscuity was at all unusual. She was particularly vehement in her insistence that she enjoyed sex, that she had orgasm with every sexual encounter, and that each affair was more exciting than the last. All this insistence notwithstanding, her condition continued to deteriorate. She began to drink heavily, became obviously more depressed, and began to voice thoughts of suicide.

Only after she slept with a boy whom she said she despised did her facade of sexual satisfaction and enjoyment crack What emerged was a poignant history that had begun with an intense affair with the first boy who had ever asked her out more than twice. When he eventually broke off with her, she denied her devastating disappointment by initiating a series of promiscuous affairs, typically with boys whose social status was lower than hers and who frequently treated her with disdain and contempt. This sequence was endlessly repeated, sustained by her fantasies that the next affair would be like the first, but at a terrible cost to her self-esteem, her ability to work, and her mental health.

Her excessive need for a loving relationship as proof of her own worth not only drove her prematurely into an involvement she was not prepared for, but left her further unable to manage the rejection and its consequences of negative judgments about her value as a lovable person. Her inability to manage this loss to her self-esteem led her into a succession of decisions that were, paradoxically, progressively more destructive. Had she had some means by which to examine the meanings of her first decision to become involved, especially after the trauma of rejection, she might have been spared the long and personally expensive course of events that followed. All of her protestations to the contrary, her sexual behavior clearly had nothing at all to do with sex as a loving and creative act.

Esther came to a large state university from a small midwest town where she had been raised by a deeply religious and controlling— but benevolent—family. She had always looked forward to college as a moment of liberation. Although she insisted that she was never happier in her life, she spent a great deal of time writing long avowals of happiness to her parents. She was apparently unaware of how lonely and homesick she felt in the wake of departing from the close-knit family where she had been the only child. She met and became deeply involved with a college senior who seemed exceedingly mature and highly attractive. When he showed some interest in her, her sense of appreciation for his attentions gave way to infatuation and then to an intensely emotional affair. What for the boy was simply a last fling before leaving college came to be her very life. When she began to fear the possibility of losing him she became pregnant, although it was clear that this event was not a conscious intentional act on her part. She had "forgotten" when her safe period was.

This event forced them into a marriage that came to be grossly resented by both and ended in divorce before she was twenty. Although she eventually recovered a more mature perspective and developed a productive and satisfactory life, it was not without considerable pain to many people, great expense, and, perhaps most tragic of all, an unwanted child.

> **Discussion groups can not only provide the benefits of multiple perspectives on common problems, but also offer that special warmth and support that only a group can provide.**

Her unrecognized and unmastered problems of separation from a close but dominating family life stimulated a series of personal decisions in which sexuality came to be the glue that would hold together a traumatized self. Since an experience as intense and ephemeral as the sexual one lacks continuity and provides no solid foundation for anything beyond biological discharge, her use of sex as a solution was foreordained to fail. It could not possibly resolve her unacknowledged conflict between her wish for independence and her wish to remain the deeply loved daughter of her parents.

In the two cases I have cited, the decision to engage in sexual behavior was powerfully influenced by conflicting but denied ideas about one's self and one's relation to other important people. The hidden nature of these persistently active conflicts led to their recreation in the setting of an affair at school, which both reactivated and failed to solve pre-existing concerns. In turn, sexual behavior became a means for simultaneously expressing these conflicts and avoiding a conscious confrontation with them that might have led to a tempering of the disastrous consequences that followed.

Of course, any of fifty other examples could have been selected, for almost every sexual decision requires that the participants face issues and questions that are rarely fully perceived, sufficiently defined, or adequately confronted. At the critical point of passionate involvement, a thoughtful appreciation of all these parts of the decision must seem impossible, and perhaps it is—then. But one act need not lead thoughtlessly to the next with no pause for contemplation between. How is one to use these moments of reflection, if one can, in fact, catch hold of them?

Since it is our capacity for thought that enables us to work out such problems and eventually make good decisions, it is critical to consider by what means one can generate problem-solving thinking in the face of the many forces that seem to discourage it. My prescription is both simple and difficult: to find the means and the opportunity to talk—to talk with one's confidant, one's allies, one's friends, one's counselors, one's psychiatrist, and even perhaps, for some of us, one's parents. It is surprising that the universality of these problems has not led to a universal appreciation of the need to share them, discuss them, consider them, talk about them, and, finally, to think effectively about them.

Unfortunately, the opportunity for such specialized forms of talking as counseling or psychotherapy are available only to a very few, and typically only when such a serious crisis has developed that more is involved than the making of a decision. What is missing is an opportunity for all of us who are concerned about these problems, but still effectively struggling with them, to talk them out. Everyone, if his ego is to maintain that optimal balance, needs to be able to talk, to be listened to.

There is a means by which this can be done to suit the needs of ordinary people troubled with experiences and feelings and doubts about their abilities to resolve them. This means is the discussion group with one's peers—appropriately moderated by someone skilled in leading group discussions and simultaneously capable of empathy and objectivity. Such discussion groups are natural on college campuses where people of similar ages are struggling with similar problems. The gregarious nature of college life helps to break down the individualistic orientation that puts a high premium on the isolation that discourages a collaborative approach to solving socio-psychological problems.

Such discussion groups can not only provide the benefits of multiple perspectives on common problems, but also offer that special warmth and support that only a group can provide. In the course of sharing experiences and doubts, one not only discovers the unreality of the *Playboy* philosophy, but finds a different kind of genuineness and personal involvement that goes beyond the initimacy of the two-party relationship—and yet contributes a greater meaning to it. In the context of groups, the important qualities of empathy, openness, candor, and the capacity to listen to one's friends as well as one's self are rewarded, reinforced, and become a basis for more effective relationships with persons beyond the discussion group itself.

In such a context, one has the means and the opportunity for learning to use words as a way of testing alternatives, analyzing problems, and developing strategies—strategies that can help us deal more effectively with the issues of sexuality which confront us all. The group enables one to use the support a consensus can provide and adds to dimensions of self-knowledge that no amount of isolated introspection or even deep discussion with one's beloved can ever yield. In such a context one can learn to think more clearly about one's self and the world he is part of and thereby achieve a better balance in his decision-making among the ever-present forces of superego, id, and environment.

Out of such experiences can come the basis for more effective living, more mutually satisfying relationships with others, and a more accurate and comforting sense of one's self. The means to create such supportive and rewarding discussion groups are at hand: what is needed is a general recognition by students and administration alike that the needs of struggling, concerned youth in search of gratifying solutions to the problem of being human can be well met by the opportunity to talk together.

EDITORS

VERA BOROSAGE is Professor of Family and Child Sciences at Michigan State University. She writes and lectures on topics relating to child development, family relationships, and human sexuality.

ELEANOR S. MORRISON is on the faculty of the Department of Community Medicine, College of Osteopathic Medicine, Michigan State University. She also designs and leads human sexuality workshops for students, clergy, educators, social workers, and medical personnel. She is co-author with her husband of *Growing Up in the Family* (1964) and with Mila U. Price of *Values in Sexuality: A New Approach to Sex Education* (1974).

CONTRIBUTORS

SANDRA LIPSITZ BEM is Assistant Professor of Psychology at Stanford University. She writes and does research on sex roles and their consequences in personal and in job-related spheres.

INGRID BENGIS is a free-lance writer and taxicab driver. She wrote *Combat in the Erogenous Zone* in 1972.

MYRON BRENTON is a free-lance writer and the author of *The American Male* (1966) and *Sex Talk* (1972).

MARY S. CALDERONE has been Executive Director of SIECUS (Sex Information and Education Council of the U.S.) since 1964. She has written and lectured extensively on the need for planned parenthood and sex education. Her most recent book is *Sexuality and Human Values* (1974).

487

LOUIE CREW has written widely as a scholar, poet, and fiction writer. In February, 1974, he and Ernest Clay were married in Fort Valley, Georgia. They live as an integrated couple in what is otherwise the white part of town.

VICTOR DANIELS is Professor of Psychology at California State University in Sonoma. He was a Public Health Research Fellow at the Systems Development Corporation in Santa Monica, and he has served as a Peace Corps consultant in Chile.

LEO DAVIDS is Associate Professor of Sociology at York University in Downsview, Ontario, Canada.

SIMONE DE BEAUVOIR is a well-known French novelist and existentialist philosopher whose latest book, *The Coming of Age*, deals with ageing and sexuality.

ALBERT ELLIS is a practicing psychotherapist and Executive Director of the Institute for Advanced Study of Rational Psychotherapy. He has written over 400 articles and books on psychotherapy, sex, love, and marriage.

JOHN GAGNON is Professor of Sociology at The State University of New York and the author of numerous articles and books dealing with human sexuality. His most recent book, co-authored with William Simon, is *Sexual Conduct* (1973).

GEORGE GILDER has been a fellow at The Kennedy Institute of Politics and has written articles and books on political affairs. He wrote the best-seller *Sexual Suicide* in 1973.

GERMAINE GREER is an internationally known writer, lecturer, and advocate of women's liberation. Among her writings is the best-seller *The Female Eunuch* (1971).

CALVIN HERNTON is a sociologist and Associate Professor of Afro-American Studies at Oberlin College. Among his prolific writings about the relationship of sex and racism are *Sex and Racism in America* (1965) and *Coming Together: Black Power, White Hatred, and Sexual Hang-ups* (1971).

RICHARD HETTLINGER is Professor in the Department of Religion at Kenyon College. Among his books are *Living With Sex* (1966), *Sexual Maturity,* and *Sex Isn't That Simple* (1974).

LAURENCE HOROWITZ is Professor of Psychology at California State University in Sonoma and Director of the Ananda Institute in Santa Rosa. He is a practicing psychologist and has acted as a consultant for several public school districts in Northern California.

TOM HURLEY lives with five other men in the Boston area and teaches part time at several universities. He writes news articles for the *Gay Community News* and works on his own poetry and prose.

CAROL NAGY JACKLIN has been a research associate at Stanford University since 1972. Her interests and writings are in the development of sex differences and infant learning and perception. She is co-author with Eleanor E. Maccoby of *The Psychology of Sex Differences* (1974).

KARLA JAY writes for *The Lesbian Tide, Win,* and many other publications. She was Chairwoman of the Gay Liberation Front in 1970 and was a member of Radicalesbians.

DON D. JACKSON was a psychiatrist and author of several works on communication and marriage.

FRED A. JOHNSON is a psychologist. He conducts courses on human sexual behavior at the Counselling Center of American University, Washington, D.C.

VIRGINIA E. JOHNSON is co-director of the Reproductive Biology Research Foundation in St. Louis, Missouri. With William H. Masters, she does research and writes in the field of human sexual response and human sexual inadequacy, and treats sexually dysfunctional persons.

HERANT A. KATCHADOURIAN is Professor of Psychiatry at Stanford University. He served on a committee on university health and, with Donald T. Lunde, undertook an innovative course on human sexuality for Stanford University undergraduates. The textbook *Fundamentals of Human Sexuality* grew out of that course. He was recently appointed Vice Provost and Dean of Undergraduate Studies.

IRVING KRISTOL is Henry Luce Professor of Urban Values at New York University. He is co-editor of *The Public Interest* magazine and a prolific writer and commentator on American mores.

ZIVA KWITNEY is associate editor of *Catalog of Sexual Consciousness* (1975) and facilitates groups dealing with sexuality and sex roles.

WILLIAM J. LEDERER is a writer, retired captain of the U.S. Navy, and co-author of several books including *The Ugly American* and *Mirages of Marriage* (with Don D. Jackson).

CAROL B. LEFEVRE is Associate Professor of Psychology at St. Xavier College and a psychotherapist. She writes and does research on the life styles and identity of women.

SUZANNAH LESSARD is an editor of the *Washington Monthly* and a penetrating commentator on the American scene.

JACK LITEWKA is a free-lance writer of poetry and essays who is interested in men's liberation vis-à-vis the movement for liberation of women.

DONALD T. LUNDE is Senior Attending Physician, Clinical Associate Professor of Psychology and Behavioral Sciences, and Cooperating Associate Professor of Psychology and Law at Stanford University. The course he developed with Herant Katchadourian drew over a thousand students the third time it was offered, becoming thereby the largest single course at Stanford. He is co-author with Dr. Katchadourian of *Fundamentals of Human Sexuality*.

ELEANOR EMMONS MACCOBY is Professor and Chairman of the Department of Psychology at Stanford University. She has done extensive research and writing in many areas of developmental child psychology. Her latest book (with Carol Nagy Jacklin) is *The Psychology of Sex Differences*. In 1974 she was elected a Fellow of the American Academy of Arts and Sciences.

WILLIAM H. MASTERS is co-director with Virginia Johnson of the Reproductive Biology Research Foundation in St. Louis, Missouri. Among their writings are *Human Sexual Response* (1966), *Human Sexual Inadequacy* (1970), and *The Pleasure Bond* (1974).

ROLLO MAY is a psychotherapist and the author of numerous articles and books about sex and the human dilemma, including *Love and Will* and *The Courage to Create* (1975).

BARRY W. McCARTHY is Associate Professor of Psychology at the Counselling Center of American University, Washington, D.C., where he conducts courses on human sexual behavior.

ROY W. MENNINGER is a psychiatrist famous for his work and writings on mental health. He is President of the Menninger Foundation in Topeka, Kansas.

THOMAS ODEN has taught at several universities and studied abroad at Heidelberg University. He now teaches interpersonal theology at Drew University. His main interest is exploring the interfaces of psychology, ethics, and religion. Among his books are *The Structure of Awareness* (1967) and *Game Free* (1974).

BETTY ROSZAK is a free-lance writer who has contributed various articles to magazines such as *Peace News, Manas, Ballet Review,* and *The Daily Californian.*

THEODORE ROSZAK is Professor of History at California State University in Hayward. He is the author of *The Making of the Counter Culture* (1972) and *Beyond the Wasteland*.

MARY RYAN is a psychologist who conducts courses on human sexual behavior at the Counselling Center of American University, Washington, D.C.

WILLIAM SIMON is Professor of Sociology at the University of Houston, and Director of the Institute for Urban Studies. He has written extensively for professional journals; his most recent book, co-authored with John Gagnon, is *Sexual Conduct* (1973).

PHILIP SLATER is Professor of Sociology at Brandeis University. He writes and does research on families and small groups. Among his books are *The Temporary Society* (1968), *The Pursuit of Loneliness* (1970), and *Earth Walk* (1975).

GEORGE WEINBERG is a psychotherapist who has wide contact with homosexuals in both his practice and the gay movement organizations. He is the author of *Society and the Healthy Homosexual* (1972).

CODY WILSON was Executive Director and Director of Research for the Commision on Obscenity and Pornography.

INDEX

Abbott, Sidney, 251

Abortion, xi, 110, 124, 273; attitudes toward, 300-302, 304-305, 308, 309-310, 313; counseling, 305-306, 308; and the fetus, 302-304, 307, 312, 314; legal, 176-178, 274-275, 305; and rape, 284-285; research into, 311-312; teenage, 309-311, 312

Abortion Rap, 312-313

Adolescence: and homosexuality, 338-339; juvenile crime, 352; late, 23-24; and masturbation, 49-50, 52, 61; moral reasoning in, 69-70; and parents, 69-71; pressures in, 72-73, 476; and pornography, 343, 344-346, 350; and racism, 275-276; sexuality in, 4, 10, 15-17, 40-41, 224, 227-229, 473. *See also* Men— adolescent; Women—adolescent

Advertising, *see* Media

Age discrimination, 159, 344-346, 368-369, 403. *See also* Child

molesters; Elderly

Aggression, 32, 37, 66, 76. *See also* Rape

Alienation, 23, 60, 244, 395-396

American Civil Liberties Union, 336

American Dilemma, An, 316

American Law Institute, 45

American Psychiatric Association, 276

American Sexual Tragedy, The, 431

Amour et Vieillesse—Chants de Tristesse, 92

Androgen, 43

Androgyny, 110, 116-172 *passim*

Anxiety, *see* Guilt

Aphrodisiacs, 93

Ardrey, Robert, 66

Arieti, Silvano, 67

Astor, Bart, 169

Autoeroticism, *see* Masturbation

Bach, George R., 450, 462

Baker, Jack, 332-333, 338

Baldwin, James, 260

Fielding, Henry, 365
Flaubert, Gustave, 103
Foreplay, 11, 81, 99, 227-229
Freedman, Mark, 191, 192
Freeman, Harry, 333-334
Freud, Sigmund, 39, 281, 325, 393, 397; on masturbation, 58; on sexuality, 92; theories of, 3, 9, 11, 19; on women, 22
Fromm, Erich, 382, 423

Gagnon, John, 3
Gay liberation, 126, 128, 131, 246, 249, 276. *See also* Homosexuality; Homosexuals; Lesbians; Marriage, gay
Gender roles: genetic, 43-44; and heterosexuality, 69-70; homosexual, 251-252, 253-254; learning, 4, 14; male, 116-118; sex-typed, 171-172; and social class, 150-151; stereotypes, 107, 110, 126, 137, 138-139, 143, 158, 161, 162, 165-168; women, 117
Germany (West), 354
Gerontophilia, 100
Gibran, Kahlil, 428
Gide, Andre, 103-104
Gilder, George, 108
Ginsberg, Dorothy, 170
Girls, *see* Women—adolescent
Go Tell It on the Mountain, 260
Great Britain, 354, 373
Greer, Germaine, 273-274
Griffin, John, 319
Guilt, xi, 24; and abortion, 305-306, 311, 315; masturbatory, 17-18, 55, 59, 61; sexual, 13-14, 72-73, 281-282, 296, 299, 391, 394, 395, 474,

475, 478, 480; sources of, 18-19; of working women, 109, 155, 156-157

Hammerstein, Oscar, 27
Hardin, Garrett, 309
Harroff, Peggy, 388
Hefner, Hugh, 128
Hernton, Calvin, 275, 276
Hettlinger, Richard, 6, 64
Hippocrates, 57
Hitler, Adolf, 261
Homophile Community Health Service, 335, 336, 338
Homophobia: academic, 262-263; heterosexual, 126, 128, 132, 133, 233, 242-243, 321-322, 328-330; legal, 247-248, 276-277; male, 286, 322, 326, 327-328; reasons for, 323-330
Homosexuality, xi, 3, 5, 77, 125, 273, 343, 346, 351, 363; attitudes toward, 45-46, 126, 276, 321-322, 325-328; exhibitionistic, 102; latent, 385; origins of, 329-330; prevalence, 76, 249, 262; and religion, 323-324, 329; and social class, 19; and stress, 25-26. *See also* Homophobia; Lesbians
Homosexuals: and children, 336-339; closeted, 191-192, 249, 259, 262, 263-264, 335; and gay goals, 191, 257, 259-260, 264, 326-327; jealous, 255-256; and the law, 331-339; lifestyles, 248, 249-250, 253, 276, 334; myths about, 321-322, 329-330; and nonreproductive sex, 328-329, 330; radical, 248, 249-250, 333; pressures on, 192, 261-262, 276, 322, 323-324; self-hatred of, 321, 324-325;

255. *See also* Homosexuality; Homosexuals

Lesbian Mothers, 335

Lesbian/Woman, 334, 336-337

Lessard, Suzannah, 275

Lewis, C.S., 365

Libido, 9, 11, 73, 88, 89, 90, 103, 395, 396

Litewka, Jack, 190

Lopata, Helena Z., 148, 150

Lorenz, Konrad, 65, 66

Love, Barbara, 251

Love: agape, 429, conscious, 427-429; definition of, 440, 441, 443; and gender values, 130; and marriage, 438-445; myth of, 174-175; object-centered, 423-424; projective, 424-427; romantic, 20, 21-22, 125; and sex, 195-196, 382, 395, 396-397, 432-437, 479

Love Is an Attitude, 427

Lunde, Donald T., 5

Lyon, Phyllis, 251, 334, 336-337

Maccoby, Eleanor Emmons, 4

Machismo, *see* Masculinity

Magazines, *see* Media

Mahé, Georges, 102

Mailer, Norman, 128, 389

Male magazine, 124

Malinowski, Bronislaw, 286-287

Marcus, Steven, 79

Marcuse, Herbert, 369

Marriage: age of, 23, 184-185; and capitalism, 125, 248; childless, 128, 181, 186; companionate, 185; computer, 185; conflict in, 462-463; conservatism of, 70; contracts, 127, 178, 179, 181, 196, 333; counselors,

410-411, 413, 439, 442; and dating, 290; dual-career, 109-110; equal-sharing, 153-154, 157, 175-176, 254; fidelity in, 25, 388; gay, 190-191, 246-256, 276, 331-339; group, 182; legal view of, 332; manuals, 62, 127-128, 254, 410; models of, 177-178, 181-182, 185; open, 127-128; and pornography, 348, 349, 353-354; prevalence of, 136; sex in, 24-25, 51, 52, 54-55, 89-91, 137, 138-139, 398, 407-422 *passim*, 431, 432, 480; and society, xi, 118, 147-151; trial, 110, 181-182, 195-196; unhappy, 438-445

Martin, Del, 251, 334, 336-337

Martinerie, Andrée, 100

Martyna, Wendy, 170

Masculinity: and class values, 19; cult of, 69, 108-109, 112-113, 119-120, 123, 125, 138, 165, 166, 172, 190, 233, 237, 240, 290-291, 326, 408, 479-480; defined, 5; limitations of, 169-171, 202, 204, 242, 322, 391

Maslow, Abraham, 23, 82, 451

Masochism, *see* Sadomasochism

Masters, William H., ix, 3, 12, 39, 42, 45, 65, 69, 76, 77, 78, 79-80, 99, 108-109, 389

Masturbation, 5, 76, 124, 210, 215, 216, 224, 225, 294; attitudes toward, 5, 45-46, 52, 54, 57-58, 59, 60-62, 67; and doctors, 57-58, 222-223; first, 49-50, 52-53, 56; guilt about, 18, 55, 59, 61; and health, 57-62; and marriage, 25, 54-55, 90-91; motivations for, 55, 60, 243-244; and pornography, 367, 368-369; prevalence and frequency, 15, 50-57, 90;

public, 102; and religion, 55-56; and social class, 53-54

Matriarchy, 121

Mattachine Society, 324

Maugham, Somerset, 259

May, Rollo, 72-73, 124-125, 380, 382

McCarthy, Barry W., 380, 381, 383

McConnell, Mike, 332-333, 338

McGaw, Don, 336, 338-339

McGrady, Mike, 149, 154

Mead, Margaret, 110

Media, 231, 275, 372; and marriage, 438-439; selling of sex, 317-318, 472; violence, 363

Men: and aggression, 32, 35-36, 37; black, 275, 283, 317-320, 326, 342; elderly, 87-88, 89-98; and the Feminine Ideal, 385-387; group bonding of, 291; homophobia of, 286, 322, 326, 327-328; and marriage, 137, 138, 147, 149, 153-154; and masturbation, 16, 17-19, 50-51, 52, 55-56; middle-aged, 348; middle-class, 25, 291, 292; myths about, 28-32, 117-118, 122-123, 145-146, 162, 209, 319-320; objectified, 286-287, 294-295; orgasms of, 50, 241-242, 244, 384-385; and pornography, 343-344, 367-368; self-image of, 29, 388; sexual pressures on, 36, 79, 121, 138-140, 213-215, 218, 225, 402; sexual socialization of, 14-15, 17-20, 21-22, 24-25, 27, 71, 190, 223-238 *passim*, 289, 294, 295, 310, 322, 385-386; sexuality of, 73, 209, 115-116, 385-390; woman hatred of, 235, 239-240, 274, 279, 286, 288-290, 291-293, 295-296, 321, 385, 387; and work, 118-125. *See also*

Fathers; Masculinity; Penis
————adolescent: black, 275-276; and competition, 35; masturbation of, 10, 16-17, 19, 49, 51, 52-53; middle-class, 18, 19; myths about, 28-33; and pornography, 345-346; sexual socialization of, 14, 15, 21-22, 166, 227, 380, 482; sexuality of, 16, 17-20; transvestite, 338

Mencken, H. L., 326

Menninger, Roy W., 381, 383

Menopause, 7, 158

Menstruation, 17, 43, 49, 117, 229, 294

Metropolitan Community Church, 324

Middle age, sexuality in, 6-7

Middle class: marriage, 147-150, 182, 197-198; and masturbation, 53-54; and pornography, 348, 366; sexual attitudes of, 15, 73-75; sexuality of, 25, 91

Miller, Henry, 94

Millett, Kate, 126

Money, John, 42, 43, 44

Morality: and abortion, 305-308; Christian, 55-56, 68, 128, 323, 345; codes of, 323; and masturbation, 55, 58, 60; and pornography, 349, 352-353, 354, 356-357; and rape, 282; and reason, 67-69; sexual, 6, 41-42, 66-67, 88, 89, 139. *See also* Religion

Morris, Desmond, 65-66

Moss, Howard, 14

Mothers: and daughters, 315, 322; lesbian, 336-337; middle-class, 148-150, 155; as role models, 155-157, 198, 315, 322; working, 154-157; working-class, 150-151, 155

Ms. magazine, 126

Mulvey, Mary C., 158

Murphy, Lois B., 156
My Secret Life, 291, 297
Myrdal, Gunnar, 316-317

Narcissism, 88, 91, 92, 98, 101, 381, 480
National Gay Task Force, 338
Newman, G., 45
New York Times, The, 368
Nichols, C. R., 45
Nietzsche, Friedrich, 369
1984, 110
Nixon, Richard M., 277, 355
Nye, F. Ivan, 154
Nymphomania, 242

Obscenity, *see* Pornography
Oden, Thomas C., 381, 382
Oedipal stage, 59
Old people, *see* Elderly
O'Neill, Nena and George, 127, 128
Open Marriage, 127
Orgasm: fantasy of, 392; first, 45;
    frequency of, 3, 25; masturbatory,
    16, 17, 44-45, 50, 244; men's, 50, 78,
    241-242, 244, 384-385; multiple, 3,
    12, 77, 78; nocturnal, 55; and rape,
    286; simultaneous, 384-385, 399;
    tyranny of, 77-81, 140, 213, 379,
    380-381, 389-391, 398, 399, 480;
    vaginal, 388, 392; women's, 17, 25,
    45, 50, 69, 76, 77-78, 79-80, 99, 139,
    212-213, 241, 266, 286, 384-385, 389,
    391, 413. *See also* Penis, premature
    ejaculation
Our Bodies, Our Selves, 78
Out From Under, 126
Ovaries, 5, 42-43, 57

Packard, Vance, 74
Parents: authority of, 69-71; education

for, 149, 162, 183-186; foster, 338;
    gay, 336-339; and the generation
    gap, 69-70, 71, 273, 481; involun-
    tary, 310; licensing of, 110, 177,
    178-179, 182-186; myth of, 173-175;
    as sexual socializers, 4-5, 18, 40,
    43-44, 45, 47, 179, 183-184, 310, 406.
    See also Fathers; Mothers
Parsons, Talcott, 21
Patriarchy, 155, 180, 185
Pedophiles, *see* Child molesters
Peeping, *see* Voyeurism
Penis: absence of, 44, 230-231; as
    alter ego, 90; erected, 17, 42, 90, 98,
    116, 214, 218, 224-226, 228, 229,
    231, 232-233, 234-235, 279, 287, 384;
    focus on, 190; friction, 228, 232, 243;
    myths about, 275; objectified, 233-
    234, 243; premature ejaculation, 79,
    241-242; and privilege, 235-236,
    274, 288-290, 297, 388. *See also*
    Orgasm, men's
Permissiveness, 6, 54, 70-71
Perry, Troy, 324, 332
Petroni, Frank A., 275
Petting, 65, 80, 227-229, 381, 401, 406.
    See also Courtship; Dating
Physicians, *see* Doctors; Psychiatrists
Piaget, Jean, 67
Picasso, Pablo, 94, 103
Plath, Sylvia, 198, 295
Playboy magazine, 5, 52, 61, 65, 73,
    124, 385, 480, 486
Pornography: as art, 365, 373-374;
    attitudes toward, 340-341, 364-365;
    and censorship, 277, 362-375 *pas-
    sim*; effects of, 277, 341, 348-355;
    experience with, 341-348; hard-
    core, 47; laws on, 351, 354-357, 364,
    372-375; market controls on, 368;

myths about, 350; research into, 340-357 *passim*; soft-core, 294; and social hypocrisy, 354-357, 364; sources of, 347-348; U.S. Commission on Obscenity and, 277, 341, 348, 351

Portnoy's Complaint, 62, 369

Pregnancy: motivations for, 311, 312; and rape, 138, 285, 287; unwanted, 139, 174, 175, 287, 300, 311, 314-315, 383, 483-484. *See also* Abortion; Contraception

Premature ejaculation, *see under* Penis

Prescott, James, 274

Prime of Life, The, 199

Promiscuity, 74, 75-76, 131-132, 195, 206, 246, 290

Prophet, The, 428

Prostitution, 75, 90, 93, 227, 234

Protestants, 56, 128, 390. *See also* Catholics; Morality, Christian; Religion

Psychiatrists: failure of, 222-223, 385, 388-389, 392; homophobia of, 276, 329; and masturbation, 58-60. *See also* Doctors; Women, and psychiatrists

Psychology of Sex Differences, The, 4

Psychology Today magazine, 342

Puberty: female, 20; and hormones, 44; male, 16-17; and masturbation, 17, 45, 58, 59; onset of, 56, 58

Rabelais, François, 373

Racism, 273; and pornography, 346; sexual, 237, 275, 316-320, 325-326; southern, 316

Rape, xi, 102, 179, 243, 274, 351; attitudes toward, 278-280; consent to, 281-283, 291-293; crisis centers,

298; fear of, 281; homosexual, 363; legalized, 260; motivations for, 293; and pornography, 349, 354; and racism, 283, 317; research into, 284; statutes, 282-283, 284; and suicide, 287; and woman hatred, 274. *See also* Crime, sexual

Raushenbush, Esther, 156

Reiss, Ira L., 70-71

Religion: and homosexuality, 249, 323-324, 329; and masturbation, 55-56; and morality, 69; and pornography, 344, 356, 357; and rape, 285, 293. *See also* Morality

Reuben, David, 72, 80

Rheingold, Joseph, 20

Richelieu, Duc de, 92, 93

Rinder, Walter, 427

Rodgers, Richard, 27

Rogers, Carl R., 461, 463

Rook, Karen, 168

Rossi, Alice, 148, 156

Roszak, Betty and Theodore, 107

Rothschild, Amalie, 310

Rubin, Jerry, 369

Rubino, Richard, 333-334, 335-336, 337-338

Rudd, Mark, 370

Ryan, Mary, 380

Sade, Marquis de, 365, 374

Sadomasochism, 26, 47, 91-92, 197, 286, 343, 346, 364, 368, 391

Saga magazine, 124

Schaefer, Leah Cahan, 69, 79, 80, 81

Schopenhauer, Arthur, 103

Schulder, Dianne, 312

Science Digest magazine, 318-319

Second Sex, The, 305

Sensuous Couple, The, 409

Sensuous Woman, The, 409

Sex: attitudes toward, 4-5, 138-139, 221; and body image, 88-89, 91, 92, 94, 95, 101; casual, 211; compulsive, 97, 102; and death, 328-329, 366-367, 392; drive, 65, 69, 87, 89, 99, 432, 474, 479; education, xii, 5, 44, 349, 353, 393, 394; exploitative, 19, 76, 367-368; goal-oriented, 77, 81, 116, 139-140, 379, 380, 390, 398-399, 406; group, 26; interracial, 275, 317; language of, 217, 234, 236, 241, 278, 290, 296, 346, 365, 447-448; manuals, 62, 72, 124, 126, 131, 389, 390, 394-395, 409-410; negotiating for, 416-422; nonmarital, 3, 5, 45-46, 137; nonreproductive, 129, 131, 175; and nudity, 400-401, 403, 404; oral, xii, 126, 343, 344, 346, 401, 421; and performance syndrome, 138-140, 380, 389, 390, 394-395; power of, 196, 396; public, 363, 367, 400; reciprocal, 140-142; reproductive, 128-129, 132, 327, 328-330, 392; research, 3, 6, 28, 42, 45, 50-53, 76-77, 79-80, 99, 108, 139; scripted behavior, 11-12, 13, 14, 18; surgery, 5, 43-44; taboos, 54; talking about, 214-215, 381-382, 383, 401-406, 407-422 *passim,* 464-465, 485; techniques, 126, 395, 401-406, 421-422; therapy, 381. *See also* Crime, sexual; Intercourse; Marriage, sex in; Orgasm

Sex and Racism in America, 275

Sex and the Significant Americans, 388

Sex roles, *see* Gender roles

Sexes: differences between, 21, 32-33, 35-36, 37, 49, 55, 89, 90, 98-99, 115, 133, 135, 146, 194, 201, 367; equality between, xi, 4, 107, 110, 134, 135-137, 138, 142-143, 195, 235

Sexism, 107, 273; economic, 152-153, 161; male, 146, 239-240; and pornography, 367-368. *See also* Men, woman hatred of

Sexology magazine, 90

Sexual Wilderness, The, 74

Sexuality: attitudes toward, 6, 10-11, 13-14, 18, 22, 44, 45-47, 115, 357, 367-368; and body image, 396-397; and creativity, 103, 479; and culture, xi, 6, 44, 67, 116, 131, 245, 386, 387, 480; double-standard, 379, 384, 386; economics of, 118-125; emotional, 4, 20, 21-22, 80, 139-141, 210, 367, 379, 380, 391, 397; fashions in, x, 77-78, 81, 126; fears about, xi, 47; gay, 258; genital, x, 4, 15, 17, 19, 22, 82, 87, 92, 126, 190, 192, 269, 380-381, 446-447; and intimacy, 399, 446-468 *passim;* and law, 45, 47; learned, x-xi, 21-22, 67; lifelong, x; myths about, 28-32, 40-42, 480; "normal," 92; peer pressure on, 6, 29; and personality development, 472-486 *passim;* physiology of, ix-x, 3, 9-10, 77, 89, 98, 146, 210, 433; polymorphous, 87, 92, 129; power of, x, 21; repression of, 20, 21, 102, 114, 393, 396; self-contained, 232-233; and self-worth, x, 24, 25, 69, 88-89, 142, 229, 232, 233, 242, 290, 319, 478, 482-483; and sensuousness, 380-381, 389-391, 398, 399-406, 463-464; and social class, 5, 365-366, 373, 375, 463-464; socialization of, 3-4, 13, 23, 43-44; values of, 64-82 *passim,* 88, 91

Shanahan, Claire, 334-335

of, 158, 161; elderly, 88, 89, 98-103; emotional dependence on men, 123-124, 199-202, 205-208, 266, 268-269, 290; and marriage, 136-138, 147-152, 207-208; and masturbation, 5-6, 16, 17, 20, 49, 50, 51-56, 100, 266, 267; mental health of, 146, 151, 152, 158, 198, 284, 285, 286, 297, 313; middle-aged, 157-160; and motherhood, 116, 128; myths about, 28-32, 110, 118, 130, 138, 146, 279-280, 286, 287-288, 296, 297, 320; orgasms of, 25, 45, 50, 69, 99, 139, 212-213, 241, 266, 286, 384-385, 389, 391, 413; and pornography, 277, 294-295, 343-344, 352, 353, 356, 367; pressures on, 121; and psychiatrists, 388-389, 392, 482-484; "psychology" of, 385-386; role models for, 197-199; self-defense of, 280, 299; self-image of, 29, 142, 149, 150, 156-157, 158, 270, 284, 287, 289, 292-293, 298, 304; as sex objects, 89, 99, 101, 142, 161, 190, 217, 227-229, 230-232, 233, 234, 236-237, 240, 294, 317-318, 368, 386, 389, 435; sexual socialization of, 14-15, 17, 20-24, 27-28, 44, 194, 231, 233, 239, 240, 280, 314-315, 326; sexuality of, xi, 3, 99-101, 139-141, 386, 388-389, 390, 391; single, 51, 52, 71, 279; suicides of, 198, 287; virginity of, 71-74, 194, 195, 205, 388; wages of, 119-120, 153; and

welfare, 151; working, 109, 119-120, 147, 152-157, 176. *See also* Abortion; Feminists; Femininity; Lesbians; Mothers; Pregnancy; Rape; Sexism

Women—adolescent: and abortion, 309-311, 312; black, 275-276, 284-285; and masturbation, 49-50, 52-53; and parents, 71; and pornography, 345-346; sexual abuse of, 351; sexuality of, 13, 14, 15, 17, 20-22, 281-282; socialization of, 28-33, 160, 166; working-class, 174; of working mothers, 155-156, 157

Women in Transition, 337

Women's liberation movement: impact of, 107, 108, 223; male fear of, 119, 125, 135-137, 239; on marriage, 175, 251; on pornography, 368; on sexuality, 131, 132, 133; on working women, 120, 143, 147. *See also* Feminists

Woolf, Virginia, 198

Woolston, Florence, 108

Workentin, John, 444

Working class: mothers, 150-151, 155; and pornography, 342, 345-346; sexual attitudes of, 15, 19, 25, 54, 91

Yankelovich, Daniel, Inc., 74

Yin-yang, xi

Yorburg, Betty, 75

Youth, *see* Adolescence; Children; Men—adolescent; Students; Women—adolescent